Unpopular Sovereignty

Unpopular Sovereignty

Rhodesian Independence and African Decolonization

LUISE WHITE

The University of Chicago Press   Chicago and London

The University of Chicago Press, Chicago 60637
The University of Chicago Press, Ltd., London
© 2015 by The University of Chicago
All rights reserved. Published 2015.
Printed in the United States of America

24 23 22 21 20 19 18 17 16 15   1 2 3 4 5

ISBN-13: 978-0-226-23505-9 (cloth)
ISBN-13: 978-0-226-23519-6 (paper)
ISBN-13: 978-0-226-23522-6 (e-book)
DOI: 10.7208/chicago/9780226235226.001.0001

Library of Congress Cataloging-in-Publication Data
White, Luise, author.
   Unpopular sovereignty : Rhodesian independence and African decolonization / Luise White.
       pages ; cm
   Includes bibliographical references and index.
   ISBN 978-0-226-23505-9 (cloth : alk. paper)—ISBN 978-0-226-23519-6 (pbk. : alk. paper)—ISBN 978-0226-23522-6 (e-book) 1. Zimbabwe—History—1965–1980. 2. Zimbabwe—History—Autonomy and independence movements. 3. Decolonization—Zimbabwe. 4. Zimbabwe—History—1890–1965. I. Title.
   DT2981.W45 2015
   968.91'04—dc23

                                                           2014030670

♾ This paper meets the requirements of ANSI/NISO Z39.48-1992 (Permanence of Paper).

Contents

Acknowledgments

I first went to Zimbabwe with a project in medical history, but even as I prepared to do that research I found myself drawn to the sheer amount of white writing—memoirs and novels and polemics—written about Rhodesia's renegade independence during it and after Rhodesia ceased to exist. As the medical history project became increasingly untenable, I thought I would write a book about Rhodesian independence based on these published materials. What made me think more critically about what such a project might entail and what I might find in archives and libraries were the conversations I had when I was a fellow at the Woodrow Wilson International Center for Scholars in 1997–1998. James Hevia, Douglas Howland, and David Gilmartin demonstrated by example the imaginative potential of political history. This encounter with scholars of East and South Asia convinced me that what was at stake in this project could not be expressed in the binary of published versus unpublished or even primary versus secondary sources. Doug Howland in particular encouraged me to rethink how I read texts and also to attend to the genealogies of language in which the historical experience of power and privilege was recorded. For the next decade, however, I imagined I could write a history of Rhodesian independence without addressing the complications of the five constitutions Rhodesia had between 1961 and 1980. I had hoped to write a book without learning the minutiae of voter qualifications, the question of dual voters' rolls, and the byzantine rules for cross-voting. At the Shelby Cullom Davis Center for Historical Studies at Princeton

University in 2007 I had the time and the library resources to read franchise commissions and constitutions. To my surprise I discovered that the minutiae of voter qualifications were a way to talk about history and difference at the end of the colonial era; separate voters' rolls for Africans and Europeans were a late colonial fiction about ending racial politics; cross-voting was a territorial mechanism for keeping racial politics buoyant. The organization of this book emerged out of that fellowship, and I am grateful to Michael Gordin and Gyan Prakash for their support.

I was able to explore the overlapping histories of states and votes and voters in three conferences. The Center for Twenty-First Century Studies at the University of Wisconsin–Milwaukee funded Doug Howland and me to organize a conference historicizing sovereignty. At the University of Florida, the Center for the Humanities and Public Sphere funded two workshops, one on decolonization and the franchise and one co-organized with my colleague Alioune Sow on the production of memoirs in Africa since 1980. I am grateful to the participants for their papers and discussion. This research was funded by the Social Science Research Council, the Wenner-Gren Foundation for Anthropological Research, the Woodrow Wilson International Center for Scholars, the National Endowment for the Humanities, and the Shelby Cullom Davis Center for Historical Studies. The John Simon Guggenheim Memorial Foundation allowed me the time to write this book. Such a list masks the colleagues who have, time after time, written the letters that recommended me for funding. Over many years and no small amount of disk space, Fred Cooper and Ivan Karp have supported me and my research in ways I can only call unfailing. Ivan did not live to see this book. He never really approved of this project, but his belief that a scholar's engagement could trump his own sensibilities has served as an example of uncompromising professionalism and is one of the many reasons he is so sorely missed.

This book was written at the University of Florida, where the Department of History has supported my work and helped me secure funds for research from the College of Liberal Arts for research trips. At Florida I am affiliated with a Title VI Center for African Studies. Title VI centers are relics of the Cold War, to be sure, but like relics of old they have been given a special and somewhat different meaning by the people who revere them. At Florida this has meant a sense of place and possible futures for Africa shared by a truly interdisciplinary group of scholars. The center's directors and associate director—Michael Chege, Abe Goldman, Todd Leedy, and especially Leonardo Villalón—have been only too eager to turn scholars' ideas into research trips and conferences and invited speakers. Steve Davis began graduate work in African history at Florida in 2003, when I had just begun to think seriously about this book. He finished his dissertation years before I finished this manuscript, but not before I learned an enormous amount from him.

Writing about the history of a state that no longer exists has required a triangulation of archives and libraries. I have been helped along this circuitous path by Ivan Murambiwa at the National Archives of Zimbabwe, Shirley Kabwato at the Cory Library at Rhodes University, John Pinfold at Rhodes House in Oxford, Hilary McEwan at the Commonwealth Secretariat in London, Chris Webb at the Borthwick Historical Institute in York, Marja Hinfelaar at the National Archives of Zambia, and Kelebogile Pinkie at the Botswana National Archives. In the United States I am grateful for the assistance of Jennifer Cuttleback at the LBJ Archives in Austin, William McNitt at the Gerald Ford Library in Ann Arbor, Carol Leaderham at the Hoover Institution Archives at Stanford University, David Easterbrook at Northwestern University, Dorothy Woodson of the Sterling Library at Yale University, and most of all, Dan Reboussin at the University of Florida.

My research outside the United States would not have been possible without the friendship and hospitality of Irene Staunton and Murray McCarthy in Harare, Helen and Robert Irwin in London, Judy Butterman and Roger Tangri in Gaborone, Megan Vaughan in Oxford, Diana Jeater in Wick, Bill Freund in Durban, and Isabel Hofmeyr, Jon Hyslop, and David Moore in Johannesburg. Colleagues, journalists, former Commonwealth officials and Rhodesian officials in Zimbabwe, and those in what Zimbabweans call "the diaspora" have been exceptionally generous with their time and insight. Many asked not to be cited by name, and so I refer to these conversations as my field notes. I want to thank the named and unnamed—friends and informants and participants in various seminars in various countries—for their comments and suggestions.

At the University of Chicago Press David Brent was enthusiastic about this book before it was done. Once it was, his respect for an author's voice matched his regard for an author's need to attend to timetables. I am grateful to him, Priya Nelson, and Ellen Kladky for guiding me through editorial processes and procedures with wondrous speed and good will and for making sure this book could be available in Africa. Jocelyn Alexander, Josiah Brownell, Elizabeth Dale, Abdoulaye Kane, Robert McMahon, Pius Nyambara, and Leonard V. Smith read individual chapters for me. Steve Davis, David Gilmartin, Doug Howland each read several chapters, sometimes more than once. This is a stronger book for their comments. Kate Law and Frederick Cooper read the manuscript for the press. Fred was the reader on my first book; then and now I am grateful for the clarity he brought to the study of work and labor in East African history. Almost twenty-five years later, both of us found ourselves engaged with the politics of belonging and citizenship in twentieth-century Africa. Again, I am grateful for his clear and wide-ranging thinking about empires and the promise and problems of decolonization, and the place of Africans therein. I thank Fred for his many years of helping me see what was weak and what was important in my work and for his insistence that a commitment to Africa's future be central to the writing about its past.

I first wrote these acknowledgments in Harare; I revised them in Gainesville. This is a journey I have made many times, but in recent years Harare has seemed vulnerable not only to the conditions of the present but to its understanding of its past. I do not imagine that this book will make Harare seem any less defenseless, but I hope it is a first step in a history in which the present does not explain the past and in which the past is allowed to be in the past, an object of study and inquiry that informs everyday politics but does not control it.

Gainesville
May 2014

A Note on Sources

There are no archives for independent Rhodesia. While there is a trove of documents in Zimbabwe, almost nothing has been made available since 1995 or 1996. The oral history and manuscript collections cover longer periods, but given the thirty-five-year ban on accessioning material and persistent understaffing, the archive stops around 1961. Partly for this reason, many of the histories of Rhodesia written in the 1980s and 1990s relied heavily on newspapers and parliamentary debates. (I have complained that this produced a historiography that is of one note, but it has been very helpful to me.) What has become available in the last fifteen years are the Rhodesian cabinet papers, bound volumes of minutes and memoranda, which together with some prime minister files from the 1970s were given—still in their National Archives of Zimbabwe boxes—by Ian Smith to his alma mater, Rhodes University. These have been available to researchers since Smith's death in 2007. In addition, there is extensive material on the first year of Rhodesian independence and worldwide optimism about sanctions in the Lyndon Baines Johnson Library in Austin, Texas, and there is rich material on the events leading up to Rhodesia's internal settlement in the Gerald Ford Library in Ann Arbor, Michigan. There are sizable collections of Rhodesia ephemera and government pamphlets in both the Sterling Library at Yale University and the Melville Herskovits Library at Northwestern. There are, or were, the papers of the Rhodesian Army Association. These were hastily packed-up papers taken to South Africa in February 1980 that were deposited, uncataloged, in the

British Empire and Commonwealth Museum in Bristol in 2001. These papers were closed to the public in 2010 after a dispute about who would archive them; the museum closed soon thereafter because of legal issues. There are a number of manuscript collections in Britain and the United States. The papers of Sir Roy Welensky, Sir Edgar Whitehead, and Professor Terence Ranger are all in Rhodes House, Oxford. The papers of the Capricorn Africa Society and the Centre Party are in the Borthwick Historical Institute in York, England, and there is some Capricorn correspondence in the National Archives of Zambia. The papers of Diana Mitchell, the woman who was the institutional memory of the Centre Party, and those of George Loft, who represented the American Friends Service Committee in Central Africa in the 1960s, are in the Hoover Institution Archives at Stanford University. Material on the Lancaster House conference in 1979 and the 1980 election has only recently been made available by the National Archives of the United Kingdom at Kew; the Commonwealth Secretariat in London also released the papers of the Commonwealth Observers Group for the 1980 election after thirty years had elapsed.

All this has also encouraged me to see the hodgepodge of Rhodesian political thought a bit more clearly than I might have done otherwise, or if I had access to a complete national archive and censorship-wary newspapers. It has also required some triangulation. With the exception of conscription, almost every other debate with which this book is concerned had to be pieced together from multiple sources in various archives and personal papers. "Piecing together" may be the wrong concept: it implies that a whole picture emerged from the process. What I have learned is how deep the fissures were and, I hope, how to avoid patching them over; fragments have allowed me to see fragmented ideas. The archival constraint has also allowed me to use a range of sources that historians do not often use when writing political history. I have relied extensively on Rhodesian memoirs and Rhodesian novels. The publication of both genres—of which not only the novels seem fictive—has become something of a cottage industry starting in the late 1980s and has provided a density of material that has allowed me to see how Rhodesians debated what it meant to belong to that nation and what they would do in order to belong to it. I also rely on journalists' accounts. Rhodesia was ground zero for a certain kind of literary journalism in the 1960s and 1970s: David Caute, Christopher Hitchens, Jan Morris, and Calvin Trillin all visited. This writing provided a level of insight that was missing in some of the histories of the era.

Place Names, Party Names, Abbreviations, and Currency

The convention of historical writing about the country of which I write is to give a list of place names in the front matter, with Rhodesian names on one side and the Zimbabwean names on the other. I will not do that here. The country I write about had four names between 1960 and 1980; what these were and how they changed are discussed at the start of the first chapter. I avoid such lists because of my concerns about a notion of before-and-after in history: a list of place names and their changes suggests a too-pat transformation from colony to nation, from bad to good, from minority to majority rule. It also suggests that transitions are instantaneous, as if a threshold has been crossed. For the record, however, Rhodesia became Southern Rhodesia from mid-December 1979 to April 1980, when it became Zimbabwe; Salisbury, the capital, became Harare in 1982. More common and never part of any list has been the tendency to use "Rhodesian" to mean white and "Zimbabwean" to mean African. I have tried to avoid this as often as I could throughout this book

Political parties in Rhodesia and Zimbabwe, white and black, changed their names frequently; in the case of white political parties this was because they were fairly fluid coalitions, and in the case of African nationalist parties in the 1950s and 1960s this was because they had been banned. The Zimbabwe African Peoples Union (ZAPU) was the new name for the banned National Democratic Party (NDP), which itself was the new name for the banned Southern Rhodesia African National Congress (SRANC). In 1963 the Zimbabwe African National Union (ZANU) was formed by dissidents in ZAPU. In 1976 the two parties formed a united front with which to negotiate at all-party conferences. This was the Patriotic Front that negotiated both at Geneva in 1976 and at Lancaster House in 1979. In preparation for the 1980 elections, ZANU left the Patriotic Front but kept the name in parentheses: then and now the party is ZANU(PF). ZAPU was left with the name Patriotic Front, under which it contested the election. After the election it returned to ZAPU. In my chapter on the 1980 election I will most often call ZAPU ZAPU: most of the sources I use did so, as did almost every cadre. The African National Council (ANC) was formed in late 1971 to protest the visit of the Pearce Commission to Rhodesia in 1972. It was so successful that the party briefly became the umbrella group under which the armies of ZANU and ZAPU fought from exile. After disputes about who led the party it became the United African National Council (UANC) in 1976, under which it contested the 1979 and 1980 elections.

Against editorial advice, I do not have a list of abbreviations at the beginning of this book. However helpful such lists are designed to be, they take names out of context and give a false equivalency to each and every group that had an acronym. In the following chapters I discuss those parties and organizations that did not last a year, but they and the long-lasting parties they sought to challenge lose their specificity if they are listed as if they were words in a glossary. Nevertheless, ZANU, ZANU(PF), ZAPU, and the UANC are the tip of the very large iceberg of the acronyms of party names in Rhodesia and in many African nations. The states neighboring Rhodesia or those sheltering the guerrillas trying to overthrow it were all ruled by parties the acronyms of which were pronounced as words, as ZANU and ZAPU were. There was UNIP (United National Independence Party) in Zambia, TANU (Tanzania African National Union) in Tanzania (independent Tanganyika from 1961 to 1964), and FRELIMO (Frente de Libertação de Mozambique) in Mozambique.

The European, or white, parties in Southern Rhodesia and Rhodesia tended to be broad coalitions with even broader names. This book begins in 1957 when the United Federal Party (UFP) was the ruling party of Southern Rhodesia; it had grown out of the United Party. In 1953 dissidents in the UFP formed the United Rhodesia Party (URP). The URP lost the 1958 election; its more progressive elements regrouped as the Central African Party (CAP), which moved closer and closer to the NDP in 1960–1961. There were many segregationist parties that came and went. By the late 1950s the most successful of these was the Dominion

Party (DP), which went into the Rhodesian Front (RF) when it was formed in 1962. The Rhodesian Front had a stranglehold on white politics until 1980: several other parties, many of which found the Rhodesian Front too liberal on matters pertaining to race, came and went, but never mounted meaningful opposition.

African political parties were all but illegal in the country after 1964. The two periods in which there were openings—1972 and 1979—saw a variety of African political parties, most of which were funded by the Rhodesian Front government. Those that were not were creations of ZANU and ZAPU or the remnants of the multiracial movements of the 1950s, most notably the Capricorn Africa Society (CAS). Most of the African organizations from 1972 did not last a year: groups such as COSS (Committee to Organize Support for Settlement), PARD (People against Racial Discrimination), and the RSF (Rhodesia Settlement Forum) were more noteworthy for their genealogies than for anything they accomplished. The election of 1979, won by a regrouped UANC, featured two other parties that were close to the Rhodesian Front regime, ZUPO (the Zimbabwe United People's Organization) and a party claiming it was the authentic ANC. In the 1980 election, however, the Rhodesian Front did not determine which parties contested the election. There were several small parties—the Zimbabwe Democratic Party (ZDP), for example, and the party that had claimed it was the authentic ANC and now claimed it was the original ZANU—but none of these managed to win any seats. More significant during the election was the Commonwealth Observers Group (COG), which provided perhaps the most comprehensive overview of the campaign and the voting.

Rhodesian security had as many acronyms as its politics. The British South African Police (BSAP) began as the police force for Cecil Rhodes's company; it kept the name until 1980. The oldest infantry regiment in the country was the Rhodesian African Rifles (RAR) formed from volunteers in 1940 to fight overseas. Rhodesia's SAS (Special Air Services, founded by the same World War II hero who founded the Capricorn Africa Society) began as Rhodesian volunteers who went to fight in Malaya in 1951. They became first the Malaya Scouts and then C Squadron of the SAS. The first all-white regiment for national servicemen was the Rhodesian Light Infantry (RLI) formed in 1961. The army called guerrillas CTs (communist terrorists).

The British had perhaps fewer acronyms, but these were no less confusing. The Colonial Office oversaw Britain's colonies but the Commonwealth Relations Office (CRO) was in charge of Southern Rhodesia during the Central African Federation. The Foreign Office became the

Foreign and Commonwealth Office in 1968 when the CRO was folded into it, in part because of the comings and goings of member states furious over Britain's handling of Rhodesia. The convention is that when the name of the body is written out it is Foreign Office but when it is abbreviated it is FCO.

The Central African Federation had its own currency, the Rhodesia and Nyasaland pound, pegged to that of Great Britain. With the breakup of the federation, Rhodesia named its currency the Rhodesian pound (£). Cast out of the sterling zone shortly after it took its own independence, Rhodesia valued its pound at US$2. In 1970, Rhodesia adopted the dollar as its currency. It was designed to be valued at half a British pound and between 1970 and 1980 hovered at about US$1.50. This currency—most often written as R$—was not convertible out of Rhodesia, however, so almost all foreign trade went on in South African rand (ZAR) or in other African or European currencies.

ONE

"The last good white man left": Rhodesia, Rhonasia, and the Decolonization of British Africa

In November 1965, when almost all British territories in Africa had been granted their independence, Rhodesia's white minority government made a Unilateral Declaration of Independence from Britain. This was UDI, an acronym that would serve both to mark the event and to describe the period of Rhodesian independence, which lasted until 1980. Or 1979: Rhodesia, which had been Southern Rhodesia until 1964, became Zimbabwe-Rhodesia in 1979, with a no less independent government with an elected African head of state. It became majority-ruled independent Zimbabwe in 1980. These four names have been collapsed into two—Rhodesia and Zimbabwe—and have produced some discursive flourishes that have generated two histories, a before-and-after that literally makes the past a prologue, an exception to the natural order that was decolonization, an interruption that slowed down the history of what should have happened. These two histories have been routinely deployed as an example of the well-wrought story of a colony becoming an independent nation. In the story of Rhodesia becoming Zimbabwe it is one of the success of guerrilla struggle and the valiant triumph of universal rights. But it is a story that even at its best leaves out the peculiarities of local politics and difference,

1

not to mention one or two of the country's names. The result is a history in which Rhodesia was the racist anomaly, an eager if secondhand imitation of South Africa's apartheid. Rhodesia—and Southern Rhodesia, and Zimbabwe-Rhodesia—hardly merits any analysis beyond the racism of its renegade independence. It is an example or an occurrence; it has no specific history.

The Country No One Can Name

At the level of popular and academic history and at the level of diplomacy, Rhodesia was the place that no one could even name: for years after the country took its own independence Britain referred to it as Southern Rhodesia while much of the historiography refers to "colonial Zimbabwe," although Rhodesia had never really been a formal colony in the way that Kenya or Gabon had been. On one hand, not calling Rhodesia Rhodesia was a way to show how illegitimate it really was. On the other, calling Rhodesia colonial Zimbabwe served—as did talk of the decolonization of Algeria—to change its history, to return clumsy governance and messy episodes to the normal, linear story of colony to nation.[1]

The two names make for a definitive break. This is the literature of *The Past Is Another Country,* the title of a journalist's account of the events and negotiations that ended white rule; it is in a genre of crossing a threshold, from oppression to freedom.[2] Authors and activists announced, with pride or sadness depending on the circumstance, that they would never return to Rhodesia, only to arrive in Zimbabwe at the start of the next chapter.[3] Indeed, once Rhodesia became Zimbabwe it became a commonplace for history texts to begin with a before-and-after list of place names. Obviously a before-and-after list cannot do justice

1. See Todd Shepard, *The Invention of Decolonization: The Algerian War and the Remaking of France* (Ithaca, NY: Cornell University Press, 2006), 2–5.

2. Martin Meredith, *The Past Is Another Country: Rhodesia UDI to Zimbabwe* (London: Pan Books, 1980). The problem of such analyses is well known to a younger generation of Zimbabwean historians; see Brian Raftopoulos and Alois Mlambo, eds., *Becoming Zimbabwe: A History from Pre-colonial Times to 2008* (Harare: Weaver, 2009).

3. Peter Godwin, *Mukiwa: A White Boy in Africa* (London: Macmillan, 1996), 321–25. When Guy Clutton-Brock of the interracial and progressive St. Faith's Mission was deported in 1971 he said the regime was temporary but he himself was "a continuing citizen of Rhodesia" who expected "to return to Zimbabwe again"; quoted in Judith Todd, *The Right to Say No* (London: Sedgwick & Jackson, 1972), 15–16.

to all the names of the country, but I have dispensed with such a list altogether because of my misgivings about the whole before-and-after enterprise. Place names and how they change are important, to be sure, but all too often the then-and-now lists that show that African names have replaced those chosen by settlers (Harare for Salisbury, for example, but see Mutare for Umtali, or Kadoma for Gatooma) suggest that a new name represents a resolution, a wrong that has now been righted.

Almost as common as the list of place names is a chronology or time line in the front matter of a text. A few begin the country's history with the building of Great Zimbabwe, but most start the chronology with European contact in 1509 or with the first white settlers in 1890. Even the most African nationalist books have chronologies that begin in 1890. Chronologies may have been required by publishers who thought Central Africa too remote for many readers, but the ways these chronologies begin suggest a desire to historicize the land—even if it cannot be named—and establish a claim to territory whoever the population is and whenever it got there. Rhodesia's territory was never really contested, but who lived on it, and where they lived, was. One critical argument of this book is that the idea of place—as in "patria" and "locus"—was in flux for much of the 1960s and 1970s. Independent Rhodesia was likened to Britain at its best, or to Britain in the 1940s, or to Sparta, or to the European nations handed to Hitler by Neville Chamberlin, or to Hungary in 1956.[4] In the rhetoric of its independence, what located Rhodesians firmly in Africa was not its African population, but its white one. Party hacks called upon the genealogy of brave pioneers who had tamed the land bare-handed. "The Rhodesian was the last good white man left," recalled P. K. van der Byl, a post–World War II immigrant who was to hold several portfolios in the Rhodesian cabinet.[5]

But good white men or bad ones, the fact was that the white population of Southern Rhodesia (and Rhodesia) was small, never amounting to as much as 5 percent of the total population of the country. There were fewer than 34,000 Europeans in Southern Rhodesia in 1921 and the numbers gradually increased to about 85,000 in 1946. Within six years the population was almost 140,000; it peaked at 277,000 in 1961. These

4. These comparisons are widely cited; see John Parker, *Rhodesia: Little White Island* (London: Pittman Publishing, 1972), 13; Kenneth Skelton, *Bishop in Smith's Rhodesia: Notes from a Turbulent Octave, 1962–70* (Gweru: Mambo Press, 1983), 87; Michael Evans, The Role of Ideology in Rhodesian Front Rule, 1962–1980, Ph.D. dissertation, University of Western Australia, 1993, 113, 280–83.

5. Hannes Wessels, *P. K. van der Byl: African Statesman* (Johannesburg: 30 Degrees South, 2010), 79–81.

figures are misleading, however, as they do not show how peripatetic the white population was: of the seven hundred original pioneers who arrived in 1890, only fifteen lived in the country in 1924. Many came and went because of changing opportunities in regional industries, particularly mining, while others used South Africa, Northern Rhodesia, or Britain as a base from which to launch new careers. These were the men called "Good Time Charlies" in the press and "rainbow boys" in parliament. This pattern intensified as the population trebled: there were almost equal numbers of white immigrants and white emigrants for most of the early 1960s. It was only during the boom years of 1966–1971 that white immigration exceeded white emigration by significant amounts. After that, more whites left the country than came to live there.[6]

This book, then, is a history of Rhodesia's independence and its place—clumsy governance and messy episodes and all—in what was everywhere else postcolonial Africa. Caroline Elkins has argued that after 1945, white settlers in Africa dug in against the colonial retreat and claimed a popular sovereignty for themselves alone, insisting that they constituted a people who had the legitimacy to trump empire and to make claims equivalent to those independent nations could make.[7] This book argues something quite different, that white settlers and white residents and whites who were just passing through utilized a hodgepodge of institutions and laws and practices in Rhodesia to maintain what they refused to call white rule but instead relabeled as responsible government by civilized people. They did not claim to be "the people" worthy of sovereignty but instead proclaimed membership in an empire, or the West, or an anticommunism that had no national boundaries. I am writing against, for want of a better term, the story of Rhodesia becoming Zimbabwe, which is itself a version of colonies becoming nation-states: I am writing a history of how Rhodesia and its several names disrupt that narrative and show how awkward and uneven it was.

6. Colin Leys, *European Politics in Southern Rhodesia* (Oxford: Clarendon Press, 1960, 14); A. S. Mlambo, *White Immigration into Rhodesia: From Occupation to Federation* (Harare: University of Zimbabwe Press, 2002), 4–11; Josiah Brownell, *The Collapse of Rhodesia: Population Demographics and the Politics of Race* (London: I. B. Taurus, 2011), 3, 73, 89.

7. Caroline Elkins, "Race, Citizenship, and Governance: Settler Tyranny and the End of Empire," in Caroline Elkins and Susan Pedersen, *Settler Colonialism in the Twentieth Century: Projects, Practices, Legacies* (New York: Routledge, 2005), 203–22, esp. 206–7; Leonard V. Smith, "Wilsonian Sovereignty in the Middle East: The King-Crane Commission Report of 1919," in *The State of Sovereignty: Territories, Laws, Populations*, ed. Douglas Howland and Luise White (Bloomington: Indiana University Press, 2009), 56–74.

Southern Rhodesia: A Short History

Southern Rhodesia was founded as a chartered colony of the British South Africa Company in 1890. It was Cecil Rhodes's attempt to find more gold and to create a buffer against the Dutch in South Africa. Thirty years later a rebellion had been vanquished, South Africa was British, the gold mines were not wholly successful, and a chartered colony did not fit easily with the imperial world after the Treaty of Versailles. Indeed, Jan Smuts, an architect of the mandate system of the League of Nations, wanted Southern Rhodesia to join the Union of South Africa, but a white electorate of less than fifteen thousand, fearing an influx of white Afrikaaners, rejected this in 1922. In 1923, the British government expropriated the British South Africa Company, which then ceased to administer both Northern and Southern Rhodesia. The company maintained some rights in Northern Rhodesia but Southern Rhodesia was annexed to the crown as a colony but would have responsible government. This had a specific and limited meaning in 1923: Britain had the right to make laws for Southern Rhodesia but the colony could legislate its own internal affairs so long as these did not affect African land rights and political rights, such as they were. The assembly was elected, and the cabinet was chosen from ministers all of whom were appointed by the governor, including the prime minister. In a very short time the Southern Rhodesian government presented all draft legislation to Britain and amended or abandoned them if the United Kingdom objected, thus making the limits of responsible government barely visible.[8]

This version of responsible government did not give Rhodesia dominion status, as many white politicians were to insist forty years later. Dominion status was itself very indistinct: it was an ambiguous term used to convey that some self-governing states—Canada, New Zealand, Australia, and the Union of South Africa after 1910—were to some degree subordinate to Britain. At its most clear-cut it marked a space between internal self-government and full independence, and as such it proved a useful procedural route to the independence of the Indian subcontinent. It was South Africa, and the union Southern Rhodesia rejected, that had

---

8. Robert Blake, *A History of Rhodesia* (London: Eyre Methuen, 1977), 189–93; Martin Chanock, *Unconsummated Union: Britain, Rhodesia, and South Africa, 1900–1945* (Manchester: Manchester University Press, 1977), 136–37,172–77; Ian Phimister, *An Economic and Social History of Zimbabwe, 1890–1948* (London: Longman, 1988), 116–70; J. R. T. Wood, *So Far and No Further! Rhodesia's Bid for Independence during the Retreat from Empire, 1959–1865* (Victoria, BC: Tafford, 2005), 9.

dominion status with responsible government. Southern Rhodesia had responsible government without dominion status.[9]

Throughout the 1920s, commercial agriculture expanded. Even as Britain regarded Southern Rhodesia's African policies as more progressive than those of South Africa, the Land Apportionment Act of 1930—the cornerstone of settler society, wrote Victor Machingaidze—evicted thousands of Africans from their farms to guarantee that land was available to new white farmers. A few years later the government of Southern Rhodesia created Native Purchase Areas, to compensate Africans not necessarily for their loss of land, but for their loss of the right to purchase land anywhere in the country. The scheme never managed to settle the fifty thousand African farmers Rhodesian officials both hoped and feared would create a propertied African middle class, but the ten thousand Purchase Area farmers who took advantage of the scheme occupied a unique space in how Rhodesians imagined African politics, as chapters 6, 9, and 11 show.[10] This pattern, of openings for white immigrants yet to come that closed down opportunities for Africans, was to be repeated for years, especially after World War II, when the white population grew rapidly as commercial agriculture became once again profitable.

In 1951, Southern Rhodesia introduced the Native Land Husbandry Act (NLHA). Funded by the World Bank, it marked a significant shift in thinking about Africans, as Jocelyn Alexander has argued: Africans were no longer communal tribesmen, but rational actors operating within an impersonal market. Each man was a yeoman farmer. There would be fewer but more productive farms in the reserves; rural Africans should not be intermittent farmers, nor could they lay claim to land they had not worked for years. Urban Africans were to live in townships and rely exclusively on their wages: The actual implementation of the act was slow, however, and gave chiefs considerable latitude about how to protect their own land and cattle while safeguarding their rights over land redistribution. African opposition to the act was intense.[11] The Southern

9. W. Donald McIntyre, "The Strange Death of Dominion Status," *J. Imperial and Commonwealth History* 27, no. 2 (1999): 193–212; A. G. Hopkins, "Rethinking Decolonization," *Past and Present* 200 (2008): 211–16.

10. Chanock, *Unconsummated Union*, 218; Phimister, *History of Zimbabwe*, 193–94; Victor E. M. Machingaidze, "Agrarian Change from Above: The Southern Rhodesia Native Land Husbandry Act and African Response," *International J. African Historical Studies* 24, no. 3 (1991): 557–88; Allison K. Shutt, "Purchase Area Farmers and the Middle Class of Southern Rhodesia, 1931–1952," *Int. J. African Historical Studies* 18, no. 3 (1997): 555–81; Jocelyn Alexander, *The Unsettled Land: State-making and the Politics of Land in Zimbabwe, 1893–2003* (Oxford: James Currey, 2006), 32–34.

11. Alexander, *The Unsettled Land*, 44–51; Machingaidze, "Agrarian Change," 565–88; Donald S. Moore, *Suffering for Territory: Race, Power, and Place in Zimbabwe* (Harare: Weaver Press, 2005), 83–87; Ian Phimister, "Rethinking the Reserves: Southern Rhodesia's Land Husbandry Act Reviewed,"

Rhodesia African National Congress (SRANC) and its successor, the National Democratic Party (NDP), made land, not voting, the center of their political platforms, and their actions in towns and countryside brought about a range of repressive legislation that was to shape the history of Rhodesia. A state of emergency was declared in early 1959. Many leaders of the SRANC were detained. In prison they founded the NDP and continued to direct party affairs, as we shall see in chapter 3. The Law and Order (Maintenance) Act of 1960 strengthened not only executive power but that of security forces just as trade unionists struggled with—and sometimes against—nationalists while political parties sent youth leagues into townships to rally support, often with great violence and always with easy accusations that rivals had collaborated with the regime.[12] By the time the NLHA was withdrawn in the early 1960s the rapidly overcrowded reserves were once more under the authority of chiefs and headmen.

Even as the government planned for a new kind of African farmer, officials in London, Salisbury, and Lusaka planned ways for new white immigrants to live in Africa. This was the Central African Federation, established in 1953. Federations within the British Empire had been promoted first in the 1880s, a way to secure British greatness in a way that made the nation global and British nationality the basis for political organization. There was one population—Anglo-Saxon—that could bring stability to a chaotic colonial world.[13] As the idea of an imperial federation waned in Britain, the idea of merging of Southern and Northern Rhodesia in some way took shape in the 1920s. There were fantastic ideas with fantastic maps.[14] The Central African Federation created in the early 1950s was in large part a product of pressure exerted by mining companies on the Colonial Office, which itself grappled with how the

---

J. Southern African Studies 19, no. 2 (1993): 225–39; William A. Munro, *The Moral Economy of the State: Conservation, Community Development and State Making in Zimbabwe* (Athens: Ohio University Press, 1998), 112–16; Heike Schmidt, *Colonialism and Violence in Zimbabwe: A History of Suffering* (Oxford: James Currey, 2012), 117–20.

12. Brian Raftopoulos, "The Labour Movement in Zimbabwe, 1945–1965," in *Keep on Knocking: A History of the Labour Movement in Zimbabwe, 1900–97*, ed. Brian Raftopoulos and Ian Phimister (Harare: Baobab Books, 1997), 55–90, and "Nationalism and Labour in Salisbury 1953–65," in *Sites of Struggle: Essays in Zimbabwe's Urban History*, ed. Brian Raftopoulos and Tsuneo Yoshikuni (Harare: Weaver Press, 1999), 129–50; Timothy Scarnecchia, *The Urban Roots of Democracy and Political Violence in Zimbabwe: Harare and Highfield, 1940–1964* (Rochester, NY: University of Rochester Press, 2008), 94–113; Terence Ranger, *Writing Revolt: An Engagement with African Nationalism, 1957–67* (Harare: Weaver Press, 2013).

13. Duncan Bell, *The Idea of Greater Britain* (Princeton, NJ: Princeton University Press, 2007), 92–93, 117–19.

14. The best summary of these plans is in Wood, *No Further!*, 15–16.

new white immigrants would live in Africa: in old colonies or in new kinds of states. In the end the Colonial Office agreed to a federation of Southern and Northern Rhodesia so long as it included Nyasaland. The widespread joke in Southern Rhodesia was that the federation was a "marriage of convenience" between a wealthy bride (copper-rich Northern Rhodesia) and a hardworking husband (the not-so-coded reference to white settlers in Southern Rhodesia). Impoverished Nyasaland was accepted "as the unavoidable mother-in-law in the matrimonial home." But many whites in Southern Rhodesia were elated: the goal of some kind of merging with Northern Rhodesia, a tobacco farmer said, was that "the copper mines could pay for the development of the whole area . . . the same as the coal mines did in Britain and gold in South Africa."[15] What was to distress many whites in Southern Rhodesia was the degree to which the question of Southern Rhodesia's status was mooted by the creation of the federation.

The structure of the federation disrupted the familiar hierarchies of colonial rule, in which the Colonial Office appointed a governor to oversee the territory and to act according to the reports of district and provincial officials. In the Central African Federation, Southern Rhodesia came under the supervision of the Commonwealth Relations Office (CRO); the federal government which oversaw the administration of Northern Rhodesia and Nyasaland was located in Salisbury while the two territories were nominally under the control of the Colonial Office. The federal government and those of the two northern territories were often in conflict; the Colonial Office usually did not support the federal government, about which officials in Salisbury complained loudly.[16] This made Southern Rhodesia's status as a British possession even more ambiguous than it had been, and it made party politics layered. The federation introduced a tiered political system of federal and territorial assemblies and political parties that operated at both levels. It also required a determination of who, if anyone, would elect representatives to these bodies. There were federal electoral commissions and territorial franchise commissions. As chapter 2 shows, these did not promote universal adult suffrage but instead worked out convoluted imaginaries by which each territory would have something called nonracial politics that eventually would lead to parity between black and white

15. Bennie Goldin, Q. C., *The Judge, the Prince and the Usurper—from UDI to Zimbabwe* (New York: Vantage Press, 1990), 15; Carl Herbert Fox, Salisbury, November 7, 1973, National Archives of Zimbabwe [hereafter NAZ]/ORAL/F02.

16. Philip Murphy, *Party Politics and Decolonization: The Conservative Party and British Colonial Policy in Tropical Africa* (Oxford: Clarendon Press, 1995), 20–21.

in legislative bodies. The franchise commission in Southern Rhodesia, where voter qualifications had not changed since the 1930s, did not seek to expand or to limit African voting so much as it sought to hone it, to make sure that voter qualifications met African experiences, and to make sure Africans did not vote based on appeals to their emotions, emotions all too often triggered by talk of race. It is easy enough to read these commissions as a last gasp of white supremacy, but that would flatten the very active debates about race and politics that they engendered. There was a range of multiracial organizations, as we will see in the next chapter, and a social world, best chronicled by Philip Mason, of Salisbury dinners in which white people argued about the ideas of Burke and Mill and who should be allowed to vote.[17]

By the time the recommendations of the 1957 franchise commission were debated and reworked, events in Nyasaland and commissions from London sounded the death knell for the federation. The Monckton Commission recommended a few, halfhearted life-saving techniques: a complete reorganization of the structure of federation, moving the capital, parity of whites and blacks in the federal assembly, and changing the federation's name altogether.[18] Only in Southern Rhodesia were these recommendations taken seriously. In 1961 the Southern Rhodesia organizing secretary for the ruling United Federal Party (UFP) suggested a contest to change the name of the federation. He understood that Africans hated the term, so perhaps the party rank and file could come up with a better name. He himself liked "Rhonasia. . . . Friends, let us love 'Rhonasia.' Let us build it into a glorious country. Let us be big enough to forget this silly bickering about race."[19]

No other territory and certainly not Britain was as concerned with how to save the federation: Northern and Southern Rhodesia elected antifederal parties in 1962, when both Northern Rhodesia and Nyasaland were on track to become independent states in a few years. Southern Rhodesia was another issue entirely. Starting in January 1961 the debates about the new constitution became debates about the status of Southern Rhodesia. As chapter 3 shows, throughout 1961 white and

17. Admittedly these were the dinners to which the head of the Institute of Race Relations would be invited. Philip Mason, *Year of Decision: Rhodesia and Nyasaland in 1960* (Oxford: Oxford University Press, 1960), 70–71.

18. John Darwin, *Britain and Decolonisation: The Retreat from Empire in the Post-War World* (New York: St. Martin's Press, 1988), 272–73.

19. Steve Kock, *Ukuru!*, vol. 1, 1961 mimeograph, Salisbury, Rhodesia. Kock did not want anyone to recommend any "silly names like 'Zimbabwe'!" Sir Edgar Whitehead papers, personal file October 1960–September 1962, Rhodes House, Oxford [hereafter RH] Mss Afr s 1482/2.

African political parties, and factions therein, demanded that the new constitution should promise independence, or dominion status, or majority rule soon, or majority rule in a distant future. As Northern Rhodesia and Nyasaland were readied for independence, the question of Southern Rhodesia's status became acute. As that status was debated and disputed, older ideas were given renewed and powerful emphasis as talk of standards, responsible government, and voter qualification began to circulate from Salisbury to London, shaping the vocabularies with which the country demanded its independence. In 1963, however, no one in London or Salisbury thought the future of Southern Rhodesia would be a peaceful one. Six months before its dissolution, the Conservative government in Britain handed over most of the federation's military assets to Southern Rhodesia. The Royal Rhodesian Air Force was given to Southern Rhodesia in its entirety. The official explanation was that this force had originated in Southern Rhodesia and thus should return there, but in the United Nations and in African capitals it was understood that Southern Rhodesia had been given the only force capable of repelling an invasion from Britain or a liberation army.[20]

Rhodesia: A Short History

Southern Rhodesia officially became Rhodesia before UDI, on May 24, 1964, when Northern Rhodesia became Zambia: government offices and businesses were instructed to drop the "Southern" from its name.[21] Residents had already been doing this for years, speaking as if "Northern Rhodesia" were a branch, not the real Rhodesia. By then the NLHA had been repealed and African settlement or resettlement in the reserves had intensified; such tribesmen were to live under the customary authority of chiefs and headmen. Also by 1964 the successor to the National Democratic Party, the Zimbabwe African Peoples Union (ZAPU), had been banned, and the party that broke from it, the Zimbabwe African National Union (ZANU), was launched in exile. Leaders of both parties

20. Wood, *No Further!*, 215; Philip Murphy, "'An intricate and distasteful subject': British Planning for the Use of Force against European Settlers in Central Africa, 1952–65," *English Historical Review* 131, no. 402 (2006): 764–65; Carl Peter Watts, *Rhodesia's Unilateral Declaration of Independence: An International History* (London: Palgrave, 2012), 62–63.

21. Cabinet minutes, May 27, 1964. Ian Smith deposit, Cory Library, Rhodes University, Grahamstown, South Africa [hereafter CL/Smith]/17. By the date of UDI, Britain had not ratified the change of name; see Daniel McNeil, "'The Rivers of Zimbabwe Will Run Red with Blood': Enoch Powell and the Post-Imperial Nostalgia of the Monday Club," *J. Southern African Studies* 37, no. 4 (2011): 734.

were either in prison or otherwise restricted, or else in exile in Zambia or Tanzania. Before UDI and again in the early 1970s, a great deal of African politics took place in Rhodesia's jails, as we shall see in chapters 3 and 7.

The legal political parties, all of which were white and almost all of which considered themselves nonracial or multiracial, grew out of long genealogies of shifting coalitions with names that were as broad as they were interchangeable, such as the United Federal Party (UFP). After the 1961 constitution was accepted, several new parties were formed, the most important of which was the Rhodesian Front. Formed by members of the segregationist Dominion Party and disaffected but well-placed members of the UFP, and funded by wealthy landowners, in 1962 it actively opposed the new constitution that some claimed would lead to majority rule too soon and others claimed should merit independence at once. The history of the Rhodesian Front and the history of independent Rhodesia are very much entwined, but in 1962 it looked like one of the many political parties that had a fleeting moment in Rhodesian electoral politics: it was thought to be the kind of "rusty, crusty old fashioned right-wing party" that never won an electoral victory in Southern Rhodesia.[22] In 1962 it did win, however. Despite its narrow margin of victory, the new government began planning for independence at once: civil servants who were members of the party conducted affairs of state but in private planned UDI. The Rhodesian Front government was considered a "seismic shift" in white politics and an equally seismic shift in African politics.[23] The change in white politics has been explained by everything from a history of anticommunism that predated UDI, to events in the newly independent Congo, to the embrace of right-wing ideologies imported from the United States or a reworked version of British fascism.[24] All of these explanations are shorthands, of course, and all are somewhat flawed, as this and subsequent chapters argue. The Rhodesian Front was a party of wealthy farmers, recent immigrants, and experienced parliamentarians: it was only anti-establishment in that it demanded a break from Britain. At the same time, all observers

22. *The Central African Examiner*, quoted in Evans, Rhodesian Front Rule, 33–34.
23. Blake, *Rhodesia*, 343–44, 367; Donal Lowry, "The Impact of Anti-communism on White Rhodesian Political Culture, c. 1920–1980," *Cold War History* 7, no. 2 (2007): 177.
24. Desmond Lardner-Burke, *Rhodesia: The Story of a Crisis* (London: Ouldborne Book Co., 1966), 11–12. Evans, Rhodesian Front Rule, 41; Wood, *No Further!*, 100–101; Daniel McNeil, " 'The Rivers of Zimbabwe Will Run Red with Blood': Enoch Powell and the Post-Imperial Nostalgia of the Monday Club," *J. Southern African Studies* 37, no. 4 (2011): 731–45; Lowry, "Impact of Anti-Communism," 169–94.

attributed its victories either to how whites voted or to how Africans did not vote, as we will see in chapter 3.

The Rhodesian Front was returned by an overwhelming majority in 1964, when it promised to seek independence, with or without Britain's approval. Shortly thereafter, it replaced its leader with Ian Smith, formerly the chief federal whip of the UFP, who demanded independence and was to be Rhodesia's prime minister until 1979. Smith and Rhodesian Front stalwarts were to insist that the 1961 constitution promised independence, or that British diplomats had done so, or that independence was what Rhodesia deserved after Britain had abandoned the federation. After a year of increasingly argumentative negotiations, first with a Conservative and then with a Labour government in Britain, and after months of "quiet" in rural Rhodesia and its townships, Rhodesia took its own independence on November 11, 1965. Between 1965 and 1972 was the era of Harold Wilson's "five principles," the requirements that Rhodesia would have to meet in order to have its independence recognized by Britain. One of these was that the "whole" population of Rhodesia had to approve of independence so taken. Rhodesian Front officials argued that they had already fulfilled these principles, especially by the meetings of chiefs. The Rhodesian Front regarded chiefs both as its agents in rural Rhodesia, the men who implemented what agricultural policies the state had, and as the true, authentic representatives of rural people as we shall see in chapters 6 and 8. Chiefs of the 1960s and 1970s were anything but this, but the idea of chiefs and what they could do for the Rhodesian state was a powerful one for a political party that argued with increasing frequency that Africans were primarily rural tribesmen.

Rhodesia was the first pariah nation. Mandatory sanctions were imposed on it right after UDI, and no other country recognized it. Rhodesia was to struggle for some kind of recognition for its entire history, but it legitimated itself in 1966. In a court case in which detainees challenged the legitimacy of the 1965 constitution, the high court found that Rhodesia was "de facto independent." The term seemed as good as any—Ian Smith was delighted; de facto was better than illegal—because UDI was not necessarily straightforward nor was its meaning clear to anyone on the ground in Rhodesia. Journalists noted how glum everyone seemed: instead of parades and celebrations the atmosphere seemed "menacing."[25] Six weeks after UDI, the president, Clifford Dupont, held

25. Marion Kaplan, "Their Rhodesia," *Transition* 23 (1965): 32.

an anguished meeting with the American consul general; if sanctions prevailed he could see no future for the country unless it became a fifth province of South Africa.[26] Calvin Trillin visited Rhodesia in early 1966. He was the first of many visitors to disparage what Rhodesians bragged about, particularly their working telephones. Trillin was told over and over again that telephone service was so bad in neighboring Zambia that businessmen preferred to drive hundreds of miles to the Copperbelt rather than wait for a connection. Trillin saw something "constricting" about a country "where the national aspiration can be stated in terms of preserving an efficient telephone system."[27]

The first years of UDI were those of the Rhodesian Front's "cowboy cabinet." There are multiple meanings of "cowboy" and almost all of them applied: in this case most ministers were farmers and only a few had political experience.[28] Although the business community had only reluctantly supported UDI, commerce and industry were able to usher in a period of extraordinary economic growth (1966–1972) during which white immigration was greater than white emigration and "sanctions busting" provided the renegade nation with heroes. These were men who could break laws made by Britain but who could be, and were, compared to James Bond. A James Bond would have lived comfortably. The Rhodesian economy, stagnant in the early 1960s, grew at an unprecedented rate, averaging over 9 percent per year between 1966 and 1974. Under sanctions, local industries flourished by producing goods that had been imported a few years before. Profits stayed in Rhodesia, not because of patriotism but because the Rhodesian Front government assumed increasingly tight control over foreign-exchange transactions. Rhodesia managed to export its most profitable commodities for much of the period of UDI, as chapter 5 shows. Despite complaints by manufacturers that the intense conscription of the late 1970s removed young

26. Consul General, Salisbury to State Department, Washington DC, January 22, 1966. Dupont admitted that this meeting was "to blow off steam," which he could safely do with an American diplomat because "you wouldn't dare tell your people in Washington you had come to see me." Lyndon Baines Johnson Library, Austin, Texas [hereafter LBJ]/NSF Country file/97.

27. Calvin Trillin, "Letter from Salisbury," The New Yorker 42 (November 12, 1966): 139, 162. Ten years later David Caute interviewed a company director who had the usual praise for Rhodesia's standards of sanitation, hygiene, and "telephones that work." David Caute, Under the Skin: The Death of White Rhodesia (London: Allen Lane, 1983), 27.

28. The first president, Clifford Dupont, thought "the inexperience helped us a great deal because . . . it was to our advantage that we didn't know the protocol of being a minister." Clifford Dupont, Salisbury, June 1976 and January 1977, NAZ/ORAL/DU4. Nathan Shamuyarira noted the many meanings of cowboy: Rhodesian satirists used it to describe members' inexperience, and the British press used it to refer to the number of farmers in the cabinet; see Nathan Shamuyarira, Crisis in Rhodesia (London: Andre Deutch, 1965), 210.

men from the labor pool available to Rhodesian industries, black labor was substituted for white labor and was paid lower wages. Rhodesia's economic decline in the late 1970s was due to high oil prices, drought, war, and diminishing access to foreign exchange—problems that beset many African countries after 1972. What made the downturn in Rhodesia different, and in some ways more acute, was that it was war that was draining the country's foreign exchange and that manufacturing had saturated local markets. There was a gradual decline in domestic investment. Shortly after the failure of a proposed settlement with Britain, Rhodesian economists observed "the general feeling" that "something always seemed to be going wrong." Currency was another matter. The Rhodesian dollar was a source of great pride to the regime, even though it had three small devaluations between 1975 and 1979. The Reserve Bank took great pains to keep the money supply buoyant and its value stable. And for all the Rhodesian Front's insistence that multilateral organizations were too close to the Afro-Arab bloc in the UN, or somewhere, to be trustworthy, the World Bank worked quietly with the regime to repay the loans incurred by the Native Land Husbandry Act. In 1975 it provided funds for a foundation that would provide capital to Africans who wished to buy farms.[29]

Throughout the 1960s there were dramatic conferences between the Rhodesian Front and Harold Wilson's government—on yachts on the high seas so as not to give implicit recognition to Rhodesia—and less exciting but constant negotiations in Salisbury with British representatives.[30] The boom years of the late 1960s shielded Rhodesia from compromising in any way even as moderates and the business community spoke of the need for an "honorable settlement" (see chapters 6 and 8). In 1969 Rhodesia produced a new constitution that pushed segregation to giddy and unworkable heights: its goal was not simply to create separate provincial councils for the three "races"—Europeans, Shona, and Ndebele—but to remove all rural Africans from participation in the institutions of representative government. Such a constitution was impossible to implement, but it was adopted by the new republic of Rhodesia. This so alarmed the new Conservative government in Britain that it began negotiations with the Salisbury government in order to bring Rhodesia back into the fold of modern nations. The 1971 White

29. John Handford, *Portrait of an Economy under Sanctions, 1965–1975* (Salisbury: Mercury Press, 1976), 26, 29; Patrick Bond, *Uneven Zimbabwe: A Study of Finance, Development, and Underdevelopment* (Trenton, NJ: Africa World Press, 1998), 126–36, 137–41.

30. UN representatives had come and gone in 1963; see Evans, Rhodesian Front Rule, 47.

Paper offered Rhodesia formal independence in exchange for a return to the 1961 constitution, the release of many political prisoners, and modest compromises on public meetings. The only requirement was to satisfy Wilson's fifth principle, to show that "the population of Rhodesia as a whole" approved. As chapter 8 shows, Africans made it clear to Britain's Pearce Commission that they did not approve. The campaign to reject the proposals was led in part by an African grassroots organization, the African National Council headed by Bishop Abel Muzorewa, whose increasingly sordid history is told in chapters 8, 9, and 11. When the White Paper was rejected, the Rhodesian Front returned to the 1969 constitution but in a few years the efforts of a war fought against two guerrilla armies, based in neighboring countries, took their toll: by 1976 Britain, the United States, and South Africa and many in the Rhodesian Front had good reason to fear Rhodesia's isolation. Rhodesian officials went to an all-party conference in Geneva in 1976, met with British and American diplomats throughout most of 1977, and eventually agreed to an "internal settlement" with a timetable to majority rule. In early 1979 there was a multiracial government elected by a clear majority, led by the party that had organized resistance to the Pearce Commission, and with a new name, Zimbabwe-Rhodesia, which Salisbury wags and British journalists quickly changed to "Rhobabwe."[31]

The government of Zimbabwe-Rhodesia, with Muzorewa as prime minister, gave a freer hand to its military than Rhodesia had done and began to bomb the camps—said to house guerrillas by Zimbabwe-Rhodesia and said to house refugees by the guerrilla armies—in Mozambique and Zambia. The raids and the fact that Zimbabwe-Rhodesia—a name only a few officials and generals bothered to use—had a government elected by a process that included Africans provided the nations that sheltered the guerrilla armies with reasons with which to argue for a negotiated end to the war. When Conservatives won the British election of May 1979 the Foreign and Commonwealth Office set about once again finding a solution to what was by then called "our terrible problems with Rhodesia."[32] After a remarkably few weeks of negotiations with various heads of state, a cease-fire agreement and a draft constitution were worked out at the Commonwealth Heads of Government Annual Meeting in Lusaka in August. Parties in exile and the Zimbabwe-Rhodesia government were

---

31. Caute, *Under the Skin*, 191; Xan Smiley, "Confusion in Rhobabwe," *The Spectator*, May 19, 1978, 7.

32. Sir Anthony Parsons of the Foreign and Commonwealth Office quoted in Michael Charlton, *The Last Colony in Africa: Diplomacy and the Independence of Rhodesia* (Oxford: Blackwell, 1990), 21.

invited to a constitutional conference at Lancaster House in London. In three months of great drama and empty threats the conference agreed to the Lusaka proposals. Zimbabwe-Rhodesia returned to being called Southern Rhodesia and was for the first time brought under direct British control, to supervise the elections scheduled for February 1980. Six weeks later, in April 1980, it became independent again, as Zimbabwe.

This summary gives scant attention to the guerrilla war Rhodesia fought against the armies of the two political parties in exile, the Zimbabwe African National Liberation Army (ZANLA) of ZANU and the Zimbabwe Peoples' Liberation Army (ZPRA, sometime written as ZIPRA) of ZAPU. This is not because I think the war was unimportant but because this book argues that it was not always central to the internal politics of Rhodesia. Indeed, some of the politics discussed in this book took place as if the war were something that could be ignored. Certainly how Africans' access to the vote was reckoned had little to do with the war—to the absurd point of Rhodesia's 1979 election that took place during a civil war. (This was probably true of the 1980 election as well; see chapter 11.) The idea of normalcy, of defending literacy in one constitution and debating the possibility of emulating Switzerland in another, was an almost daily practice in Rhodesian domestic politics. One of the texts that started my thinking along these lines was a book that described how school athletes and garden clubs in a city on the border with Mozambique managed their competitions during the war.[33] Lancelot Bales Smith, among the first to join the Rhodesian Front and eventually known as a moderate member of parliament (MP), described party congresses as "bonkers." Even as MPs described the pressures under which Rhodesia was made to participate in the Geneva conference in 1976, the rank and file demanded increased segregation of toilets in public parks.[34] In 1977, Christopher Hitchens was struck by how much Victoria Falls, surrounded by armed patrols, had the feel of a scaled-down European resort. In 1978, after mortar fire hit Umtali, on the border with Mozambique, schoolgirls marched through the main streets wearing banners that proclaimed "Umtali is super!" The art school designed posters reading "Umtali can take it!" An entrepreneur designed a T-shirt showing a beer bottle with fins and the caption "Come to Umtali

---

33. James MacBruce, *When the Going Was Rough: A Rhodesian Story* (Pretoria: Femina, 1983).
34. Lancelot Bales Smith, Banket, November 22, 1985, NAZ/ORAL/29.

and get bombed."[35] Journalists and visitors offered this as proof of the pitiable insularity of white Rhodesians. I disagree. I think the demands at party meetings and the banners and slogans suggest the extent to which Rhodesians literally sought to make the war transparent, something they could look through to see a "real" Rhodesia, with its proud cities and segregated public conveniences. More important, perhaps, and critical to the argument of this book, is that Rhodesia made up its governmentality as it went along: sometimes schoolgirls were in order.

One casualty of the historiographic binary of Rhodesia and Zimbabwe has been military history, however. Although publications chronicling one side or the other have appeared regularly since the early 1980s, there are texts, often in the form of memoirs, about the Rhodesian bush war in which African guerrillas and the barest mention of African politics are a background. There are fewer texts and a growing number of memoirs about the conflict that everyone else calls the liberation struggle in which white soldiers and white politics are the background.[36] The exception is J. R. T. Wood's encyclopedic history of Rhodesia from 1965 to 1969, with its day-by-day account of politics and war.[37] Whatever the historiography, I am also wary of writing a history that shows the guerrilla war to be a constant. Barbarians were always imagined at Rhodesia's gates, to be sure, but the war Rhodesia fought against African nationalists had significant down times, especially 1975–1976, when ZANLA policed itself and ZIPRA struggled under the "umbrella" of Muzorewa's African National Council. When the war effort began anew, with increased Eastern bloc funding and arms, it was when an economically weakened Rhodesia had intensified its own war effort, through a massive conscription of its white population that I shall discuss at length in chapter 7. There have been various arguments that by 1979, even as Muzorewa

35. Denis Hills, *Rebel People* (New York: Africana Publishing, 1978), 109; Christopher Hitchens, "Salisbury Diary," *New Statesman* 47, no. 16 (September 1977): 365; Meredith, *Another Country*, 240–41; David Pike, *My Part in the Downfall: Being Civil in the Rhodesian War* (Pietermaritzburg: David Pike, 2009), 48.

36. A basic list would include David Martin and Phyllis Johnson, *The Struggle for Zimbabwe* (London: Faber & Faber, 1981); Paul L. Moorcraft and Peter McLaughlin, *Chimurenga! The War in Rhodesia, 1965–1980* (Johannesburg: Sygma/Collins, 1982); Lt. Ron Reid-Daly, *Selous Scouts: Top Secret War* (Alberton: South Africa, Galago, 1982); N. Bhebe and T. Ranger, eds., *Soldiers in Zimbabwe's Liberation War* (Harare: University of Zimbabwe Press, 1995). Chris Cocks, *Fireforce: One Man's War in the Rhodesian Light Infantry* (Weltevreden Park, South Africa, 1997); Wilfred Mhanda, *Dzino: Memoirs of a Freedom Fighter* (Harare: Weaver, 2011); and a number of novels I will discuss in chapter 7.

37. J. R. T. Wood, *A Matter of Weeks Rather Than Months: The Impasse between Harold Wilson and Ian Smith, Sanctions, and Aborted Settlements and War, 1965–1969* (Victoria, B. C.: Tafford, 2008). See also R. S. Roberts, "The Armed Forces and Chimurenga: Ideology and Historiography," *Heritage of Zimbabwe* 7 (1989): 31–47.

took office, the war was at a stalemate. It was not: the war effort by both Rhodesian and guerrilla forces intensified after 1979, but that is only part of the story.[38] The rest is that there was international pressure in and out of Africa, and a new Conservative government in Britain saw in the internal settlement an opportunity to push ZANU and ZAPU and the Rhodesian Front to negotiate an end to the war. Diplomacy was not the only kind of accommodation taking place, however. In 1978 Tom Wigglesworth, a retired British army officer who had come to Rhodesia in 1974, was captured by ZANLA on his farm on the Mozambique border. The guerrillas were passing through; they had not intended to capture anyone but assumed he was some kind of mercenary. Marched through Mozambique, he was frequently interrogated; each time he demanded to know why he had been taken prisoner. An exasperated cadre told him why: "hundreds of whites all over the country" were helping ZANLA but he was not. He then named Wigglesworth's neighbors who gave food to his comrades and did not report their presence on the border. This troubled Wigglesworth. "Some of them were very vociferous supporters of Smith and the Rhodesian Front party."[39]

Decolonization

However it is told, the history of Rhodesia (or Southern Rhodesia) becoming Zimbabwe is a heroic one: either the small brave white-ruled nation standing alone in a hostile world or the inevitable victory of guerrilla armies fighting on behalf of African masses and defeating minority rule. This chapter and the two that follow it are about another story, that of Southern Rhodesia becoming Rhodesia. I argue that the link between the two is neither white Rhodesians' intransigence nor the rise of African nationalism, but the decolonization of Africa. And decolonization, as Frederick Cooper has shown for French Africa, was not so much a political fact as it was the principled ideas and piecemeal reforms that lay between the "colonial" and the "postcolonial."[40]

Historians of sub-Saharan Africa have come slowly to the study of decolonization. In part this is because African history began as an academic discipline when African nations became independent. The sub-

38. Mathew Preston, "Stalemate and the Termination of Civil War: Rhodesia Reassessed," *J. Peace Research* 41, no. 1 (2004): 65–83.

39. Tom Wigglesworth, *Perhaps Tomorrow* (Salisbury: Galaxie Press, 1980), 28, 31.

40. Frederick Cooper, *Citizenship between Empire and Nation: Remaking France and French Africa, 1945–1960* (Princeton, NJ: Princeton University Press, 2014).

ject matter of African history was to show how different it was from imperial history or anthropology, and in its first years most doctoral research was into the history of precolonial Africa as if this was a way to historicize African independence and the sovereignty thereof.[41] By the end of the 1970s there was a critical shift to twentieth-century African history, often showing Africans' constant and varied resistance to colonial rule. It may be too much of a leap to argue that the idea of African nationalism lurked behind studies of colonial Africa, but by and large these studies implied that colonialism was something to be struggled against, whether in small private acts or in public protests: colonialism generated African nations and thus African nationalism. This led to a tendency to write of African independence and the decolonization of Africa as if they were one and the same, as if both emerged from nationalism and a reformed, some said retreating, imperialism. This was tempered by new archives: what made decolonization different from the inexorable triumph of nationalism was that it involved a change in metropolitan thinking. As Frederick Cooper pointed out almost twenty years ago, by the late 1940s the imperial world (London and Accra, Paris and Bamako) was a jumble of ideas and actions—some political, some social, and almost all of them anxious about what the future would hold—that could not be flattened into nationalism or decolonization.[42]

This decolonization described something different from the imperial retreat, a term that does not do justice to the changing ideas about empire in both colonial and European capitals that sought alternatives to colonial rule, such as the pro-colonial Monday Club and the Capricorn Africa Society, which figures in chapter 2. Imperial retreat does not allow for the frequency with which African nationalists sometimes tried to delay independence, as we shall see in chapters 10 and 11. In 1955, for example, the governor of the Gold Coast complained to his wife how difficult it was to give Africans "the independence for which they have been clamoring all these years. Now they are going to have it whether they like it or not."[43]

Imperial historians have tended to argue that decolonization was a fairly even process, not wholly directed from London and Paris but very much shaped by concerns there. Based on a first exploration of new

41. This was first articulated by John Lonsdale, "States and Social Processes in Africa: A Historiographical Survey," *African Studies Review* 24, no. 2/3 (1981): 139–225.

42. Frederick Cooper, *Decolonization and African Society: The Labor Question in French and British Africa* (Cambridge: Cambridge University Press, 2006), 173–75.

43. Jean Marie Allman, *Quills of the Porcupine: Asante Nationalism in Emergent Ghana* (Madison: University of Wisconsin Press, 1993), 146.

British archives, in 1988 John Darwin argued that World War II, and colonial economies' involvement therein, created new political conditions that made colonies harder to rule. By the 1950s—and certainly after 1957—Britain did not have the resources to fully repress anticolonial movements. More important, perhaps, was that such repression would have weakened a number of Britain's alliances in Europe and North America. Economic relations between Britain and her former possessions did not necessarily change because of decolonization, but they were governed by new sets of rules.[44] Imperial historians writing a few years later honed these points. In 1995 Philip Murphy published a detailed and subtle study of the Conservative Party and the decolonization of Africa in which he showed not only the complexity of Conservative opinions and ideas about African independence but also the ways various lobbies shaped and undermined policies and plans.[45] Five years later Nicholas White's research of business records showed that British policy at the end of empire in Africa was shaped as much by relations with Washington as they were by corporate interests fearful of African violence.[46]

African historians, working with local and metropolitan archives, reported something else, Africans' continual reworking of metropolitan openings and opportunities. Decolonization took place in fits and starts, with overtures exploited and procedures scaled back. There was occasional—and eventually violent—disdain for the very notion of the nation-state. The exiled king of Buganda complained that the only person in Uganda who wanted a unitary state was the British governor, while a newspaper on Zanzibar cautioned its readers against the new, strange idea that they were "Zanzibaris." Veteran politicians in the Gold Coast wanted a federal state with more representation for Asante, while new metropolitan gestures toward multiracial elections—"the fancy franchises" we will see in chapter 3—were manipulated by shrewd politicians to bring about independence in poor colonies.[47] Even

44. Darwin, *Britain and Decolonisation*, 16, 21–23.

45. Philip Murphy, *Party Politics and Decolonization: The Conservative Party in British Colonial Policy in Tropical Africa, 1951–1964* (Oxford: Clarendon Press, 1995).

46. Nicholas J. White, "The Business and the Politics of Decolonization: The British Experience in the Twentieth Century," *Economic History Review* 53, no. 3 (2000): 544–64. Washington did not seem to take its cues from London on the decolonization of Central Africa, however. A CIA document from mid-1965 predicted "race riots" in the Copperbelt if Rhodesia took its own independence; Central Intelligence Agency, "Zambia and Its Refugee Nationalist Problem," July 3, 1965, LBJ/NSF 102/1.

47. Mutesa II, Kabaka of Buganda, *Desecration of My Kingdom* (London: Constable, 1967), 12–22; Jonathon Glassman, "Sorting Out the Tribes: The Creation of Racial Identities in Colonial Zanzibar's Newspaper Wars," *J. African History* 41, no. 3 (2000): 395; Allman, *Quills of the Porcupine;*

the best-intentioned colonial regimes followed "madcap" policies like Tanganyika's disastrous groundnut scheme, and the least progressive became imperial embarrassments. In the wake of Mau Mau, Kenya seemed tragically out of step with imperial goals, a pathological example of policies that had to be reversed so that Britain could end its empire with grace and pride.[48]

A new generation of diplomatic and European historians has taken decolonization in another direction altogether, arguing that the very embrace of the concept in the 1950s and 1960s made a critical distinction between anticolonial movements and the civil rights movement in the United States. Focusing on the sovereignty of states rather than on race and its historical deployments removed debates about decolonization from its Pan-African roots and created a discourse in which politics in Africa was something that should be conducted without reference to race. We will see this again in chapters 2 and 3, but these ideas were inverted by many Rhodesian politicians before and during UDI. Not only was it Africans and the British who were racists, insisting that races be represented in specific ways, but Americans in particular failed to understand Rhodesia's unique place in the world precisely because they confused the struggle there with the civil rights movement.[49]

Within Rhodesia, and certainly within the Rhodesian Front, the end of empire required no subtlety and no African or Pan-African history to understand, however: decolonization was seen as a top-down enterprise, another way that a weakened socialist and permissive Britain was willing to placate the United Nations or the Commonwealth or whoever and abandon their kith and kin. Britain and its naïve insistence on majority rule was the problem, not African nationalism. In November 1965

John Iliffe, "Breaking the Chain at Its Weakest Link: TANU and the Colonial Office," in *In Search of a Nation: Histories of Authority and Dissonance in Tanzania*, ed. Gregory H. Maddox and James L. Giblin (Oxford: James Currey, 2005), 168–97; Daniel Branch, *Defeating Mau Mau, Creating Kenya* (Cambridge: Cambridge University Press, 2009).

48. I owe "madcap" to Frederick Cooper, "Mau Mau and the Discourses of Decolonization," *J. African History* 29, no. 2 (1988): 313–320; David Anderson, *Histories of the Hanged: The Dirty War in Kenya and the End of Empire* (New York: Norton, 2005), 328–30.

49. I take this point from Shepard, *Invention of Decolonization*, 60–61. See also Penny M. von Eschen, *Race against Empire: Black Americans and Anti-Colonialism, 1937–1957* (Ithaca, NY: Cornell University Press, 1997), 145–66; Mathew Connelly, *A Diplomatic Revolution: Algeria's Fight for Independence and the Origins of the Post–Cold War World* (New York: Oxford, 2002), 119–24, 142–54. There has been a development within American history to re-insert race into the history of U.S. relations with Rhodesia; see Andrew DeRoche, *Black, White and Chrome: The United States and Zimbabwe, 1953–1998* (Trenton, NJ: Africa World Press, 2001); Gerald Horne, *From the Barrel of a Gun: The United States and the War against Zimbabwe, 1965–1980* (Chapel Hill: University of North Carolina Press, 2001); Francis Njubi Nesbitt, *Race against Sanctions: African Americans against Apartheid* (Bloomington: Indiana University Press, 2004).

Rhodesia's Special Branch—a body well informed about the extent of African nationalist and trade unionist organizing—was quick to reassure the cabinet that the antigovernment demonstrations had been directed from abroad by exiled leaders encouraged to do so by Britain.[50]

In the next few chapters, I refer to what Rhodesia rebelled against as the orderly process of decolonization. By orderly I do not mean a political transition free of riots and repression, but orderly in terms of the idea of African territories crossing a threshold by which they would become nation-states and take a newly claimed rightful place in the community of nations, the UN, the Commonwealth, and even the Organization of African Unity (OAU). For many Rhodesian politicians, not all of whom supported UDI, this made for a dangerous new world. The imagined power and reach of these new coalitions problematize some of the literature on decolonization and the idea that a straightforward political independence was its end point. Another journey to independence—at least for some colonies and possessions—was through multilateral organizations. The United Nations had a particular role in decolonization, especially in the first years of decolonization. Algeria's Front de Libération Nationale (FLN) and its "battle of New York" may be the best-known example, but in 1964 Sir Roy Welensky, by then the former prime minister of the Central African Federation, feared that the "voting strength" of African nations in the UN would lead to intervention in the domestic affairs of Rhodesia and South Africa. Rhodesian Front hacks saw a "new colonialism" emerge from the UN; it was "a new empire." They feared that the creation of the OAU in 1963 would create "too many difficulties." Indeed, it was the founding of the OAU, some officials claimed, that made it necessary for Rhodesia to break with Britain "and take the consequences. Let us paddle our own canoe rather than there be an opportunity every now and then for some kind of special enquiry into what we were doing." Dominion status was not enough. "We took a calculated risk and went whole hog, taking our independence."[51]

This raises another question, however: if Rhodesia did not take its own independence, who would? By definition decolonization required that there would have to be someone to give independence to. There

50. Special Branch HQ, Salisbury, Organization of anti-government demonstrations, November 13, 1965. Cabinet memoranda, pt. 4, CL/Smith/20.

51. Connelly, *Diplomatic Revolution*, 125–30; Roy Welensky, "The United Nations and Colonialism in Africa," *Annals of the American Academy of Political and Social Science* 354 (1964): 145–52; Evans, Rhodesian Front Rule, 116; William Joseph Cary, Gwelo, September 1971 and February 1972, NAZ/ORAL/CA4.

would have to be political parties representing all Rhodesian peoples, there would have to be voters and elections, a government would have to form, and *then* independence could be given to that government. In Rhodesia in 1965 the two major African political parties were embattled: both had been banned and their leadership detained or exiled, so for these or any other political parties to hold elections and form a government meant that Britain would take direct control of Rhodesia until African political parties could legitimately form a government. In order for Britain to prepare Rhodesia for independence, it would first have to make it a colony. As discussed in chapters 10 and 11, this is precisely what happened in 1979, but in 1965 it did not even seem imaginable, let alone possible.

Several chapters in this book revisit this ideal of decolonization to look closely at the mechanics of the last colonial elections. Political scientists call these "foundational" elections in that they would instill democratic practices in the electorate; they were to make the "last stage of colonial government" become the first stage of African government.[52] Before anyone could practice democracy in any way, he or less often she had to fill out forms, register, and mark the ballot in the prescribed way. These were not uncomplicated or uncontested acts. First of all, threatened boycotts were sometimes as powerful as votes, as we shall see. Second, the ability to read and write was not the same as the ability to fill out forms. In the Nyasaland election of 1961, qualified voters had to be able to fill out the forms in English unaided (or have paid taxes for ten years and be able to fill out the form in one of the territory's African languages); many literate people were baffled by the forms and copied the instructions in the space reserved for answers.[53] In the Northern Rhodesia election of 1962 the literacy requirement followed that of Southern Rhodesia, the ability to fill out the form in English unaided. Kenneth Kaunda's United National Independence Party (UNIP) organized classes to give instructions on how to fill out the form to electors who had met all the other requirements. The Northern Rhodesia branch of the UFP demanded that the government outlaw these "registration schools," but the government refused: what was the difference

---

52. Staffan I. Lindberg, *Democracy and Elections in Africa* (Baltimore: Johns Hopkins University Press, 2006), 8–12; W. J. M. MacKenzie and Kenneth Robinson, eds., *Five Elections in Africa: A Group of Electoral Studies* (Oxford: Clarendon Press, 1960), 463–65.

53. Lucy Mair, *The Nyasaland Election of 1961* (London: Athlone Press, 1962), 23.

between students studying for examinations and a voter practicing how to register?[54]

The elections of the 1950s and early 1960s with their orderly lines and secret ballots and the secure ballot boxes elected a national government, to be sure, but they also gave proof that the colony was ready for the transition to nation. Peter Pels, writing about late colonial Tanganyika, and Justin Willis, writing about Sudan in 1953, have argued that such elections were performances, demonstrations of Africans' ability to be modern, to make political choices that were new and separate from clan and countryside.[55] The audience for the conduct and the results of these elections was as much in Africa as it was in the metropole. The electoral defeat of federalist parties in the late 1950s and early 1960s was heralded in London and Accra and Nairobi as the triumph of nation over tribe and region.[56] This triumph was the promise of "impartial" elections, so critical to territories on the cusp of independence. Years before "free and fair elections" and "imagined communities" became mantras of different sorts, K. W. J. Post wrote that although independence was "phrased as nationhood," there was "very little common sentiment that can bind all citizens together in allegiance to a new political system." Yet by "the casting of a vote" people demonstrated their willingness to be part of the new political system. Voting alone would not guarantee democracy, but it was the method by which "the mass of the people" would come to identify with the political system.[57] These kinds of elections took place almost twenty years later in Rhodesia than they did anywhere else in Africa and perhaps for that reason they were even more invested with the same imaginary of inculcating democratic values. Indeed, the Rhodesian elections were thought to encourage democracy and bring an end to war, all by allowing Africans in huge numbers to vote.

54. David C. Mulford, *The Northern Rhodesia General Election, 1962* (Nairobi: Oxford University Press, 1964), 55–56.

55. Peter Pels, "Imagining Elections: Modernity, Mediation and the Secret Ballot in Late Colonial Tanganyika," in *The Hidden History of the Secret Ballot*, ed. Romain Bertrand, Jean-Louis Briquet, and Peter Pels (Bloomington: Indiana University Press, 2006), 100–113; Justin Willis, "'A Model of Its Kind': Representation and Performance in the Sudan Self-government Election of 1953," *J. Imperial and Commonwealth History* 35, no. 3 (2007): 485–502, and "'We Changed the Laws': Electoral Practice and Malpractice in Sudan since 1953," *African Affairs* 109, no. 435 (2010): 191–212.

56. Allman, *Quills of the Porcupine*, 159–62; David M. Anderson, "'Yours in Struggle for Majimbo': Nationalism and the Party Politics of Decolonization in Kenya, 1955–64," *J. Contemporary History* 40, no. 3 (2005): 547–64.

57. K. W. J. Post, *The Nigerian Federal Election of 1959: Politics and Administration in a Developing Political System* (London: Oxford University Press, 1963), 24.

Imagined Continuities

A term I do not use in this book is settler colonialism. It is a category that received some defensive attention in the 1960s—including an edited collection called *White Africans Are Also People*—and has been resuscitated as new metropolitan archives were opened to reveal the extent to which colonial secretaries struggled with the demands of white settlers.[58] The newly revived term has been used in some wide-ranging and important comparative studies, but for my purposes whatever is gained by writing about, say, Australia, Israel, and Rhodesia in the same frame disrupts the very specific questions this book asks. My questions are less to do with settlers than they are to do with the fissures and fractures in the political ideas these specific settlers used to rule. Racism is not a sufficient explanation for fourteen years of renegade independence and constitutions that invoked John Stuart Mill, Switzerland, and Africans under the sway of diviners and chiefs.

The Rhodesian Front claimed there was nothing racist about UDI. Officials insisted that they were forced to take the country's own independence because of the racism of decolonization—the idea, dear to Britain and African nationalists alike, that independence for African territories had to be based on universal suffrage, which would mean majority rule, which would mean the rule by one race, and that would be racist. Rhodesians maintained that their independence was not based on race, but on the need to maintain "standards," to stand up for "civilization," and to struggle against the communist menace or the Afro-Arab bloc in the UN. Such generalizations made Rhodesians' ideas about their country's own statehood somewhat vague and relative. Rhodesia was far better than the African states that Europe had summarily abandoned to independence and one man, one vote, it was said, and a lot better than the Britain that had done the abandoning. There was a political imaginary that white Rhodesians, however long they or their forebears had been in the country, were the only "true Britons" left. Many whites scoffed at this, but it matched a sensibility in the Colonial Office that settlers in Africa demonstrated a kind of Anglo-Saxon rugged self-reliance

---

58. See Sarah Gertrude Millin, ed., *White African Are Also People* (Cape Town: Howard Timmons, 1966); Lewis Gann and Peter Duignan, *White Settlers in Tropical Africa* (Baltimore: Penguin Books, 1962); Caroline Elkins, *Imperial Reckoning: The Untold Story of Britain's Gulag in Kenya* (New York: Henry Holt, 2005); Anderson, *Histories of the Hanged*; Elkins and Pedersen, *Settler Colonialism*.

that could no longer be found in the metropole.[59] David Caute, who began reporting on Rhodesia for the *New Statesman* in 1976, was often told that if Winston Churchill were alive, he would immediately immigrate to Rhodesia: only there could he find the qualities he had once loved about Britain.[60] Most of the leadership of the Rhodesian Front and a great many federalists boasted that Rhodesia in the early 1960s was the heir of the British Empire.

There was no clear consensus of what that meant, of course, but the imaginary was to last well into the 1970s. Years before scholars coined the term "imperial retreat," Rhodesian politicians repeated the story of a 1962 meeting with the Conservative Commonwealth secretary, Duncan Sandys, who told them that Britain had lost the will to rule. The Rhodesians were sickened; an otherwise moderate parliamentarian blurted out, "But *we* haven't."[61] This encounter was to shape one of the narratives of UDI. Britain was now weak and impotent, but Rhodesia was strong enough to rule.

But what could it possibly mean to be successor to empire in the mid-1960s? There was hardly any empire left, and imperial powers were now welfare states. In 1965 could anyone imagine that even the older, whiter Commonwealth—Australia, Canada, and New Zealand—could unite in action, and perhaps even use force, after Suez and Sharpeville? The right wing of the Rhodesian Front seemed to believe this was a possibility, that there was an empire which was loyal and unified. Nathan Shamuyarira, editor of the *Daily News,* Salisbury's one African newspaper in the early 1960s, was a former member of the Capricorn Africa Society and by the time of UDI a member of ZANU. He gave the example of Lord Angus Graham, whose shifting political affiliations paralleled his own. Graham had had a cattle ranch in Rhodesia since 1930; he was a Dominion Party member who was a founder (and funder) of the Rhodesian Front. Throughout 1965 Graham gave speeches across the

59. Murphy, *Party Politics*, 10; Brigadier A. Skeen, *Prelude to Independence: Skeen's 115 Days* (Cape Town: Boekhandel, 1966), n. p. Robert Tredgold was scathing about such sentiments. How was it that "this little pool of white people in the heart of Africa has become the repository of all those qualities" that made Britain great? Sir Robert Tredgold, *The Rhodesia That Was My Life* (London: George Allen & Unwin, 1968), 255.

60. David Caute, *Under the Skin*, 89–90.

61. Exchange between Duncan Sandys, Commonwealth secretary, and Julian Greenfield, quoted in Sir Roy Welensky, *Welensky's 4000 Days: The Life and Death of the Federation of Rhodesia and Nyasaland* (London: Collins, 1964), 319; J. M. Greenfield, *Testimony of a Rhodesian Federal* (Bulawayo: Books of Rhodesia, 1978), 251. According to Welensky, Lord Alport, British high commissioner to the Federation, went home and vomited, so sickened was he by this rejection of empire. Alport later wrote that he was angry, not sick or mortified. Lord Alport, *The Sudden Assignment: Central Africa 1961–63* (London, Hodder & Stoughton, 1965), 168.

country about the glories of the empire exemplified by his father, the sixth duke of Montrose, who was playing cricket when he learned that war had been declared in 1914. He left the match, ran home, put on his naval uniform, and went to war. For Graham, this was the empire, membership and participation because of loyalty and oaths and action. The Rhodesian Front rank and file loved the speech, but they, like Graham, must have understood that it was spoken with great longing. The empire of the Great War and stately homes turned into convalescent hospitals could no longer be located in mid-1960s Britain, where widespread immigration from the West Indies and the Indian subcontinent meant that talk about empire had become a way to talk about race. Only in Britain's white-ruled possessions could empire mean a British nationality that black and brown people could not claim. Shamuyarira understood how self-serving this was. Rhodesian Front supporters who were on the verge of treason could now imagine they were the "*only* loyal Briton" wherever they came from and whatever passports they carried.[62]

Could Rhodesians be members of the empire, true Britons, while being Rhodesians? Graham's vignettes did not travel well outside Rhodesian Front campaigns. Imperial citizenship—belonging as much to the collectivity of the British Empire as to one of its territories—was based on ideas about inclusion that were largely absent from Rhodesian Front rhetoric in the early 1960s. The claims to loyalty and tradition and action were challenged, if not replaced, by the clever illegalities of sanction busting, of ordinary men defying the UN, as I show in chapter 5. The idea of imperial citizenship never took hold in the white dominions or even between white dominions.[63] The Rhodesian press mocked the men who left India after its independence and came first to Kenya and then to Rhodesia: they were "Bengal Chancers." Ian Smith was unmoved when Harold Wilson suggested that if Rhodesia took its own independence it would endanger whites elsewhere in Africa.[64] Whatever the claims to loyalty and empire, being Rhodesian was a local matter. "The mantle of the pioneers has fallen on our shoulders," Ian Smith told the nation in 1965.[65] Belonging to Rhodesia, that nation of holders of many passports, was never a straightforward category, however. Not all the people who called themselves Rhodesians were citizens and not all of them wanted to be citizens. Beginning in the late 1940s, citizenship in Rhodesia was

62. Shamuyarira, *Crisis*, 223–24.
63. Daniel Gorman, *Imperial Citizenship: Empire and the Question of Belonging* (Manchester: Manchester University Press, 2006), 19–21, 205.
64. Lowry, "Anti-communism," 171.
65. Quoted in Godwin, *Mukiwa*, 72.

one of several modes of being part of and at odds with a state. During UDI, when Rhodesia became more of a cause than a country, belonging was detached from Rhodesian laws and Rhodesian history. A fictional soldier from the United States explains to the Rhodesian army unit he joins, "I may sound like an American but I'm a Rhodesian" and "I feel more like a Rhodesian than an American."[66] Such appropriations of membership were about racial policies, not a place or its past, but in the following chapters we will see Rhodesians animate residency, dual citizenship, belonging, and history (whether or not it was their own history) to make a claim about being Rhodesian.

What did this make Rhodesia? If it was an imagined community it was imagined all over the globe—in the empire, in disaffected Americans—and was not always able to keep pace with the comings and goings of so many white Rhodesians. Between 1973 and 1979, an annual average of just over 13,000 whites left the country while an annual average of 7,500 immigrated. Many of the whites who emigrated did so quietly—otherwise, said a mechanic planning his return to Scotland in 1977, "the revenue office will be breathing down your neck to see if you're fiddling some extra cash out"—and the government periodically banned the publication of emigration figures, fearing that the figures themselves would intensify white anxieties. What did these comings and goings mean for patriotism, a commitment to the Rhodesian cause? Josiah Brownell has looked to Albert Hirschman's model of voice and exit, that members of an organization who disapprove of its policies either voice their concerns or exit from it, to read in the rate of emigration Rhodesians' "shallow loyalties" to the Rhodesian Front.[67] I am not so sure. Such a model may not hold for Rhodesia, since the Rhodesian Front was fractious in the extreme, and in addition to the number of whites who were detained and deported, there were those who sought ways for Rhodesia to end its rebellion and bring more—not all, but more—Africans into government. The larger question, however, is how do we distinguish between whites who left during UDI and the historical patterns of comings and goings from the territory? How do we disaggregate the white people who left because they could not abide Rhodesian Front racism and those who left because national service had become too onerous or because they had better opportunities in Bristol or Brisbane? This question will come to

66. Robin Moore, *The White Tribe* (Publishers Encampment, WY: Affiliated Writers of America, 1991), 23, 187.
67. Brownell, *Collapse*, 75–80, 83.

the fore in chapter 7, but now it serves to open the space between the fragility of the white Rhodesian population and the stamina of the idea of white-ruled Rhodesia. Duncan Bell, in an article that takes historians to task for failing to distinguish between history, myth, and memory, proposed the idea of "mythscape," the translation of a specific national narrative over—and I would add into—time. Rhodesia had a national imaginary and a sense of purpose constituted with images and ideas that could easily be appropriated by anyone who wanted to claim them as his own.[68] This was the "mantle of the pioneers." A few months after Smith told Rhodesians that they were a determined people who had been called upon to play a role of worldwide significance, a British journalist wrote that the country was "a suburb masquerading as a nation."[69]

The suburb was a potent image for describing Rhodesia, and, as chapter 4 argues, sanctions busting required that Rhodesia masquerade as many nations, not just itself. This book charts a path that may be best understood as standing outside national identity, showing that Rhodesians were men and women who could, as chapters 4 and 7 describe, become British or South African at a moment's notice.[70] By the 1970s being Rhodesian came to be promoted as a set of personal qualities that made the nation, not the other way around. Before fictional characters announced they felt like Rhodesians there was an officially sanctioned hyperbole, best exemplified by the speeches of P. K. van der Byl. Being Rhodesian had become mystical, grandiose, and above all personal. In 1977 van der Byl articulated the problem of an unstable white population and an all-too-stable national project. He condemned draft dodgers and emigrants, people who left "because they are tired of being called up, or because of the inconvenience and indeed the danger of living in Rhodesia during her present time of trouble." "I am a Rhodesian. This is a breed of men the like of which has not been seen for many a long age and which yet by virtue of the example that it sets

68. Duncan S. A. Bell, "Mythscapes, Memory, Mythology and National Identity," *British J. Sociology* 54, no. 1 (2003): 63–81.

69. Ian Smith, *The Great Betrayal: The Memoirs of Ian Douglas Smith* (London: Blake, 1997), 106; Paul L. Moorcraft, *A Short Thousand Years: The End of Rhodesia's Rebellion* (Salisbury: Galaxie, 1979), 18. The suburb remark has been attributed both to Alan Coren of *Punch* and David Astor of the *Observer*. Author's field notes, Harare, July 22, 2001.

70. The Rhodesians who left were caricatured as "Whenwes," because they began every sentence with "When we were in Rhodesia . . ." I am inclined not to regard them as a postcolonial people in the sense that Algeria's Pied Noir were: men and women who had lived in Rhodesia never formed a constituency anywhere else. They were instead the butt of jokes, and at least one book of cartoons; see Louis Bolze and Rose Martin, *The Whenwes of Rhodesia* (Bulawayo: Books of Rhodesia, 1978).

may go some way towards redeeming the squalid and shameful times in which we live."[71] The mythscape had become a home movie.

Van der Byl had not been in the country for fifteen years when he began to demand its independence. Indeed, a sizable proportion of the white electorate had been in the country less than twenty years.[72] But men like van der Byl joined with the original cowboys. They were the settlers who came to the country after World War II, men who were inexperienced in government—and proud of it—but with a deep and abiding faith in what it meant to be Rhodesian even when they learned it secondhand or made it up.[73] P. K. van der Byl came in 1951. He had visited Rhodesia many times as a youth; when he read about the profits from tobacco he "suddenly got a rush of blood to the crotch about the tobacco boom and decided I was going to go up there and make the family fortune in a place I liked and wanted to be in." The tobacco boom waned; he lost £10,000 the first year. He then "drifted" into politics: Everything about the country had "a tremendous emotional appeal then. The Rhodesian was the last good white man left; we were the renaissance people."[74] William Harper was a Bengal Chancer: he was born in India, came to Rhodesia in 1947, and by 1962 was the leader of the segregationist Dominion Party before it joined with the Rhodesian Front. Clifford Dupont, the first president of independent Rhodesia, and Brigadier Andrew Skeen, Rhodesia's last high commissioner to Britain, came in 1948. Dupont opened his 1962 campaign with a loud promise to stop "the black flood" at the Zambezi; Skeen opposed federation because it did not serve the needs of Southern Rhodesia's whites; he joined the Rhodesian Front in 1962 because it did. Three years later he was appointed high commissioner because he "knew the psychology of the British public" as well as anyone in Rhodesia did.[75]

Post–World War II immigration was immigration to a land of opportunity. Many young men—including Leo Solomon Baron, whom we will meet again—came for the Empire Air Training Scheme and returned a

71. Quoted in Moorcraft, *Short Thousand Years*, 3; Hills, *Rebel People*, 204–5.

72. Given the comings and goings of whites in Rhodesia, the actual number of immigrants who stayed is almost impossible to reckon, but between 1941 and 1961 more whites—twice as many 1951–61—came to Rhodesia than were born there. Mlambo, *White Immigration*, 4; Brownell, *Collapse*, 75.

73. Clifford Dupont thought "the inexperience helped us a great deal because . . . it was to our advantage that we didn't know the protocol of being a minister." Clifford Dupont, Salisbury, June 1976 and January 1977, NAZ/ORAL/DU4.

74. Hannes Wessels, *P. K. van der Byl: African Statesman* (Johannesburg: 30 Degrees South, 2010), 79–81.

75. Dupont interview, NAZ/ORAL/DU4; Skeen, *115 Days*, 3, 7–10.

few years after the end of the war. Retired officers found a place where a pension would go far.[76] Progressive South Africa lawyers moved to Salisbury and Bulawayo in the grim years following the Treason Trial.[77] John Parker was a journalist who came to Rhodesia in 1955. He left in 1966 and wrote a scathing condemnation of the tragic insularity of white Rhodesians in which he could not contain his pride at the impact of postwar immigrants. Salisbury was the most "cosmopolitan capital" south of the Sahara, he boasted. Every day he encountered White Russians, Greeks, and Italians, apparently without knowing the zeal with which the government limited the number of non-British immigrants.[78] By the 1960s, most immigrants to Rhodesia came from the United Kingdom.[79] Derek van der Syde had worked in Europe and Africa before coming to Rhodesia in 1959. By 1964 he was at the consular desk of the Ministry of Foreign Affairs. In 1966 he became Rhodesia's consul in Mozambique after UDI and later oversaw sanctions-busting air traffic to and from Gabon.[80]

British immigrants imagined Rhodesia to be all that Britain was not. When James Barlow arrived in 1961 he immediately saw "how happy" Rhodesians were. It was he who was "weighed down by the sorrow of editorials, the UNO, trade unions, pundits, culture and the rest." John Tagel came in 1966; he considered it his "duty" to support Rhodesia "as the last part of the British empire in Africa which still flew the Union Jack." Dick Pittman came in 1972. "Anything was better than being ground to a powder under the crushing weight of income tax and creeping bureaucracy."[81] There were storied assassins and teachers and

76. Leo Solomon Baron, London, August 5 and 16, 1983, NAZ/ORAL/239. The Empire Air Training Scheme is well known to readers of Doris Lessing's Martha Quest novels. For retired officers, see Skeen, *Prelude to Independence*, 3–5; Tom Wigglesworth, *Perhaps Tomorrow* (Salisbury: Galaxie, 1980); Lauren St. John, *Rainbow's End: A Memoir of Childhood, War and an African Farm* (London: Hamish Hamilton, 2002), 4–16.

77. Isie Maisels, *A Life at Law: The Memoirs of I. A. Maisels, QC* (Johannesburg: Jonathan Ball, 1998), 223–36.

78. John Parker, *Rhodesia: Little White Island* (London: Pitman, 1972), 11; Denis Hills, *The Last Days of White Rhodesia* (London, Chatto & Windus, 1981), 42–44; Mlambo, *White Immigration*, 64–67.

79. Caute, *Under the Skin*, 87–89, 114–16; Brownell, *Collapse*, 103. A scheme to encourage immigrants from the decolonizing north had not worked well. Smith's secretary alerted the chair of the public service board to the difficulties that civil servants from African colonies had in finding employment in Britain, where they would be ribbed for leading a life of luxury in Africa. G. B. Clarke to S. E. Morris, chair, Public Service Commission, January 3, 1966, Loyalty to Rhodesian Government, NAZ/S3279/1/211.

80. Derek Arthur Collings van der Syde, Harare, November 27, 1987, NAZ/ORAL/267.

81. James Barlow, *Goodbye, England* (London: Hamish Hamilton, 1969), 94; John Tagel, *Bolt from the Blue* (Cape Town: Howard Timmins, 1979), 165; Dick Pitman, *You Must Be New Around Here* (Bulawayo: Books of Rhodesia, 1979), 1. Tagel's book was published in 1979, when the Union Jack

journalists. Denis Hills, whose lyrical accounts of teaching and traveling in the Eastern Highlands I cite in chapter 11, came to Rhodesia in 1975. He had escaped a death sentence in Idi Amin's Uganda and had been deported from Northern Nigeria. When he took up a teaching position in Rhodesia he felt "safe" among the Yorkshire accents, swimming pools, and superb gardens.[82]

Escapes from dictators and taxes notwithstanding, how do all these experiences add up to a nationality, a claim to a history and its possible futures that were, almost all immigrants acknowledged, unlike those of other countries? The idea of Rhodesia as a place where white men did what needed to be done was a strong one, but the actual governing of the country required something else—a sense of place, an understanding that a few Africans were needed to help rule the country. Many Rhodesian Front politicians, and many of their opponents, had deep roots in the country. This group includes Ian Smith but also Robert Tredgold and the brothers Jack and Roger Howman, all of whom we will meet in subsequent chapters, and all of whom regarded the participation of some Africans in some aspect of government as a necessary if not a good development. They described a Rhodesian past of humility and inclusion. When Lord Alport was appointed high commissioner to the federation in 1961 he was repeatedly told about earlier times— before the boom, before "immigrants and sophistication"—when white men worked alongside Africans on road gangs.[83] These men—especially Ian Smith—had long careers as federalists. Smith in particular had the language of partnership and multiracialism down pat: he could speak of gradualism, of African advancement, his knowledge of Africans, and what they would do if they were enfranchised. Ian Smith was one of many Rhodesian Front leaders who knew how to talk about minority rule without talking about race. Instead he invoked a Rhodesia that was an exemplar of progress, of efficiency, of modern conveniences that could be maintained only by the hard work of qualified men and women. That these men and women were white was the coincidence of history that made Rhodesia what it was. These people knew how to work alongside Africans.

"no longer flies in Rhodesia, but there is still the glimmer of that ghostly figure riding ahead in armour and drawn sword."

82. Peter Stiff, *See You in November: Rhodesia's No-Holds-Barred Intelligence War* (Alberton: Galago, 1985), 88–90. Hills, *Rebel People*, 1–66;

83. Alport, *Sudden Assignment*, 138.

Race, Place, and UDI

Rhonasia was to vanish without a trace, but its short life in a party newsletter suggests that a term like white supremacy does not fully address all the fissures and fictions in Rhodesians' ideas about being white. Rhodesian Front officials, for example, had concerns about who was called white and what privileges that would give them. Many had never approved of the eager inclusion of Afrikaaners—and speeches in Afrikaans—in federal politics, and many more never overcame their disdain for non-British immigrants.[84] Rhodesian-born men often called themselves African. Robert Tredgold, a jurist we will meet in the next chapter, was born in Bulawayo in 1899; he frequently referred to himself as a "White Matabele." Ian Smith was born in Selukwe in 1919 and loved to say "I am an African just as much as any black man is."[85] But being African and being white was not the same as being Rhodesian. Between 1967 and 1971 the number of Portuguese immigrants from Mozambique more than doubled; by 1971 they constituted 11 percent of all immigrants. The government had been informed that many of the men frequented African prostitutes. Cabinet ministers believed this was a direct result of Portuguese colonial policy, which "contradicted" the Rhodesian way of life. They suggested strongly worded propaganda for the Portuguese community, to be followed by more selective immigration.[86] Being Rhodesian, at least for its long-term residents, was a matter of history and culture. In 1973 Smith asked the Department of Internal Affairs (formerly Native Affairs) to form a committee that could declare individuals white, just as there were committees to classify Africans and "Coloureds," the long-established term used for people of mixed race. He was concerned about the case of two children who could not be admitted to the government school in a provincial town. Their mother's father had married a "creole" woman, but their mother had married a white man and was accepted as white in the European community of Fort Victoria. It was necessary that there be a committee that could

84. George Willburn Rudland, Sinoia, September 5, 1972, NAZ/ORAL/RU3; Barry Shutz, "European Population Patterns, Cultural Persistence, and Political Change in Rhodesia," *Canadian J. African Studies* 7, no. 1 (1973): 3–26; Mlambo, *White Immigration*, 64–67; Brownell, *Collapse*, 107–10.

85. Caute, *Under the Skin*, 88; Peter Godwin and Ian Hancock, *"Rhodesians Never Die": The Impact of War and Political Change on White Rhodesia c. 1970–1980* (Harare: Baobab Books, 1995), 20.

86. Miscegenation, Prostitution, and Allied Problems, Cabinet Minutes, August 24, 1971, CL/Smith/24.

declare people white because there were similar problems throughout the country.[87]

What does this do to the idea of whiteness, which historians of the United States have shown to be critical to understanding how race and racism operates? Labor historians in particular have argued that whiteness was constructed in opposition to an imaginary of blackness–servile, foreign, erotic—even as whiteness had no fixed constituency. Throughout the nineteenth century certain white European immigrant groups, such as Irish and Italians, came to be called white only through a long and contentious process.[88] Rhodesia's immigration figures throw an equivalent notion of whiteness into question. If most of the new immigrants circulated between the United Kingdom, South Africa, Rhodesia, and possibly Mozambique, how well could the mechanics of exclusion and subsequent inclusion operate? If whiteness was not an immutable fact, could it be decided by a committee? Warwick Anderson's work on Australia may provide the greatest insight. Anderson has argued that for Australia "white" was at first an imprecise term, at once too simple and too ambiguous. It came to mean an identifiable assemblage of physical, cultural, and political traits only after generations of Australian doctors and researchers used the term as the entry point into the debates of the day about what white bodies could and could not do in an alien land. The resolution of these debates fixed membership in a community.[89]

In Rhodesia, especially after 1960, these debates were not about the vulnerability of white bodies in the colonies, but about the vulnerability of white polities therein. The term white was not as simplistic as it was vulgar; it was much better to say responsible or civilized. The bureaucratic power to declare someone white—or black, or Coloured—was the discursive ability to mark Rhodesians in place; it was a way to animate heritage and history. A set of rules, in and of themselves, by which someone could become fully white was too close to some of the evolutionary models behind so much decolonization. The fact of being white—or "creole"—was not in and of itself a basis for privilege and

87. Cabinet minutes, June 23, 1973, CL/Smith/26.

88. David Roediger, *The Wages of Whiteness: The Making of the American Working Class* (London: Verso, 1990); and Noel Ignatiev, *How the Irish Became White* (New York, Routledge, 1996); John Hartigan, "Establishing the Fact of Whiteness," *American Anthropologist* 99, no. 3 (1997): 495–505; Peter Kolchin, "Whiteness Studies: The New History of Race in America," *Journal of American History* 89, no. 1 (2002): 154–73.

89. Warwick Anderson, *The Construction of Whiteness: Science, Health, and Racial Destiny in Australia* (Melbourne: Melbourne University Press, 2002).

favor; being white only became a social fact when the white person in question practiced a Rhodesian way of life. I build this argument on two recent books, both of which deploy whiteness as an organizing principle. Both David McDermott Hughes and Rory Pilossof argue that white farmers constructed their own sense of place and power not by making skin color or even heritage their center, but by articulating their place in Africa in specific imaginaries and languages. In the 1950s white farmers remade the high veld landscape by irrigation: they created European-like farmlands with lakes and dams. Fifty years later white farmers deployed the thirty-year-old language of UDI and the bush war to describe being driven from their farms.[90] What follows builds on the work of Hughes and Pilossof. I argue that being white in Rhodesia was never in and of itself the right to rule or to do much else. What mattered was being white and laying claim to the history of civilization and responsibility that had so capably maintained standards for the last forty years.

But—and this is a big but—whoever immigrated and whatever history they claimed, there were just not very many white Rhodesians at all. As liberals joked during UDI, "There weren't enough whites to run Aberdeen, let alone a country."[91] The Rhodesian careers of many new immigrants suggest as much, but the fact that there were not many whites—and of those, not many white electors—meant that there had to be an inclusion of some Africans in political life, first to provide Rhodesian politicians and their supporters in London evidence that theirs was not a wholly racist regime and second simply to make the work of government credible and possible. The Rhodesian Front had always been an uneasy alliance, and its ideas about who should do the work of government were to divide the party over the 1969 constitution.[92] Several authors have insisted that the UDI government kept a tight rein on dissent and that Rhodesians were neither allowed access to accurate information about domestic politics nor allowed to protest.[93] I disagree. The Rhodesian Front could not keep itself together all the time, as we shall see, and the idea that it controlled how its citizens (and residents and want-to-be nationals) thought seems to be too easy an explanation for why the very outmoded ideas of Rhodesian politics lasted

90. David McDermott Hughes, *Whiteness in Zimbabwe: Race, Landscape, and the Problem of Belonging* (New York, Palgrave Macmillan, 2010); Rory Pilossof, *The Unbearable Whiteness of Being: Farmers' Voices from Zimbabwe* (Harare: Weaver, 2012).
91. Author's field notes, Harare, July 21, 1995.
92. Wood, *No Further!*, 100; Godwin and Hancock, "*Rhodesians Never Die*," 19.
93. Moorcraft, *Short Thousand Years*, 197–99; Evans, Rhodesian Front Rule, 87–92; Hancock and Godwin, "*Rhodesians Never Die*"; Brownell, *Collapse*, 75–78.

as long as they did. The problem of this book is how to join boasts about working telephones to Ian Smith's pointless anguish over the independence of Zambia and Malawi: it was "absurd," he told the nation, that Rhodesians, "who have ruled ourselves with such an impressive record for over forty years, are denied what is freely granted to other countries," some of which had not ruled themselves for more than a year.[94] How do I reconcile this obsession with the empty rhetoric of empire at least a decade after it ended? How do I discuss the practices of political independence when the independent state was so often represented in the vocabulary of responsibility and efficiency and when reliable telephone service was equated with a civilization that was a stand-in for talking about race? One strategy I use in some of the following chapters is the history of political parties. The Rhodesian Front could never contain all the tensions of older residents, new immigrants, and foreign soldiers. The party was fractious, as we shall see, without any singular notion of race but with a very singular idea about racialized rule. Another strategy I use is to interrogate debates about the African franchise. For all the hodgepodge of Rhodesian political thought—at one point Smith announced that the country had long been a "meritocracy"—there was no one who openly supported universal adult suffrage. These fractions and debates, in political parties and outside of them, do not make Rhodesia any more or less racist than is generally thought, but they require a book that historicizes ideas about the vote as much as it historicizes ideas about race.

94. Smith, *Betrayal*, 101, 104–6.

TWO

"Racial representation of the worst type": The 1957 Franchise Commission, Citizenship, and the Problem of Polygyny

In the first years of the Central African Federation, years of increasing white immigration into the region, the vocabularies of imperial rule changed. There was a firm if grudging belief that Africans now were to be civic actors who would vote in elections that would choose people to speak for their interests. This was a far cry from self-determination, but it joined a language of citizenship that had not been in place before. This citizenship was of a specific kind, however. To allow postwar Africans citizenship that was equivalent to that of Europeans in Europe would be to offer all the benefits of a welfare state.[1] The citizenship on offer to most inhabitants of Britain's African territories was a set of obligations very much like what they had before—except for the absence of forced labor—but an entirely new set of rights. Determining which rights were to be granted and how often they could be exercised was of great concern to Southern Rhodesia in the late 1950s.

---

1. Jane Burbank and Frederick Cooper, *Empires in World History: Power and the Politics of Difference* (Princeton, NJ: Princeton University Press, 2010), 422.

The Rights of Citizens

In the last twenty years, scholars have grappled with citizenship in part because of a renewed attention to the end of colonial rule in Africa. In 1996 Mahmood Mamdani published *Citizen and Subject*. The book is perhaps more about indirect rule than it is about the nature of citizenship. He identified as citizens those late colonial Africans who had rights—urban, literate elites who were a postwar ideal of African advancement—and those without them, subjects, rural villagers who lived under the chiefs of indirect rule. Taken together, these two groups produced a "bifurcated state" and a society that was never fully unified or civil.[2] Mamdani's terms took hold as tropes of late colonialism, despite the constraints on late colonial chiefs and the fuzziness with which colonial officials defined "natives" or "subjects."[3] Indeed, the gap between urban elites and rural tribesmen may not have been great. Literacy was not always an either/or condition, as Jonathon Glassman has argued persuasively for Zanzibar: the importance of newspapers was not that some people could read them and others could not, but that the debates around their content, by those who had read and those who had heard about it, shaped the concerns that would appear in the next issue. Citizens did not always use their rights for exclusion. In the Kenya election of 1960 there was universal adult suffrage for everyone over forty; anyone younger had to meet certain qualifications. Urban professionals seeking political office realized that they could most easily win rural constituencies by demanding absentee ballots for older, illiterate migrants working in distant cities. They did this to win elections, of course, but it joined the needs of rural, illiterate subjects to those of

2. Mahmood Mamdani, *Citizen and Subject: Contemporary Africa and the Legacy of Late Colonialism* (Princeton, NJ: Princeton University Press, 1996), and "Beyond Settler and Native as Political Identities: Overcoming the Political Legacy of Colonialism," *Comparative Studies in Society and Hist.* 43, no. 4 (2001): 651–64. See also Atieno Odhiambo, "Woza Lugard? Rhetoric and Antiquarian Knowledge," *Canadian J. of African Studies* 34, no. 2 (2000): 387–96.

3. For different ideas about chiefs, see John Tosh, "Colonial Chiefs in a Stateless Society: A Case Study from Northern Uganda," *J. African History* 14, no. 3 (1973): 473–90; and David Gordon, "Owners of the Land and Lunda Lords: Colonial Chiefs in the Borderlands of Northern Rhodesia and the Belgian Congo," *International J. African Historical Studies* 34, no.1 (2001): 315–38. For what were at best loose and partial definitions of "native" and "subject" in places as diverse as Senegal, Nyasaland, and Nigeria, see Gregory Mann, *Native Sons: West African Veterans and France in the Twentieth Century* (Durham, NC: Duke University Press, 2006), 70–72; Christopher Joon-Hai Lee, "The 'Native' Undefined: Colonial Categories, Anglo-African Status and the Politics of Kinship in British Central Africa, 1929–38," *J. African History* 46, no. 3 (2005): 455–78; Mair, *Nyasaland Election*, 15–16; Post, *Nigerian Federal Election*, 192–94.

urban elites. In the one man, one vote election in Northern Nigeria in 1959, for example, elite politicians were able to register a large number of underage and illiterate voters.[4] Nationalist politicians were keenly aware of the power of not exercising the rights they had been given, such as boycotting or threatening to boycott an election.[5]

Also in 1996 and in subsequent years, Frederick Cooper made a substantially different and more nuanced argument about citizenship in late colonial Africa. He demonstrated that while the allocation of citizenship was critical to colonial imaginaries of Africans after 1945, Africans had instrumental ideas about citizenship that went beyond colonial platitudes. Citizenship was not an end in itself, but a platform from which claims could be made—about the workplace, about the household, about politics—because of the equality inherent in the status. Citizenship was not simply about rights, but about belonging to a political unit, one that could and indeed should make demands on its citizenry.[6]

In this book I use citizenship in a limited but straightforward way, to mean political rights bestowed by a legal authority, most often a constitution. It is not a synonym for nationality, membership, belonging, or community, or whatever category applies to the men who felt "like a Rhodesian." I want to expand Cooper's argument, that the citizenship offered to Africans (and whites) was an imaginary in itself, sometimes of rights and obligations but almost always of conditions of belonging and membership. In its practice in Rhodesia—more often before UDI than after—it meant that some Africans were given citizen rights when they acquired the qualifications and characteristics that many white people had. This was citizenship that was also membership but it did not convey full political rights, even for all whites. Ian Smith, at least, said he had "never believed in one man, one vote in any country, including the UK."[7] Well into the 1970s, citizenship did not automatically allow for

4. Glassman, "Sorting Out the Tribes," 395–423; Post, *Nigerian Federal Election*, 205–6; George Bennett and Carl Rosberg, *The Kenyatta Election: Kenya 1960–1961* (Oxford: Oxford University Press, 1961), 56–58, 62–63.

5. The Tanganyika election of 1958 is a case in point; see John Iliffe, "Breaking the Chain at Its Weakest Link: TANU and the Colonial Office," in *In Search of a Nation: Histories of Authority and Dissonance in Tanzania*, ed. Gregory H. Maddox and James L. Giblin (Bloomington: Indiana University Press, 2009), 168–97.

6. Frederick Cooper, *Decolonization and African Society: The Labor Question in French and British Africa* (Cambridge: Cambridge University Press, 1996), 266–68, "Alternatives to Empire: France and Africa after World War II," in *The State of Sovereignty: Territories, Laws, Populations*, ed. Douglas Howland and Luise White (Bloomington: Indiana University Press, 2009), 94–123, and *Africa and the World: The McMillan-Stewart Lectures* (Cambridge, MA: Harvard University Press, 2014), 72–73, 97–99.

7. Quoted in Caute, *Under the Skin*, 92.

voting rights: not all citizens could vote, and more often than not all voters were not citizens.

Citizenship is a slippery category, one that changes over time, as in the allocation of citizen rights to women, and one that is often specific to the regime, as in Idi Amin's expulsion of Ugandan Asians.[8] In the case of Rhodesia, the advantages of citizenship were not always obvious, as we shall see. New immigrants received public assistance while second-generation Rhodesians did not. The overlap of citizenship with nationality was often challenged by the creation of new nations.[9] The British Nationality Act of 1948 actually simplified citizenship for Britain but not necessarily for its former colonies. The act distinguished between citizens of the United Kingdom and those of Commonwealth countries, but both had the status of British subjects. Whether men and women from former colonies were called subjects or Commonwealth citizens, both categories had identical rights, including that of entry and settlement in Britain.[10] Once resident in Britain, citizens of colonies and former colonies had the same rights as citizens of the United Kingdom. In late colonial Africa, the very fact of elections brought residency into questions of citizenship: the issue was not simply one of who could vote, but where they could vote, and who could and could not stand as a candidate.[11] At the end of the colonial era, many African nationalists tried to lengthen the residency requirements by which Asians or Europeans could become citizens.[12] Place of birth did not always guarantee citizenship. Ghana bestowed citizenship on Lebanese who were born there; Zanzibar did the same for all Africans born on the island, but in Southern Rhodesia the children and grandchildren of migrant laborers from Nyasaland could not become citizens even when they were born there.[13]

8. Etienne Balibar, "Propositions on Citizenship," *Ethics* 98 (1988): 723–30; Mahmood Mamdani, *From Citizen to Refugee: Ugandan Asians Come to Britain* (London: Francis Pinter, 1973).

9. W. Rogers Brubaker, "Citizenship Struggles in Soviet Successor States," *International Migration Review* 26, no. 2 (1992): 269–91.

10. Robert Miles, "Nationality, Citizenship and Migration to Britain, 1945–1951," *J. of Law and Society* 16, no. 4 (1989): 428–29.

11. I take this point from Peter Geschiere and Stephen Jackson, "Autochthony and the Crisis of Citizenship: Democratization, Decentralization, and the Politics of Belonging," *African Studies Review* 49, no. 2 (2006): 4.

12. SRANC: statement of principles, policy and programme, Salisbury 1957, in *Zimbabwe Independence Movements: Select Documents*, ed. Christopher Nyangoni and Gideon Nyandoro (New York, Barnes & Noble, 1979), 10; James R. Brennan, *Taifa: Making Nation and Race in Urban Tanzania* (Athens: Ohio University Press, 2012), 155–56.

13. Emmanuel K. Akyeampong, "Race, Identity and Citizenship in Black Africa: The Case of the Lebanese in Ghana," *Africa* 76, no. 3 (2006): 297–322; Jonathon Glassman, *War of Words, War of Stones: Racial Thought in Colonial Zanzibar* (Bloomington: Indiana University Press, 2011), 155–56.

A central question for the early chapters of this book is how to reconcile the fine-grained concerns about who could vote in Southern Rhodesia and the rather opaque notion of citizenship deployed by whites who lived there. Sir Robert Tredgold—who headed the franchise commission I will discuss—believed that men like himself, who had been born in the country in 1899 and who literally grew up with it, had a special link to the nation.[14] For many longtime residents, these ties remained emotional. Doris Lessing was born in Persia in 1919; in 1925 her parent immigrated to Southern Rhodesia. She left for Britain in 1949 and returned for the first time in 1956, her trip paid for by the *Daily Worker.* She was not permitted to enter South Africa at all and only allowed to remain in Southern Rhodesia because of the intervention of an old friend; were she to travel to Northern Rhodesia or Nyasaland, she was told, she would be deported. She was "upset" about this, but did not invoke the language of rights to convey her distress: "To be refused entry into a country one knows and loves is bad enough, but to be . . . on sufferance in a country one has lived in nearly all one's life is very painful."[15] Legal rights were also not the issue for the immigrants who came in the 1960s and 1970s. Their ideas about belonging to Rhodesia tended to be impressionistic and sentimental, not unlike the concept of nationality but frequently ahistorical and almost always quirky.[16] These were the new arrivals who "felt at home" amidst the Yorkshire accents and the men who formed a national identity around Rhodesian independence and its prattle about breeds of men and Sparta, and the men who claimed to feel like a Rhodesian.[17]

This is only part of the ahistorical aspect of Rhodesian citizenship. The willingness of successive constitutions to deal with displacements was another. The question of dual citizenship was for years at least as important as national citizenship. In Central Africa the history of the movement of people over borders was matched by what Rogers Brubaker called the movement of borders over people.[18] Both as a chartered colony and as a responsible government, Southern Rhodesia could not give citizenship to its residents. The Central African Federation could give federal citizenship after 1953, but territories could not. Once Rhodesia had

14. Tredgold, *The Rhodesia*, 13.
15. Doris Lessing, *Going Home* (New York: HarperCollins, 1996 [1957]), 76–82.
16. I take this point from Rogers Brubaker, "Migration, Membership, and the Modern Nation-State: Internal and External Dimensions of the Politics of Belonging," *J. of Interdisciplinary History* 41, no. 1 (2010): 61–78. For more examples, see Hughes, *Whiteness in Zimbabwe*, 1–26.
17. Moorcraft, *Short Thousand Years*, 3; Hills, *Rebel People*, 66; Moore, *White Tribe*, 187.
18. Brubaker, "Citizenship Struggles in Soviet Successor States," 269–91.

its own citizenship, this was both a basis for making claims on the state and a basis for the state to make claims—often extensive claims—on its citizens. Some of those obligations could be met by the emotional ties of belonging, especially since Rhodesian citizenship did not always demand more obligations than residency did for white people, in large part because the legal rights of white residents were so extensive and elastic. After UDI, as we shall see, very few people, including citizens, wanted Rhodesian citizenship with any exclusivity.

The question for Rhodesia from 1957 to 1979 was not only what did citizenship mean, but how useful was the category to the states that gave it and how useful was it to the individuals who could claim it? Before UDI, territories understood the ways that citizenship constrained their ability to regulate residents; it was frequently withheld to allow a state greater control over individuals. Terence Ranger, who will figure as an actor and as historian in subsequent chapters, was deported from Southern Rhodesia in 1963. He had come to teach at the University College of Rhodesia and Nyasaland in 1957. He had been active in three of the political parties discussed in the next chapter. He and his wife applied for federal citizenship—there was no citizenship in individual territories—as soon as they could, in 1959. They were refused and did not re-apply. One key requirement for federal citizenship was a "satisfactory" security record, which meant avoiding support for or association with African nationalists. In 1961 Ranger organized a campaign to integrate Rhodesia's restaurants, barbershops, and swimming pools. There had been frequent calls from MPs to deport him, but as he was a British subject and thus not legally alien he could not be deported unless he imperiled public safety. In 1962, when the Zimbabwe African Peoples Union was banned, Ranger, a member, was restricted to a three-mile radius of his home.[19] When his period of restriction ended, the moribund federal government declared him a prohibited immigrant. Ranger had done nothing illegal; his defense was that he was a resident in Southern Rhodesia and that the federal government had no jurisdiction over his

19. The group was imprecisely called Citizens against the Colour Bar. "Sitters and Citizens," *Central African Examiner* 5, no. 2 (July 1961); "Not Proven," *Central African Examiner* 6, no. 5 (October 1962): 31; Claire Palley, *The Constitutional History of Southern Rhodesia, 1888–1965, with Special Reference to Imperial Control* (Oxford: Clarendon Press, 1966), 567; Tapiwa Zimudzi, "Spies and Informers on Campus: Vetting, Surveillance and Deportation of Expatriate University Lecturers in Colonial Zimbabwe, 1954–63," *J. Southern African Studies* 33, no. 1 (2007): 194; Terence Ranger, *Writing Revolt: A Rhodesian Memoir, 1957–1967* (Harare: Weaver Press, 2013), 110–20. One government minister recalled that he could have deported Ranger on several occasions, but "I didn't think he should have the satisfaction." H. J. Quinton, Salisbury, May 1977 and May 1978, NAZ/ORAL/QU2.

status. Two of the three judges argued that later laws gave the federal government jurisdiction; a third did not and argued that the status of prohibited immigrant should be reserved for new immigrants. The court voided his residency permit.[20] The next year the government of Southern Rhodesia revised its citizenship law in anticipation of UDI so that anyone acting against the interests of the country could be deprived of his citizenship; those who lost their citizenship could then, and only then, be declared prohibited immigrants.[21]

When Rhodesia became a republic in 1970, questions of citizenship changed dramatically. When could citizens be naturalized, could birthright citizens be deported, and above all how could anyone other than citizens be conscripted? By 1970, however, Rhodesia was an outlaw state, and almost every immigrant or resident avoided or delayed becoming a citizen for as long as he or she could. In the chapters that follow, we will see contests around citizenship that are not only about who can be declared a citizen but also about how long that process should take and how long it could be reasonably postponed. We will see constitutions in which only citizens can vote and constitutions in which citizens and residents can. In this chapter we will see that debates about who could become a citizen were less important than debates about whether or not to enfranchise the wives in polygynous marriages.

Creating Voters, 1896–1953

Ian Smith insisted that Rhodesia had never been a racialist state because it had had a common voter roll since 1896. In order to provide for the election of four representatives to the newly created legislative council, two electoral districts were created. Each would have two representatives. Franchise qualifications followed those of the Cape Colony in South Africa. Males twenty-one or over could vote, providing they were

20. "The Ranger Case," *Central African Examiner* 6, no. 10 (March 1963): 7; Ranger, *Writing*, 142–28; Terence Ranger, personal communication, January 6, 2013.

21. W. J. Harper, Minister of Internal Affairs, Deportation Act 1964, Cabinet Memoranda 1964/1, CL/Smith/18; van der Syde interview, NAZ/ORAL/267. A few years later, however, when Claire Palley, a young university lecturer, gave a speech critical of the Rhodesian judiciary on radio in Botswana the attorney general of independent Rhodesia was at a loss of how to deport her. Too many constitutional issues were in the courts to do so, however good an idea that was, but could she be struck off the advocate's rolls? Could there be a new law forbidding citizens from making radio broadcasts from Botswana? T. A. T. Bosman to Minister of Justice, Broadcast of Dr. Claire Palley's opinion by Francistown Radio, November 23, 1967. Cabinet memoranda, 1967. CL/Smith/21.

British subjects by birth or naturalization or if they had taken the oath of allegiance and if they had lived for six or more months in the electoral district in a building valued at £75, or owned a mining claim, or received wages of at least £50 per year, and if they could write their name, address, and occupation in English. This last was to become the minimal definition of literacy in subsequent voter qualification, the ability to fill out the registration form unaided. Even in 1899 the problem for the British South Africa Company was that there were not enough white people to govern or even be governed. In order to make sure that all male settlers could vote and that "aliens" were not excluded, it relaxed the rules for naturalization so that aliens were eligible to vote after they had lived in Southern Rhodesia for one year.[22]

Despite two women's antisuffrage groups, both of which wanted women's participation in local but not national elections, white women were given the right to vote in 1919. In a practice that would continue for more than fifty years for African and European voters, women qualified to vote with their own or their husbands' property, not their husbands' literacy.[23] The 1896 qualifications remained intact even as the number of elected legislators increased. In 1922, when an electorate of fewer than twenty thousand voted not to join South Africa, Southern Rhodesia was granted "Responsible Government" status beginning in 1923. The actual legal meaning of this status was vague, but in practice it meant that Southern Rhodesia would have its own army and civil service, but that the British government had oversight for certain kinds of legislation, most especially that regarding Africans. This was the "reserve clause." British oversight tended to be behind the scenes. The British government, or governor, saw draft legislation; bills were negotiated before they went to parliament for a vote, so that there was no overt conflict between the governments of the United Kingdom and Southern Rhodesia. For many years this served to discourage Southern Rhodesia from attempting to limit the African franchise. In 1928, for example, in anxious anticipation that the Native Purchase Areas to be established in the early 1930s would create a group of well-off African farmers, a bill was introduced that would raise the property qualification to £500. The British government objected, and the property qualification remained

22. Palley, *Constitutional History*, 135–36, 203.
23. Donal Lowry, "'White Woman's Country': Ethel Tawse Jollie and the Making of White Rhodesia," *J. Southern African Studies* 23, no. 2 (1997): 261–64.

£150. A few years later, the prime minister asked the British if the voting rolls could be closed to further African registration. Britain refused.[24]

There were no significant attempts to change voter qualifications until the 1950s, after the postwar influx of thousands of white immigrants. Many were to leave in a few years, but those who sought a legal relationship to Southern Rhodesia soon learned how partial "responsible government" was. In matters pertaining to citizenship and nationality Southern Rhodesia acted as an agent for Great Britain, receiving and forwarding applications for nationality and naturalization until 1949, when Southern Rhodesian citizenship was created.[25] The Southern Rhodesia law of 1949 continued to allow citizens of Southern Rhodesia to be British subjects, and it permitted dual or even triple nationality for people resident in Southern Rhodesia.

Nationality applied primarily to white people; its multiplicity reflected the circular nature of white settlement and skilled labor migration in the region. A Polish-born British citizen resident in Southern Rhodesia might be married to a South African–born woman whose parents were from Lithuania. Their children might have been born in Northern Rhodesia but were residents of Southern Rhodesia. Residents could become naturalized citizens after two years, British-protected persons after four years. Citizenship was not offered to African migrants, no matter how long they lived in Southern Rhodesia. This was to become critically important thirty years later in the election of 1979, when African residents were allowed to vote, but throughout the 1950s and 1960s farm workers from Nyasaland who married in Southern Rhodesia, and whose children were born there and now worked there, were British-protected persons until they became Malawian nationals. White Rhodesians could lose their citizenship if they became citizens of another country if it was not the country in which they already had dual citizenship. Plural marriage, both in the 1949 act and in its amended versions of 1958 and 1963, seemed to require the most specialized restrictions. If a citizen of Southern Rhodesia married one woman in another country, both she and the children of that union were citizens by marriage and descent. But if a citizen of Southern Rhodesia married more than one wife in a country in which polygyny was legal, none of the wives or children could become citizens, either by marriage or descent.

24. Palley, *Constitutional History*, 242–44.
25. Brownell, *Collapse*, 3–4; Palley, *Constitutional History*, 224–25.

Why did plural marriage, which was surely declining in the years after 1949, become a practice that denied wives and children citizenship?
In part I submit this was because of some of the emotional aspects of citizenship that seem to have characterized Southern Rhodesia more than
many places: citizens were the kind of persons upon whom the state
wanted to bestow rights and duties,[26] men whose grandfathers might
have married a "creole" woman years ago, but not men from Portuguese
Africa who sought out African prostitutes. Although later versions of the
polygyny clause may have been aimed at the families of African civil
servants who had worked in Northern Rhodesia or Nyasaland, the 1949
act seemed also to be aimed at whites who had "gone native," an anxiety that remained in Southern Rhodesia long after it was an apparent
social problem.[27] But beyond the circulation of white laborers in Central
Africa, polygyny had a renewed importance in British law. As Jordanna
Bailkin has recently shown, colonial migration to the welfare state of the
1950s required new laws and new court rulings to address polygynous
unions. The rights of co-wives and their children, not the least of which
was who was entitled to pensions and survivors' benefits, joined questions of citizenship and domicile.[28] Southern Rhodesia in the 1940s and
1950s was not a welfare state but its lawmakers were as keenly aware of
legal developments in the United Kingdom as they were fearful of the
kinds of practices new immigrants might bring with them.

Citizenship did not guarantee voting rights, however: specific qualifications did. In 1951 the Southern Rhodesia legislature was finally able
to raise the franchise qualifications: the property qualification was increased to £500 and income, however it was reckoned, to £240 per year.
All voters had to be citizens and all applicants had to be able to speak
and write English, apart from the literacy required to fill out the form
unaided. All voters already on the roll could re-register whether or not
they met the new requirements, which would have kept poor white immigrants off the roll and allowed what African middle class there was
on it.[29]

26. I take this point from Balibar, "Propositions."
27. In 1957 the Southern Rhodesia parliament debated and extended the law banning sexual
relations between white men and African women to white women and African men; see Hardwicke
Holderness, *Lost Chance: Southern Rhodesia 1945–58* (Harare: Zimbabwe Publishing House, 1985),
184–87.
28. Jordanna Bailkin, *The Afterlife of Empire* (Berkeley: University of California Press, 2012),
137–51.
29. Palley, *Constitutional History*, 308–10; Mlambo, *White Immigration*, 64–69.

Federation and Decolonization

The Central African Federation was one of many federal plans with which various metropoles imagined an end to colonialism. In 1945, for example, the Netherlands proposed—and backed down from—a Commonwealth of the Netherlands, Surinam, Curaçao, and Indonesia. The British had created and almost lost the Malayan Federation. France, which had restructured its African empire in 1944 and again in 1958, created the Mali Federation, a union of Senegal and Mali that actually was granted independence as a unit in 1960. It did not survive the year, but in its two years of existence it marked a moment when the nation-state could be secondary to regional unions. The Central African Federation was not wholly a British idea, as we have seen, but as late as 1957, Harold Macmillan's government was convinced that it could promise a brighter African future. A 1957 report suggested that if the "pipe dream" of a West African federation was possible, the small states of Gambia and Sierra Leone might secure independence within it. Frederick Cooper has called these "alternatives to empire."[30] They were, just as they were ways to protect the most important economic resources of the region, but for men and women on the ground in Central Africa, they were something more.[31]

The Central African Federation was a hoped-for way to protect whites in Africa with a political ideology about the place of race in politics. This was a watered-down politics of inclusion that was first known as multiracialism, which had different qualifications for different racial groups, and then as nonracialism, which emphasized that qualifications had to be the same for all. The difference between the two was to be very important in terms of the franchise but not in terms of political talk: multiracialism and nonracialism were often used as synonyms, the meaning of which was always subsumed in the federal buzzword "partnership." No one quite knew what it meant, and however limited it was in practice, officials often had to deny Africans a place in it. Sir Geoffrey Huggins, the Southern Rhodesia prime minister who had brought the territory into the federation, was known to reassure white audiences that

30. Cooper, "Alternatives to Empire"; Burbank and Cooper, *Empires*, 415–18; Ritchie Ovendale, "Macmillan and the Wind of Change in Africa, 1957–1960," *The Historical Journal* 81, no. 1 (1995): 460.
    31. Murphy, *Party Politics*, 73–80.

it meant "the partnership between the horse and its rider."[32] Although multiracialists hoped that more and more Africans would gradually qualify to vote and maintain stability, and that more and more responsible Africans would serve in the federal parliament, federalists generally maintained that partnership should be about economic growth.[33] Roy Welensky, the Southern Rhodesian trade unionist who was to become prime minister of the federation, said this was his core argument. "If we are genuinely concerned about the Africans let us give them economic development and political rights can come later."[34] Not everyone in the territories agreed, however. In a novel the plot of which spans the federal era, when a well-intentioned magistrate must prosecute his trusted servant who has been blackmailed into terrorist acts by African nationalists, he reflects on the rights and reforms of federation, designed to preserve Southern Rhodesia "by the new ideal, Partnership. Partnership between the races. . . . Trying to stop it going black like Ghana, trying to stop it going berserk and bloodstained like Kenya."[35] By the late 1950s, however, terms like "partnership" and "multiracialism" came to be used in opposition to majority rule, most especially one man, one vote.

The creation of the Central African Federation in 1953 made questions of franchise more complex and more urgent than they had previously been. It also changed the political landscape in Southern Rhodesia. Political parties had long had interchangeable names and shifting memberships; they now stood candidates for territorial and federal parliaments. In 1953 and 1954, when many believed the federation would become independent soon, the most experienced and perhaps most ambitious politicians sought federal offices. They vacated seats and positions at the territorial level and created a space for several parties on the right and the left—terms defined solely by their degree of

32. Ovendale, "Macmillan," 457; Luise White, *The Assassination of Herbert Chitepo: Texts and Politics in Zimbabwe* (Bloomington: Indiana University Press, 2003), 4.

33. For a different view, see John David Leaver, "Multiracialism and Nationalisms: A Political Retrospective on 1950s Southern Rhodesia ('Colonial Zimbabwe')," *J. of Third World Studies* 23, no. 2 (2006): 167–88.

34. Welensky, *4000 Days*, 35; for British civil servants blatantly lobbying on behalf of federation, see Murphy, *Party Politics*, 125–26. Kwame Nkrumah's refrain, "Seek ye first the political kingdom" may have been a well-placed response against Anglo-American Corporation, the mining company with holdings both on the Gold Coast and in Northern Rhodesia that supported federation but opposed him. Murphy, *Party Politics*, 98.

35. John Gordon Davis, *Hold My Hand I'm Dying* (London, Diamond Books, 1989 [1967]), 30. Davis was a Rhodesian-born prosecutor and based his first novel on the trial of the first group of guerrillas who infiltrated the country; see Anthony Chennells, "Rhodesian Discourse, Rhodesian Novels, and the Zimbabwe Liberation War," in *Society in Zimbabwe's Liberation War*, ed. N. Bhebe and T. Ranger (London: James Currey, 1995), 102–29.

support for African advancement—to both develop and merge. Party membership was equally fluid. Garfield Todd, for example, was perhaps the best-known white liberal politician in the country. He came to Southern Rhodesia in 1934 as a missionary from New Zealand; he was first elected to parliament in 1946 as a United Party MP. He acquired dual citizenship in the late 1940s. When the United Party became the United Federal Party, Todd joined and was elected head of the United Rhodesia Party (URP) in 1953. The URP had grown out of the collapse and transformation of the very segregationist Rhodesia Party (formerly the Liberal Party) and the more progressive Rhodesian Labour Party.[36] Throughout the 1930s and 1940s political parties had emerged from parties that had similar policies, but after 1953 new parties were often coalitions of conflicting interests. Thus, the URP stood progressives and conservatives for parliament in its first campaign in February 1954. The party platform reflected the coalitions on which it was based. The URP promised to appoint a special commission to look into ways to expand the African franchise, to make English the sole language of the federation, and to seek dominion status for the federation as a single unit. It won twenty-five out of thirty seats.[37] Over the next two years there was an expansion of political parties that almost matched the expansion of positions within political parties: this signaled the range of new political alliances in Southern Rhodesia that were as unstable as they were broad.

Creating and Categorizing Voters, 1956–1958

Even as white political parties regrouped and reorganized, the question of who might be a citizen of the federation, and who had the right to vote for its governance, had to be worked out. In 1956, as the Gold Coast prepared for independence and as a multiracial electoral system was put in place in Tanganyika Territory that would lead to independence in a few years, federal and territorial electoral laws came under review.[38] This was not without urgency. Nyasaland had no electoral law; the Africans who sat in territorial and federal assemblies were appointed. Throughout 1956 committees and subcommittees sought ways

36. Leys, *European Politics*, 140–41; Hancock, *White Liberals*, 2–3, 38–39.
37. Colin Leys, *European Politics*, 142; Holderness, *Lost Chance*, 12–32; Hancock, *White Liberals*, 38–39.
38. Inter-Governmental Committee on Citizenship and the Franchise, October–December 1956, Cabinet Memoranda 1956, CL/Smith/5; Greenfield, *Testimony of a Rhodesian Federal*, 152; John Iliffe, "Breaking the Chain."

to allow Africans to elect their own representatives in both Nyasaland and Northern Rhodesia. This would help the federation win the African support it had not yet enjoyed and would bring Africans "into the political system and end racial politics."[39]

The federal Committee on Citizenship and Franchise met late in 1956. It was tasked with developing a notion of citizenship that fit all three territories, two of which had been protectorates, while accommodating British laws that now made being a British subject synonymous with the category of Commonwealth citizen. The committee was not overly concerned about defining citizenship, which they conferred on all "belongers." This was as close as anyone in the country came to asserting natural rights: belongers were men and women resident in the territory and wanting to become citizens of it and those with deep familial ties to the territory. Most commonly this meant a father born there, and in Southern Rhodesia that included Africans and Europeans. In Nyasaland and Northern Rhodesia, however, Africans were British-protected persons, a status that Africans were said to prefer to that of becoming British subjects.[40] The committee struggled over the franchise, however. The question of the franchise was the question of what role Africans would play in national politics; it was the flash point of African aspirations and white fears. This was not a case of governments being mandated to enfranchise Africans and how they avoided doing that, but of governments seeking to enfranchise Africans who were not "primitive and backward" in order to have a government that was multi-something and was based on a population large enough to make claims on the metropole.[41] The question was not just one of who might vote, but for whom one could vote. The African representatives to the federal and territorial assemblies had been appointed, but by 1956 this was seen as harmful to the successful workings of a party system. More to the point, if Africans were appointed to legislative bodies by European committees, surely their ability to represent African interests would be seen as "diluted"? If Africans were elected, as they were in Southern Rhodesia by a common roll that was 99 percent white, these representatives were considered compromised by Africans: some needed police protection when they visited townships. The committee sought new ways to elect African representatives and new voters to elect them.

39. Report of the Sub-Committee, Inter-Governmental Committee on Citizenship and the Franchise, December 1956, CL/Smith/5.

40. Inter-Governmental Committee on Citizenship and the Franchise; Greenfield, *Rhodesian Federal*, 149.

41. Holderness, *Lost Chance*, 176.

The voting rolls that emerged from these concerns had two overlapping points of origin. First, of course, was the assertion that talk of race generated a set of issues that got in the way of the supposed real issues of the day, which were invariably left unspecified but seem to have been some version of Welensky's argument for the primacy of economic development.[42] Throughout the region African politicians complained about the "fancy franchises" that were designed to encourage Africans to vote for European candidates and Europeans to vote for African ones as a way to make race obsolete.[43] Such social engineering was part and parcel of late colonialism, of course, but such a grand—and ahistorical— imaginary for elections meant that voters could never quite be sovereigns themselves but always objects to be arranged in a specialized order by another, more knowledgeable sovereign. The fiction of the voter protected from external pressures by a secret ballot marked in the privacy of a voting booth was just that: the candidates had been selected for them; voters exercised something other than agency and choice.[44]

The second point was simply to have more voters. There were less than a quarter of a million whites in Southern Rhodesia in 1956. As they understood at the time and as everyone else appeared not to notice, the country had never achieved a sizable or a stable white population. Josiah Brownell's careful research has shown that between 1955 and 1979, a total of almost 256,000 whites entered the country and a total of 246,000 left.[45] The problem for Southern Rhodesia was that if the electorate was entirely white it would also be too small to legitimate a claim for any kind of special standing, least of all dominion status or full independence. In the late 1950s there had to be, with considerably

42. The idea of race in British Empire circles was categorically different from the racial thought being deployed in Africa at the same time. The Colonial Office understood race to be about phenotypes and skin color: in their African territories there were blacks, whites, and perhaps Indians or Lebanese. Among Africans however there was racial thinking and racial categories that were not derived from colonial ideas: race in these cases may or may not have been described as lighter skin, but most often was described as a history of slave owning, exploitation, and being foreign. See Michael Lofchie, *Zanzibar: Background to Revolution* (Princeton, NJ: Princeton University Press, 1965), 127–80; Bruce S. Hall, *A History of Race in Muslim West Africa, 1600–1960* (Cambridge: Cambridge University Press, 2011), 1–5, 276–90; Glassman, *War of Words*; Brennan, *Taifa*, 159–95.

43. Inter-Governmental Committee on Citizenship and the Franchise; Leys, *European Politics*, 212–13, 227; Mason, *Year of Decision*, 85; Eshmael Mlambo, *Rhodesia: The Struggle for a Birthright* (London: Hurst, 1972), 122; Shamuyarira, *Crisis in Rhodesia*, 152–52; Newell M. Stulz, "Multi-racial Voting and Nonracial Politics in Colonial East and Central Africa," *Phylon* 33, no. 1 (1972): 67–78.

44. I take these points from Edmund S. Morgan, *Inventing the People: The Rise of Popular Sovereignty in England and America* (New York: Norton, 1988), 85; and David Gilmartin, "Towards a Global History of Voting: Sovereignty, the Diffusion of Ideas, and the Enchanted Individual," *Religions* 3 (2012): 407–23.

45. Brownell, *Collapse*, 3, 73.

more urgency than there had been in the past, some attempt to include enough Africans in the electorate to strengthen the case for an independent government. The solution was something that would be called "parity" that was to happen in the future, when, eventually, there would be the same number of African representatives as there were white ones. The path to parity was to begin with doubling the number of African representatives and white representatives, which meant that African representatives would increase from two to four just as white members in Southern Rhodesia would increase from twelve to twenty-four. Thus, parity would be achieved in some distant future but Africans should be reassured that there would be no discrimination in the proportion of increase. The question that was to drive debates about the franchise in Southern Rhodesia was how—and how many—Africans might be found qualified to have the same political status as white voters.

In 1956, only Southern Rhodesia insisted on a common voters roll. Nyasaland and Northern Rhodesia and the federal intergovernmental committee wanted two voting rolls, one for Africans and one for whites. The committee debated and dismissed several possible electoral systems—multiple voting, fractional voting, an electoral college dominated by whites—as a way to praise the idea of two racialized voters rolls. The committee proposed an A roll, primarily for Europeans, which would elect three-quarters of members, and a B roll, which would "have a strong admixture of less mature voters" and would elect one-quarter. As long as the upper roll voters had greater influence than those of the lower roll it could allay European fears about the number of Africans in the enlarged federal assembly. Everyone on the committee agreed that the very fact of the two voting rolls, in and of themselves, would lead to the development of nonracial political parties. Moreover, if Africans could elect their own representatives this would "satisfy" their "widespread desire" for a secret ballot.[46]

The desire that could not be satisfied was that of universal adult suffrage: it was simply not considered. In the absence of one man, one vote, the question was one of which Africans should be allowed to vote? The federal committee simplified Southern Rhodesia's 1951 requirements to property or income totaling £500 per year and simple literacy in English, the ability to fill out the form unaided. It recommended an alternative qualification of property or income of £300 per year and a Cambridge School certificate or its equivalent. The committee was not fully satisfied

46. Inter-Governmental Committee on Citizenship and the Franchise.

that education and means were the only measurements by which a "deserving" African might be allowed to vote. It suggested a point system that would find a way to assess Africans' vote-worthiness by measuring their judgment and civic worth. Education alone should allow African teachers and clergymen to vote, and the first wife in a polygynous marriage should be allowed to vote on her husband's income.[47]

The 1957 Franchise Commission

At the end of December—two weeks after it rejected the idea of two voter rolls—Southern Rhodesia appointed its own franchise commission. Headed by Sir Robert Tredgold, chief justice of the federal court, its other members were Sir Charles Cummings, former chief justice of colonial Sudan and participant in the drafting of the constitution for independent Sudan, and John Murray, chief justice of Southern Rhodesia and the man who had encouraged progressive South African lawyers to come and practice there. The commission began hearing testimony in mid-January 1957 and published its report three months later, having heard from thirty-six witnesses and read fifty-six memoranda, some from outside the country. Even so, the published report echoed many of the findings and even more of the concerns of the Inter-Governmental Committee. The franchise commission's *Report* received great praise— according to Tredgold one minister called it "a work of genius"—and over the next ten years most authors applauded its reasoned statements in defense of voter qualification.[48] Only the young researcher Colin Leys was appalled at the smug assertions the commission made and the condescension it showed the African electorate and the notion of universal suffrage. Leys was to prove prescient, as I shall show, but for the next few pages let me concern myself with Tredgold's commitment to the idea of a common roll, his modes of reckoning voter qualification, and the audience for whom those reasoned statements about voter qualification were intended.

Although the Inter-Governmental Committee had dismissed the segregationist parties' franchise proposals, the Tredgold commission considered them. It accepted testimony from the Segregation Society, the League of Empire Loyalists, and the Dominion Party (DP), which was

47. Inter-Governmental Committee on Citizenship and the Franchise.
48. Iliffe, "Breaking the Chain," 174; Holderness, *Lost Chance,* 177–79; Tredgold, *The Rhodesia,* 212, 218; Palley, *Constitutional History,* 308–9.

the most recent and fastest-growing of the segregationist parties that had frequently constituted the opposition in Southern Rhodesia's parliament. The Dominion Party, led by William Harper, wanted to maintain a common roll, one for which Africans could not easily qualify. Under the DP's proposals, Africans would have to submit ten letters of recommendation from members of the common roll and one from a magistrate or native commissioner. These letters would certify that the individual African lived "a civilised manner of life" and was "of good general repute" for ten years and able to understand "the implications of a liberal democracy." A five-member board was to be appointed to evaluate the recommendations; if the applicant received three votes cast on a secret ballot, he was able to register on the common roll. If he did not, there was no appeal.[49]

The commission heard testimony from the Southern Rhodesian African National Youth League—formerly the City Youth League and soon to be the Southern Rhodesia African National Congress (SRANC) and then the National Democratic Party (NDP), which I will discuss at length in the next chapter—and several African trade unions. It also received submissions from the best-known parties of the multiracial movement, the most prominent of which was the Capricorn Africa Society (CAS). Founded by war hero David Stirling, the CAS linked the colonies of Northern and Southern Rhodesia and sometimes Nyasaland (i.e., the Tropic of Capricorn) and added Tanganyika Territory and Kenya for good measure. Stirling had extensive diplomatic and journalistic contacts, which gave the organization credit when the Colonial Office did not. Laurens van der Post was a frequent fundraiser, for example. In Salisbury Stirling was close to African politicians and professionals, not all of whom were CAS members.[50] Liberals scoffed at the Capricorn conference of 1956, at "white Rhodesians hobnobbing with black ex–Mau

49. The DP looked forward to a nation of 20 to 30 million whites by the year 2000, none of whom would have to prove their understanding of liberal democracies; see Leys, *European Politics*, 170–72.

50. Activities of the Capricorn Africa Society in relation to native affairs in East and Central Africa, June 16, 1952, The National Archives, Kew [hereafter TNA]/CO822/340. The CAS was often in financial trouble; Stirling's contacts helped it obtain overdrafts in London, but officers in Southern Rhodesia were sometimes paid by wealthy white members instead of by the organization; see A. G. C. Pilavachi, CAS Southern Rhodesia Branch to David Stirling, October 24, 1957, Borthwick Historical Institute, York, CAS(SR)/307A. Van der Post occasionally claimed to have founded the CAS; see J. D. F. Jones, *Storyteller: The Many Lives of Laurens van der Post* (London: John Murray, 2001), 252–55. In 1958 Stirling asked George Loft of the American Friends Service if a Quaker-managed building society in Bulawayo could loan Joshua Nkomo money; see George Loft papers, Hoover Institution Archives, Stanford University [hereafter Hoover]/Correspondence/Whitehead; author's field notes, Harare, July 8, 2001, August 15, 2012.

Mau from Kenya," but for African businessmen and African politicians the CAS offered opportunities and a platform unlike anything they had previously enjoyed. Progressives in and out of Africa understood this: Julius Nyerere was an early supporter, and Capricorns were able to create a short-lived political party in Northern Rhodesia in 1957. During her 1956 visit Doris Lessing attended a Capricorn meeting, where she saw what she could not have imagined a decade earlier, a white audience applauding a black speaker.[51] Most of its white membership in Southern Rhodesia and all its office staff were recent immigrants, men and women who came to the country in the early 1950s and believed in Stirling's "touch of genius" or the promise of a multiracial future. Its African members included Leopold Takawira and Herbert Chitepo, both of whom we shall meet in the next chapter. Takawira was a member much longer and more prominently than Chitepo was. The Capricorns were unequivocal about what motivated their philosophy of inclusion: Stirling wanted a multiracial party that could thwart the emergence of an "effective African nationalist movement whose purpose would be to push Europeans out of Africa," something the Colonial Office was by 1950 too tainted to achieve.[52] The Capricorns owed most of their ideas to nineteenth-century liberalism; they believed that the leadership necessary to achieve public good had to be privileged before any particular public could be wholly included in political affairs. Capricorns wanted to increase the number of African voters; they championed home ownership for urban Africans as a way for more Africans to obtain the property qualifications to allow them to vote.[53] Part of Capricorn's appeal was that it took a great many positions. David Stirling has been credited with encouraging Harold Macmillan's Conservative cabinet to embrace decolonization at the same time he was extremely cautious in Southern Rhodesia. In 1957, for example, when the local CAS chairman

---

51. Holderness, *Lost Chance*, 170–73; Leaver, "Multiracialisms and Nationalisms," 169–74; Bizeck Jube Phiri, "The Capricorn Africa Society Revisited: The Impact of Liberalism in Zambia's Colonial History, 1949–1963," *Int. J. African Hist. Studies* 24, no. 1 (1991): 65–83; Peter Mackay, *We Have Tomorrow: Stirrings in Africa, 1959–1967* (Wilby: Michael Russell, 2008), 90–91; Murphy, *Party Politics*, 176; Lessing, *Going Home*, 98–99; Richard Hughes, *Capricorn: David Stirling's Second Africa Campaign* (London: Radcliffe Press, 2003), 108–13; Michael West, *The Rise of the African Middle Class in Colonial Zimbabwe* (Bloomington: Indiana University Press, 2002), 197–98; White, *Assassination of Herbert Chitepo*, 68–69.

52. Hancock, *White Liberals*, 42; Holderness, *Lost Chance*, 171; Murphy, *Party Politics*, 175–76; David Stirling, London, to Margery Perham, Oxford, September 14, 1953, Rhodes House, Oxford [hereafter RH]/MSS Perham 713/1.

53. The idea of urban African householders took hold in 1950s British thinking as a way to stabilize African labor and African politics; see Luise White, *The Comforts of Home: Prostitution in Colonial Nairobi* (Chicago: University of Chicago Press, 1990), 212–16.

threatened to resign when he saw a draft document demanding universal suffrage, the office explained that this was a typing error.[54]

The Capricorn Africa Society never favored universal suffrage. Instead, the plural, or multiple, vote was at the center of its proposals. Although some of its most prominent supporters later thought the idea "a bit potty," in the 1950s Capricorns claimed that the plural vote demonstrated that the privilege of voting was based on experience and education, not race.[55] There was to be a common roll with a limited "qualitative" franchise based on ten qualifications. Any three of these would qualify for one vote; anyone with additional qualifications would get an additional vote, but under no circumstances could any individual have more than seven votes. These qualifications were being twenty-one or older, completing secondary school, a university degree, five years' military service, an income of £120 or property worth £500, having been elected an elder of the tribe, being awarded a civil or military decoration, five years' service on an African district council or court, and having a master farmer's certificate or a women's club badge. The Inter-Governmental Committee dismissed multiple voting out of hand. No single set of criteria, however lengthy, could determine who was qualified to vote in communities "which are at markedly different stages of development." More troubling was that the Capricorn proposals would allow illiterates to vote if they met other qualifications: the committee insisted that literacy should be the minimum qualification for a vote.[56]

The Tredgold commission found plural voting a useful foil for its outright rejection of universal suffrage, however. It did not defend literacy as much as it derided the mechanics of allocating multiple votes: "It is hard enough to judge whether a man should be entitled to a vote at all"; trying to decide who was eligible for multiple votes was a quagmire. The commission's *Report* listed some of the obvious problems: if a man earned £1,500 a year was he entitled to one vote more than a man earning £1,000? Was an achievement in commerce worth the same number of votes as secondary education? Should a major be given more votes than a captain? It concluded that multiple voting would not solve the

54. Ovendale, "Macmillan," 456–56, 472; Murphy, *Party Politics*, 174–76; David Mowbray to Aleco Pilavachi, September 17, 1957, CAS (SR)/307A, Borthwick Historical Institute, University of York.

55. Denis Acheson to Monica Hinfelaar, February 2, 1987, National Archives of Zambia, Lusaka HM73.CAS/Correspondence.

56. Inter-Governmental Committee on Citizenship and the Franchise, CL/Smith/5. Philip Mason attended several Capricorn meetings where he found African members opposed to multiple voting. "Why not one man one vote?" they asked. "That is what *you* have in England. If it's good for you, why not us?" Philip Mason, *A Thread of Silk* (London: Michael Russell, 1984), 83–84.

problems specific to Southern Rhodesia, where the "numerical superiority" of men with one vote would neutralize the effect of multiple votes, so that however carefully plural voting had been assigned and applied, it would be insignificant.[57]

Southern Rhodesia's local multiracial party, the Interracial Association, which had a foothold in the ruling party, made broad recommendations to the Tredgold commission. Founded in 1953 by professionals and businessmen, it held that the ultimate goal for the country should be universal adult suffrage. This was not immediately possible, but every effort should be made to progress toward this goal. The Interracial Association—and many members of the territorial government—wanted to keep the common voters roll "because it already exists, is simple and workable, and gives hope to Africans, and lessens the possibility of future racial politics." In this vein, it wanted to make sure Africans had the right to own homes in urban areas; this would enable them to meet the property requirements of the franchise. It opposed multiple voting for all the reasons the Inter-Governmental Committee had: it was cumbersome, and as the proposals stood they were unfair to Africans.[58]

The Mystical Power of One Man, One Vote

It was around the issue of universal suffrage that the *Report* was most articulate and most scolding. Universal adult suffrage was the ideal system for a democratic government, the commission agreed, but it was not at all clear that it could function without certain conditions in place. These were a "homogenous electorate, at a fairly high standard of civilization" separated only by "political divisions" based on the records of government and opposition "and not confused by differences, such as race or colour, that tend to create artificial divisions cutting across the real issues." The idea that democracy must be based on universal suffrage "has involved so much emotion, not to say passion," that the commission considered it necessary to explain the principles of government to its audience. The commission had heard many such "aphorisms" in the memoranda submitted to it. These treated concepts like "democracy" and "self-government" as "mystic," as "fetishes" to be followed. Some claimed that "self-government was more important than good

57. Southern Rhodesia, *Report of the Franchise Commission* (Salisbury: Government Printer, 1957), 7.

58. *Franchise Report*, 7–8; West, *Middle Class*, 194–95; Holderness, *Lost Chance*, 150–54, 177–84.

government," which simply elevated "'self-government' to something approaching transcendental status." All these concepts vested government with "quasi supernatural attributes" and concealed the principle that "government was made for man, not man for government." The object of government, the *Report* intoned, was to give an individual the opportunity to lead the good life "as he sees it." Every man had the right to have a say in government, but no one should be able to use that right to harm another, which the *Report* insinuated would happen under majority rule. In any case, the *Report* had a trump card: universal suffrage was qualified. Even the most "ardent advocates" of universal adult suffrage saw "no logical inconsistency" in excluding mentally deficient people from voting, or those who were below a certain age. Among the many advocates of universal adult suffrage the commission heard, only a very few thought that African women should be franchised immediately. "The more reasonable" admitted that, given the "tutelage" in which African women had been held for generations, they "were not in a position to exercise the franchise intelligently." Yet women represent more than half the African population of the country. Once such a large section of the people is excluded it is impossible to argue that everyone is entitled to the vote "by virtue of his humanity alone."[59] The subordination of women, and the meaning of that subordination for their ability to vote, was to become commonplace in discussions about universal suffrage in Southern Rhodesia.

Having dealt with the theory of universal adult suffrage, the *Report* turned to the practice. A common roll with adult suffrage was out of the question. "It would mean that the overwhelming majority of the voters would be African." There would be implicit racial representation on such a roll, "and racial representation of the worst type" as only one race would be represented. If such a roll were introduced at this time, it would place the European minority "entirely" in the hands of the African majority—a majority who are "for the most part uneducated and backwards." Recent events in other parts of the continent—presumably Mau Mau—should alert any observer "not obsessed with particular political doctrines" of the danger that many Africans would give in to the emotional appeal of African nationalism and readily "sacrifice their own best interests, let alone interests apparently opposed to their own." Europeans' fears may have been exaggerated, but the commission

59. *Franchise Report*, 2–3.

"could not close our eyes to the fact that they exist." If European fears could be allayed with a qualified franchise, then it would be possible to have an electorate who approached every problem with an open mind, "for there is no greater disturber of a man's judgment than fear."[60]

Who did the commission imagine was the audience for this level of clarity and condescension? No one in the government that created the commission considered universal suffrage a possibility, and no African political party actually demanded it in 1957. It would be another year before the SRANC would list universal suffrage as fifteenth in a twenty-one-point program.[61] In 1957 was there anyone in the country in need of such a lecture on race, history, and responsible government? The parliamentary debates about the proposals never questioned Tredgold's broad principles but concentrated instead on how to allocate votes to the people who deserved to have them all the while slowing the "forced pace" of African advancement.[62] The audience for these pages seems to have been the Colonial Office: the commission began its work just as the secretary of state for the colonies arrived in the federation, fresh from social and electoral engineering in the Tanganyika Territory.[63]

According to the Tredgold *Report* Southern Rhodesia was a country "amply justified" in confining the franchise to those who were capable of exercising it with "reason, judgment and public spirit." Voting was thus not an innate right or a privilege, but a skill. Skill—as in maintaining telephones—was to become as powerful a trope in debates about the franchise as African women were. And, as Colin Leys noted at the time, since African wealth and education lagged behind that of Europeans, there was ample "evidence of a general lack of all skills, from plumbing to conveyancing" that should deny Africans the vote. Philip Mason was more precise: by calling voting a skill the commission repudiated "with scorn the idea of a 'natural' or 'inalienable' right to vote."[64] The commission, however, both promoted these generalizations and struggled against them: its concerns were to find a just mechanism that could measure people's "capacity to vote." Standards had to be flexible enough to allow for the deficiencies in African education and broad enough to measure "the qualities of mind and character" that enabled a man to vote intelligently. A means test was appropriate; if a man earned beyond

60. *Franchise Report*, 5.
61. SRANC Statement, *Zimbabwe Independence Documents*, 4–11.
62. Leys, *European Politics*, 215–16; Holderness, *Lost Chance*, 189–94.
63. Iliffe, "Breaking the Chain," 184–85.
64. Leys, *European Politics*, 221; Mason, *Year of Decision*, 78.

subsistence he had obviously accomplished something. An educational test was justifiable as well: a man with a "trained and disciplined mind" should be able to make better decisions than his untutored fellows. The commission heard many submissions that certain professions should have a special right to vote, but decided not to compare the capacity to vote of a schoolmaster with that of an industrialist, or a sergeant-major, or a building foreman.[65]

In the end the commission retained the common roll, to which it proposed four "doorways," three ordinary and one special. The three ordinary doorways reflected the complexities of assessing a voter's capacities in the plural society Southern Rhodesia had become in the 1950s. The first doorway required an income of £60 per month or occupancy of immovable property valued at £1,500 and sufficient literacy in English to fill out the registration form unaided. The second required a monthly income of £40 or occupancy of immovable property valued at £1,000 and the completion of standard VI in school. The third doorway required an income of £25 per month or occupancy of immovable property valued at £500 and the completion of form IV in school. Married women qualified through the property of their husbands, but not through their husbands' schooling. A wife had to have adequate literacy to fill out the form unaided.[66]

The third doorway was not specifically designed for African electors. Only a handful of Africans qualified under the third doorway, but there were intense debates about how many wives of polygynous Africans could qualify with their husbands' property. The concerns about polygyny were twofold. Despite women's political activism in Salisbury's townships in the early 1950s and despite the strong influence of John Stuart Mill on Rhodesia's next two constitutions, federal committees held to the idea that women voted however their husbands instructed them to.[67] Polygyny thus did not prove a man uncivilized and incapable of exercising the rights offered to civilized men; rather, it allowed him too many votes.[68] A polygynous wife, whether she was the first wife or

65. *Franchise Report*, 6.
66. *Franchise Report*, 4.
67. For women's activism, see Scarnecchia, *Urban Roots*, 49–68. The 1961 and 1969 constitutions followed some of Mills's proscriptions exactly. The authors had to have known that he argued that women would learn independence of thought by the very exercise of the vote. Indeed, he thought that husbands instructing their wives on how to vote would in fact generate a discussion of who to vote for and thus each vote would reflect two opinions rather than one. John Stuart Mill, *Considerations on Representative Government* (New York: Harper & Bros., 1862), 191–94.
68. The national condemnation of enfranchising women in the territory of Utah was that it allowed polygynous wives to vote as their husbands and church dictated; see Sarah Barringer Gordon,

the fifth, was a dominated wife, and as much as these issues had their origins in British legal theories they became in Southern Rhodesia a new way to argue that African men were unfit to vote: Tredgold's assertion that the tutelage in which African women were kept rendered them unskilled voters would become, in a very short time, proof that African men did not deserve the vote. In federal committees Southern Rhodesia agreed that women should either qualify on their husband's income or qualify on their own, but did not want to enfranchise any wives in polygynous unions. Nyasaland and Northern Rhodesia rejected this out of hand: such a policy would exclude too many women.[69] For much of the 1950s, polygyny remained the indelible marker of difference in colonial debates. In French West Africa, for example, it took several years of intense debate—and far-fetched ideas about how many wives a waged worker might have—before family allowances were allocated to African workers.[70] In British Central Africa, social life was seen as a precondition for civic life. In the debates that followed the publication of the Tredgold report, it was decided that a woman had to meet the educational qualifications if she was to qualify on her own, but the wife in a monogamous marriage or the first wife in a polygynous marriage could qualify on their husband's income.[71]

Only the fourth, or special, doorway had the specific goal of increasing the number of Africans who could vote. The special doorway was open for Africans who earned £15 per month. There would be a few exceptions, of course, but the commission was satisfied that an African with a monthly income of £15 "has proved himself as a citizen." This was the salary of an agricultural supervisor, a building overseer, a clerk, an interpreter, a clergyman, an editor, or a journalist. This would include only state-registered nurses who had passed several examinations and teachers who had school certificates and many years' experience. It was open to only those policemen who had been promoted to the rank of noncommissioned officer or who had served for at least ten years. In short, "an African drawing £15 per month has passed well beyond

"'The Liberty of Self-Degradation': Women, Suffrage and Consent in Nineteenth-Century America," *J. American History* 83, no. 3 (1996): 815–47.

69. Southern Rhodesia also wanted the voting age raised to twenty-five. Minutes of meetings, January 30 and 31, 1957, Inter-Territorial Committee on Federal Franchise Requirements, CL/Smith/6.

70. Cooper, *Decolonization*, 281, 315–16.

71. J. M. Greenfield, Minister of Law and Order, Memorandum on the Federal Electoral Bill, May 30, 1957, CL/Smith/6.

unskilled labor and may be regarded as a reasonably responsible citizen." No "fair-minded person" could deny him the vote.[72]

Counting Votes in 1958

What kind of citizenship was this, that had to demonstrate its worth and responsibility? Tredgold's use of the term has less to do with law—something he knew very well—than with the broad concept I discussed earlier, an ahistorical condition of experience that proved something that could not be established by place of birth or residence. Citizenship here means specific political rights that have been earned and that demonstrate a combination of experience and expertise most Africans did not have. And even though these "reasonably responsible citizens" might be able to vote, their votes were to be devalued. In an extraordinarily cumbersome reckoning, the commission recommended that the total number of special qualification votes should never count for more than half of the votes cast by voters with ordinary qualifications. This was fractional voting in which, for example, there might be a total of 3,000 votes in a district election. If 1,200 were special qualification votes and 1,800 were ordinary qualification votes, the 1,200 special qualification votes could count as only 900, half of 1,800. But in another hypothetical 3,000-vote district there might be 1,000 special qualification votes and 2,000 ordinary qualification votes. In that case all votes would count equally in the final tally. Yes, the *Report* admitted, the special qualification voters would be primarily Africans who would be aware of the diminution of their votes, but fractional voting would allow them immediate participation in the electoral process with the promise of full inclusion on the voters roll "should they advance sufficiently." Still, the *Report* maintained the various doorways to the franchise were not about race, but a way to end racial politics: since all constituencies had voters of all races, no candidate could appeal to any one race without risking defeat and political parties could not appeal to racialism without risking the loss of marginal seats. With fractional voting, Europeans could not fear being overwhelmed "by the backwards and illiterate sections of the African population"—who were not enfranchised—while Africans would have gradually increasing participation in political affairs and learn the traditions of parliamentary government. Africans should not

---

72. *Franchise Report*, 12.

think they were getting a devalued franchise, either. They should understand that they have reached a stage where they are "entitled to some
say in the affairs of the country," but until they advanced further "in
education and responsibility" it is not "right" that they assume control
of those affairs.[73] At the time, however, Colin Leys and Philip Mason
disagreed: these proposals were designed to keep " 'extremist' Africans"
out of parliament: they would expand the number of African voters so
as to strengthen support for moderates. The African representatives thus
elected were in fact the people European voters "thought suitable to lead
them."[74] Both men may have been overly generous: several members of
the Southern Rhodesian parliament thought it best to limit the number
of special doorway voters.[75]

Fractional voting, which was to survive in a modified form, fit well
with Southern Rhodesia's new electoral districts. In 1951, on the eve of
federation, Southern Rhodesia set up a commission to increase the number of electoral districts. Headed by Tredgold, it established forty electoral districts—each averaging about thirteen hundred voters—replacing
the thirty that had been in place since 1938. Given the increase in urban
population, and given the weight this system had historically given the
agricultural sector, the commission declared that fourteen of the forty
districts would be in rural areas and the remainder in towns. Because so
many African townships were in fact peri-urban areas, the commission
suggested that further delimitations would soon be necessary.[76] The next
delimitation was in 1961, by which time Southern Rhodesia had adopted
a standardized vocabulary for elections, in which urban districts became
constituencies. Rural areas continued to have electoral districts.

When the territorial governments met to discuss the Tredgold *Report*, they all found most of its recommendations—especially devalued
votes—impracticable. The federal government, Northern Rhodesia,
and Nyasaland all read the *Report* as making a case for two rolls, since
the special qualification amounted to an African roll. Why not form
two separate rolls, in which the African roll, with lower qualifications,
elected fewer representatives than the European roll? Two rolls would
meet the conflicting demands of Nyasaland, which sought lower

73. *Franchise Report*, 9–11.
74. Leys, *European Politics*, 227; Mason, *Year of Decision*, 86.
75. Holderness, *Lost Chance*, 194.
76. Southern Rhodesia, *Report of the Commission Appointed to Re-Divide the Colony and Electoral
Districts, 1952* (Salisbury: Government Printer, 1952); Leys, *European Politics*, 192–93; Anthony
Lemon, "Electoral Machinery and Voting Patterns in Rhodesia, 1962–1977," *African Affairs* 77,
no. 309 (1978): 516.

qualifications, and Northern Rhodesia, which sought simpler ones, and could perhaps resolve some of the "difficulties" the federal government had with the Colonial Office. Only Southern Rhodesia resisted two rolls. Garfield Todd, prime minister of Southern Rhodesia, insisted that two rolls "would consolidate racism." The proposed common roll "did away with racialism, notwithstanding that the special voters would, in fact, be Africans." And of course those Europeans who could only qualify for the lower roll would not want to vote for Africans at lower-roll elections. Neither Northern Rhodesia nor Nyasaland had such concerns about European voters; they wanted to increase the number of enfranchised Africans. The government of Northern Rhodesia proposed that married couples—not polygynous households—be allowed to qualify by combining the incomes of husband and wife. The committee rejected this: qualification was to be based on the husband's income, nothing more.[77]

But did a federal franchise require federal citizenship? The federal committee was not entirely sure. Was everyone—excluding Africans in Nyasaland, who were British-protected persons—required to be a federal citizen or would being a British subject suffice? If federal citizenship was required to be able to vote, how long should it take to get it? The federation required two years' residence (with exceptions made for wives), but Southern Rhodesia now required three years and Northern Rhodesia two.[78] Throughout the 1950s, Southern Rhodesia had revised its citizenship laws to get rid of citizens who left: a citizen who resided in another country for seven years could lose his or her citizenship, as could any citizen who committed acts that were contrary to "the public good." Those ex-citizens could be declared prohibited immigrants and deported if they tried to return.[79]

The federal committee was more certain of what to do with the special qualification. It was to be available to anyone who earned £20 per month and had the required literacy or to anyone who earned £10 per month and had completed ten years of education. Enrollments under special qualification would be closed when the number of special voters equaled 20 percent of the ordinary electorate. Tredgold claimed his proposals had been "fatally maimed." As Southern Rhodesia debated the franchise proposals the federal government produced statistics predict-

77. Minutes of meeting on Constitution of Federal Assembly and Franchise Proposals, Lusaka, March 30, 1957, Cabinet Memoranda 1957 CL/Smith/6.

78. J. M. Greenfield, minister of law, memorandum on federal election bill, May 30, 1957. Cabinet memoranda, CL/Smith/6.

79. Palley, *Constitutional History*, 564–66.

ing that with the lower qualifications 12,000 Africans would be enfranchised immediately, and that 30,000 Africans and 128,000 Europeans would be qualified to vote in Southern Rhodesia by 1963. Tredgold called these figures "fantastic" but they gained traction when Todd proposed that all Africans with ten years of schooling be given the vote, making it clear that the wives of such men could not qualify on their husbands' education.[80]

Party Politics in 1958

The very idea of an expanded African franchise in Southern Rhodesia caused established white political parties to contract. Todd's proposal split his party, the United Rhodesia Party (URP). Todd resigned the party leadership after he was accused of abandoning the rhetoric of federation and of putting African advancement before economic advancement. His resignation and broader recriminations led to a realignment of the party. The URP of Southern Rhodesia became the Southern Rhodesia division of the United Federal Party (UFP) in early 1958. The UFP was a party of veteran politicians, and as such it wasted no time replacing Todd with a compromise candidate, Sir Edgar Whitehead. Those who left the UFP formed a streamlined URP that was stripped of its more right-wing and segregationist elements. In the 1958 election the URP stood progressive candidates on a platform that demanded the implementation of the Tredgold proposals. One of their pamphlets asked if white voters could be relied on to support reasonable legislation or were they "as people overseas imagine them—like the platteland voters in the Union?" Although Tredgold was optimistic that a more liberal regime was at hand, all the URP candidates lost. In one of the many contingencies with which the origins of UDI were explained, URP stalwarts insisted that if the Tredgold proposals had been in place, the party would have benefited from the expanded African voters rolls, and the hope for white and black Rhodesians finding common ground would have lived on a while longer.[81] The UFP moved even further to the right after the

80. J. M. Greenfield, CL/Smith/6; Leys, *European Politics*, 141–43; Mason, *Year of Decision*, 192–95; Tredgold, *The Rhodesia*, 218–19; Holderness, *Lost Chance*, 216–21; Ian Hancock, *White Liberals*, 65.

81. Blake, *Rhodesia*, 307–13; Leys, *White Politics*, 142–43; Holderness, *Lost Chance*, 195, 216–21, 227–30; Hancock, *White Liberals*, 69–70; George Loft, notes on conversation with Sir Robert Tredgold, March 2, 1958. George Loft Papers, Hoover/Correspondence/Tredgold.

1958 election, and the URP reconstituted itself as the Central African Party (CAP), which was headed by Todd and which welcomed Africans.[82]

In its final version the electoral act did not adopt all the Tredgold proposals. Voter qualifications were to be raised at the same time that the special qualification became more difficult to attain and less worthwhile to exercise. The new law provided an immediate increase in the number of African voters up to a point: once the special voters reached 20 percent of the ordinarily qualified electorate, the special voters' roll would be closed. For Africans to qualify for the franchise after that, they would have to meet the new, higher ordinary qualifications. Under the new law, the special qualification was an annual income of £120 for two consecutive years and two years of secondary education, or an annual income of £240 for two consecutive years. The only long-term expansion of the African franchise was that of wives in polygynous marriages: the senior wife of a polygamous man would qualify under her husband's income. The new ordinary qualifications, based on property ownership— not occupancy—and two years' earnings, were beyond the reach of all but perhaps four thousand Africans. The new, higher qualifications were two years of an annual income of £720 or ownership of immovable property worth £1,500, or completed primary education and an annual income of £480 for two years or owning immovable property worth £1,000 or four years' secondary education and £300 annual income for two years or owning immovable property worth £500.

The law also introduced multiple-preference voting (sometimes called alternative voting), in which each elector would vote for two candidates in order of preference. Once the first-preference votes were counted, the candidate who received the most second-preference votes would be awarded the votes from the candidate who received the least second-preference votes and then from the candidate with the next least votes, until one candidate received an absolute majority. Multiple-preference voting and the bizarre arithmetic it required was designed to encourage inter-racial alliances, at least in theory, but in practice it precluded the election of an African candidate if the European vote was split. In Southern Rhodesia it tended to favor those European parties who received some African votes. Indeed, in 1958 the ruling United Federal Party was returned to power by four seats, all won by the redistribution of votes.[83]

82. Mlambo, *Rhodesia*, 136–37.
83. Palley, *Constitutional History*, 309–11; Greenfield, *Rhodesian Federal*, 152–53.

This electoral result demands two separate concluding remarks. First, the franchise proposals that were conceived as a way to shift voters away from race and toward the real issues of party politics became—in less than a year—a law that allowed political parties to make sure European candidates could win. Second, had there been no multiple-preference voting the Dominion Party would have won. According to Jon Fraenkel's research, the Dominion Party won almost 46 percent of the first-preference votes. The UFP won 42 percent and the URP won 11 percent. The URP vote was transferred to the UFP so that it won 53 percent of the vote.[84] This seems to have encouraged the Dominion Party, which—unlike most parties in the territory—was to wait four years to merge with another political party. This also made the UFP wary of the white vote and generated a new frame for political debate in the early 1960s: that white extremists were as dangerous as African ones.

84. Jon Fraenkel, " 'Equality of rights for every civilized man south of the Zambesi': The Origins of the Alternative Vote as a Tool for Ethnic Accommodation, Southern Rhodesia 1958–65," unpublished essay.

THREE

"European opinion and African capacities": The Life and Times of the 1961 Constitution

By the early 1960s Rhodesia's claim that it was not racist in any way was reinforced by a specific and specialized vocabulary. There was the Cape franchise, government in responsible hands, the common roll, partnership, and parity. Each of these terms was part of a language of potentials and offerings that would eventually provide what the present-day electorate would not. The 1961 constitution became part of this language almost at once, even though it was itself a product—many thought the finest product—of the fiction that Rhodesia was not racist. Within a few years it became just another vocabulary term, another imagining of how to make Rhodesia, and its electorate, less racist.

Constitutional Commissions and Local Knowledge

The conventional narrative of 1958 to 1961 in the region is one of white retrenchment and African nationalism, of the gradual evisceration of multiracial coalitions and the rise of a segregationist alliance in Southern Rhodesia.[1] The conceit

---

1. This is the point of Holderness, *Lost Chance*, and Leaver, "Multiculturalism and Nationalisms"; see also Hancock, *White Liberals*, 4–5.

of this chapter is to look specifically at ideas about the franchise in this period, ideas that both underscore and complicate the conventional narrative. As the Central African Federation weakened—especially after the imperial panic and violence in Nyasaland in 1959—royal commissions and constitutional advisory committees descended on the land, hearing testimonies and written evidence and generally finding reasons to pronounce an already unpopular political construct terminally ill.[2] Private individuals, businessmen and representatives of political parties all gave evidence. There is no causal link I can discern between this testimony and UDI a few years later: individuals seemed unconcerned with the possible independence of Northern Rhodesia or Nyasaland. All of the testimony was given a few months before the Belgian Congo became independent, before its "chaos" became a favored local example of the evils of majority rule. Rhodesians across a broad political spectrum were to argue that the events in the Congo "hardened" their attitudes and made them determined never to suffer government by the "immature and ill-trained."[3] The following pages reveal something else, that the attitudes about the impossibility of African self-rule were in place well before events in the Congo or anywhere else. These were the attitudes that had given the Dominion Party its near victory in 1958 and that allowed new members to claim the Rhodesian Front emerged from "the very soil" of Rhodesia.[4] Only after 1964 did the events in the Congo become a shorthand for ideas that had been commonplace outside of most political parties for several years. Indeed, most of the individuals who gave testimony did not think race was a superficial issue. They often told anecdotes to show why Africans should not vote. Political parties, however, gave statements that were considerably less condescending than Tredgold had been on the subject of universal suffrage but were far more specific: what everyone now called adult suffrage was not suitable for Southern Rhodesia no matter what was happening anywhere to the north.

A broad spectrum of political parties gave oral and written evidence in which they all abandoned the language of partnership. That particular version of nineteenth-century liberalism in which political inclusion was based on certain groups allowing those less equal than themselves to pretend that they had the same rights, as in Tredgold's special doorway,

2. Murphy, *Party Politics*, 182–85.

3. The two quotes are from Michael Auert, quoted in Keith Meadows, *Sometimes When It Rains: White Africans in Black Africa* (Bulawayo: Thorntree Press, 1998), 205; and Desmond Lardner-Burke, *Rhodesia; The Story of a Crisis* (London: Ouldborne Book Co., 1966), 11–12.

4. Evans, Rhodesian Front Rule, 41.

did not survive the Nyasaland emergency.[5] The Dominion Party, which had never championed partnership, admitted that "the franchise question is getting more difficult and explosive every day" but proposed a redesigned federation in which the industrial areas—Salisbury, Bulawayo, and the Copperbelt—would be enfranchised. Everywhere else would be a protectorate in which African residents would be governed directly both by the United Kingdom and by "their chiefs" so that there would be no "interference" with their way of life. The League of Empire Loyalists reminded the advisory committee that the African tribes of Southern Rhodesia had been separate races in the nineteenth century, so that an ideal system might be a federal one in which each race had internal self-government. The progressive Central African Party (CAP) wanted suffrage for anyone who could fill out the form in English unaided, which it claimed would add twenty-five thousand Africans to the roll. The Southern Rhodesian branch of the UFP, the beneficiary of multiple-preference voting two years before, opposed universal suffrage. Echoing and perhaps intensifying the language of the Tredgold *Report*, the UFP identified the "modern shibboleths" of "democracy, self-government, and adult suffrage." In some places these might well be "eternal and immutable truths," but they could not work everywhere. The flaw of believing in adult suffrage, or self-government, was that people forgot that these are not ends in themselves, but means—a "means" that would insure that a "just, incorruptible, responsible government" would govern fairly. Repeating many of Tredgold's clichés—voting age, votes for African women—the UFP memo claimed that whatever happened elsewhere in Africa, universal adult suffrage was literally impossible in Southern Rhodesia, where, after all, whites had come to stay and had built a society "based on Western Civilization," which would be imperiled if government should fall into irresponsible hands. Voting was not a right but a skill, the UFP reminded the committee members in the terms Leys predicted: it was dangerous when used by unprepared hands. In their oral evidence, party members admitted that "shibboleths" cut both ways, however. Each franchise proposal was a calculus, a formula with

5. Uday Singh Mehta, "Liberal Strategies of Exclusion," in *Tensions of Empire: Colonial Cultures in a Bourgeois World*, ed. Frederick Cooper and Ann Laura Stoler (Berkeley: University of California Press, 1997), 59–85; and *Liberalism and Empire: A Study in Nineteenth-Century British Liberal Thought* (Chicago: University of Chicago Press, 1999), esp. chaps. 1 and 2.

which to make sure that no change was so rapid that it might exceed "European opinion and perhaps African capacities."[6]

The individual testimonies rarely laid claim to Western civilization or the state of European opinion. Most individuals repeatedly pointed out the exceptionalism of Southern Rhodesia: the committee members who had been in the northern territories would notice that there were no police barricades or protesters outside the building. This was "a free country, there was no intimidation." The idea and fact of intimidation was to dominate white thinking about African politics in a very short time, but in 1960 private citizens assured the commissioners that the problems of Southern Rhodesia came from outside: "Moscow, Britain, and Ghana."[7]

Africans Have No Word for Vote

The advisory committee heard dozens of white witnesses, many of whom spoke in intensely specific terms: they made no claims to know about governance, but they knew about Africans. Many were personal, using anecdotes about their servants to explain why Africans were not ready for self-government.[8] There was not any single ideology to be heard, but there were variations on set themes, the most important of which was something political parties did not mention, Africans' "awe at chiefs." This was to have a stranglehold on Rhodesian thinking about African politics by the late 1960s; in the previous decade chiefs had been granted increased authority in rural areas, but few villagers were said to be in their thrall. Indeed, the Tredgold commission did not hear testimony from chiefs. Another theme was one from the Tredgold commission, the subjugation of African women. Captain Klewman de Kock, a member of one of the parties that merged into the United Federal Party, held forth. All over the continent Africans "looked down on their women. There is no word for 'vote' in their language; they had been used to doing what they were told by their chiefs. Now they are asking for adult suffrage." Mr. Beaton had recently arrived from Northern Rhodesia, where he found urban Africans backward and with little concern for what was going on around them. The situation was the same in

---

6. Advisory Committee on the Review of the Constitution of the Federation and Nyasaland, *Report and Appendix VIII, Evidence v. IV,* Cmnd. 1151-III (London: HMSO, 1960), 167–70, 300, 316–17, 64–66.

7. Advisory Committee, *Evidence v. IV,* P. S. Reynolds, 123–24.

8. Advisory Committee, *Evidence v. IV,* J. Duncan, 124.

Bulawayo, where he now lived, and township elections were almost impossible by "the lack of suitable men" to run for office. Another witness reported that in the medium-size town he knew best, Africans had no real interest in voting. In fact, more African women voted than did men, "because they were sent to do so by their political leaders." E. D. Richter, a farmer, wanted government by "civilized people," by which he did not mean only Europeans. Nevertheless, his experience with the five hundred Nyasaland Africans he employed was that "very few" Africans were responsible. He had found that "the average African" could not draw a straight line between A and B, but could draw circles and semicircles. He thought it possible that Africans applied the same circular course of thought to education and government. T. A. J. Braithwaite, manager of Wankie Colliery, thought Africans had not had sufficient education to reach the level of skilled supervisory staff; A. B. Brown, manager of Africans at Rhodesian Iron and Steel noted that it was Africans' treatment of women that both contributed to and demonstrated their "irresponsibility." Few observers understood Africans' skills as well as he did, he said: it was "farcical" to assume that a man who could dig a cable trench might soon qualify as an electrician. There were an "isolated few" who had qualifications to vote, but if they stood for office, "by virtue of being lionized and lauded by persons not qualified to understand or appreciate the position" they "will bring chaos." J. P. Valentine, manager of fifteen stores in a rural district, worried that education was fairly meaningless for Africans because of how easily they would revert to an "early way of life." If his cook returned to his village for six months he forgot all he had learned, "like a bucket being emptied." But "an African with a little knowledge" will intimidate and exploit his uneducated brothers at every opportunity: Valentine did not understand how Africans could vote. In the district he knew best there were between twenty and thirty thousand Africans, perhaps twelve of whom understood what federation was. One of his African clerks testified as well, speaking through a translator who was also an employee of Valentine's. "He was perfectly happy and saw no reason why he should have a vote." Reverend Grey had a rural parish; he thought 80 percent of Africans had no interest in politics and were "incapable of exercising the vote."[9] A. H. E. Davies, a Bulawayo advocate and appointed federal representative for African interests, favored the current voter qualifications. Money and education were not "perfect" measurements, but they were "the least objectionable

9. Advisory Committee, *Evidence v. IV*, 73, 86, 133, 139–40, 142, 157, 259.

of many" and it was difficult to see what could replace them. He too told the advisory committee that saying government should remain in responsible hands was not the same as saying it should remain in European hands. A. J. Labuschange, a UFP committeeman, called color prejudice "a fly in the ointment" that stood between federation and "utopia." Even so, he was "100% in favour" of the present franchise qualifications. It was up to Africans to better their lot enough to qualify to vote.[10]

Harry Reedman, whom we shall meet again, feared adult suffrage was inevitable, but what was more important than suffrage was the election of parliament. Following Cecil Rhodes's "equal rights for all civilized men," he proposed "No-Party, Best Man, Non-racial" government. This would be based on proportional representation of trades and professions. "Everyone will have a vote but will be required to vote not for a party but for particular people who best understand his day to day problems." Many white people failed to understand this, Reedman said. They asked him if both he and his cook were to seek nomination, would his cook not win because of there were more Africans to vote for him? Not at all: Reedman produced a chart to show how this would work. In Best Man voting, it was impossible for a cook and his employer to stand against each other because every household could be broken down into trades and professions, as his chart indicated. The father's interests were represented by engineers, the mother's by teachers, the son's by lawyers, the daughter's—a typist in the chart—by commerce, the cook's by the catering trades, and the gardener's by agriculture. This was a system that allowed universal suffrage, but voters would vote as occupational groups; they would elect a council that would in turn elect an executive committee, a parliament, and a prime minister. Everyone would vote for the candidate who would guarantee their continued employment.[11]

In the individual testimony, there was little in the way of calculus. Property and literacy hardly mattered; there were no special votes available to special Africans. Even among MPs, who regularly debated the minutiae of voter qualifications, income and specific years of schooling were replaced by broad percentages. The Dominion Party MP from Shabani described his district. There were 400,000 Africans and 5,000 Europeans, out of which 52 Africans and 1,500 Europeans were qualified to vote. This was a good thing, he said, because many of the Africans in his district were so backward they did not know what or where

10. Advisory Committee, *Evidence v. IV*, 92–94, 120.
11. Advisory Committee, *Evidence v. IV*, 216–21.

Great Britain was. L. M. N. Hodgson, MP, thought a lower educational qualification—completing primary school—was fine for Nyasaland, but not for Southern Rhodesia. Only UFP parliamentarians insisted on more schooling for Africans. The MP (and M.D.) M. I. Hirsch was troubled that many Africans who were qualified to vote did not do so; apparently they "lacked political awareness" and for this reason he opposed a fixed percentage of Africans in government. The best way to get Africans to take electoral politics seriously "was to educate them as fast as we could."[12]

What was important about this testimony was the ways in which the ideas of the Tredgold *Report* were repeated and reformulated. How Africans treated African women, for example, shifted from being a reason to disenfranchise African women to a reason to disenfranchise African men. There were also new ideas about Africans and their politics that were to shape white political thought for almost twenty years. Africans' intimidation of other Africans was now said to be crucial to what kinds of African organization—and what kinds of Africans—were to be allowed. There was less and less commitment to the idea of creating an African electorate through education. Chiefs had been critical to the implementation of agricultural policies for years, but in these testimonies there were suggestions of how they were to be seen as controlling rural Africans—an idea that was to take a powerful hold on Rhodesian political thought. Rural areas were renamed Tribal Trust Lands in the 1961 constitution, and ideas about reworking the countryside so that voters would be physically segregated from those who were incapable of doing so would be in the foreground of the 1969 constitution.[13] Best-man government would die a quick and painless death, but Harry Reedman would become the first minister of immigration in the first UDI cabinet.

The 1961 Constitution

The greatest source of angst and anger for white Rhodesians was African nationalists' rejection of the 1961 constitution. The story of the constitutional negotiations and the subsequent referenda is usually told as a tragic narrative, in which either whites offered too little too late or African politicians became intransigent. In either narrative, the conduct of one side alone shaped the next twenty years. This is too narrow and

12. Advisory Committee, *Evidence v. IV*, 122, 166, 101.
13. Alexander, *Unsettled Land*, 68.

too linear for the fits and starts, and the grudging give and take within political parties, of this history. I argue that the defeat of the Tredgold proposals marked a rearrangement of multiracialist parties, while the electoral success of the 1961 constitution marked the demise of the party that campaigned for it, the UFP.

The 1961 constitution, and its promise of eventual parliamentary parity—a term that meant more in Rhodesia than it did anywhere else— and its subsequent rebuff by African nationalists allow me to write about African politics and white politics in a single frame. For much of this period and for most of its historiography white politics and African politics were considered separate worlds, parallel tracks that intersected only in revolt and repression. This book argues something different, that white and black politics often—not frequently, but often—overlapped and became entangled. We have seen the seepage of white and African Capricorns and we will see the seepage of white and African members of Garfield Todd's Central African Party to African political parties in this chapter, while the larger politics around the 1961 constitution— the value of African votes, the politics that take place in prison, and the quarrelsome negotiations with Britain—would shape the next two decades. The events surrounding the 1961 constitution also make visible a rupture in the neatly choreographed pattern of white politics in Southern Rhodesia since 1923, in which the party in power articulated a more moderate line toward African rights than it practiced, in large part because the audience for such a performance was in Britain. The party in opposition, with its shifting array of names, was occasionally more moderate in racial matters than the government party but more often more segregationist: it was also too small, and too fragile a coalition, to accomplish anything.[14]

There are, of course, multiple layers to this story. One was discursive: if some of the ideas presented to visiting commissions and committees seemed to come out of the proverbial woodwork, Rhodesian moderates wanted to drive them back in. Another was objective: however neutral advisory committees and commissions imagined their tasks to be, they took evidence in the shadow of the Mau Mau and Nyasaland emergencies in the year in which seventeen African countries became independent. Africans in Salisbury and Bulawayo rioted; many whites said they feared for their lives. Whether or not they were led by the National

14. I take this point from Leys, *European Politics*, 131–33, 162–68.

Democratic Party (NDP; successor to the SRANC), angry youths, whatever their influences, threw petrol bombs; a general strike was called for July. NDP leaders Michael Mawema and James Chikerema were arrested; Leopold Takawira fled to London.[15] There was also the practical layer. Shortly after the NDP arrests, Sir Charles Cummings—formerly of the Sudan supreme court and the Tredgold commission—convened a constitutional conference in Salisbury. It was modeled on Cecil Rhodes's *indaba,* or meeting of elders, a "hallowed" if illusory tradition in Southern Rhodesia's history of governmentality.[16] There were 174 delegates, seventy-two of which were Africans. Southern Rhodesia's newspapers crowed that it was an example of what was "unique and fantastic" about Southern Rhodesians, how hard they worked, how tolerant they were, and how easily, at buffet meals "men and women of different races . . . sat on the carpeted floor" when there were not enough chairs.[17]

The conference made broad recommendations about Africans' rights and status. It asked for the abolition of pass laws, the repeal of the Land Apportionment Act, the legalization of liquor sales to Africans, and for townships to be incorporated as municipalities. It recommended a bill of rights incorporated into the constitution. It suggested a broadening of the franchise, including a mechanism by which Africans with "experience and judgment" could qualify to vote without having to fulfill the educational requirements. Echoing Tredgold's special doorway to the franchise, they recommended that chiefs, headmen, agricultural demonstrators, clergy, teachers, and master farmers all be allowed to vote whatever their qualifications.[18] Nevertheless, the conference did not envision more than five African MPs in a parliament of thirty.[19]

15. Mlambo, *Birthright,* 147–49; Evans, Rhodesian Front Rule, 18–20, 27–28. For more recent analyses, see Scarnecchia, *Urban Roots,* 95–100; Terence Ranger, *Bulawayo Burning: The Social History of a Southern African City, 1893–1960* (Harare: Weaver Press, 2010), 238–43, 330–33. When Takawira was arrested in July 1960 Capricorns in Britain and the federation raised £400 for his defense. Col. David Wolfe-Murray, CAS London, to members, July 20, 1960, Borthwick Historical Institute, University of York, CAS/26.

16. Those chiefs who met with Rhodes, J. F. Holleman pointed out, were not proud warriors meeting Rhodes on equal terms, but the "pitiful remnants" of a defeated and demoralized military state who made a "desperate appeal" that at least some of their homelands be returned to them, J. F. Holleman, *Chief, Council and Commissioner: Some Problems of Government in Rhodesia* (Assen: Royal VanGorcum, 1969), 341.

17. Shamuyarira, *Crisis,* 154–55.

18. Quoted in Shamuyarira, *Crisis,* 154–55; Palley, *Constitutional History,* 314.

19. Mlambo, *Birthright,* 149.

A Bill of Rights for Southern Rhodesia

The official constitutional talks began in January 1961. By then the Central African Federation had been given a death sentence, and from its demise Northern Rhodesia and Nyasaland were to be given independence as separate states. For the ruling United Federal Party in Southern Rhodesia, this seemed the perfect moment to press for some kind of autonomy, most specifically removal of the reserve clause by which Great Britain could veto any legislation Southern Rhodesia made. Such autonomy was not really viable in the world of 1961, but white political parties bargained for scenarios in which it might be. Thus, the UFP was willing to compromise on the African franchise to get the reserve clause removed, even if it meant ratcheting up European anxieties over African advancement. For the first time, constitutional talks involved an African political party, the NDP, which claimed to have boycotted the indaba—it had not in fact been invited—because nothing decided there would be binding on the government. Despite its new name, the NDP was an experienced party; after political violence in Southern Rhodesia and recent events in Africa its leaders demanded that they be included in talks in London.[20] The NDP was the successor to the SRANC (founded in 1957 and banned in 1959), which had made broad demands for African advancement but no aggressive demands for universal suffrage. A month after the SRANC was banned, in January 1960, George Nyandoro and James Chikerema, both of whom were in detention, founded the NDP. Its primary goal was one man, one vote.[21] Several whites quickly left the CAP or the progressive factions of the UFP to join the NDP precisely because it demanded one man, one vote: the "only tolerable way to run a modern state," John Reed, a lecturer at the University College of Rhodesia and Nyasaland, wrote. Universal adult suffrage had "a proud history." That Whitehead had scoffed at this—he called demands for universal suffrage a "parrot cry"—revealed his ignorance: one man, one

20. The NDP's official statement invoked "another Congo" if there was not African participation in future elections. Mlambo, *Birthright*, 149.

21. Mlambo, *Birthright*, 154–55; Maurice Nyagumbo, *With the People* (London: Allison & Busby, 1980), 135; Joshua Nkomo, *The Story of My Life* (London: Methuen, 1984), 90–91; John Day, "Southern Rhodesian African Nationalists and the 1961 Constitution," *J. Modern African Studies* 7, no. 2 (1969): 221–22.

vote would give Southern Rhodesia a "real continuity of institutions and traditions" rooted in the nineteenth century.[22]

As the constitutional conference was being planned, however, the NDP was more concerned with its own representation than it was with a broader African franchise. Sir Edgar Whitehead announced that he, not the NDP, would choose who would represent the party. He chose Herbert Chitepo, Southern Rhodesia's first African barrister, who had been an NDP member since June 1960, when many people thought he still belonged to Todd's Central African Party.[23] He did not choose Joshua Nkomo, head of the party, who will figure in several of the following chapters. Nkomo was a veteran politician by 1960. Born in Matabeleland in 1917, he attended secondary school in South Africa. He had worked for Rhodesian Railways, first as a social worker and then as head of the African railway workers' union, the membership of which doubled under Nkomo's leadership. Local politicians took notice: in 1952 he was elected head of another, earlier Southern Rhodesia ANC.[24] In 1954 he stood for the one African seat in Matabeleland but was defeated by the UFP candidate. A few months after the NDP was formed, Nkomo was elected president, most likely the compromise candidate. When the NDP was banned in 1961, he formed the Zimbabwe African Peoples Union (ZAPU). When ZAPU was banned he formed the Peoples' Caretaker Council—ZAPU in all but name—but there were many complaints about his autocratic leadership, both in Southern Rhodesia and in Dar es Salaam, where the banned ZAPU had its headquarters. In 1963 a group split off from ZAPU to form the Zimbabwe African National Union (ZANU). Although in later years this would be cast as a Shona-Ndebele split, at the time most of the ZANU leadership—Chitepo, Takawira, Ndabaningi Sithole, but not Robert Mugabe—had been involved in multiracial parties such as the CAP or had been Capricorns. ZANU was banned in 1964. Nkomo, Mugabe, and Sithole were all to spend the next ten years in restriction in an isolated preventative detention in a camp in the southeast of the country. When Nkomo was released it was to head an umbrella organization—another ANC, this time the African National Council that he had in fact helped to set up (see chapter 8)—based in Lusaka. When the ANC fell apart, Nkomo re-

22. John Reed, "Joining the N.D.P.," *Dissent* 21, August 4, 1960, 10–12.
23. Letters to the editor, *Central African Examiner* 4, no. 4 (July 1960): 16; Ranger, *Writing Revolt*, 62.
24. This ANC grew out of the Southern Rhodesia Bantu Association, which became the Southern Rhodesia Bantu Congress and then the African National Congress of Southern Rhodesia between 1945 and 1948. See West, *African Middle Class*, 150–55.

mained in Lusaka to head ZAPU. He proved himself a prodigious fundraiser. His critics called him the "eternal chameleon," someone who was "equally at home in the Kremlin, in the Lonrho boardroom, and the White House," but his travels paid off: ZIPRA cadres were well-armed and well-fed. Nkomo brought ZAPU into the unworkable Patriotic Front with ZANU in 1976. Between 1977 and 1980, Nkomo demonstrated a willingness to talk to everyone. He had secret negotiations with Ian Smith and open discussions with the British governor in 1980, as we shall see.[25] Mugabe had a somewhat more straightforward trajectory. Educated at missions in Southern Rhodesia and Fort Hare in South Africa, he taught in Ghana and returned to Southern Rhodesia in 1960 to take charge of publicity for the NDP and then for ZAPU in 1961. He was one of the key figures in the formation of ZANU in 1963. A year later he was arrested in Southern Rhodesia and remained in some form of detention until 1974. He then went to Lusaka as part of détente exercises and to establish himself with ZANU in exile. He was not well received by Kaunda. After travels to London and Dar es Salaam, he gradually took over the party leadership by 1977.

The NDP paper quickly denounced Whitehead for not choosing Nkomo: "Sir Edgar reveals his imperialistic mentality of 'divide and rule.'" The NDP would choose its own representatives or would not attend the conference.[26] Whitehead backed down: Nkomo and Ndabaningi Sithole represented the NDP in February 1961; Chitepo and George Silundika served as their advisers. The Dominion Party, which demanded independence under minority rule, was also represented. Duncan Sandys, Conservative Commonwealth secretary, attended as an adviser, but he was an active participant in debates. He spent a day in an African primary school in order to weigh in on educational qualifications.

In the first days of the conference the NDP became mired in the debates about a bill of rights. This debate and the contentious positions taken in it allow me to locate Southern Rhodesia's constitutional issues in both global processes of decolonization and distinctively local concerns. Bills of rights were an important part of the battery of conventions and declarations of rights that emerged and were refined after 1945—after the defeat of fascism, the founding of the UN, and the

25. Robert Cary and Diana Mitchell, *African Nationalist Leaders in Rhodesia: Who's Who* (Bulawayo: Books of Rhodesia, 1977), 1830; Nkomo, *My Life*; Moorcraft, *Short Thousand Years*, 168; Martin and Johnson, *Struggle for Zimbabwe*, 286–88; White, *Herbert Chitepo*, 16–17; author's field notes, Harare, July 16, 2001.

26. Mlambo, *Birthright*, 146; *Democratic Voice* 1, no. 8 (November 1960): 12; Mimeograph, Terence Ranger Papers, RH.

beginning of decolonization. Bills of rights, however, were powerfully aspirational, although as a rule they could not be contested in courts. In and of themselves they did not guarantee rights—as the United States in early 1961 made clear—but the presence of such a list allowed citizens to lay claim to their protections.[27] More important was that the rights in bills of rights were natural rights; they were a powerful rejoinder to the idea of skill and qualification that determined Africans' rights in Southern Rhodesia. Bills of rights protected individual, not group rights, however: as Samuel Moyn has shown, for the most part nationalist movements in Asia and Africa tended to oppose them and sought instead to locate individual freedoms in the collective self-determination of subject peoples.[28] The work in American history that argues that the meaning of bills of rights in late colonial constitutions represents an export of U.S. jurisprudence or a performance of Cold War ideologies flattens decolonization and does not take into account the very specific negotiations that bills of rights engendered.[29] The NDP, for example, had hoped that by demanding a bill of rights it might encourage whites to believe that Africans wanted a body of legal rights that would move them away from the imagined backwardness of their tribes. Instead, the Dominion Party expressed concerns that if Africans had the right to a private life it would soon mean the right to miscegenation.

The most intense arguments against a bill of rights for Southern Rhodesia came from African and white progressives. Writing from detention, Maurice Nyagumbo thought a bill of rights "will not work as it does in Britain and other Commonwealth countries. Here it is going to work in the sense the settlers will find necessary." Claire Palley, a lecturer in law at the University College of Rhodesia and Nyasaland, did not think a bill of rights was worth the struggle. In an article published in Shamuyarira's *Daily News,* she argued that bills of rights were artifacts of the eighteenth-century political philosophy that shaped the U.S. constitution. It was adopted by European nations after World War I and gradually by British colonies, starting with India in 1931. Many former colonies—Nigeria, Pakistan, Malaya—amended their bills

---

27. Roland Burke, *Decolonization and the Evolution of International Human Rights* (Philadelphia: University of Pennsylvania Press, 2010); Hendrick Hartog, "The Constitution of Aspiration and 'The Rights That Belong to Us All,'" *J. American History* 74, no. 3 (1987): 1013–34.

28. Samuel Moyn, *The Last Utopia: Human Rights in History* (Cambridge: Harvard University Press, 2010), 84–114.

29. Thomas Borstelmann, *The Cold War and the Color Line* (Cambridge: Harvard University Press, 2005); Mary L. Dudziak, *Exporting American Dreams: Thurgood Marshall's African Journey* (Oxford: Oxford University Press, 2008), 73–74, and *Cold War, Civil Rights: Race and the Image of American Democracy* (Princeton, NJ: Princeton University Press, 2011 [2000]).

of rights, making them weak. The NDP took no notice of the article; Chitepo was in fact so impressed by how well the bill of rights was working in the Nigerian constitution that he offered to replace Silundika with the attorney general of Nigeria. Whitehead refused Nigerian advisers; he opposed a bill of rights, at least in the first days of debate. Like most of the UFP delegation, he tended to disparage anything that seemed to be part of Britain's decolonizing constitutions. At the same time the UFP and other white delegations wanted the reserve powers removed. Whitehead thought he could achieve this by creating a senate, an upper house that would review all legislation and thus make the reserve powers unnecessary. Africans would be appointed to the senate, which he hoped would dampen Africans' demands for a wider franchise. A. W. Stumbles, speaker of the legislative assembly, thought a bill of rights might be a useful way to bargain with Britain. What would Britain give up if Southern Rhodesia accepted a bill of rights? Stumbles read the Nigerian constitution and once he explained how easily a bill of rights could be amended or suspended, the UFP was keen to incorporate one in the new constitution in the hope that the reserve powers could be removed in exchange.[30]

Who Should Vote in 1961

The conference adopted a bill of rights that outlawed discrimination but struggled over the question of universal suffrage. The NDP demanded one man, one vote, but had no timetable for its implementation. The Central African Party said that such a demand was premature, while the UFP wanted to retain voter qualification. The CAP proposed a franchise based on literacy in any language. Whitehead and others in the UFP wanted at least two years of secondary school: completing standard six was too low a qualification. Sandys disagreed: Africans who had completed primary school had essentially learned a foreign language and should qualify to vote without question. Another group in the UFP wanted to enfranchise "the older and more stable section of the African community" whose work and service amply demonstrated that they would vote responsibly even if they had no formal schooling.[31] Another

---

30. Stumbles, *Rhodesian Speaker*, 91–93; Shamuyarira, *Crisis*, 137; Mlambo, *Birthright*, 153–54; Wood, *No Further!*, 70; Ranger, *Writing Revolt*, 92.

31. Dr. I. M. Hirsch, *Focus on Southern Rhodesia: The Constitution and Independence* (Bulawayo: Stuart Manning, 1964), 11–13; Mlambo, *Birthright*, 153–54.

UFP faction proposed fifteen seats reserved for Africans as a compromise. The NDP responded first by claiming that it was only interested in shaping the electoral law so that no one party could manipulate it and then demanded parity immediately. Parity became the buzz word of the conference, and it seems to have provided the UFP and the CAP with the logical basis for more complicated and racialized voter qualifications than anything that had gone before.[32]

The new voter qualifications grew out of those of the Tredgold *Report* but were designed for two voter rolls rather than one. These were to be labeled A and B, rather than European and African. Voters on both rolls had to be citizens who had resided in the country for two years and at their current residence for three months. They all had to be twenty-one or older and have "adequate" knowledge of English, which meant they had to be able to fill out the registration form unaided. The A roll had higher qualifications than the B roll did, and there were several ways to qualify for the A roll. The simplest was by appointment: anyone appointed chief or headman could register for the A roll. Indeed, chiefs and headmen were the only voters exempt from the requirement of filling out the registration form. Other A roll voters, almost all of whom were white, qualified on some combination of income and education. One set of A roll qualifications required a voter to have earned at least £792 during each of the previous two years or to own immovable property valued at £1,650 and to have completed primary school. The other required an income of at least £528 during each of the two previous years or owning immovable property valued at not less than £1,000 and having completed four years of secondary school. The B roll qualifications were both more nuanced and more restricted—as in higher—than what had been proposed by Tredgold's commission, much to the chagrin of NDP members in detention. Kraal heads with a following of twenty or more families and ordained ministers with either five years' training or two years' service were allowed to vote on the B roll. Other B roll voters had to prove that their income for the previous six months was the equivalent to £264 a year or that they owned immovable property valued at £495. Men who had completed two years of secondary education could register for the B roll, providing their income for the previous six months was equivalent to £132 per year or that they owned immovable property valued at £275. Men and women over thirty who had completed primary school were eligible for the B roll, as were men and

---

32. Mlambo, *Birthright*, 154–55; Day, "1961 Constitution," 225–29; Shamuyarira, *Crisis*, 137–38; J. R. T. Wood, *A Matter of Weeks*, 448.

women whose income for the previous six months was equivalent to £198 per year or who owned immovable property valued at least £385. Whitehead insisted that these requirements would bring fifty thousand Africans onto the rolls. Educational qualifications were vetted by a special board; there was no appeal. The board understood that Africans were discriminated against in education and rarely attended schools as good as to those available to whites, but for this reason Africans had to have more years of schooling than a European, not less. To qualify for either the A or the B roll, Africans had to have one more year of primary or secondary school than white voters had.[33] Thus "African capacities" was unpacked: African qualities were acquired and not innate, and difference was the product of history, not race. Nevertheless, few Africans could qualify to vote.

The new draft constitution devised a new way to talk about race, one that was to determine how A and B rolls elected representatives. The country was to be divided into fifty constituencies and fifteen electoral districts. This increase of twenty constituencies was designed in 1959 to increase African representation, but in fact it added only two African seats. The two separate bases for representation would retain their original character—although now there would be eighteen rural constituencies—but the delimitation commission took up as its charge that every constituency should have an equal number of A roll voters and every electoral district should have the same number of B roll voters. The slate of candidates was the same in constituencies and electoral districts.[34] To make sure that the constituencies and electoral districts retained the specificity of voter rolls, the constitution had a provision to devalue votes which amounted to a refined version of the fractional voting federal committees had rejected a few years before. If B roll votes in any constituency exceeded the total number of A roll votes by one-fourth, they were devalued by one-fourth, or until they became equal with the number of A roll votes. In electoral districts, if A roll votes exceeded the number of B roll votes by one-fourth, they were devalued by one-fourth so that the elected member will have received a proportion of A roll votes equal to one-quarter of the B roll votes he received. In other words, A roll voters had up 25 percent influence in electoral district elections, and 75 percent influence in constituency elections,

33. Mlambo, *Birthright*, 154–55; Shamuyarira, *Crisis*, 155–61; Palley, *Constitutional History*, 416–22, 434; Ranger, *Writing Revolt*, 90–92.

34. Cabinet Minutes, October 31, 1961, CL/Smith/13; Hirsch, *Constitution and Independence*, 15; Palley, *Constitutional History*, 415n.

while B roll voters had the reverse. Because there were now fifty constituencies and fifteen electoral districts, A roll voters had the greatest say in electing the legislature.[35] This turned all the franchise proposals into somewhat of a hoax; progressive sources reckoned that it would take fifteen years before there were sufficient African voters on the A roll to win two constituencies. Nevertheless, the UFP insisted that majority rule was fifteen years away.[36]

Both the UFP and the NDP accepted the draft constitution, and both claimed doing so was a victory. Although Sandys was relieved that the constitution was accepted—he called it a miracle—he later inserted the equivalent of reserve powers because of irresponsible statements by UFP MPs. Even so, Whitehead announced that this constitution brought Southern Rhodesia "so near to complete independence" that no British government "could put the clock back." For the first six months of 1961 he was cautious, saying that the new constitution would give Southern Rhodesia the same status that New Zealand had before the Statute of Westminster, or the same status as Australian states. Stumbles told the legislative assembly that the 1961 constitution provided "90 percent independence" and that Southern Rhodesia had "virtually become a Dominion."[37] The NDP claimed the opposite was the case. The party's publicity secretary, Robert Mugabe, boasted that by accepting the constitution the NDP stopped the "settlers getting the independence they wanted." Whatever the NDP objections to the new franchise, Nkomo said, "we don't stand in its way."[38]

Rejecting the Constitution

Nkomo's actions infuriated many in the NDP. The day after the constitution was signed, Leopold Takawira, former Capricorn and NDP

---

35. Palley, *Constitutional History*, 414–16.

36. "Weighing Up Sandys' Bag," *Central African Examiner* 4, no. 18 (March 1961): 4; Shamuyarira, *Crisis*, 167. Years later, Claire Palley estimated that the earliest majority rule could be achieved under the 1961 constitution was 2012; Claire Palley, "Rhodesia: The Time-Scale for Majority Rule," *Issue: A J. of Opinion* 2, no. 2 (1972): 52–64.

37. Shamuyarira, *Crisis*, 160–61; Prime Minister's Office, *Rhodesia: Independence under the 1961 Constitution* (Salisbury: Government Printer, 1965). The introduction to the pamphlet notes that at no time did the British government contradict these statements, which they would have done if they were contrary to Britain's intentions. The Statute of Westminster gave legislative autonomy to the dominions; see Hopkins, "Rethinking Decolonization," 214–15.

38. Scarnecchia, *Urban Roots*, 104–5. Twenty years later—too late for anyone to believe him—Nkomo claimed Sandys lied when he said the NDP would support the franchise proposals. Nkomo, *My Life*, 92–93.

representative in London, and Michael Mawema, appealing a four-year prison sentence in Salisbury, and the trade unionist Ruben Jamela all demanded that Nkomo reject it. In an angry telegram, Takawira called the proposed constitution "diabolical and disastrous" and the NDP leadership "docile" for accepting it. The outside world was shocked, he wrote, that the NDP failed to represent African interests and betrayed "friends and supporters," most especially the nationalist parties in Northern Rhodesia that demanded universal suffrage.[39] A few days later, Takawira issued a more detailed statement: given the new B roll qualifications, it would take African voters "fifteen or twenty years to equal the number of European voters." The new educational requirements would slow the rate of Africans eligible to vote. To qualify based on a primary school education, an African had to be thirty years old, so that a child who left school today at thirteen or fourteen would have to wait sixteen years to vote. There were not enough Africans currently enrolled in secondary school to impact the future B roll. The annual average wage of African workers was £81, well below the £120 required to qualify for the B roll; the average wage of a white worker was on the other hand well above what was required to qualify for the A roll. The UFP had butchered a democratic franchise. Takawira demanded that Nkomo reverse his position, and for the British parliament to reject the 1961 constitution.[40] In a statement for the House of Commons, Takawira positioned the NDP against white domination. It would be easy enough for the party to win the fifteen seats allotted to the 3 million Africans under the constitution, but that would preserve minority rule, and the "Africans of Southern Rhodesia do not want to be governed by a minority race; they want to govern themselves." The NDP would not be "lulled into political inactivity" by the "mere" abolition of discrimination. Takawira invoked Algeria, where there "was no discrimination . . . yet Algerians have been fighting for years for self-determination." He asked for a new constitutional conference that would provide for majority rule and protect Southern Rhodesia's economy by protecting "the skills and know-how of Europeans."[41]

Nkomo was slow to reject the constitution, in large part because the NDP seemed divided on the issue. At first, as Chitepo and Silundika wrote to Sandys, the NDP executive committee wanted to reject the

39. Day, "1961 Constitution," 229–31; Ranger, *Writing Revolt*, 94–96, 125–27.

40. NDP, "Southern Rhodesia Constitution a Fraud," Statement, London, March 9, 1961, in Nyangoni and Nyandoro, *Zimbabwe Independence Movements*, 43–44.

41. London Office, NDP to House of Commons, mimeo., n.d. Various papers relating to the NDP and 1961 constitution, NAZ/MS734/3.

franchise but accept everything else in the constitution. This simply was not enough for NDP members in Southern Rhodesia's jails or public meetings, who opposed the entire constitution with increasing vehemence. Mawema was expelled from the executive and set up a new party, the Zimbabwe National Party (ZNP), to oppose the constitution. Nkomo defended his position, at least at first, with the help of the NDP founders still in detention, James Chikerema and George Nyandoro, who urged the rank and file to rally behind Nkomo. After years of struggle, they argued, this constitution gave them an opportunity to pressure the system from inside. Yet Chikerema and Nyandoro wrote their defense of Nkomo only after they had been removed to Salisbury prison, where they were taken for protection. Detainees held at Marandellas voted to reject the constitution. Amidst rumors that Ghana had threatened to withdraw financial support if he did not reject the constitution, Nkomo visited London—where he seems to have failed to discipline Takawira—and then Cairo, assuring funders in both places that this was a minor internal party issue. On his return he denounced Takawira as a "Tshombe" and an "imperialist" (but not a Capricorn) who sought to divide the NDP and slander its leadership, but now he too rejected the constitution.[42]

At a press conference in mid-February, Nkomo repeated Takawira's figures. Few urban Africans could meet the income requirements or had completed two years of secondary school. He expressed dismay that Britain hailed the proposed Southern Rhodesia parliament of fifty Europeans and fifteen Africans as nonracial but called the demands for an elected African majority government in Northern Rhodesia "racial."[43] At the party congress in March 1961, the NDP rejected the entire constitution with an almost unanimous vote. Mawema was welcomed back to the NDP, although a ZNP group was to survive for several years. Nkomo denounced the "clever fancy franchise" designed to deny the NDP political influence while Ndabaningi Sithole, who had been an NDP delegate to the constitutional conference, described it "as a deception from start to finish." Sithole was to have a troubled career in the NDP and then in ZANU. Trained at a mission school by Garfield Todd, he had been a CAP member before joining the NDP; when ZANU was created he was its first president. He was detained in 1964, during which time he

42. "Challenge in the NDP," *Central African Examiner* 4, no. 18 (March 1961): 15; Mlambo, *Birthright*, 158, 188; Shamuyarira, *Crisis*, 163–64; Nyagumbo, *With the People*, 137, 147–50; Ngwabi Bhebe, *Simon Vengayi Muzenda and the Struggle for the Liberation of Zimbabwe* (Gweru: Mambo Press, 2004), 128–30; Ranger, *Writing Revolt*, 93–98.
43. Nkomo Press Conference, February 17, 1961, NAZ/MS734/3/4.

wrote two novels in Shona. In the early 1970s he was deposed as party president and replaced by Mugabe, who was also in prison in Rhodesia. When Sithole was released in 1974 no one was willing to back him. Although he was appointed to the ANC central committee in Lusaka, he drifted in and out of ZANU: he formed the Zimbabwe Leadership Council in Dar es Salaam and eventually claimed to reconstruct the ZANU of 1963, which became part of the internal settlement and stood candidates in 1980.[44] In 1961, however, he wanted the NDP to boycott the referendum. The NDP sought to "dissuade" Africans from registering on the B roll, and this soon became—and was to remain—the proof of African intransigence, policies that doomed Africans to struggle outside the constitution.[45]

NDP members still in detention, notably Nyandoro and Chikerema, hoped to garner white progressive and African moderate support for the constitution, however. They asked the editors of *Dissent,* a mimeographed journal founded by Terence Ranger and John Reed in 1959, to urge a "yes" vote on the referendum. Ranger had been one of the NDP members originally dismayed that Nkomo accepted the constitution, but he and Reed—leader of the NDP's Salisbury branch—tossed a coin to see who would write an article supporting the constitution and who would write against it. Fifty years later, Ranger could not tell who wrote which one. The case against the 1961 constitution was a case for the NDP; it was a party issue, not a racial or national one. It was essential that the NDP maintain itself as a unified, revolutionary party at all costs. It could not do so if it accepted the proposed franchise, with its reducible vote, although that was better than Tredgold's special door. Under the proposed constitution, the NDP could win every B roll seat and have no real parliamentary say; the best it could hope for would be to be a sometimes ally of the UFP against the segregationist excesses of the Dominion Party. If there was a tragedy in the NDP's rejection of the 1961 constitution it was not that it opted out of parliament, but that the party would probably split and a more revolutionary party would spring up to its left. The case for the constitution, and against the NDP's decision, lay in the regional context in which the NDP sought to place itself. The idea that the NDP might betray the nationalist parties of Northern Rhodesia or Nyasaland simply ignored the differences between the three

44. Cary and Mitchell, *Who's Who,* 135–46; Martin and Johnson, *Struggle for Zimbabwe,* claim that Sithole stepped down in favor of Mugabe, 31, 147–51; White, *Herbert Chitepo,* 18–19, 56–59.

45. "NDP Congress: Facing Facts and Gaining Time," *Central African Examiner* 4, no. 19 (1961): 6–8; Wood, *No Further!,* 75; Nkomo, *My Life,* 92–94; Shamuyarira, *Crisis,* 163–67; Day, "1961 Constitution," 230–42; Scarnecchia, *Urban Roots,* 105.

Central African territories. "Southern Rhodesia is *not* Nyasaland; here there is no Colonial Office to yield very sensibly to a show of force but 'settlers' determined to fight if needs be." The NDP had every reason to consider the franchise totally inadequate, but that inadequacy offered some way forward: the NDP could have maintained "resolution and radical principle" by participating in an imperfect system. Had the NDP accepted the 1961 constitution, it would have had a choice of working within the system "or turning to frankly revolutionary techniques." Now it had no choice.[46]

A few years later, Nathan Samuyarira, another former Capricorn, wrote that many progressives in Rhodesia and Britain began to think of the NDP as "inept." Had the party not rejected the 1961 constitution, had it taken part in elections, it would have had enough influence to keep its leaders out of detention and to keep itself from being banned. He went so far as to argue that white progressives blamed the 1962 victory of the Rhodesian Front on the NDP: why welcome Africans into the political process, he imagined them asking, if they were only going to slap your face in return?[47] He was not far wrong. In 2005, J. R. T. Wood noted that Ian Smith had not been a signatory of the draft constitution but that Nkomo had been. He offered another imaginary, that if Nkomo had not rejected the constitution "he would have found himself in reasonable time the President of the independent state of Zimbabwe," and the years of bloody armed struggle could have been averted.[48]

However the argument is cast, a great deal of weight is placed on the NDP: the party was either revolutionary or capricious to reject the 1961 constitution. These poles misrepresent the politics of African nationalism in 1961. Shifting and fluid do not adequately describe the actions of people who were involved in two distinct political movements at once; sometimes the goals of these movements dovetailed and sometimes they did not. The comings and goings of Michael Mawema are one example; Chitepo's possible membership in the Capricorn Africa Society and simultaneous membership in the NDP and CAP is another. This was no less true for white politics. Terence Ranger was on the CAP executive committee while he was close to the NDP. ("The situation here is confused," he wrote to John Reed.) After the referendum on the

---

46. Ranger, *Writing Revolt*, 90–96; "Southern Rhodesia Constitutional Agreement: For and Against; the Case Against," *Dissent* 24 (March 1961): 5–10; "Southern Rhodesia Constitutional Agreement: For and Against; the Case For," *Dissent* 24 (March 1961): 11–14.

47. Shamuyarira, *Crisis*, 165–67.

48. Wood, *No Further!*, 74.

1961 constitution both he and Garfield Todd left the CAP to join the NDP.[49] All the while, the NDP struggled with the vocabularies of universal rights and something as local as the idea of parity. Mrinalini Sinha has argued for the history of women's suffrage in colonial India that proposals and debates about the franchise were not just about the allocation of rights, but about how to imagine and then represent political constituencies, both communal and constructed. These constituencies and their representation were often in tension—and often outside the country or in prison within it.[50] For the NDP, the question was not one of the franchise in and of itself, but how to accept a racialized voters' roll and remain a nationalist party that had legitimacy anywhere else in the world. In the era of African decolonization, no nationalist parties were exclusively national. The NDP was located, in every sense of the term, in the regional and international arenas where decolonization and majority rule were synonymous. The NDP may have negotiated with the UFP and the British government, but it was also concerned with establishing itself as a nationalist movement with the United National Independence Party (UNIP) in Northern Rhodesia, London, and Salisbury, where UNIP and the Nyasaland Congress Party had a larger membership among foreign workers than the NDP had among black Rhodesians.[51]

In Southern Rhodesia, even in an era of universal rights, there was not wholehearted support for universal suffrage. African trade unionists had argued for voter qualifications for years because the property qualification would encourage a stable and skilled workforce: men would stay at their jobs longer. In December 1961 The *Central African Examiner* published opposing views on the one man, one vote. It had clearly been planned for earlier publication, but two African MPs, both UFP members, had declined to write. The journal finally went to Charles Mzingeli, veteran trade unionist, who wrote in favor of voter qualification. He repeated many of the Tredgold staples about responsibility and qualification; he feared that universal suffrage would bring about the same kind of "chaos" now raging in the Congo. Mzingeli believed African politicians and voters were "immature." Such politicians

49. Ranger, *Writing Revolt*, 60–65.
50. Mrinalini Sinha, *Specters of Mother India: The Global Restructuring of Empire* (Durham, NC: Duke University Press, 2006), 197–30.
51. Lucy Mair was told that the Nyasaland Congress Party was at least as strong in Southern Rhodesia as it was at home. Mair, *Nyasaland Election*, 16; David B. Moore, The Contradictory Construction of Hegemony in Zimbabwe: Politics, Ideology and Class Formation of a New African State. Ph.D. dissertation, York University, 1989, 84.

would buy votes with free drinks and then, once in power, change the slogan to "one-vote-for-one-man."[52] Why was Mzingeli willing to go beyond what was acceptable rhetoric for African politicians? Timothy Scarnecchia sees this as a moment of pathos, in which an established trade unionist became the politician he had once despised, a man used by white politicians to make their case for them.[53] I do not disagree— Mzingeli was to serve on the 1968 constitutional commission—but I think making his statement a personal one ignores the history of voter qualification in Southern Rhodesia and its emphasis on property and thereby on a stable and skilled labor force. The case for universal suffrage was made by Edwin Litchtenstein, a young lawyer who had left the Central African Party for the NDP because it was the only party demanding universal suffrage. He made a straightforward argument: not only was it moral, it was "realistic and practical." India, not the Congo, was proof that backward voters were not swayed by unscrupulous politicians.[54]

Two Referenda

The NDP was not alone in rejecting the constitution. Ian Smith, chief whip of the UFP in the federal parliament, opposed it because it did not guarantee independence; the Dominion Party opposed it for the same reason and because the franchise was too easily obtained. Todd and Tredgold—who founded their own short-lived party to oppose the constitution—rejected it because of the racially restricted franchise. The UFP scheduled a referendum for July. In May the new constitution was mailed to each of Southern Rhodesia's eighty-four thousand voters. There was the inevitable question of whether there should be an African language version of the constitution, but the cabinet decided that as the official language of Southern Rhodesia was English, and some English was required to be given the franchise, all voters should be able to read English. Eventually it was decided to print a summary in African languages.[55] The UFP made much of the NDP's defection; UFP pamphlets reminded voters that the "so-called African nationalists have thrived on

52. Charles Mzingeli, "Qualified Responsibility," *Central African Examiner* 5, no. 7 (1961): 17.

53. Scarnecchia, *Urban Roots*, 109–10.

54. Edwin Litchtenstein, "One Man—One Vote," *Central African Examiner* 5, no. 7 (1961): 17–18; Edwin Alan Litchtenstein, London, November 20, 1983, NAZ/ORAL/243.

55. Cabinet Minutes, Southern Rhodesia Constitution: White Paper, May 19, 1961/3, CL/Smith/13.

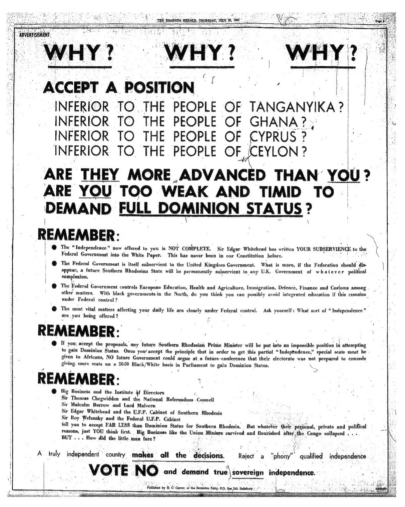

1   Dominion Party advertisement against the 1961 constitution, *The Herald,* July 20, 1961, 3.

the weakness of whites," who had failed to understand how dangerous one man, one vote would be in a country most of whose population was "backwards and primitive."[56] Southern Rhodesia needed a government that would not fail to take "just and drastic disciplinary action" against the violence of African nationalists.[57] The Dominion Party accused

56. R. Auret, "Towards a Rhodesian Nation," mimeo., Belingwe, June 1961. Sir Edgar Whitehead Papers, RH Mss Afr s. 1482.

57. Hancock, *White Liberals,* 76; Ian Smith, *Betrayal,* 45.

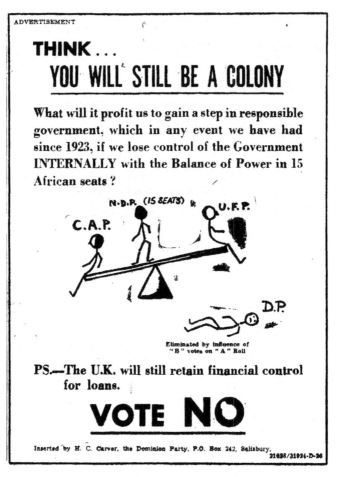

2 Dominion Party advertisement against the 1961 constitution, *The Herald,* July 21, 1961, 4.

the British of duplicity ("Shifting Sandys" one ad began) and worried about the influence of the Central African Party. Its ads complained that Tanganyika was promised independence but Southern Rhodesia was not ("Why? Why? Why?" was the first line). The UFP's advertisement threatened a white exodus if the constitution was rejected. As the day of the referendum neared, posters appeared in Salisbury and Bulawayo proclaiming "Vote No for Nkomo."[58] In the end, 80 percent of the electorate

58. The Dominion Party, the UFP, and the NDP all denied authoring these; "Whose Is Illegal 'Vote No for Nkomo' Poster?" *The Herald* (Salisbury, Southern Rhodesia), July 24, 1961, 1.

voted almost two to one for the new constitution: 42,000 voted "yes" and 22,000 voted "no."[59]

This was not the only referendum of the constitution, however. Three days before the official one, the NDP hastily organized their own referendum; it was to be the "voice of the people," an election in which all adults, "literate or not," could participate. Mugabe said the party expected eight hundred thousand voters; he invited a number of observers: journalists; Lord Alport, Britain's high commissioner; the U.S. consul general; and the assistant high commissioner for India.[60] As the NDP threatened a general strike on the day of the official referendum, there were fears of intimidation and threats of reprisals by the government.[61] But the actual NDP poll went on without any difficulties. Although some rural polling places did not open before late morning, and others did not have any ballot boxes until late in the day, or did not have enough ballot boxes, thousands of Africans—and a few urban whites—voted. There were long lines in urban areas. In rural areas the staff was often disorganized, but they took great pains to explain the process, especially to African women: a white card (white for Whitehead) for the constitution and a pink card against it. Many journalists were concerned by the lack of privacy in rural voting booths, and how visible ballots were before they were put in boxes, but overall voters were "quiet and good humored."[62] The NDP announced that 467,000 voted against the constitution and 600 voted for it.[63] Lord Alport believed that everyone who voted did so voluntarily and with clear purpose. Perhaps they did not understand the constitution but they knew they were rejecting something "contrary to their rights."[64] The *Central African Examiner* went further. "For Africans, the NDP referendum had far greater meaning than that staged by the

59. For advertisements, see *The Herald*, July 21, 23, and 24, 1961; Mlambo, *Birthright*, 160.

60. "NDP to Hold Referendum to Assess African Opinion on Colony's Future," *Central African Daily News*, June 19, 1961, 1; "Tough Talk in the NDP," *Central African Examiner* 5, no. 2 (July 1061): 6; "Stage Is Now Set for NDP Referendum," *Central African Daily News*, July 22, 1961, 1.

61. Statement issued by Prime Minister, Southern Rhodesia, July 18, 1961, Cabinet minutes, CL/Smith/13; "Bid to Call Strike Will be 'Crushed by Force,'" *The Times* (London), July 19, 1961, 8; "Rhodesia Ban on African Meetings," *The Times*, July 22, 1961, 7.

62. "Heavy Polling in NDP Referendum Reported: Firm 'No' Vote Expected," *Central African Daily News*, July 24, 1961, 3–4; "NDP Referendum Goes Off Quietly," *The Herald*, July 24, 1961, 1; "Four Incidents in NDP's Mock Poll," *Bulawayo Chronicle*, July 24, 1961, 1; "Garfield Todd Tells Why He Cast His Vote," *Bulawayo Chronicle*, July 24, 1961, 1.

63. H. J. Quinton, Municipal Native Administration, Salisbury to Whitehead, July 15, 1961, Whitehead Papers, RH Mss. Afr s. 142; Nkomo, *My Life*, 96; Wood, *No Further!*, 86.

64. Lord Alport, *Sudden Assignment*, 74–75.

government."[65] Nevertheless, the two referenda undergirded the story of black and white—and black or white—intransigence.

Who Could Vote in 1961

Once the constitution was accepted, the government set about the task of how to make the new voter qualifications work. There were discussions with Britain, of course, while political parties were asked to make comments and suggestions, especially on the matter of how to secure African support.[66] A few political parties offered comments and complaints, most of which were about how to include more voters on the A roll and exclude some of those already on the B roll. Committees honed some of the proposals. The idea that people should reside in a district or constituency for three months before voting, for example, was a concern suited more to politics in the northern territories than in the south. In Nyasaland and Northern Rhodesia it was feared that political parties transferred large numbers of voters into electoral districts right before the election. Southern Rhodesia closed its voters' rolls at various points in the year and had more rigorous delimitation than elsewhere in the federation, so such a requirement would be unnecessary. And of course the 25 percent influence of A roll voters in constituencies and B roll voters in electoral districts meant that large transfers of population would not matter. The real problem with the three-month-residency requirement was that it made white professionals—road overseers, tsetse fly officers, and railway track inspectors—ineligible to vote. To ensure their franchise, the residency requirement was changed to three months in the country, rather than in any specific constituency.

Income was another problem. The federal franchise had only counted wages as income, but Southern Rhodesia had been casual on the common roll and counted any regular receipt of money—a scholarship, a pension, and rents from lodgers—as income. This worked perfectly when there was a common roll and it was only necessary for the applicant to have reached a specific figure, but with two rolls applicants had to fill out a much longer form that would allow a committee to ascertain on which roll they could register. There was no simple way to help applicants compute income, especially on a form already seven pages long,

---

65. "The Birth of a Nation?" *Central African Examiner* 5, no. 3 (August 1961): 3.

66. "By all accounts," the Cabinet was told, moderate Africans now favored the government over the NDP. Cabinet minutes, July 28, 1961. CL/Smith/13.

so it was decided to ask applicants to declare only the lowest income that would qualify them for the A or B roll. The actual question about income had to be reworked; instead of asking the rate of income for the previous six months, it asked if a man had earned between £60 and £75 in the previous six months. This would be easier for the applicant but meant there would have to be more income categories on the form.[67]

Property proved to be the most difficult part of the form. The form should state that property meant land and buildings, so that Africans could understand the concept. Whites too might become confused: were mining claims property? These had to be included. The form asked for property ownership; this meant a deed or proof that the applicant had paid 10 percent of the purchase price, but would Africans understand about interest or legal fees? The original wording—"How much of the purchase price have you repaid?"—would trouble even "the most conscientious European," who probably could not accurately calculate the amount on the spot. "An African would hardly be expected to know the answer." The question would have to be reworded so that interest and stamp duties and conveyancing fees were included. The Central African Party was concerned that all this might keep women from registering to vote. How many married women, white and African, were able to report their husbands' particulars? They could not ask their husbands because the instructions insisted they fill out the forms unaided. Some registering officers allowed wives to ask their husbands for practical information—his date of birth, his income—while filling out the form, but the CAP wanted two forms, one a wife could fill out unaided and one for information she could only get from her husband. The minister of internal affairs objected; there had to be one common form, with questions a wife could ask of her husband marked by an asterisk. All this was part of that larger problem of Africans' wives, and which wife of which man would qualify to vote. Again, wives qualified on their husbands' property in Southern Rhodesia; only the senior wife of a polygynous man could qualify.[68] Education—which was not transferable from husband to wife—added more problems. This too had never been an issue on the common roll, but the new qualifications required that the lowest earnings were combined with the most education. Those with the lowest income to be eligible for the A roll had to have completed secondary

67. Electoral Act: Amendments in conformity with the new constitution, Confidential, September 1, 1961, Minister of Justice and Internal Affairs, CL/Smith/14.

68. Minister of Internal Affairs, Claims for registering a voter for the Southern Rhodesia legislative assembly, Confidential, September 1, 1961, Cabinet Memoranda, CL/Smith/14.

school, the second lowest two years of secondary school, and those with the highest income were only required to have completed primary school. The minister of justice wanted to know what completing school meant. The federation had always taken it to mean years of schooling, but Southern Rhodesia thought it meant sitting a final examination.[69]

Whitehead was ecstatic about both referenda: he told visiting diplomats that extremist Africans and extremist whites had been defeated; he told the local press that African nationalism was now dead. Under the new franchise the extremists "in both wings" would find it difficult to win enough support to be elected to parliament. Nevertheless, for months before the NDP referendum, Whitehead accused the NDP of township violence. After the referenda he said it had become increasingly undemocratic, falling back on "the old tribal ideal" of not tolerating opposition.[70] Beginning in February Whitehead attempted to ban NDP meetings or at least limit them to the "stable environment" of the Purchase Areas. By the end of the year, however, intimidation was increasing in the townships, and in rural areas ordinarily law-abiding Africans were "stirred up" and encouraged to burn down schools and destroy dip tanks.[71] Once the new franchise requirements and registration forms were remade for Southern Rhodesia, however, Whitehead banned the NDP and left the white extremists of the Dominion Party intact. Whitehead understood that the NDP leadership would create a successor party, but he hoped that the new party would not repeat the violence of its predecessors and would work through constitutional channels. He went on to call for an end to all discrimination in the country; this would benefit Europeans most of all, as they had the most to lose from political turmoil.[72] Nkomo only learned of this in Tanganyika, where he went to represent the NDP at the independence celebrations. The day after the ceremony Julius Nyerere—whose relationship with Nkomo was to continue to be troubled—made a harsh joke: "You shouldn't be here," he told Nkomo. "You don't represent anybody."[73]

69. Electoral Act: Amendments and Conformity with New Constitution, September 1, 1961, Cabinet Memoranda, CL/Smith/ 14.
70. Notes of a meeting between Prime Minister and Mr. G. Mennen Williams, U.S. Asst. Secretary of State for African Affairs, Salisbury, August 24, 1961, CL/Smith/14; "Whitehead's short-term victories," *Central African Examiner*, 5, no. 3 (August 1961): 5–7; Shamuyarira, *Crisis*, 165.
71. Cabinet minutes, February 13 and July 18, 1961, CL/Smith/13.
72. Public Relations Department, Southern Rhodesia, Sir Edgar explains why the NDP was banned, December 15, 1961, NAZ/MS 734/3/4.
73. Nkomo, *My Life*, 97.

Two New Parties

Eight days after the NDP was banned, Nkomo formed ZAPU. His was not the only new party formed at the end of a tumultuous 1961; the other was the Rhodesian Front.[74] Many UFP MPs said they left the party over its support for the 1961 constitution and its separate voting rolls: Lancelot Bales Smith, for example, wanted a fair, common roll that would allow African businessmen and Africans with education and good jobs a say in government but he joined the Rhodesian Front even though it too maintained two voter rolls.[75] How does someone, or many people, leave one party for another that advocates exactly what they objected to in the party they left? The answer can be found in Colin Leys's almost sixty-year-old description of white political parties in Southern Rhodesia and how they consisted of shifting alliances, amalgamations of factions that changed their names more often than they changed their policies. Once a party formed a government, Leys observed, the constraints of Southern Rhodesia's situation determined common characteristics. Ruling parties all spoke of gradual African advancement, the need to maintain standards in all walks of life, but especially of a vague need to expand the franchise: these ruling parties did whatever was required to keep Britain's oversight at arm's length. Opposition parties tended to be more segregationist, or very occasionally more progressive. These were invariably too small, and too short-lived, to accomplish anything, but they had no official dealings with Britain and were often very outspoken. All white political parties tended to be very fluid, groupings of allies and opponents who were willing to stick together for the purpose of an election. When the Central African Federation was formed political parties operated at both the federal and territorial levels, which intensified this volatility and fluidity.[76] The Rhodesian Front (RF) was both such a party and a departure from this pattern. Over the years scholars have claimed that the RF replaced a moderate white electorate with a "pro-white one," that it was made up of farmers, rural Afrikaners, white artisans, and white women, or that it was a party of Anglo-American white

---

74. There were responses at the metropolitan level as well. In November the newly formed Monday Club approached Welensky, who was impressed by their "sensible attitude" toward decolonization. Federal High Commissioner to Roy Welensky, November 23, 1961; Welensky to J. J. F. Francis, British Museum, March 5, 1962. RH Mss Welensky 522/3, Monday Club. See also McNeil, "'The rivers of Zimbabwe,'" 731–45.

75. Lancelot Bales Smith, Banket, November 22, 1985, NAZ/ORAL/250; Wood, *No Further!*, 93.

76. Leys, *European Politics*, 134–44; Bowman, *Politics in Rhodesia*, 33–34.

supremacy.[77] Such claims make parties and platforms much more rational and stable than they seem to have actually been in 1962 and fail to adequately describe the ways that the ideas of the Rhodesian Front were themselves ways of maintaining a coalition. What may have marked a turning point in Rhodesian politics was not the ideas of the Rhodesian Front, but how long they lasted.

In his 1997 memoirs, Ian Smith devoted a scant three pages to the creation of the Rhodesian Front. He had opposed the 1961 constitution; he disliked the two voter rolls with their "racial connotation" but believed that a new franchise was a step forward on the road to independence. But as there was no written guarantee of independence, and no sense that it would be secured when federation was dissolved, after the July referendum Smith thought it time to return to territorial politics. Although he had been the UFP chief whip in the federal parliament—he was to joke that the Rhodesian Front had more federalists and Welensky supporters in it than the UFP had—he portrayed himself in the vocabularies he was to favor in future years. "Our political world was riddled with compromise, appeasement, indecision" which permeated society: "I felt strongly about this permissiveness." Smith maintained that he had always put Southern Rhodesia before the federation and by the end of 1961 these feelings led him to organize a new party. He first asked Winston Field, of the federal Dominion Party, to join him, as well as D. C. ("Boss") Lilford, a man of great wealth and stature who would soon become one of the largest landowners in Rhodesia, and Angus Graham, seventh duke of Montrose and a loyal member of the territorial Dominion Party, to fund him. All three men agreed, and the party grew by the defections of prominent UFP MPs and Dominion Party members. Field became party leader, and the Rhodesian Front was able to soften some of the DP's racial rhetoric, replacing it with promises to strengthen tribes and the rule of chiefs, ideas that would come to the fore in a few years. The RF promised to keep the government of Southern Rhodesia in responsible hands. The alliance between the Dominion Party and defectors from the UFP was no easier than other alliances in the country's history, but the Rhodesian Front grew rapidly. By March 1962 three UFP

---

77. Stephen E. C. Hintz, "The Political Transformation of Rhodesia, 1958–1965," *African Studies Review* 15, no. 2 (1971): 173–83; Alport, *Sudden Assignment*, 215–16; Evans, Rhodesian Front Rule, 38–40; Horne, *From the Barrel of a Gun*, 21–22, 44–45, 103; and Alexander, *Unsettled Land*, 71. The Rhodesian Front had the ambivalent support of commercial farmers. Pilossof, *Unbearable Whiteness*, 19.

branch committees had resigned to join the RF, taking many of their members with them.[78]

The Rhodesian Front stood candidates in the territorial elections of 1962. Whitehead, buoyed by the success of the referendum, began his "Build a Nation" campaign, which introduced a new and strident rhetoric of nationality. The vague ideas of the 1940s about belonging were replaced by a nation of equals, where every resident of the territory—"be he a Scot, a Matabele, a Greek . . . or an Indian"—regards himself "as first and foremost a Rhodesian."[79] At the same time, many UFP loyalists, including Steve Kock, who had professed his love for Rhonasia only a year earlier, insisted that middle-class African support was essential to the success of any elected regime in Southern Rhodesia and all but implored eligible Africans to register on the B roll, hoping to strengthen the UFP's position. In the last weeks of his campaign Whitehead predicted that one day an African might serve in a UFP cabinet, and then he predicted that there could be as many as six Africans in his government.[80] If the audience for these predictions was the ten thousand B roll voters, more than half of whom were schoolteachers, they fell on deaf or at least absent ears: many had been discouraged to register by ZAPU and many had refused to vote after ZAPU was banned.[81] Even more than the NDP, ZAPU was accused of widespread intimidation: petrol bombs and threats of petrol bombs in townships probably kept many African voters from the polls and may have convinced many white voters that the UFP could not control African townships.[82] They could not, but for the most part neither could the ZAPU leadership: having created youth leagues to attack their enemies, they were unable to call them off when they wanted to. The "Jamela incident" is a case in point. The trade unionist Ruben Jamela had already broken with ZAPU when the party's executive accused him of taking bribes from industrialists to register B roll

78. For Smith's jokes and disclaimers, see Evans, Rhodesian Front Rule, 39, 41; P. K. van der Byl's biographer says that Lilford called the meeting; Wessels, PK, 94; Smith, Betrayal, 45–46; Palley, Constitutional History, 808–9; Wood, No Further!, 97–100; Angus Shaw, Mutoko Madness (Harare: Boundary Books, 2013), 56–57.

79. UFP, Southern Rhodesia Division, The Build-a-Nation Campaign in Southern Rhodesia, n.d., but filed for February 1962. Whitehead Papers, RH Ms. Afr. s. 1482.

80. Hancock, White Liberals, 95–99.

81. "Voting in a Vacuum," Central African Examiner 6, no. 6 (November 1962): 9. The Central African Party asked members to vote in the election; see "Why We Shall Vote," but A roll and B roll ZAPU boycotted it; see "Why We Shall Not Vote," Central African Examiner 6, no. 7 (December 1962): 7.

82. S. A. Kock, Salisbury, Problem of Casting B Roll Votes in the Forthcoming Election, October 25, 1962, Whitehead Papers, RH Mss. Afr. s. 1482; Alport, Sudden Assignment, 150–51; Wood, No Further!, 115–18.

voters for the 1962 election. When he attended the funeral of an old comrade, Nkomo and Mugabe were unable to shield him from an assault by ZAPU youths.[83]

The Rhodesian Front won the 1962 election with a majority of five seats. Multiple-preference voting hardly mattered, because the election was essentially between two parties and many Africans did not vote.[84] Robert Blake blamed Nkomo, "the true architect of the Rhodesian Front victory." The Rhodesian Front won, by narrow margins, in mining areas and provincial cities and many rural constituencies. The UFP became the party of the wealthier suburbs of Salisbury and Bulawayo; it had not had the support of the B roll voters who cast ballots in cross-voting constituencies.[85] Winston Field's cabinet was very different from the one Whitehead envisioned: all but two cabinet ministers—one of whom was Ian Smith—were former Dominion Party members. This clearly encouraged a hard line on various racial issues, including urban segregation and selling land to Africans, but it also may have kept the Dominion Party rhetoric in line.[86] William Harper, a longtime DP stalwart, was made minister of water and irrigation.[87] Many Rhodesian Front MPs had campaigned on the issue of independence and the promises of the 1961 constitution, but Field believed that a unilateral declaration of independence would be disastrous. The cabinet became increasingly frustrated with his leadership, regarding Field as too close to the British governor. He resigned under pressure from the wing of his party variously called right-wing or pro-independence. He was replaced by Ian Smith in 1964.[88]

Smith believed he ushered in a new era in Rhodesian politics. He had been born in the country. He often called himself an African and

83. Shamuyarira, *Crisis*, 140; Scarnecchia, *Urban Roots*, 109–11, 116–18. Mugabe shouted "not here!" at the youths to no avail: the incident was one of the reasons used for banning ZAPU. "All Quiet on the Southern Front" and "Not Proven," *Central African Examiner* 6, no. 2 (October 1962): 7, 31.

84. Leaver, "Multiculturalism," 177; Fraenkel, " 'Equality of rights.' "

85. Blake, *Rhodesia*, 344; Shamuyarira, *Crisis*, 213; Hancock, *White Liberals*, 100.

86. No one seemed able to keep Lord Graham entirely under control. Early in 1965, when he was minister of agriculture, he sought a reduced sentence for a young African sentenced to three years' hard labor for inciting a riot at a beer hall over the short, tight skirts worn by young women there. The young man's action was entirely justified, Graham said. A key "technique of communist subversion" was the "lowering of standards of dress and behavior." Such skirts contributed to an overall decline in morals, and some young women required a "good spanking." *Regina v. Mafunga*, Cabinet Memoranda 2/1965, CL/Smith/19.

87. Shamuyarira, *Crisis*, 215–16; "The Front's front men," *Central African Examiner* 6, no. 8 (February 1963): 5.

88. Sir John Caldicott, Salisbury, March 12, 1976, NAZ/ORAL/CA 5. Smith, *Betrayal*, 50–63; Alan Megahey, *Humphrey Gibbs: Beleaguered Governor: Southern Rhodesia 1929–69* (London: Macmillan, 1998), 90.

noted that for men like him, there was no return or retreat to the United Kingdom. Many other RF members felt the same, despite the fact that they had been in Southern Rhodesia for little more than a decade. The Rhodesian Front leadership spoke of themselves as Scotsmen, or Cornishmen, or Britons, terms that gave more power to their rebellion against the Queen but marked a return to the unstable notion of citizenship that had long been so much a part of the Rhodesian project. The cowboy cabinet issued a report on citizenship in 1963. It praised dual citizenship because it recognized the "emotional attachments" people had to their country of origin. Federal citizens who were not citizens of Southern Rhodesia should become British subjects, at least until Nyasaland and Northern Rhodesia enacted citizenship laws. It was fairly easy to become a citizen of Southern Rhodesia. Perhaps in anticipation of independence the RF found a way to restore citizen rights to those who had left either because of political uncertainty—which in this case meant fear of black rule—or because of older patterns of skilled labor migration in the region. Anyone who was not born there, or whose father was not born there, could apply for citizenship if he or his father was a resident of the territory or had been on the voters' roll before March 1958.[89]

Ian Smith was firmly, if not publicly, committed to independence, which between 1962 and 1964 was still linked to that of the other territories of the federation, "territories that had not experienced one day of responsible government," Smith complained. What he saw as Britain's "pandering to black politicians" only strengthened his resolve. There were many points of conflict, but the one that seemed most grating to Smith was the meaning of the 1961 constitution. Even though he and most of his party's leadership opposed the constitution, Smith spent 1964 and 1965 insisting that Rhodesians believed—as Whitehead had told them—that the 1961 constitution would lead to independence when the federation was dissolved. When the British reinserted reserve powers they denied Rhodesia true independence, or at least dominion status. This was an example of "'Perfidious Albion' at its best." Had Rhodesians understood such British duplicity, they never would have voted for the 1961 constitution.[90] But Rhodesians did vote for it, and

89. Dissolution of the federation, committee A, 53rd report, October 29, 1963, Citizenship and related subjects, Cabinet Memoranda, 1963/6, CL/Smith/17; Brownell, *Collapse*, 74–75. Northern Rhodesia, following the Southern Rhodesian constitution, banned migrants from Nyasaland from voting if they did not have federal citizenship; see "Citizenship Farce," *Central African Examiner* 6, no. 1 (June 1962): 6.

90. Smith, *Betrayal*, 43, 70–71.

it was in place when Smith became prime minister. In his memoirs, he offered the 1961 constitution as proof of how eager Rhodesians were to make progress toward majority rule. It was true, he wrote, that the B roll was "a debased franchise especially designed to cater to our black people," but the A roll remained open to all, regardless of race or color. In this way the 1961 constitution "facilitated and encouraged" African participation: no one in Southern Rhodesia interfered with Africans' access to voter rolls. There was no attempt to entrench minority rule. All Rhodesians wanted was exactly what Britain demanded, a peaceful transition to majority rule.[91]

UDI and the 1961 Constitution

Once Nyasaland and Northern Rhodesia became independent in 1964, demands for Rhodesian independence intensified, as did British demands for majority rule or some approximation thereof. Between September and October 1965 British and Rhodesian officials debated the likelihood of majority rule in Rhodesia, which was in fact a debate about the content and meaning of the 1961 constitution. The fate of the B roll was at stake. In meetings in London in October, Smith insisted that Rhodesians all thought the 1961 constitution was an "acceptable" basis for independence; they assumed Britain agreed. Harold Wilson and Arthur Bottomley, secretary of state for Commonwealth Relations, replied that the issue was not one of independence in and of itself, but of independence based on democratic electoral processes. There should be no independence before there was majority rule.[92] The 1961 constitution, let alone its supposed promise of independence, had not been voted on by all racial groups in Rhodesia. Smith reminded Wilson and Bottomley of the history of African political participation after 1961, that Africans had rejected even the limited opportunities they had to vote. Bottomley complained that even when the B roll had been expanded—"almost one man, one vote," said Smith—there were no new plans for improving African political participation.[93] Smith thought the complaint justified, but so long as Africans did not act "in a constitutional

91. Smith, *Betrayal*, 102–3.
92. This was NIBMR, no independence before majority rule, the acronym that quickly was amended to be NIBMAR in Southern Rhodesia, no independence before African majority rule, which proved how racist Wilson was.
93. Arthur Bottomley, secretary of state for Commonwealth Relations to Ian Smith, September 21, 1965, *Southern Rhodesia: Documents Relating to Negotiations between the United Kingdom and*

manner and are not prepared to take advantage of the present constitution" his government would make no further efforts to enfranchise
them.[94] Wilson saw this as an opening. If Africans were willing to work
within the 1961 constitution, he said, their advancement would depend
on their educational and economic qualifications: how long would it
then take for Africans to dominate the A roll? Smith refused to guess.
Indeed, he was adamant that Rhodesians should not accelerate the educational or economic development of Africans so they might secure a
vote: that would be like bribery. Besides, Africans did not take full advantage of the opportunities they were offered already; there were more
vacancies in African secondary schools than there were in those reserved
for Europeans. Wilson suggested that this meant that under the 1961
constitution majority rule was far off. Smith said it was. His government
wanted a majority rule that was "reasonable and responsible." He added
what was already a Rhodesian theme that nowhere in newly independent African nations was there a democratic process.[95]

Wilson clarified his position, which he reminded Smith was identical
to that of the Conservative government in 1964. Britain could not grant
independence to a country that limited African voting rights in the present or in the future. The example of South Africa was irrelevant: it had
been an independent country before it denied voting rights to the majority of its population. Its policies were condemned, but they were not
illegal. Rhodesia however had announced its intention to sever its ties
with Britain in order to maintain minority rule. This would be illegal,
and it justified the British government retaining reserve powers for the
same reason it had always claimed them, to protect the African franchise.
Smith said this was unnecessary: there was a "blocking mechanism" of
awkward design even by the standards of the 1961 constitution. There
were to be twelve chiefs in the senate, and they, along with the fifteen
African B roll members of the legislature, would provide a blocking third
to all amendments to the constitution that required a two-thirds majority. The chiefs, however, would not be elected, but appointed. Since
their only governmental function would be to provide a blocking mechanism, there was no need to elect chiefs. Rhodesia's minister of justice,

---

Southern Rhodesian Governments, November 1963–November 1965 (London: HMSO, 1965), 66–67. See
also Wood, *No Further!*, 367–411.

94. Smith to Bottomley, September 27, 1965, *Southern Rhodesia*, 68.

95. This was less accurate in 1965 than it was to be in later years, as Smith noted with increasing self-righteousness. His supporters in Britain were at pains to show the hypocrisy of the United
Nations. See Luise White, "What Does It Take to Be a State? Sovereignty and Sanctions in Rhodesia,
1965–1980," in Howland and White, *State of Sovereignty*, 154–58 and chap. 4.

Desmond Lardner-Burke, insisted that this was not a matter of simple representation. The combination of chiefs and elected B roll representatives ensured "what mattered," that candidates for the senate would be "responsible individuals." And since Africans had already rejected the "opportunities for representation" offered by the 1961 constitution there was no reason to believe that lowering qualifications would increase the number of Africans who voted.[96]

Wilson was not impressed. How could a country be ready for independence but not for democracy? How could there be independence before majority rule? Was there no way to have a referendum on independence involving the expanded B roll and the A roll? Smith repeated what he had said at earlier meetings, that this was not possible. In an ordinary election, voters had only to exercise a choice between two candidates: "this was something the average African could easily do." Deciding on the complex issues of an independence constitution was a very different matter, as "it involved sophisticated judgments which the ordinary African could not comprehend." Wilson might believe that the ordinary African might be able to say "yes" or "no," Smith said, but Africans simply could not understand what they were being asked to decide. This was why the 1961 constitution gave A roll votes to chiefs but not to other Africans.[97]

The conventional narratives of 1961–1965 are of the tragedy of white intentions, or the tragedy of the intransigence of African response, or of white attitudes calcifying over events in the Congo and further north. None of these adequately tells this story, in which personal testimonies to constitutional commissions in 1960 became the basis for electoral policies a few years later. The eccentric detours that preceded the exclusions of the 1961 constitution were to be welcomed in the rhetoric and the cabinet of the Rhodesian Front, as in the itinerary of Harry Reedman, but they were not the only itineraries of this period. There were also the journeys of Ian Smith, Steve Kock, and Terence Ranger, and the journeys of Charles Mzingeli, Michael Mawema, Leopold Takawira, and Joshua Nkomo: the political positions these men took, and the parties in which they took them, do not so much mark changes in an individual's politics as they reveal how parties offered political spaces to accommodate and articulate ideas about who to govern and how to do so.

96. Duncan Sandys to Winston Field, PM of Southern Rhodesia, February 22, 1964; Record of a meeting held at 10 Downing Street, October 11, 1965, *Southern Rhodesia*, 10–13, 92–93.
97. Record of meeting held at 10 Downing Street, October 7 and 26, 1965, *Southern Rhodesia*, 69–79, 105–6.

FOUR

"A rebellion by a population the size of Portsmouth": The Status of Rhodesia's Independence, 1965–1969

The notion of empire touted by Lord Graham in 1965 was that of the Victorian era, the idea of a Greater Britain—Ireland, Canada, Australia, New Zealand, and South Africa—populated by prosperous white people bringing civilization and commerce to the lands they ruled. Its antecedents were classical: Pax Britannica was in Latin because Pax Romana was.[1] Despite the many references to Sparta, despite appeals to the history of conquest—"Saying Africa belongs to Africans is a bit like saying England belongs to the Welsh"[2]—once in power the Rhodesian Front shied away from Graham's grand vision and instead spoke of "kith and kin." This was the imagined community of English-speaking white people who should have honored Rhodesian policies rather than seeking to end them. The first half of this chapter and much of chapter 7 argue that the idea of kith and kin backfired. It allowed for the already indistinct ways of belonging to Rhodesia to be belonging

1. Duncan Bell, *Idea of Greater Britain*; Burbank and Cooper, *Empires*, 300.
2. Lancelot Bales Smith, Banket, November 22, 1985, NAZ/ORAL/250.

to somewhere else. It also seems to have encouraged a characterization of independent Rhodesia as a kind of lesser Britain, out of step with the times and more like a midsized British city than anything else. In 1966 the Liberal MP Jeremy Thorpe accused Harold Wilson of being incapable of "putting down a rebellion by a population the size of Portsmouth."[3] Others used Harrow as the comparison. There were the jokes about suburbs and Aberdeen. Most recently, to make his point about the instability of the white Rhodesian population Josiah Brownell explained that it was as "the percentage equivalent of the entire cities Birmingham, Leeds, Liverpool and Manchester being completely replaced by new people every year."[4]

States of Emergency

The Rhodesian Front was returned to power by a massive majority in May 1964. It was "almost a referendum," said Clifford Dupont, its first president: the question was not should Rhodesia be independent, but should it take its own independence without any endorsement from Britain? Even before the disastrous meetings in London in October 1965—after which Dupont thought it was "fairly obvious" that the "only solution" was UDI—Rhodesia had moved to a gradual, if piecemeal, status of independence.[5] Because of its quasi-dominion noncolonial status, Rhodesia was overseen by the Commonwealth Relations Office (CRO). Rhodesia had a high commissioner in London; everywhere else its diplomatic relations were handled by Rhodesian representatives in British embassies. In what J. R. T. Wood has called "the first act of defiance," Harry Reedman—of Best Man government proposed in 1960—was appointed accredited diplomatic representative in Lisbon in August 1965. This outraged the CRO and made Rhodesia's relations with Britain worse than they were before.[6]

The choice of November 11 for Rhodesian independence was not symbolic but practical. The tobacco crop, for example, would not be

3. Quoted in Martin Bailey, *Oilgate: The Sanctions Scandal* (London: Coronet Books, 1979), 117.

4. Carl Watts, "Killing Kith and Kin: The Viability of British Military Intervention in Rhodesia, 1964–5," *Twentieth-Century British History* 16, no. 4 (2005): 391; Brownell, *Collapse*, 3, 73.

5. Clifford Dupont, six interviews, June 1976–January 1977, Salisbury, NAZ/ORAL/DU4.

6. Philip Murphy, "'An intricate and distasteful subject': British Planning for the Use of Force against the European Settlers of Central Africa, 1952–65," *English Historical Review* 131, no. 492 (2006): 750; Wood, *No Further!*, 344–61.

ready until the following March; if there were to be sanctions Rhodesia had time to make new trade arrangements.[7] More important, however, was that the preventative detention bill was due to expire in November 1965. This would mean the release of one thousand Africans in detention, many of whom had been accused of intimidation and all of whom opposed Rhodesian independence. The bill could be renewed only by royal assent, which of course was not forthcoming: the only way to keep the detainees in detention was a state of emergency. On November 1 the cabinet met and voted to take UDI. On November 3 Smith went to see the governor, Humphrey Gibbs, carrying a proclamation of a state of emergency and an affidavit by the commissioner of police stating his "deep apprehension" for the future security of the country because of the number of guerrillas being trained and armed in Tanzania and Zambia. Gibbs knew Rhodesia was calmer than it had been for months, and he knew that a declaration of independence would most likely be preceded by the proclamation of a state of emergency. Nevertheless, he signed the proclamation, asking only that Smith promise that his government would deny that the proclamation had anything to do with UDI. The proclamation was not dated for a week, during which there were several anxious phone calls and visits between London and Salisbury. It was finally dated on November 11. Years later Dupont said that the state of emergency was not in preparation for UDI, but "to keep the shape of the state" the same as it had been under federation.[8]

What shape was that? The state Dupont wanted to preserve had nothing to do with the feeble liberalism of federation. When he opened his campaign in 1962 he promised "categorically" to stop "the black flood at the Zambezi,"[9] by which he meant African nationalism, not African people. The shape desired by Dupont and others in the Rhodesian Front leadership was a minority-ruled state that was legal in the eyes of Britain and the various ministries that attended to its former possessions. The shape of the state Dupont wanted was one that could maintain independence without making new laws to guarantee it.

Much of the work to make an independent Rhodesia secure was done well before November 1965. The Rhodesian Front forced the resignation of the party leader, Winston Field, in April 1964 because he did

---

7. Robert C. Good, *U. D. I.: The International Relations of the Rhodesian Rebellion* (Princeton, NJ: Princeton University Press, 1973), 69.

8. Clifford Dupont interview, NAZ/ORAL/DU4; Megahey, *Humphrey Gibbs*, 106–8; Flower, *Serving Secretly*, 292–93.

9. Clifford Dupont interview, NAZ/ORAL/DU4.

not pursue independence vigorously enough. As it planned Rhodesian independence, the party evaluated the attitudes of civil servants and soldiers and purged those who might oppose UDI. Loyalty to fellow white men, even those who shared ties of history and schools and regiments, was secondary to ascertaining individual loyalty to a specific political goal. In 1964 and 1965 government departments conducted business on two levels, one for the ordinary affairs of state and one for an inner circle that evaluated bureaucrats for their loyalty to the Rhodesian Front and UDI.[10] Party stalwarts boasted of whom they had forced to resign. "We assessed the feelings of the army," said William Cary, a Dominion Party MP who eagerly joined the Rhodesian Front in 1962. "Where we found obstruction as in the case of Brig. General Anderson, we got rid of him." Otherwise "it would have been the simplest matter for the army to have stepped in and had a coup." Years later Ken Flower of Rhodesia's Central Intelligence Organization (CIO)—who had his own list of whom he considered disloyal—wrote that Anderson was simply indiscreet in the officers' mess; had he not been asked to resign he would have done his duty as a soldier for Rhodesia. Flower lamented that the government listened to criticism of military officers from men of junior rank. Between April 1964 and November 1965 Rhodesian Front apparatchiks made "very careful" and "very deliberate" inquiries and appeals "to find if the army was with us and whether in fact the civil service was with us." Those who did not approve of UDI were given the opportunity of resigning and taking their pensions right away. Those who did support UDI worried that they would have to sign loyalty oaths; those who did not said they were barely tolerated: some left the country as soon as they could afford to; others called it the worst years of their lives.[11]

The economy was also planned, as we shall see, to make sure an independent Rhodesia could withstand sanctions. What was not planned, or may have been overestimated or not estimated carefully enough, was how Britain would respond and which other nations would recognize Rhodesia as a legitimate state.

10. Blake, *Rhodesia*, 367.
11. Shortly after he resigned, Anderson told the press that he was "not alone" in the security forces opposing UDI. See Watts, "Kith and Kin," 393; Flower, *Serving Secretly*, 40–41; Wood, *No Further!*, 243–44; William Joseph John Cary, Gwelo, September 1971, February 1972, NAZ/ORAL/CA 4; Rupert Meredith Davies, Hampshire, November 17, 1983, NAZ/ORAL/241; M. J. Thompson, Ag. Secretary, Public Service Board, to C. H. W. Banger, Bulawayo, December 8, 1966, NAZ/S3279/11/211, Loyalty to Rhodesian Government; author's field notes, Harare, July 13, 2001.

Kith, Kin, and the Use of Force

Leaving Rhodesia at the end of October 1965, Harold Wilson announced he would not authorize the use of force if the Rhodesian Front took UDI. In Britain many officials and diplomats doubted the strategic wisdom of announcing this in advance, while in Rhodesia white moderates complained that this curtailed any possibility of internal resistance.[12] Since then there have been several explanations for and considerable hand-wringing about Wilson's inaction. Some argued that the British feared that their troops would not fight their "kith and kin," while others insisted that Rhodesian forces would fight to the death, and still others maintained that they would not fight at all. As new archives were opened, new research has been possible; between 2005 and 2006 three publications addressed Wilson's decision. In these, both Philip Murphy and J. R. T. Wood showed how Wilson's critics ignored how many times he had said this. Both noted how much Britain knew about how little Smith trusted the loyalty of his senior officers, although they used their material to different ends. Murphy argues that by the end of October Wilson thought the best hope of a settlement was persuading Nkomo and Mugabe to participate in the 1961 constitution: when he said "there will be no thunderbolt," he was speaking to men in detention or in exile. Wood disagreed. Following Ken Flower, he argued that Wilson was speaking to Nkomo and Mugabe, not to begin negotiations but to begin guerrilla incursions and thus cow Rhodesia into a settlement.[13] Carl Watts also found that a British invasion could have been successful had Wilson's cabinet been willing to mount one, but his research involved the question of whether or not Rhodesian troops would defend Rhodesia. In 1999 several former combatants told him they would have fought the British tooth and nail.[14] For all their misgivings about the loyalty of the army, Rhodesian officials imagined ways that an invasion might be to their advantage.

12. Denis Healy, *The Time of My* Life (New York: Norton, 1990 [1989]), 332; Robin Renwick, *Unconventional Diplomacy in Southern Africa* (New York: St. Martin's Press, 1997), 3; Edwin Albert Litchtenstein, London, November 20, 1983, NAZ/ORAL/243; Leo Solomon Baron, Harare, August 5 and 16, 1983, NAZ/ORAL/239; author's field notes, June 25, 1999.

13. Flower, *Serving Secretly*, 51–52; Murphy, "Distasteful Subject," 746–77; Wood, *No Further!*, 413–15.

14. Watts, "Killing Kith and Kin."

The fragmentary archives available in the United States and Zimbabwe suggest as much. There were rumors Smith had threatened to blow up the power installations at Kariba Dam if the British attacked.[15] Rhodesian officials dismissed the possibility of an invasion out of hand: it would take the British at least twenty-four hours to land an airborne division in Rhodesia and "we knew damn well they couldn't do it without prior warning."[16] Some thought British troops could be deployed to help Rhodesia survive. Less than two weeks after UDI, officials in Salisbury circulated a memo about the possibility of British troops in Zambia. Kenneth Kaunda was under pressure to confront Rhodesia; he wanted to allow British troops into Zambia but not OAU ones. But if British troops were there, "nationalists" would do everything they could to bring about an "explosive" situation to justify an invasion of Rhodesia. Zambian or British troops could occupy Kariba and control Rhodesia's electric power. The best way to avoid a confrontation on the border would be to invite British troops to join Rhodesian troops protecting Kariba. This was impossible, however, not because British troops would not cooperate but because Rhodesian publics might object: white Rhodesians might see this as a surrender to British force and African nationalists would condemn the occupation of Kariba. Worse still, this would try the support available from Portugal and South Africa, neither of which would become involved in a confrontation with a major power.[17]

I am less concerned with the question of a British invasion than I am with the question of who and what Britain would have invaded. That was the question of kith and kin and the entire lexicon with which the invasion was deemed a dangerous enterprise, despite the weakness of Rhodesian forces. This was literally the historical conditions of impossibility that British troops would not fight against their "kith and kin." This was—or was made into—a reference to the incident at Curragh in Northern Ireland in 1914, when British officers, many of whom were from Belfast, resigned their commissions rather than fight against Ulster volunteers. The comparison was rich in imperial trappings—a claim to British heritage and ideals, Ulstermen's opposition to home rule—but it was also largely anecdotal: British officers denied ever asking their troops

15. American Consul General, telegram to Washington, December 4, 1965, LBJ Library, NSF Country File/97.
16. George Wilburn Rudland, Sinoia, September 5, 1972, NAZ/ORAL/RU3. This part of the interview was to be sealed for twenty years.
17. British troops in Zambia, points for discussion, November 22, 1965, Use of Force against Rhodesia, NAZ/S 3287/76/40.

if they would wage war against white Rhodesians. Years after the idea of an invasion was credible, Paul Moorcraft asked cadets at Sandhurst if they were prepared to fight against white Rhodesian troops. Almost all said they would not have been—not because of Curragh but because of the number of Rhodesians on the roll of honor in the Sandhurst chapel.[18] The differences between Northern Ireland and Central Africa were great, and by 1965 "kith and kin" was not a description of populations, but was both a way to argue against a British invasion and a way to talk about what being Rhodesian meant and to whom it had a meaning. In this fictive kith and kin Rhodesians were members of an imperial community that would approve of Rhodesian independence and that, should any members be ordered to invade the country, would refuse to shoot white Rhodesians. And this added kith and kin to the already opaque notions of belonging in Rhodesia, even as it mocked the speeches about how unique Rhodesians were or how someone could feel like a Rhodesian when they were in fact American. Kith and kin emphasized the ways that being Rhodesian was indistinct, that being Rhodesian was all but indistinguishable from being British or Irish or South African at the same time. Kith and kin meant belonging to something beyond a state. A case in point is Major John Anderson, who was born in South Africa of British parents. He had served in the British army and was seconded to the Rhodesian army to train troops during World War II. He married a Rhodesian woman with her own complicated history: raised by her impoverished uncle, she later suspected that the mother who abandoned her was not Portuguese or French as she been told but of mixed race. John Anderson served in Britain's counterinsurgency in Malaya and returned to Central Africa in 1957 to join the federal army of the Central African Federation. When the federation dissolved he became chief of staff of the army in Southern Rhodesia. Whether or not he had dual citizenship—he was eligible for federal citizenship in 1959—he had a home in Britain to which he could return when he resigned.[19] There were many like him: not necessarily the opponents of UDI Anderson boasted about to the Rhodesian press, but men whose nationality was unsettled, who could change from being Rhodesian or British or South African at a moment's notice.

18. Moorcraft, *Short Thousand Years*, 18n; Carl Peter Watts, *Rhodesia's Unilateral Declaration of Independence: An International History* (London: Palgrave Macmillan, 2012), 62–66.

19. Major John Anderson, London, November 24, 1983, NAZ/ORAL/244; Daphne Anderson, *The Toe-Rags: The Story of a Strange Up-Bringing in Southern Rhodesia* (London: Andre Deutsch, 1989).

Rhodesians and Britons served in the armed forces of both countries. Britain did not draw up formal plans for an invasion because there were Rhodesians on the army's planning staff.[20] Britain's air vice marshal had trained in the Rhodesian air training group during World War II; generals and majors and police officers in both countries enjoyed close if informal relations with their counterparts. A British-born Rhodesian security officer "heard from my own colleagues back home" that there would be no invasion.[21] There were stories of Rhodesians serving in the Royal Air Force who resigned immediately after UDI to go and serve in the Royal Rhodesian Air Force, and of Britons in the RRAF who resigned to return home.[22] The police—a larger group than whites in the army—had special concerns of nationality. The British South African Police (BSAP), originally the police for Cecil Rhodes's British South Africa Company, had long recruited from Britain. Former policemen recalled that there were only one or two or three Rhodesians in squads that ranged in size from sixteen to thirty white recruits. Few officials believed the BSAP would fight off a British invasion; the former BSAP officer who assured Carl Watts that he would have done so left Rhodesia to join the British army and become an officer in the Gurkhas.

In the months after UDI there was a wave of desertions from the BSAP.[23] But were these desertions in any way different from the emigration that was commonplace between 1960 and 1965? Were the deserters of those years in any way different from the thousands of whites who left Rhodesia in the uncertain years of 1961–1966? New immigrants left for personal reasons; immigration boards asserted that many left because they did not find the prosperous lifestyle promised by their brochures.[24] Did this mean that young Britons deserted the BSAP because they were unwilling to fight for a country rebelling against their queen or because the tax burden of bachelors was greater than had been expected? According to the BSAP's quasi-official history, a few long-serving members and many new recruits left it between October 1965 and early 1966. None of them blamed "the political situation" but were vague about why they were leaving. Three deserters arrested in early November

20. Michael Charlton, *The Last Colony in Africa: Diplomacy and the Independence of Rhodesia* (Oxford: Basil Blackwell, 1990), 13–14.

21. Col. Henry Melville de Berdt Romilly, London, July 24, 1984, NAZ/ORAL/247.

22. It is not entirely clear how these men would have fared under new citizenship laws, but it is also not clear if citizenship was the issue. Author's field notes, Bristol, June 23, 2003; Watts, *Unilateral Declaration of Independence*, 60; Wood, *No Further!*, 244; Beryl Salt, *A Pride of Eagles: The Definitive History of the Rhodesian Air Force 1920–1980* (Weltevreden Park: Covos-Day, 2001), 397–98.

23. Watts, "Kith and Kin," 398n.

24. Brownell, *Collapse*, 75, 79.

simply said "Rhodesia was just not what we expected it to be." Those who found their way to the Botswana border, sometimes in stolen vehicles, were taken to Zambia and then London, where they were required to repay their airfares.[25]

Rhodesia's Status

Nationality notwithstanding, Rhodesia's quasi-dominion or quasi-colonial status made the question of who had the right to invade it problematic in the extreme. Had it been a colony the governor could have asked for British troops in an emergency. This was the case with Mau Mau in Kenya and the Nyasaland Emergency in 1959. Southern Rhodesia had never been a colony; indeed at the end of federation provisions were made for its defense that were not made for Northern Rhodesia or Nyasaland. In 1963 Britain handed over the well-equipped Royal Rhodesian Air Force to Southern Rhodesia, presumably to provide both the fire power and reconnaissance to defend itself against an African uprising.[26] But however Britain dismantled the Central African Federation, debates in the Commonwealth, especially those joined by African leaders, insisted that Rhodesia was legally a colony. As such, Britain's failure to use force there contrasted sharply to her interventions in Cyprus, Kenya, and Aden, demonstrating once again the inequalities of empire and a colonial past that was simply a mask for racism. After UDI, the Commonwealth continued to call for military intervention. Again, the Commonwealth debates assumed that Rhodesia was a colony and thus should be disciplined as one. Ghana and Tanzania withdrew from the Commonwealth in protest. There was no point in negotiating with a regime that would not agree to one man, one vote, they claimed. Britain, however, sought a new weapon, sanctions. This meant treating Rhodesia as if it was an independent state, by first expelling Rhodesia from the sterling zone, then calling for an oil embargo, and eventually asking that its exports be sanctioned, all of which were unimaginable actions to take against a colony. Had Britain invaded, however, it would have meant that Britain would literally have taken over Rhodesia, to make it a colony, so that Britain could then decolonize Rhodesia.

25. Peter Gibbs and Hugh Phillips, *The History of the British South African Police 1889–1980* (North Ringwood, Australia: Something of Value Press, 2000), 291.
26. Murphy, "'Distasteful Subject,'" 764.

It was precisely because Rhodesia was not a colony that allowed for the use of a new kind of weapon, one that could do the work of military invasion and bring Rhodesia to its knees. United States archives show how powerful a tool sanctions appeared to nations in the mid-1960s.[27] As early as mid-January 1966, when sanctions had been in place for a month, the "best experts" in the U.S. State Department were no longer worried whether sanctions would work, but how quickly they would work: ideally, Smith's regime would collapse "before Kaunda and other Africans do something foolish." There were predictions that the regime would not last six months; Sir Hugh Beadle, the chief justice, told almost everyone that once oil supplies ran out Rhodesians would abandon Smith and the idea of UDI. This was in large part enthusiasm for sanctions as a new tool for new times, as something that marked the difference between 1914 and 1965. In the United States, at least, there were worries that sanctions might work too well, and too quickly. If Smith were to "cave soon other extremists will take over" and then it would be necessary for Britain to send troops to restore order.[28] In 1966 the Commonwealth agreed that there should be worldwide sanctions imposed by the United Nations and that the use of force be reserved for a later time. Only Pakistan and Malta opposed any use of force.[29] I shall discuss sanctions at length in the next chapter, but their importance as a political weapon, at least in the first months after UDI, cannot be underestimated.

Recognizing Rhodesia

Despite Rhodesia's preening boast that it had, or should have, the status of an independent nation, it did not have the traits of statehood required in the world before UDI, or even before the Central African Federation. In the 1950s the country seemed out of step with whatever

27. The United States had no real interest in Rhodesia. A few weeks after UDI, Lyndon Johnson was told as much, that Rhodesia was "critical to all the other Africans." R. W. Komer, Memorandum for the President, December 6, 1965, LBJ/NSF/Edward Hamilton/3. See also Horne, *Barrel of a Gun*, 133–44; Watts, *Unilateral Declaration*, 155–82.

28. R. W. Komer, Memorandum for the President, January 13, 1966; Ulrich Haynes to R. W. Komer, January 19, 1966; R. W. Komer, confidential memorandum, February 2, 1966; Ulrich Haynes, memorandum for Walt W. Rostow, April 4, 1966, LBJ/NSF/Ulrich Haynes/1.

29. Wilson, *Labour Government*, 116, 165, 182, 280–84, 304. Nkrumah also feared that working through the Commonwealth would undermine Ghana's ability to pursue a unified all-African government. Letter from Nkrumah to Wilson, December 11, 1965, quoted in Nkrumah, *Rhodesia File* (London: Panaf, n. d.), 119.

was constitutive of progress in the postwar and decolonizing world. In 1951, for example, Southern Rhodesia could not be a signatory to the European Convention on Human Rights, fully supported by the United Kingdom, because it allowed forced labor and prevented Africans from forming trade unions.[30] In early 1965, when the Rhodesian Front's demand for independence seemed not only possible but plausible, Rhodesia had less legitimacy for the Labour Party than did the political parties trying to take it over.[31]

Nevertheless, in early 1965 there was wishful thinking in the Rhodesian Front that the mining lobby that had failed to obtain British recognition for the breakaway state Katanga would be able to secure it for Rhodesia, or that South Africa would recognize an independent Rhodesia for sheer self-interest or that France would do so to create a precedent for Quebec.[32] Mining companies had less success arguing Rhodesia's case than they had arguing Katanga's, and neither South Africa nor France nor Portugal recognized it. Did the Smith regime believe recognition was possible by playing off one state against another, a classic eighteenth- and nineteenth-century ploy that worked well when the French supported the American Revolution but less well when Vietnam or Indonesia declared themselves independent before France or the Netherlands agreed to it?[33] Certainly in the early 1970s— the first years of the Rhodesian republic—there were desperate hopes in Salisbury that some country, somewhere, would recognize Rhodesia and other countries would follow suit.[34] But what did not work in the late 1940s failed dismally in the era of decolonization, when for the first time nonsovereign groups and territories were accorded recognized sovereign status because they were now independent.[35] In states that declared their own independence, either secessionist or Rhodesian, membership in the

---

30. A. W. Brian Simpson, *Human Rights and the End of Empire: Britain and the Genesis of the European Convention* (Oxford: Oxford University Press, 2001), 829. I am grateful to Philip Murphy for this reference.

31. Even six months before UDI, ZAPU was seen as a nationalist and refugee organization with which Britain had dealings, via Zambia. When Barbara Castle, minister for overseas development, visited Lusaka, she met with George Nyandoro. Secretary of State for Commonwealth Relations, London to Queen's Commissioner, Bechuanaland, May 1, 1965; Queen's Commissioner, Bechauanaland to CO, London, May 4, 1965; British High Commissioner, Lusaka, to H. R. E. Browne, CRO, May 14, 1965, Botswana National Archives [hereafter BNA]/ OP55/67: Saboteurs/Returning Refugees.

32. Murphy, *Party Politics*, 113–17; Goldin, *The Judge, the Prince, and the Usurper*, 19.

33. Burbank and Cooper, *Empires*, 407–10.

34. Many officials were overly optimistic about the influence of the 500 Friends of Rhodesia clubs around the world; see Evans, Rhodesian Front Rule, 128–38.

35. Mikulas Fabry, *Recognizing States: International Society and the Establishment of New States since 1776* (Oxford: Oxford University Press, 2010), 148–49.

community of nations was not automatic but depended on a state's being recognized by (at least) one other sovereign state.[36] This was almost impossible for Rhodesia: on November 20, the United Nations asked its members not to recognize "this illegal act."[37] This directive was to be a discursive thorn in Rhodesia's thin-skinned side for the next fourteen years, during which time no other country recognized Rhodesia. The importance of not being recognized was twofold in Rhodesian politics. Not being recognized cost Rhodesia an international voice, a place in international organizations; it meant its independence was not fully concrete. Not being recognized, however, allowed party hacks to continually position themselves as victims of the unprincipled politics of the day. Why was Idi Amin's Uganda recognized and not Ian Smith's Rhodesia?[38]

Rhodesian officials, like their counterparts in the United Kingdom and the United Nations, knew full well that in Africa in the 1960s independence was a specific act: it was independence from a colonial power. Recognition of each new, independent government gave the new nation a status in international law and international organizations (which included nations that did not recognize each other). Other kinds of new states were not accorded recognition.[39] Rhodesian officials were to complain that their nation was not accorded the respect given to Rwanda or Zanzibar, for example, but they understood that Rhodesia did not occupy the same legal or discursive position as did former colonies in Africa. This, of course, was a justification for UDI; when it became a complaint it tended to offer its own explanation. Recognition was an expedient, an agreed-to action (or doctrine) that had multiple audiences—the United Nations, for example, or the Commonwealth—and was not

36. Mark Bradbury, *Becoming Somaliland* (Oxford: James Currey, 2008), 249, 255.

37. Rhodesian representatives in London and Washington were stripped of their official status. For Rhodesia House in London, see Josiah Brownell, "'A Sordid Tussle on the Strand': Rhodesia House during the UDI Rebellion (1965–80)," *J. of Imperial and Commonwealth History* 38, no. 3 (2010): 471–99. The U.S. Department of State requested that the Rhodesian Information Office in Washington be closed at once, that the British embassy invalidate their passports (which said they were "in the service of HMG"), that the District of Columbia police department take away their diplomatic license plates, and that the immigration and naturalization service begin deportation procedures. Ulrich Haynes to R. W. Komer, February 24, 1966, LBJ/NSF/Chron1/Ulrich Haynes/1. The Rhodesian Information Office survived, however. Once its staff ceased to claim British diplomatic status and registered as foreign agents, there were no legal grounds on which to close the office or deport its staff; see Anthony Lake, *The 'Tar Baby' Option: American Policy toward Southern Rhodesia* (New York: Columbia University Press, 1976 [1973]), 104–7.

38. This was almost a trope in Rhodesian speech and writing. A book about the banning of Rhodesia from the 1968 Olympics, for example, was called *A Wilderness of Spite or Rhodesia Denied*. See John Cheffers, *A Wilderness of Spite* (New York: Vantage Press, 1972).

39. Anthony Anghie, *Imperialism, Sovereignty, and the Making of International Law* (Cambridge: Cambridge University Press, 2004), 75.

wholly based on the internal policies of a country, as the favorite example of Amin's Uganda shows. Thus new governments in Ghana and Uganda were recognized at once, however they came to power and whatever they did once they were there. Rhodesians used the example of Biafra carefully; they were aware that it was recognized by Anglophone African countries only after it was all but defeated in war, as a reprimand to Britain for its unwavering support for Nigeria.[40]

On the level of the passport—the level of individuals and their rights to travel—UDI created a host of concerns, most of which were anticipated and all of which were the subject of bitter complaints. In preparation for UDI Rhodesia modified its Citizenship Act in 1963 to allow Rhodesia to issue its own passports and to declare Rhodesian citizens were no longer British subjects. It was essential for Rhodesia to issue its own passports as Britain would no longer provide consular services for Rhodesians; it was hoped that removing Rhodesian citizens from British nationality would protect them from charges of treason—which UDI technically was—when they traveled to the United Kingdom or Commonwealth nations. Who was and was not a British subject could only be determined by British laws, however, some of which were amended to make it difficult for Rhodesians to travel. Immediately after UDI, the 1948 nationality act was changed so that Rhodesian citizens who wished to become British citizens could do so easily. The Commonwealth Immigrants' Act of 1962 was extended to all Rhodesians with British passports, many of whom complained that they were now treated as any other Commonwealth citizen when they tried to enter the United Kingdom.[41] New laws allowed immigration authorities to ban anyone traveling on a Rhodesian passport from entering Britain or to confiscate any passport issued by the Rhodesian government; this rarely happened, but the law was held up by the Rhodesian Front as yet another injustice from Britain.[42] Nevertheless, many officials in the Rhodesian government traveled on British passports. Some, like Ken Flower of the CIO and Sir Hugh Beadle, or Harvey Ward, the newscaster for the Rhodesian Broadcasting Corporation, came and went with ease

40. Anghie, *Making of International Law*, 78–79; Douglas Anthony, " 'Resourceful and Progressive Blackmen': Modernity and Race in Biafra, 1967–68," *J. Afr. History* 21, no. 1 (2010): 41–61.

41. Arthur R. Lewis, *Too Bright the Vision? African Adventures of a Rhodesian Rebel* (London: Covenant, 1992), 246; Caute, *Under the Skin*, 113–14, 155; Harvey Ward, London, July 4, 1984, NAZ/ORAL/246.

42. Palley, *Constitutional History*, 735–37; Derek Arthur Collings van der Syde, Harare, November 27, 1987, NAZ/ORAL/267. Two months after UDI, Rhodesians claimed only nineteen white civil servants had left the county. G. B. Clarke to Prime Minister, January 10, 1966, NAZ/S3279/11/211, Loyalty to Rhodesian Government.

while others, such as Lord Graham and a handful of distinguished World War I veterans, were banned from entering Britain.[43] By the late 1960s the workings around Rhodesian citizenship seemed to have become flexible, if not hollow. In 1967, Rhodesia streamlined its citizenship laws so that white immigrants could become citizens in two years. This did nothing to encourage more white residents to take out citizenship papers and instead seems to have sent them to the British passport office in great numbers.[44] In 1969 the Foreign and Commonwealth Office (FCO) inquired on behalf of thirty-three of the civil servants who had left Rhodesia at UDI and now wanted to return: could these men have their old jobs back? Rhodesia said no, rejecting any entitlements of belonging. Those positions had been filled, and it had no obligation to "defecting public servants."[45]

Overall, nothing happened that was as dramatic as J. R. T. Wood's assertion that Britain arranged passports for Rhodesian Africans going to Eastern Europe for guerrilla training. Britain did provide temporary passports to Rhodesian African students who were without travel documents, but often left it to other Commonwealth countries to provide passports.[46] If Britain made it difficult for Rhodesian passport holders to travel, packaged tour operators made it easy. Within a few years of UDI Portugal, Mauritius, Switzerland, and Greece advertised holidays for Rhodesian tourists; other countries, Rhodesian officials claimed, quietly allowed Rhodesian passport holders to come and go. In 1973 Cyprus and the Malagasy Republic announced all-inclusive tours in which Rhodesians could use their plane tickets as passports to avoid any problems at customs.[47]

43. Caute, *Under the Skin*, 113–14, 155; Harvey Ward interview, London, July 4, 1984, NAZ/ ORAL/246. Arthur Bottomley once requested that Beadle's British passport be withdrawn, as he considered him the "evil genius" of UDI. See Manuele Facchini, "The 'Evil Genius': Sir Hugh Beadle and the Rhodesian Crisis, 1965–1972," *J. Southern African Studies*, 33, no. 3 (2007): 677.

44. Brownell, *Collapse*, 77.

45. White paper: Anglo-Rhodesian negotiations since December 1966, Cabinet Memoranda/ 2/1969, Cory/Smith/23. Rhodesia offered an unspecified amount of compensation, which the British government rejected. It is not clear if these thirty-three men returned or not.

46. Wood, *A Matter of Weeks*, 13, 458; Byron Hove, for example, arrived in Francistown, Botswana, in mid-1966 with a scholarship in hand but no passport. Before Special Branch there could ask ZAPU in Lusaka to arrange a Zambian passport, the Colonial Office intervened and got Hove a British passport valid for six months. Interrogation reports: Byron Hove, July 21, 1966, BNA/OP55/6, ZANU and ZAPU 1965–66.

47. Harry B. Strack, *Sanctions: The Case of Rhodesia* (Syracuse: Syracuse University Press, 1978), 198.

Legalizing Rhodesia

Rhodesia's search for legitimacy quickly moved away from international recognition and international law and toward evaluating the legality of its own independence. The issues that the RF believed gave Rhodesia its rightful place in the world were not international or diplomatic, but lawsuits against the new government. In short, Rhodesia recognized itself.

On February 4, 1966, the state of emergency declared by the governor the previous November expired; the 1965 constitution gave the Rhodesian legislative assembly and the position created to replace the governor, the officer administering the government, the power to renew the state of emergency. They did so on February 3. Lawyers in the region and detainees in Rhodesia had anticipated this, and on February 4 the wife of Daniel Madzimbamuto, a ZAPU member detained in 1964, and Leo Solomon Baron, ZAPU's lawyer, detained on November 11, 1965, sued the government. The cases were linked and were argued as one: both challenged the legality of UDI. Sydney Kentridge—a South African lawyer who defended Nelson Mandela—represented Stella Madzimbamuto. Baron was represented by Oscar Rathouse, a South African lawyer who had been part of the defense team at the 1956 Treason Trial. The applicants' argument was that only the 1961 constitution was legal; any amendments or extensions made under the 1965 constitution were not. Judges who derived their authority from the 1961 constitution could not uphold as legal any changes made by the authority of the new constitution.

The government was given four months to prepare its response. During that time Desmond Lardner-Burke, then minister of law and order, wrote a memo he gave orally to the cabinet on March 15, 1966. He envisioned four possible scenarios, two of which were definitive judgments and two of which would be so "up in the air" as to leave the government with no legal means of detaining people. This might not matter to the man in the street, he wrote, but such a ruling would affect the economy by hindering the ability of the Reserve Bank to act and it would place his office and the courts in an "invidious position." The two definitive possibilities were that the 1965 constitution would be pronounced either legal or illegal. If it was declared legal that "would be fine," but the government could not tolerate the constitution being declared illegal: an action would be taken at once. There would be an appeal, of course, but that would be to buy time, during which the judges would be required to take a new oath to the 1965 constitution so that the government would continue to govern and make laws. If too few judges were willing to take the oath that would allow the courts to operate, "other arrangements will have to be made." If the judgment was vague and claimed that an invalid constitution could make laws "for peace, order and good government," or if it avoided the question of illegality altogether, the government had to be prepared to defend laws governing detentions.[48] These were not the arguments Lardner-Burke presented to the high court in June and July 1966, however. In those arguments he claimed that UDI was a revolution and according to doctrines in international law a revolution made its own laws: it swept away previous constitutions.

The judgment, delivered in September 1966 by judges appointed under the 1961 constitution, did not find Rhodesia's current government legal. There had been no revolution: the 1965 constitution usurped power. Britain, most of the justices agreed, was the rightful sovereign ruler of Rhodesia; its failure to end Rhodesia's rebellion did not make the rebellion legal. Under the 1961 constitution the cabinet and parliament did not have the authority to replace it with a new constitution, Justice Goldin wrote. "The 'assumption' of power to 'give' or 'enact' or 'declare' a new constitution had no greater validity than if a Town Management Board had presumed to do so." Nevertheless, wrote Chief Justice Beadle, "the factual position" was that the government of Rhodesia "is in complete administrative and legislative control of the country" and maintained the courts: no other government competed with the present government, and no other government made laws. Beadle argued that whatever the legality of the 1965 constitution the court had treated the laws that had thus far come before it "as if they had emanated from a lawful government." This gave the present government the status "of a fully *de facto* government." The courts were obliged to apply its laws. Doing so would not aid the revolution, Justice Goldin wrote, but would preserve peace and order and "avoid chaos and a vacuum in the law." The regime was legal in fact if not in law.[49]

48. Desmond Lardner-Burke, Memo: the judges and the courts, March 15, 1966, Cabinet Memoranda, 1966/3, CL/Smith/20.

49. Goldin, *The Judge*, 62, 65–67; Beadle quoted in H. H. Marshall, "The Legal Effects of U. D. I. (Based on Madzimbamuto v. Lardner-Burke)," *International and Comparative Law Quarterly* 17, no. 1 (1968): 1025, 1028; Claire Palley, "The Judicial Process: U. D. I. and the Rhodesian Judiciary," *Modern Law Rev.* 30, no. 3 (1967): 273–75; J. M. Eekelaar, "Rhodesia: The Abdication of Constitutionalism," *Modern Law Rev.* 32, no. 1 (1969): 22–23; F. M. Brookfield, "The Courts, Kelsen, and the Rhodesian Revolution," *University of Toronto Law J.* 19, no. 3 (1969): 331–32; Wood, *A Matter of Weeks*, 148, 296, 310.

Five justices agreed: the Rhodesian Front government was the de facto government. Even the two judges who dissented argued that while the government could not be called de facto, the necessities specific to Rhodesia in 1966 required the court to recognize its laws. Two justices argued that the RF government was the de jure government. Both argued that Rhodesia had a de facto government but that government had acquired "internal *de jure* status" in that all its laws had binding force. Rhodesians, judges and ordinary citizens alike, were required to obey the laws of the government functioning "for the time being" within Rhodesia.[50]

While judges joked that they would be removed after reaching the decision, Ian Smith was thrilled by what he called "de facto recognition." The judgment "is very good news for us," he told the royal agricultural show later that day. "It is an important milestone in our road."[51] It was not necessarily a new way of talking about the regime, however. As J. R. T. Wood has shown, the high court decision was a "legal confirmation" of ideas that had been in the Rhodesian Front air for several months. In March, for example, the ministry of information requested additional funds to "do publicity for UDI" and convince the United States, Australia, Germany, and France to accept "the de facto position" of Rhodesia.[52] The publicity may not have been necessary, as Rhodesia's status was unquestioned—as opposed to supported—by foreign countries. When Britain refused to export a quantity of Rhodesian banknotes ordered a few months before UDI, a firm in Munich was contracted to print them. In April 1966 those banknotes were seized at Frankfurt Airport at the request of the British government. The German county court released the banknotes, however, on the ground that even states that are not recognized by international law and treaties had the right to issue banknotes for use within their own territories. The decision was upheld by higher courts, which noted that given the unsettled political status of Rhodesia no country had the right to stop it from issuing its own currency.[53]

Could there be such a thing as a de facto government deserving of de facto recognition? This had happened in the mid-twentieth century.

50. Sir Sydney Kentridge, "A Judge's Duty in a Revolution—the Case of Madzimbamuto v. Lardner-Burke," *Commonwealth Judicial J.* 15, no. 2 (2003): 39; Eekelaar, "Rhodesia," 22; Marshall, "Legal Effects," 1028–29.

51. Goldin, *The Judge*, 68–69; Wood, *A Matter of Weeks*, 148–49.

52. Ministry of Information, supplementary estimates of expenditure 1965/66, Cabinet minutes, March 1, 1966, CL/Smith/20.

53. Goldin, *The Judge*, 135–36.

After World War II Britain granted de facto recognition to the Soviet client states of the Baltic, and seven countries had recognized the nationalist government of Indonesia before the Netherlands granted independence. Perhaps the best example was that of Tibet, treated as de facto independent despite its being under Chinese control. Until 1949 most European nations dealt with Tibet as if it were an independent state while recognizing Chinese suzerainty over it. I am not at all sure the cowboy cabinet was aware of this, but it is likely that many of the justices were, just as they must also have known how little difference there was between de facto and de jure.[54] The opinions in *Madzimbamuto and Baron v. Lardner-Burke* were not so much debates about the relative meanings of de facto and de jure as they were staked-out positions that were to inform each other until Rhodesia became a republic in 1970. That the government was declared de facto "until it attained de jure status" had meaning to those in the cabinet and electorate who did not believe that the Rhodesian government of mid-1966 had made a complete break with Britain.

Madzimbamuto and Baron v. Lardner-Burke has generated almost forty years of legal scholarship, almost all of which condemns the judges. The case was considered unique—it was "the okapi of justice" and "manna for jurisprudence"—and the judges were called craven.[55] They had abdicated their responsibility to the constitution, they misinterpreted legal doctrines of governance on the ground, they were ignorant of the broader context of decolonization, and they were indifferent to the fate of the African majority who would be subject to the constitution the judges empowered.[56] Most of this scholarship appeared shortly after the high court ruling. When he was interviewed by the national archives in 1972, Beadle complained that such criticisms were "so damn unjust." "We'd been trying our best to uphold the law . . . but international laws say if there is a revolution you apply the law as it exists and you do nothing to aid the revolution. That's exactly what we did." Indeed, Beadle thought the high court mediated some of the harsher laws of the RF government, "which we never could have done if we'd resigned."[57]

54. Peter Malanczuk, *Akehurst's Introduction to International Law*, 7th ed. (London: Routledge, 1997), 85, 88; I am grateful to Douglas Howland for the example of Tibet. See R. P. Anand, *Studies in International Law and History: An Asian Perspective* (Leiden: Martinus Nijhoff, 2004), 112–14.

55. The phrases are from Goldin, *The Judge*, 61–62; and Palley, "Judicial Process," 263.

56. Palley, "Judicial Process," 263–87; Marshall, "Legal Effects," 1022–34; Eekelaar, "Rhodesia," 19–34; Brookfield, "Rhodesian Revolution," 326–52; Kentridge, "Judge's Duty," 32–42.

57. Sir Hugh Beadle, February and June 1972, Bulawayo, NAZ/ORAL/BE2. Manuele Facchini has published a carefully researched rehabilitation of Beadle, showing how he tried to settle the Rhodesia crisis and end the rebellion. See Facchini, "'Evil Genius,'" 673–89.

Baron was released in April, 1967. Madzimbamuto's appeal went to the judicial committee of the Privy Council, five members of which found the Rhodesian government illegal in 1968. One of the two who found in favor of Rhodesia was Lord Pearce, whom we will meet again. When the high court refused to accept the Privy Council's judgment, two Rhodesians resigned in protest: "there was no alternative."[58]

Signs of Independence

I do not want to posit de facto and de jure as the two poles between which the state was governed. Instead they seemed to serve as a framework—rather than a frame—within which various aspects of statehood were practiced and performed. In other words, sometimes Rhodesia took the work of showing the world it was a sovereign independent nation very seriously, and sometimes it did not. To elaborate this I conclude this chapter with the debates about the signs of independence, what to name the currency, and how to choose, and perform, a national anthem.

Harold Wilson cast Rhodesia out of the sterling zone in 1966—thus sparing it the consequences of the devaluation of 1967—which brought the question of Rhodesia's currency to the fore. During the Central African Federation there had been suggestions that British pence and shillings be replaced by decimalized currency that would have a name specific to the region; these suggestions were revived during the banknote case of 1966. The recommendations of 1959 were: the dyke, the sable, the royal, the leaf, and the rhodes and the starr (for two heroes of the 1890s, Cecil Rhodes and Leander Starr Jameson), as well as an unspecified word from an African language. When the cabinet of the independent country of Rhodesia discussed these names in mid-1966, it rejected the royal because it invoked the Queen, and the rhodes and the starr on the grounds that the name of a currency should not be linked to that of a single individual. There was considerable sentiment for the rhodes, but cabinet ministers were quick to point out the problems it might cause. What would the plural be: would someone actually say "many rhodesses"? Would Rhodesia not become confused with Rhode Island, the smallest state in the United States, or with the Isle of Rhodes? And what if people spelled it "rowed" or "road"? The assembled

---

58. Wood, *A Matter of Weeks*, 296; Kentridge, "Judge's Duty," 40–42; Dendy Young's August 12, 1968, Statement, Correspondence between Dendy Young and various Rhodesian officials, May 1972, Cabinet Memoranda, 1972 CL/Smith/25.

ministers liked the leaf or the dyke as names, as both referred to tobacco and followed the South African example of naming currency after wealth—the rand—but they did not think Rhodesia should name
its currency after one sector of the economy. And everyone agreed it
would be impossible to find a vernacular word that would be acceptable to all Africans. Only John Wrathall, minister of finance, wanted a
name with international substance, the dollar. For Rhodesia to have a
"reputable position in the world" it should not have a currency that
referenced a picturesque history but one that was already recognized
around the world. Besides, the dollar was the name Rhodesia's financial
sector wanted.[59]

A new currency with a new name should signal a new nation in the
world, in control of its borders, its finances, and its trade. But given the
extent of sanctions and the necessity of breaking them, Rhodesia's trade
was invariably illegal and took place in national currencies other than
its own. The Rhodesian dollar did not replace shillings and pence until
1970, when it became as unique to Rhodesia as the rhodes would have
been, and its use abroad could only prove that trade was illegal. By the
mid-1970s in Rhodesia the dollar had competition: undated American
Express travelers checks were openly accepted in payment for goods and
services, as were British postal orders so long as they were left blank.[60]

Choosing a national anthem—lyrics and music that could link the
past and the present, or at least be played at the beginning and end
of radio and television transmissions—was postponed and postponed
again. Until 1969 Rhodesia used "God Save the Queen" without anxiety
or complaint. Once Rhodesia became a republic it was necessary to have
a new anthem to inspire national pride and, it was hoped, motivate
Rhodesian soldiers. Between 1969 and 1974 there were almost thirteen
hundred entries into government-sponsored competitions for the lyrics for the new national anthem, while the cabinet listened to record-
ings the merits and specificity of which it debated. Between 1969 and
1973 five sets of lyrics were combined to make the winning anthem. Its
lyrics were awkward but comprehensive ("Tints of our trees when the
leaves are unfolding" and "Deep as a mine be our true understanding"),
and several ministers urged that "God" be replaced by "Lord" so that
indigenous people might identify with the song. Although it was originally planned to have a second competition for the music, some in the

---

59. John Wrathall, Decimal currency: unit of currency, July 6, 1966, Cabinet Memoranda/3/1966;
Cabinet minutes, July 26 and October 4, 1966, CL/Smith/20.
60. Stack, *Sanctions*, 111.

government thought it best to import a tune. The best national anthems in the world—the French, the Israeli, and the South African, they said—were based on age-old melodies. A committee was sent to the Rhodesian Broadcasting Corporation studios and to military band rehearsals to get ideas. It did not find any appropriate music. One member of the committee suggested that a "modern" version of Beethoven's Ninth Symphony would make an ideal national anthem as it could be played as "a quick march, like the Marseilles." Everyone agreed this was the most suitable music they had heard, but several cabinet ministers worried that it might be another country's national anthem. One thought it might be that of Guatemala. The cabinet asked the South African Broadcasting Corporation's radio orchestra to record an extract from the symphony which was to help overcome copyright difficulties that were never fully explained.[61] The Rhodesian press was outraged: the music critic for *The Herald* was "dumbfounded" that the cabinet saw fit to plagiarize a melody with "supra-national associations" for "nationalistic ends." The editor of the *Umtali Post* wrote that he hoped that perhaps a Rhodesian could contribute something to Rhodesia's national anthem. By then the cabinet had rejected the proposed anthem as being "too lengthy and too much like a hymn." Another competition for lyrics was held. It took a year before the eight hundred entries were whittled down to fifteen, which the cabinet gave to the the minister for transport and power— he had a knack for poetry—who was told to take all the time he needed to choose the words for the national anthem. He seems to have taken too long, so the prize of R$500 was given to a South African–born woman in Gwelo, who had previously won a prize for naming a cocktail bar there. Her lyrics were proud and bland ("Guide us, Lord, to wise decision" and "Roaring in the mighty rivers") and were presented to the cabinet in September 1975.[62]

61. Secretary to the cabinet, the national anthem, July 23, 1969, Cabinet Memoranda/3/1969, CL/Smith/20; Cabinet minutes, July 3, 1973, October 30, 1973, CL/Smith/26.
62. Godwin and Hancock, *"Rhodesians Never Die,"* 145–46; Cabinet minutes, January 15, March 15, June 11, and August 20, 1974, CL/Smith/27.

FIVE

"A James Bond would be truly at home": Sanctions and Sanctions Busters

Whether Rhodesia was de facto independent or had de facto recognition hardly mattered. What gave Rhodesia the status of a state was the fact that it was criminalized: if nothing else, it is impossible to imagine a trade embargo against a colony. Mandatory sanctions, first by Britain and then by the United Nations, made Rhodesia a site, a locus of statehood that diplomatic recognition would have brought about. I am not arguing that sanctions legitimated Rhodesia but that by making its trade illegal sanctions provided a status that the entire world recognized. The invocation of James Bond, commonplace in Rhodesian accounts of sanctions busting, revealed membership in a global community made up of people who, even when they were not shady and corrupt, were not kith and kin.

Sanctions and Southern Africa

Rhodesia was the first pariah nation, sanctioned well before South Africa was. Despite the enthusiasm for economic sanctions in the mid-1960s, it was understood that their deployment marked a failure for Britain. What it could not achieve through the sheer weight of its influence and pressure it now had to do with the Commonwealth. Sanctions were to take the place of force.[1] Within a week of UDI, Britain sanctioned Rhodesian exports of tobacco, chrome, pig iron, copper, sugar, and much else, and it embargoed Rhodesian imports of oil. Harold Wilson told the Commonwealth conference in Lagos in January 1966 that the cumulative effect of sanctions might well end the rebellion "in a matter of weeks rather than months."[2]

Even before Rhodesians began to repeat this phrase with glee, it was clear that the oil embargo had almost no chance of succeeding. Rhodesia met two-thirds of its energy requirement with coal. With the help of oil company representatives, Rhodesia was able to secure oil through barely disguised British subsidiaries ("Oil Company of Malawi") working with Portugal and South Africa, neither of which signed onto the embargo. This gave Rhodesia access to ports from Walvis Bay in Namibia to Beira in Mozambique. In the first months after UDI, Rhodesia boasted that thirty-two tankers were headed toward Beira carrying crude oil for Rhodesia, but diplomats quickly learned these were "phantom tankers," a hoax by the Rhodesian government to prove that sanctions did not work. In methods Harold Wilson called more appropriate to James Bond than to the normal world of international commerce, oil did come to Rhodesia from Beira. The British managed to keep one ship from unloading its cargo and managed to secure a UN resolution allowing for a blockade of Beira harbor. This served to divert tankers to South African ports. It was a small victory, nevertheless, as Rhodesia maintained a refinery on the border with Mozambique.[3]

An oil embargo for Rhodesia meant an oil embargo for landlocked Zambia, however. Zambia supplied 15 percent of the copper used in the United States and Western Europe, much of it produced by mines in which the U.S. had a substantial interest.[4] Ninety-five percent of Zambia's exports and all its fuel, including petroleum, arrived by rail from Rhodesia. In anticipation of UDI and sanctions, Zambian cabinet

1. David L. Losman, *International Economic Sanctions: The Cases of Cuba, Israel, and Rhodesia* (Albuquerque: University of New Mexico Press, 1979), 98–100; David M. Rowe, *Manipulating the Market: Understanding Economic Sanctions, Institutional Change, and the Political Unity of White Rhodesia* (Ann Arbor: University of Michigan Press, 2001), 133–62; Wood, *Matter of Weeks*, 32–39.

2. Quoted in Flower, *Serving Secretly*, 61.

3. Ulrich Haynes to W. W. Rostow, Situation report for April 12 on Rhodesian Crisis, LBJ/NSF/Ulrich Haynes/1; Martin Bailey, *Oilgate*, 110–12, 146–61; Jorge Jardim, *Sanctions Double-Cross: Oil to Rhodesia* (Bulawayo: Books of Rhodesia, 1979), 69–71; Andrew Cohen, "Lonrho and Oil Sanctions against Rhodesia in the 1960s, *J. Southern African Studies* 37, no. 4 (2011): 715–30; Wood, *Matter of Weeks*, 32–34, 41–45, 70–72.

4. For U.S. involvement in Zambian mining, see DeRoche, *Black, White and Chrome*, 117–28; and Watts, *Unilateral Declaration of Independence*, 165–73.

ministers and mining company officials explored alternatives—could they substitute charcoal for coal in smelters, could they import coal in sufficient quantities from the newly opened coalfields of southern Tanzania, could they retool furnaces to run on oil instead of coal?—all of which were prohibitively expensive. Only the U.S. came up with a mildly optimistic forecast. Zambia could get by so long as it developed alternative modes of transport, to Tanzania or Mozambique in the east or to Angola in the west. In the first months of UDI, the U.S. paid for an airlift of oil to and copper from Zambia (and Katanga, as there was no runway large enough in Zambia to accommodate the cargo planes). Air transport was more efficient for exports—had the airlifts lasted a year they would have exported almost twice the tonnage that could be exported by road and rail—but much more expensive. By early April 1966 the U.S. informed Britain that it had reached its "financial limit" in supporting Zambia. Zambia then rented oil tankers from Britain and Japan to bring oil from Tanzania, but within a few years, as we shall see, there was very little enquiry into where Zambian exports went and where the country's imports came from.[5] The oil embargo continued but it was largely symbolic.[6]

The Wide World of Sanctions

Britain sought—and obtained—mandatory sanctions of Rhodesia from the United Nations at the end of 1966. This raised another set of issues. Britain's international authority was now nested in multilateral organizations, the most important of which, the UN General Assembly, had never been designed as an egalitarian body: the very fact of sanctions demonstrated that some states were powerful enough to punish others. But however much the UN had been designed to be a successor to colonial empires the General Assembly had been fashioned into an anticolonial instrument from its earliest years.[7] Sanctions against Rhodesia were not the first instance of this, but they were one of the most meaningful. Indeed, they provided the model for the UN sanctions that would

5. Good, *U. D. I.*, 89–95; Ulrich Haynes to Walt W. Rostow, memo, April 4, 1966, LBJ/NSF/Ulrich Haynes/1.
6. Bailey, *Oilgate*, 216–25; Cohen, "Lonrho," 729–30.
7. Gerry Simpson, *Great Powers and Outlaw States: Unequal Sovereigns in the International Legal Order* (Cambridge: Cambridge University Press, 2004); Mark Mazower, *No Enchanted Palace: The End of Empire and the Ideological Origins of the United Nations* (Princeton, NJ: Princeton University Press, 2009), 149–85.

become commonplace in the 1990s—against former Yugoslav republics, Libya, and Iraq—and for this reason have generated an enormous secondary literature. The frames of that literature are, in Neta Crawford's broad terms, that sanctions are either a trump card or theater, either a declaration of economic war or a performance, a statement of moral outrage enacted before the world community.[8] Opposition to sanctions is less studied, but they are no less a statement of moral outrage, not at the rogue nation but at the idea of international agencies that could assess what was criminal and what was not. Opposition to UN-imposed sanctions reveals the importance of the other Wilson and his Fourteen Points. As Erez Manela has shown, self-determination in its purest form was too risky a concept for the Treaty of Versailles, but anticolonial nationalists understood it to be embedded in the international organizations that were the legacy of the Paris Peace Conference. Rhodesian Front politicians and their supporters around the globe understood this when they complained about the UN or even the OAU that these bodies held self-determination and the idea of sovereign states for subject peoples at their core.[9]

When the United Nations banned member nations from purchasing Rhodesian exports, many Conservative MPs took the opportunity to argue that the real enemy of the rule of law was the UN, not Rhodesia. Rhodesia posed no threat, said one, but "it is a very new concept that nations may say that they so dislike what is going on in another country that they may declare it is a threat to peace." Others argued that Rhodesia was not an anomaly, that its actions were all too normal in the world after 1945. All "reasonable men," said another, were contemptuous of the UN, which had never suggested sanctions for Hungary, Tibet, or Zanzibar. Enoch Powell asked Parliament why sanctions were appropriate for Rhodesia but not for other countries "in a world half full of tyrannical regimes of various kinds."[10] These men spoke primarily to each other. The U.S. ambassador to the UN seconded the British proposals, despite mounting evidence that sanctions were not working.[11] The U.S. supported sanctions in the UN not necessarily because of their

8. Neta C. Crawford, "Trump Card or Theater? An Introduction to Two Sanctions Debates," in *How Sanctions Work: Lessons from South Africa*, ed. Neta C. Crawford and Audie Klotz (New York: St. Martin's, 1999), 2–24.

9. Erez Manela, *The Wilsonian Moment: Self-Determination and the International Origins of Anticolonial Nationalism* (Oxford: Oxford University Press, 2007), 60–61, 225.

10. Reginald Maulding and Gilbert Langdon, quoted in Miles Hudson, *Triumph or Tragedy? Rhodesia to Zimbabwe* (London: Hamish Hamilton, 1981), 58, 68; McNeil, "'Rivers of Blood,'" 737.

11. CIA Intelligence Memorandum, "Rhodesia: A Third Round of Sanctions," June 12, 1968, and "What Next for Rhodesia?" November 14, 1968, LBJ/ NSF/97; Horne, *Barrel of a Gun*, 174–93.

efficacy, but because the failure to do so would risk "domestic racial difficulties." Rhodesia was not an American concern so much as it was a platform from which the U.S. could make a diplomatic stand against racism.[12]

Outside the UN there was opposition to sanctioning Rhodesia, the most articulate spokesman for which was Dean Acheson. Acheson had been in the U.S. State Department, including serving as secretary of state, since the early 1940s. He was one of the architects of a world order in which American interests predominated. He was more romantic than the label of "cold warrior" would indicate which may have made him the ideal audience for the more flamboyant rhetoric of UDI. On leaving the State Department in 1954 he became a more cantankerous anticommunist than he had been in government.[13] He had long been pro-colonial and had no admiration for the UN of the 1960s, which he called "the international orphan asylum."[14] In a series of speeches, editorials, and letters to various editors written between 1966 and 1968, he supported Rhodesia not by praising what it was doing, but by disparaging the UN's right to sanction it. Rhodesia, he wrote, could not be punished for governing as it had done since 1923: if Rhodesia now claimed the independence in law it had practiced for over forty years there was no transgression, only the "crime" of severing its ties to Britain. Acheson argued that this was not a crime; the creation of early modern states should justify the creation of modern ones. "How fortunate were the American colonies in 1776 that there was no United Nations confronting them." As for the world after 1945, Rhodesia's domestic policies—most especially its voting laws—might be illegal in many countries in 1966, but they were not illegal in international law. It was the U.S. and not the UN that started "this Children's Crusade to universalize one-man-one-vote."[15] The U.S., the UN, and most of the Commonwealth insisted that Rhodesia was not itself a state, but part of another state, which meant that the imposition of sanctions by the legitimate sovereign could not be construed as intervention. This put Acheson on a

12. Horne, *Barrel*, 136; DeRoche, *Black, White and Chrome*, 105, 149–50; Francis Njubi Nesbitt, *Race for Sanctions: African Americans against Apartheid, 1946–1994* (Bloomington: Indiana University Press, 2004), 105–10.

13. Robert J. McMahon, *Dean Acheson and the Creation of an American World Order* (Washington, DC: Potomac, 2009), 198–208, 215–16.

14. Douglas Brinkley, *Dean Acheson: The Cold War Years, 1953–71* (New Haven, CT: Yale University Press, 1992), 303–5, 315–23.

15. This was disingenuous in the extreme. Acheson had been one of the architects of the gradual dismantling of universal suffrage in western European electoral practices after World War II, with multiple-preference voting, corrections to proportional representation, and requiring parties to win a minimum percentage of votes to compete in future elections. See Luciano Canfora, *Democracy in Europe: A History of an Ideology*, trans. Simon Jones (Oxford: Blackwell, 2006), 221–22.

train of thought that compared the UN's efforts at decolonization to Soviet aggression in the Cold War. Had not the USSR justified the invasion of South Korea by the North by saying the former was not a state? What would the world had done if the Soviet Union had appealed to the Security Council to sanction Czechoslovakia to keep it from implementing the policies it chose? If the issue was that Rhodesia's chosen policies were unacceptable to nearby nations, were not America's chosen policies unacceptable to Cuba? If the United States bestowed on the UN ("our own brainchild") the task of preventing threats to international peace, how might the U.S. look to Cuba or North Vietnam? The UN was so easily bullied by "Afro-Asian Communist delegations" that they made Rhodesia criminal, and the unintended consequences of the sanctions they imposed constituted a greater threat to peace in the region than Rhodesia's policies did.[16]

No one in the U.S. seemed to care what Acheson wrote, but he was adored in Rhodesia. He had a fawning correspondence with Lord Graham, among others, and many party hacks were pleased to call him their friend.[17] My point is less about Acheson's relative importance than it is about the way he, and the Conservatives in Britain he amplified, saw the UN as inimical to the interests of Great Britain and the United States. The argument of John Kelly and Martha Kaplan that decolonization after 1945 was shaped by the U.S. and imperial powers in multilateral organizations—which demanded the national citizenry that suited them, not the new nation—is perhaps too linear here. That of Mark Mazower may be more useful. Mazower has argued that the former colonials who did indeed take over the General Assembly—and did so on complex issues of nationality and minority rights—were as distrustful of the U.S. as they were of the British Empire, but not of the international order they had set up. As decolonization took place, new nations took the General Assembly, at least, as their own, and used it as a stage—again, the invocation of theater—for going against the will of the United States and Great Britain.[18]

---

16. These writings were reprinted as a pamphlet by the Rhodesian Information Office. *Dean Acheson on the Rhodesian Question* (Washington, DC: Rhodesian Information Office, n. d.), 5–6, 7, 12, 16–18, 21–24.

17. John Hartley Howman, Harare, six sessions June and July 1983, NAZ/ORAL/238. Dean Acheson correspondence, MS1087, Sterling Memorial Library, Yale University.

18. John D. Kelly and Martha Kaplan, *Represented Communities: Fiji and World Decolonization* (Chicago: University of Chicago Press, 2001), 18–29; John D. Kelly and Martha Kaplan, "Legal Fictions after Empire," in Howland and White, eds., *The State of Sovereignty*, 169–95; Mazower, *No Palace*, 188–91.

Tobacco Sales and Women's Stockings

Although there were regular complaints about the shortage of luxury goods—Angostura bitters and Marmite—the overall impact of sanctions on Rhodesia is difficult to gauge.[19] The figures for how much various countries imported from or exported to Rhodesia were contradictory in the extreme. At the end of 1966, for example, the Commonwealth Relations Office calculated that only the U.S., West Germany, and France were able to sanction more than 40 percent of imports from Rhodesia; Zambia was said to sanction 30 percent and the Congo, South Africa, and Portugal sanctioned none. That same year a report to the British parliament complained that both German and Japanese exports to Rhodesia increased by over 60 percent; French and Dutch exports increased by more than 20 percent. In 1968, Rhodesia's CIO claimed that only Britain and Scandinavian countries were enforcing sanctions; most other countries ignored the UN directive.[20] I shall return to Zambia's import figures later in this chapter, but the overall assessment of sanctions against Rhodesia is that they did not work, or if they did the ways in which they worked were subtle and roundabout. Andrew Cohen's 2011 article provides an excellent summary of this literature. According to Cohen there were those who considered sanctions insincere, that Wilson was simply trying to pacify African members of the Commonwealth with oil embargos and UN sanctions. Others considered sanctions insufficient to the task, that they not only failed to topple the Smith regime and did nothing to change its policies. Worse still, sanctions dissipated any calls for stronger action by the UN and unified the Rhodesian conservatives, thus making a settlement harder to achieve. A third body of literature argued that sanctions worked somewhat, that they slowed down Rhodesia's war effort by making materials harder to procure and encouraged changes in policy.[21] Indeed, the only people who claimed sanctions were effective

19. Angus Gabriel Koen, Arnot Collieries, Transvaal, August 18, 1986, NAZ/ORAL/263. As a child Wendy Kann would entertain her parents' dinner guests by singing out "Rhodesia has sanctions, and I can't have Marmite on my toast." Wendy Kann, *Casting with a Fragile Thread: A Story of Sisters and Africa* (New York: Picador, 2006), 60. Marion Kaplan was told that in anticipation of sanctions, measures were introduced to keep golfers from hoarding golf balls. Kaplan, "Their Rhodesia," 38–39.
20. Johan Galtung, "On the Effects of International Economic Sanctions: With Examples from the Case of Rhodesia," *World Politics* 19, no. 3 (1967): 378–416, from a table on 392; Handford, *Portrait of an Economy*, 21; Flower, *Serving Secretly*, 69.
21. Cohen, "Lonrho," 715–17. See also Robert B. Sutcliffe, *Sanctions against Rhodesia: The Economic Background* (London: Africa Bureau, 1966); and Rowe, *Manipulating the Market*, 133–62.

were Zimbabweans in the late 1980s eager to see mandatory sanctions imposed on South Africa. They insisted that sanctions would have crippled Rhodesia had it survived much longer.[22]

By 1968 Britain's failure to enforce the oil embargo seemed momentous, and even the U.S. lost its enthusiasm for sanctions as a weapon. Did sanctions fail because so few countries heeded them or because Rhodesians outsmarted the UN and Great Britain? Much as the Rhodesian Front wanted to think Rhodesia was admired around the globe, there was a tendency to credit a newfound sanction-busting smarts among Rhodesians. Ken Flower noted, not without some pride, that the government was willing to engage in any illegality necessary to circumvent sanctions. He quoted the chairman of Rhodesian Breweries: there was "a new and crooked generation of businessmen within Rhodesia smart enough to deal with the widest of wide boys."[23] Patrick Bond, well aware that the capitalist classes in Rhodesia were willing to engage in criminal activities, saw this as a triumph of financial controls that trapped local resources and the profits of multinational corporations. As a result, "sanctions busting became a national pastime."[24] John Handford, a Rhodesian economist, thought otherwise. Rhodesia was like Britain in the 1940s (of course). The dire predictions of economists "meant nothing in the face of the human spirit."[25]

Between the wide boys and the human spirit lay a planned economy. Before UDI the governor of the Reserve Bank moved some of Rhodesia's money into numbered accounts in Britain, which allowed Rhodesia to get most of their assets out of the United Kingdom and into European banks in the first days of UDI; a few weeks later Switzerland and the U.S. froze the assets of the Reserve Bank of Rhodesia. Rhodesia defaulted on its debts to London financial markets and the British government. Since Britain was the guarantor of some of the loans, it took over some of Southern Rhodesia's debt to the World Bank. British banks in Rhodesia moved their assets to South Africa throughout 1965: this allowed them to extend credit to Rhodesians whose accounts would have been blocked

22. William Minter and Elizabeth Schmidt, "When Sanctions Worked: The Case of Rhodesia Reexamined, "*African Affairs* 87, no. 347 (1988): 207–37.

23. Flower, *Serving Secretly*, 72.

24. Bond, *Uneven Zimbabwe*, 117–24. "We became very good at breaking laws," a journalist recalled. Author's field notes, Harare, May 3, 2014.

25. Handford, *Portrait of an Economy*, 3; Strack, *Sanctions*, 97–100.

otherwise. Rhodesia was removed from the sterling zone well before the devaluation of the British pound in 1967.[26]

The most detailed planning took place at the level of commodities. George Rudland, minister for commerce and industry, had campaigned against the 1961 constitution; he joined the Rhodesian Front right after it was founded. Along with several other ministers—John Wrathall, minister of finance, and Lord Graham, minister of agriculture—he had no questions about UDI other than "could we, or could we not, afford to take it?" For nine months he and three civil servants assessed Rhodesia's imports and exports. They filled thousands of pages of foolscap, he recalled, and listed every item imported into the country down to shoelaces and toothpaste and asked "how essential is this for the life of the country? Could we do without it? Can we do with less . . . ?" If the government prohibited or made no funds available for the import of an item, how long would it take for Rhodesian factories to produce it? Who had idle machinery that could be put to new uses?[27]

Many items were simply not imported after UDI. Andrew Dunlop, minister of transport and power and the man responsible for getting oil from Mozambique in 1966, considered sanctions "of great use to our country." They gave "a tremendous fillip to secondary industry." Cheap goods that had been manufactured for sale in Malawi and Zambia were now made with more expensive materials for sale to white Rhodesians. Local manufacturing boomed. Given the depth of Rhodesian industry before UDI by early 1967 it produced a range of goods the country had previously imported: veterinary medicines, chocolates, cosmetics, breakfast cereal, cube sugar, fifteen varieties of shampoo, and seven varieties of swimming pool paints.[28] In the first full year of UDI the value of exports fell by almost fifty million, within 3 percent of Rudland's calculations. He had not imagined that the oil embargo would be as successful as it was—"we did not consider that oil could be brought into Zambia by air"—and had underestimated the impact of sanctions on tobacco exports.[29]

By the early 1950s, tobacco was Southern Rhodesia's most valuable export, surpassing gold. By the early 1960s tobacco accounted for one-half

26. Brig. Andrew Dunlop, Salisbury, February 24 and April 13, 1972, NAZ/ORAL/DU2; Handford, *Portrait of an Economy*, 7, 18; Bond, *Uneven Zimbabwe*, 119.

27. George William Rudland, interview, NAZ/ORAL/RU3.

28. Andrew Dunlop interview, NAZ/ORAL/DU2; T. R. C. Curtin, "Rhodesian Economic Development under Sanction and 'the Long Haul,'" *African Affairs* 67, no. 267 (1968): 100–110; Handford, *Portrait of an Economy*, 7; Losman, *Economic Sanctions*, 11.

29. George Rudland interview.

of the country's agricultural production and one-third of its exports. Sanctions hit hard. For most of the late 1960s tobacco prices were so low that small farmers or those who had only begun farming a few years earlier could not survive. Large landowners, men with diversified farms, survived the first years of sanctions and bought up foreclosed farms with great speed. The remaining tobacco growers were encouraged, often with interest-free loans, to reduce their production by one-third, but by 1970 it was clear that the number of growers had declined and that many of the ones who remained would never grow tobacco again. Those who did were to take advantage of a dramatic rise in demand beginning in 1973.[30] Owners of large farms diversified even further, however, so that by the mid-1970s they supplied over 75 percent of Rhodesia's food.[31]

The economic planning took the human spirit into account. When Rudland presented this material to the cabinet, one civil servant told of a recent trip he had made to Eastern Europe. It was "dreadful," he said. "There's nothing that gets a people of a country down more than for men who are supposed to go and do a day's work and they get to their office and their secretary looks pale, no color, no paint, no powder, her hair is not waved, and she's got the same color frock as everyone else in the office." He asked that three items be added to the list: cosmetics, stockings and foundation garments. Why? Because if the project of independence required that men be asked to work "an extra three or four hours a day," in the civil service and in business, "you'll only get away with it" if the women they came home to "looks at least cheerful and attractive." If a man puts in extra hours—"and worked damn hard"—and then goes home to "a most unattractive-looking old hag of a wife, he'll say 'What the hell am I doing?'" "We took this seriously," Rudland said. "We worked this out, we said 'how much will this cost?'" And indeed, he boasted, after UDI no one could find "any girl who has not been able to get her cosmetics and stockings."[32]

---

30. British tobacco companies were the largest purchasers of Rhodesian tobacco, of which the country had an enormous stockpile in 1965; it ran out in 1968. Steven C. Rupert, *A Most Promising Weed: A History of Tobacco Farming and Labor in Colonial Zimbabwe, 1890–1945* (Athens: Ohio University Press, 1998), 9-10; C. G. Tracey, *All for Nothing: My Life Remembered* (Harare: Weaver Press, 2009), 111–12; Handford, *Portrait of an Economy*, 98, 105–6; D. C. Smith, Minister of Agriculture, Tobacco Quotas, January 22, 1970, Cabinet Memoranda, 1970 CL/Smith/24; Albert Thomas Holloway, Harare, October 24, 1986, NAZ/ORAL/255.

31. Pilossof, *Unbearable Whiteness*, 20.

32. George Rudland interview. Rhodesian women were less convinced of the availability of foundation garments but claimed to dress for patriotism: "We'd rather swing with Smith than rely on Wilson for support." Author's field notes, Harare, July 20, 1999.

With the Wide Boys

Civil servants and businessmen did work extra hours. In 1966 and 1967 Rhodesia's protective security officer—the man in charge of detentions—and five corporate directors worked overnights to unload Peugeot car kits bartered from France and illegally brought into Rhodesia by rail from South Africa. After a day's work they returned home to dine with presumably well-coifed wives. Then they changed their clothes and went to the Willowdale Ford factory, where they unloaded and unpacked boxes, returning home to sleep for a few hours before going to their offices in the morning.[33] How the car kits made it to Salisbury was the story of sanctions busting, of illegal deals and circuitous networks and tasks performed at night.

Sanctions busting did not fully account for the economic success of the early years of UDI, but it helped. By 1967 domestic investment soared, the construction industry boomed, and the business and manufacturing sectors began to cooperate with each other in activities that were often illegal. The small businesses that had almost all opposed UDI in 1964 and 1965 were now profitably linked to exporters who forged trade relations from companies in temporary quarters in the back streets of European cities. "Here a James Bond would truly be at home," John Handford wrote. Sanctions busting provided "a touch of the swashbuckle"; it was "stimulating" and sanctions busters themselves were "ingenuous, brazen, deft, and inventive."[34]

Sanctions busting was romantic; it was exciting. Two scholars writing about former Yugoslav republics have made suggestive arguments for the state-building potential of violating sanctions. Peter Andreas has argued that sanctions criminalize both domestic and international economies; they promote "uncivil society" in which smuggling is normal and smugglers heroic. Aida Hozic has argued that criminal networks created alternate political maps to those drawn and authorized by international agencies. Smugglers animate older relationships and build new alliances.[35]

33. Col. Henry Melville deBerdt Romilly, NAZ/ORAL/247; Peter Armstrong, *Tobacco Spiced with Ginger: The Life of Ginger Freeman* (Harare: Welston Press, 1987), 139.
34. Handford, *Portrait of an Economy*, 17–18, 21; Bond, *Uneven Zimbabwe*, 122–24; Godwin and Hancock, *"Rhodesians Never Die,"* 54.
35. Peter Andreas, "Criminalizing Consequences of Sanctions: Embargo Busting and Its Legacy," *International Studies Quarterly* 49 (2005): 335–60; Aida Hozic, "The Paradox of Sovereignty in the Balkans," in Howland and White, *The State of Sovereignty*, 243–60. For a somewhat more mechanistic view, see Charles Tilly, "War Making and State Making as Organized Crime," in *Bringing the State*

In Rhodesia, according to Ken Flower, Greeks and Jews "were more than willing to set up dummy companies and disguise the Rhodesian origin or destination of certain goods." Abroad, Rhodesia "found friends" in Brazil, Yemen, Mauritius, and the Soviet Union. And beyond: tons of tobacco was sold to Yugoslavia and France. West German firms developed a keen interest in Rhodesia after it was sanctioned. One company printed Rhodesian banknotes, and when that proved legally complicated, another sold printing equipment to a Rhodesian printer.[36] Taiwan offered to trade openly with Rhodesia on the condition that it ceased smuggling tobacco into the People's Republic of China. In 1970 Israel approached Rhodesia about purchasing tobacco with funds that had been set aside by the Jewish community to ensure its speedy and safe exit from the country should that become necessary. Everyone in the Central African Zionist Organization signed off on such a deal, but the Reserve Bank hesitated. It was reluctant to sell so much tobacco for local currency.[37] Flower understood that many of these new friends were commercially motivated, but he could not help but ask if they would have broken sanctions with such enthusiasm had they not believed in "what Rhodesia stood for."

All this left the dukes and their cricket matches far behind: the empire, and whatever citizenship it had left, was no longer relevant, or no longer as relevant as these new associations were. Rhodesians celebrated their unlikely friends. Any dealings with the Soviet Union delighted Rhodesian authors. Why, one wrote, did the captain of a ship of convenience ferry Rhodesian tobacco to a Baltic port? Because he appreciated the "irony of a right wing rebel government defying Britain and the United Nations to sell its product behind the Iron Curtain."[38] Biafra took on great significance in sanctions-busting stories. There were many stories of Rhodesia's helping the brave new nation, with rifles flown in by a Rhodesian who had been a mercenary in Katanga or by a legendary Rhodesian-born pilot who flew beef and small arms to Biafra and whoever else on the African continent would buy them. Flower claimed Rhodesia's CIO had operations in Biafra. What they were and what they hoped to accomplish he did not say, but that Rhodesian pilots flew

Back In, ed. Peter Evans, Dietrich Ruesdchemeyer, and Theda Stocpole (Cambridge: Cambridge University Press, 1985), 169–87.

36. Armstrong, *Ginger*, 176–78; Flower, *Serving Secretly*, 72, 75, 77; Tracey, *All for Nothing*, 109–10. West Germany admitted to violating sanctions when it kept the graphite mine it owned in Rhodesia open after UDI. Strack, *Sanctions*, 127.

37. Armstrong, *Ginger*, 189, 158–59.

38. Armstrong, *Ginger*, 151.

newly printed money for Biafra from Rome to Togo.[39] The Rhodesian state did not itself smuggle, but any number of African despots knew they could call on Rhodesia for help when they were "unlikely to find it anywhere else." Rhodesia's CIO devoted much of its time to finding the most reliable of "inherently unreliable" arms dealers.[40] Sanctions busters positioned themselves as outside politics, whatever Ken Flower imagined: they were smug and clearly thought their workings of market forces were far more civil than any society wrought by politicians. According to his biographer, Ginger Freeman was furious that there was a breach in the security of his clandestine negotiations to sell tobacco to Portugal. "Why can't these bloody politicians get themselves sorted out? Why do they have to go and stuff up a thriving industry in a beautiful country?"[41]

Sanctions busting was not reported in the Rhodesian press; tobacco sales were secret and accurate statistics nonexistent.[42] This seems to have created a space in which the James Bond figures wrested the national narrative away from the apparatchiks who prattled on about Sparta and Lepanto and evils of socialist Britain. They became larger than life, as good fictional heroes tend to be, and they inhabited a world unrestrained by the limits of kith and kin. The sanctions-busting heroes of Rhodesian fiction were debonair men at home in any European or African capital, who knowingly or unknowingly courted KGB agents, and who could secretly deal in any number of commodities while double-crossing African nationalists.[43] These men had no difficulty crossing borders. Some traveled without the inconvenience of having their passports stamped, while others had effortlessly acquired Malawian citizenship or kept their British passports.[44] Harvey Ward was a Rhodesian-born broadcaster who read the nightly news; he had been able to travel to and from Britain during UDI. In the early 1980s he wrote a novel, *Sanctions Buster,* which he claimed was "seventy-five per cent true." It ends with the funeral of the suave, sanctions-busting hero, who was killed in Britain by a member of the Baader-Meinhof gang hired by a UN sub-

39. Wessels, *PK,* 137–38; Flower, *Serving Secretly,* 75–76; Hancock and Godwin, *"Rhodesians Never Die,"* 53, 309.

40. Flower, *Serving Secretly,* 73, 76.

41. Armstrong, *Ginger,* 162.

42. Good, *U. D. I.,* 212.

43. Some or all of these traits appear in Meredith Cutlack, *Blood Running South* (London: Collins, 1972); Michael Hartmann, *Game for Vultures* (London, Pan Books, 1976 [1975]); Jack Watson, *Conspire to Kill* (Salisbury: Penn Medos, 1976); Lloyd Burton, *The Yellow Mountain* (Salisbury: Regal Publishers, 1978); Dennis Pitts, *Rogue Hercules* (New York, Athenaeum, 1978); Sylvia Bond Smith, *Ginette* (Bulawayo: Black Eagle Press, 1980); Harvey Ward, *Sanctions Buster* (Glasgow: William Maclellan Embryo, 1982).

44. Cutlack, *Blood Running South;* Hartmann, *Game for Vultures,* 245; Burton, *Yellow Mountain.*

committee to assassinate him. At the graveside an MP regrets that men such as the hero—"he was more British than anything else"—and Lord Graham were banned from entering the UK.[45]

Outside of fiction, Rhodesians dealt easily with Francophone Africa, having begun trade with Gabon a few years after UDI. Rhodesia had its own air company based there. The company went by a succession of names, Rhodesia Air Service, Air Trans-Africa, Affretair, and occasionally Air Gabon Cargo. Rhodesia supplied meat to Gabon's armed forces; it was "an open secret" that the meat trade was a cover for sending flowers to the markets of Amsterdam via Libreville and for bringing in goods, most especially spare parts for cars and machinery, back from Europe. The customs agent in charge made nominal reports to the Ministry of Foreign Affairs in Salisbury; his main job, he said, was to develop commercial contacts for Rhodesian exporters. Rhodesians used a system of thirty-day payment through a French bank; they paid in CFA francs.[46] Funds could be withdrawn in Paris or anywhere in Francophone Africa. Most of this money was to pay for fuel, which was cheaper in Gabon: Rhodesia always paid in CFA francs. "It was a very simple and elastic system. There was no problem at all." Air Trans-Africa had a small fleet of DC7s—"probably the only line in the world operating them on a regular basis"—painted green with no other markings. In 1972 it acquired a DC8 from the U.S. "by devious means" and everyone was thrilled: it could carry twice as much cargo. Air Trans-Africa had a code to tell Salisbury which plane would be flying back there, the DC8 was "Pegasus" and a DC7 was "old Ford."[47] Funds kept in Paris were also used by the Rhodesian Air Force to buy small planes. When a dozen Cessnas were purchased directly from the factory in Rheims in 1976, they were flown to Rhodesia in varied short routes across Africa so as not to arouse suspicion. To be safe, the Rhodesian Air Force made up a fictitious company and painted its colorful logo on the side of each aircraft: the Malagasy Fisheries Surveillance Team.[48]

Why Malagasy? Why not? Liisa Malkki, writing on the persistence of territorial ideas about nationhood, noted that nations are fixed on

45. Ward, *Sanctions Buster*; Harvey Ward, London, July 4 and October 17, 1984, NAZ/ORAL/246. I am not doing justice to this plot, which centers on Chinese plans to build a neutron bomb on Zanzibar to subdue Southern Africa.

46. *Communauté Financiere Africaine*, the currency used in Francophone Africa starting in 1960 and pegged to the franc in France.

47. Flower, *Serving Secretly*, 75–76; van der Syde, interview, NAZ/ORAL/267; Wessels, *PK*, 137–39.

48. Winston Brent, *Rhodesian Air Force: The Sanction Busters* (Nelspruit: Freeworld Publications, 2001), 66–70, 74–77; Beryl Salt, *A Pride of Eagles: A Definitive History of the Rhodesian Air Force, 1920–1980* (Weltevreden Park: Covos-Day, 2001), 522–27.

maps. "A country cannot at the same time be another country."[49] But it is precisely this territoriality that sanctions busting disrupts. In practice sanctions busting meant that Rhodesia managed most of its exports by labeling them the products of other countries. Zambia is a case in point. From the first British sanctions it was understood that Zambia was dependent on goods produced in or transported through Rhodesia. In 1968 and again in 1970 UN resolutions urged member nations to assist Zambia in its efforts to sanction Rhodesian imports. As we have seen, in 1966 Zambia claimed to have reduced its imports from Rhodesia by 30 percent. By 1970 the UN could report that Zambia had reduced Rhodesian imports by an astounding 81 percent, although it also reported that the amount of imports from South Africa, Mozambique, and Malawi was greater than the exports those countries traded to Zambia. It was understood that Rhodesian goods were first exported to South Africa, Malawi, and Mozambique and then exported to Zambia.[50]

The Metal and the Material

Organic products cannot be relabeled to the same extent that clothing or breakfast cereal can. The value of specific varieties of tea and coffee, to name but two examples, is determined in large part by where they are grown. Tobacco is somewhat different in that most varieties can be grown in different locales and because part of the value comes from the curing process. Rhodesia's most profitable tobacco, Virginia, was the same as the yellow-leaf, flue-cured tobacco grown so successfully in the United States and Brazil. The Rhodesian tobacco was cheaper to produce than was that of the U.S. and had lower pesticide levels than tobacco grown there or in Brazil.[51] Another variety, called Oriental or Turkish, was distinctive, but Rhodesia was one of several producers: as with Virginia, once it was blended into cigarette tobacco its place of origin was undetectable. The Rhodesian tobacco industry was crippled in the first years of sanctions. The government bought tobacco; what could not be sold was stockpiled. Very little tobacco was exported in

49. Liisa Malkki, "National Geographic: The Rootedness of People and Territorialization of National Identity among Scholars and Refugees," *Cultural Anthropology* 7, no. 1 (1992): 22–44.
50. George T. Yates III, "The Rhodesian Chrome Statute: The Congressional Response to United Nations Economic Sanctions against Southern Rhodesia," *Virginia Law Review* 58, no. 3 (1972): 534, 540; Handford, *Portrait of an Economy*, 23–24.
51. Strack, *Sanctions*, 94–95; Rupert, *Promising Weed*, 5–6, 13, 15; Hughes, *Whiteness in Zimbabwe*, 76–77.

1966 and 1967; what was exported was sold as the produce of Brazil, or sold or bartered to suppliers who relabeled it themselves. By the late 1960s, however, Rhodesian farmers claimed small but regular shipments of tobacco were sold to British manufacturers who did not question certificates of origin from Mozambique and Angola. Tobacco was most often trucked to Namibia or Angola and exported from there as Romanian or Bulgarian tobacco.[52]

Inorganic materials exported under sanctions were supposed to be transparent; they could come from anywhere. Minerals, at least copper and nickel, were to be Rhodesia's ace in the hole, so to speak: inanimate matter from beneath the earth looked just like that matter found underground in other countries. As Benedict Anderson pointed out, labeling ancient subterranean things as belonging to the country within whose borders they were found is a commonplace fiction of nationalism. Calling a dinosaur skeleton Canadian or gold South African or Russian is not historically accurate, but it is a well-established, totalizing way of describing a national patrimony, of classifying and counting what belonged to a nation and thus—and at least as important—belonged to no other nation.[53]

Rhodesia, however, sought to dispense with that fiction for the purposes of sanctions busting and planned to sell minerals slightly below the world market price so as to facilitate swift and reliable sales. In this way some minerals, like pig iron and iron ore, were exported through South Africa by French metal-trading firms. Until mid-1967—before UN sanctions came into full effect—the profits from these exports were the same as they were before UDI. After 1968 these exports still went from South Africa to Paris, but then were re-exported through a complicated network of French-owned firms. Other minerals, however, were thought to bear the taint of national origins. In 1967 the *Sunday Times*, one of the key sources for stories of sanctions busting, reported that Rhodesian copper was exported to Germany, where it was refined once more and thus made "undetectable" from that of any other nation.[54] This raises another question altogether: if Rhodesian copper could be refined to appear to be that of another country, was it still Rhodesian copper?[55] Was

52. Armstrong, *Ginger*, 145, 212–16; Strack, *Sanctions*, 93–94; Tracey, *All for Nothing*, 111–12.

53. Benedict Anderson, *Imagined Communities: Reflections on the Origins and Spread of Nationalism*, rev. ed. (London: Verso, 1991), 184.

54. Handford, *Portrait of an Economy*, 22, 125.

55. Copper ingots, whatever their origin or whatever their impurities, were sold in international commodity markets for a single price, as Zambia learned after a lengthy U.S. copper mine strike was settled. In 1968 the world price of copper plunged from seventy cents to forty-five cents, and

the nature of a metal determined by its place of origin or its chemical content?

Nowhere was the question of content and provenance greater than in the saga of Rhodesian chrome.[56] How chrome was sanctioned and then imported and once again banned by the U.S. has created the most detailed study of the practice of sanctions we have. It is a body of literature that allows me to ask what constitutes belonging to Rhodesia: if an ore comes out of an American-owned mine in Rhodesia and is sold to a country via another country, why is it Rhodesian chrome? The history of the chrome embargo is in part a story about the United States and Rhodesia and in part a story about the content of a metal. Chrome is used in the production of stainless steel; the higher the metallurgical grade of chrome used (46 percent or more chromic oxide), the higher the temperature the stainless steel can withstand, thus chrome of the highest metallurgical grade was used in the U.S. space program. The lesser grades were combined with other ores to produce linings for blast furnaces or in lead-based paints. Rhodesia's chrome mines produced all three grades of chrome, including the highest metallurgical grade. By 1963, most of these mines were owned by American companies: Union Carbide owned two large mines, Vanadium owned several smaller mines, and Foot Chemical owned a few small ones. As the demand for chrome increased Union Carbide built a smelter in Que Que so as to export ferrochrome rather than bulk ore.[57]

Whoever owned Rhodesia's chrome mines, before 1965 the U.S. purchased most of its metallurgical grade chrome from the USSR. After sanctions were imposed, there was not much change; U.S. imports of Soviet chrome increased. In 1971, after years of conservative politicians' attempts to get the U.S. to recognize Rhodesia or at least buy something from it, the Byrd Amendment to a military procurement bill passed Congress and became law. It allowed the U.S. to violate sanctions in importing those metals that were vital to national defense, including if not especially chrome. This is a story told most often by American historians as one of the U.S. flaunting UN resolutions, of U.S. dissembling about

---

continued to decline in the early 1970s. Handford, *Portrait of an Economy*, 126; C.I.A., "Troubles Ahead for Zambia," special memorandum, June 18, 1968, LBJ/NSF/102.

56. Gabrielle Hecht has written about the separation of product form provenance in the export of uranium from Namibia; see Gabrielle Hecht, *Being Nuclear: Africans and the Global Uranium Trade* (Cambridge: MIT Press, 2012), 151–70.

57. Almost all small workers' chrome mines had been sold by early 1963. A decade later, foreign firms spent over R$5 million a year prospecting and mining. Handford, *Portrait of an Economy*, 127; Strack, *Sanctions*, 94; Tracey, *All for Nothing*, 170.

national security, of Richard Nixon's indifference to laws written by racist senators from the southern states. It is the story of the U.S. once again choosing anticommunism over racism.[58] None of this is false, but I want to recast this story to write specifically about the nature of Rhodesian chrome.

Who was buying Rhodesian chrome when the U.S. was not? The UN and British figures indicate that a great deal of Rhodesian chrome was taken to South Africa and exported as South African metal. Indeed, between 1964 and 1970 Japanese chrome imports from South Africa increased by 1,775 percent, while western European chrome imports from South Africa increased by over 250 percent. Japan imported almost a hundred thousand metric tons more chrome from South Africa than the country exported.[59] Britain protested to the Japanese government that it was buying Rhodesian chrome, and the UN received formal complaints that Mexico, Brazil, Finland, and Yugoslavia purchased Rhodesian chrome.[60] The U.S. increased its imports of Rhodesian chrome after the Byrd Amendment—the tonnage more than doubled between 1974 and 1975—but continued to buy most of its chrome from the USSR. But was this really Soviet chrome? Rhodesians believed and the entrepreneur C. G. Tracey insisted that Soviet chrome was Rhodesian chrome relabeled. Starting in 1966 Tracey was involved in helping the U.S. steel industry acquire Rhodesian chrome in spite of sanctions. Chrome was stockpiled in Rhodesia and in Mozambique. Rhodesian officials began to "secretly" sell it to the USSR at a discount of 40 percent below the world market price. According to Tracey, the chrome was trucked to Lourenço Marques, in Mozambique, where it was loaded onto a Soviet ship. The captain's orders were to sail to a Black Sea port via Gibraltar. The captain was ordered to open a second envelope when he was five days out to sea: this one would instruct him to change direction and head for a U.S. port in the Gulf of Mexico.[61]

58. Raymond Arsenault, "White Chrome: Southern Congressmen and Rhodesia, 1962–71," *Issue: A J. of Opinion* 3, no. 4 (1972): 46–57; Gale W. McGee, "The US Congress and the Rhodesian Chrome Issue," *Issue* 2, no. 2 (1972): 2–7; Strack, *Sanctions*, 146–52; Lake, *The 'Tar Baby' Option*, 198–26; Horne, *Barrel of a Gun*, 150–52, and DeRoche, *Chrome*.

59. A few weeks after UDI, Salisbury industrialists told Marion Kaplan "sanctions against Rhodesia would be awkward for Japan." Kaplan, "Their Rhodesia," 38.

60. Yates, "Chrome Statue," 536–39. When countries were suspected of importing Rhodesian goods, the relevant UN committee sent letters of protest. In theory such countries could themselves be sanctioned for violating sanctions, but none were. Only Yugoslavia refused to unload a shipment of chrome after receiving such a letter.

61. Strack, *Sanctions*, 145; Tracey, *All for Nothing*, 171; Handford, *Portrait of an Economy*, 127; Wood, *Matter of Weeks*, 175.

As a James Bond story, a ship changing course after five days at sea—in the dark of night, I hope—trumps a colorful logo on a Cessna every time, but was it true? By the early 1970s Ian Smith was fond of saying he had "more than a suspicion" that communist countries were buying Rhodesian chrome and selling it as their own. Although China had made a major purchase of metallurgical chrome in 1967, there were no complaints that the USSR traded with Rhodesia. However much Smith gloated about the content of Russian chrome, such boasts made the Rhodesian mining industry indignant. Russian chrome was of a low grade compared to that of Rhodesian chrome. Although Rhodesia had many markets for its chrome in the 1970s, there were persistent anxieties that the Soviet Union was using chrome as a "Cold War weapon" with which it would create a monopoly that would leave the U.S. steel industry at its mercy.[62]

Soviet chrome did not so much create a monopoly as it did an obsession in the U.S.: how much of it was really Rhodesian chrome? Proponents of sanctions came up with indirect ways to find out. If Rhodesian chrome was sold to the USSR below world market prices, and if Soviet chrome was more expensive after 1966 than it had been before, then clearly the Soviets were exploiting sanctions for its own ends. It was impossible to prove this, however, because the price of metallurgical-grade chrome sold to the U.S. and everywhere else rose between 1966 and 1971. Proponents of sanctions interrogated the price of Soviet chrome to see if a Rhodesian price could be detected within it. This too turned out to be impossible to prove, first because between 1966 and 1971 the USSR had lowered the guaranteed chromic oxide content of their exported chrome, from 55 to 48 percent and, second, because the method of calculating the price for chrome changed during that time. All anyone could say for certain was that Soviet chrome was consistently cheaper than Turkish chrome.[63]

After the Byrd Amendment, after the U.S. continued to import chrome from the USSR, proponents of sanctions intensified their efforts to discover Rhodesian chrome in Soviet imports. By June 1972 there was a new kind of alchemy in play. Instead of a chemical process that would turn a base metal into gold, chrome was tested to find out how base it really was: was it the product of a racist, outlaw nation? Every chrome mine has a distinctive titanium fingerprint; ascertaining the titanium content of chrome should pinpoint its place of origin. Companies

62. Handford, *Portrait of an Economy*, 127.
63. Lake, *The 'Tar Baby' Option*, 252–53, 254n; Handford, *Portrait of an Economy*, 127.

performed their own tests. Colt Industries, the parent company of Crucible Steel, discovered the Soviet ore they had purchased contained Rhodesian ore. At the same time the U.S. Geological Survey—assumed to be neutral in the battle over chrome sanctions—performed its own tests and found that the Soviet ore they sampled did not contain discernible amounts of Rhodesian chrome; the titanium content was too low. Such tests came too late for opponents of the Byrd Amendment: worse still, they created grave doubts that there was a viable way to ban Rhodesian chrome imports.[64] Efforts to repeal the Byrd Amendment sought to extend sanctions to ban products used in the production of stainless steel that were not imported from their country of origin, and that might be Rhodesian in origin. The UN did not sanction steel mill products imported via a third country.[65] In 1975 the supervising chemist for Armco Steel told a congressional committee that stainless steel could not be tested for residual Rhodesian ores. The concentrations required to determine the place of origin of any element was masked by the presence of the same element in other raw materials.[66] Rhodesian chrome could indeed be brought into any country undetected.

In 1977 a change of administration in the U.S. ushered in a new, or sort of new, era in relations with Southern Africa. Even before Jimmy Carter took office, C. G. Tracey's multiple entry visa was canceled.[67] Once Carter took office, the Byrd Amendment was repealed: administration officials testified before Congress that sanctions had to be reinstated to force Rhodesia to move toward majority rule.[68] By 1977, however, Rhodesia did not have many problems finding trading partners, but the economy was stagnant and in need of capital. South Africa's Anglo-American Corporation had bought Foot Chemical's holdings in Rhodesia in 1976, but Vanadium and Union Carbide mines remained in U.S. hands.

The saga of Rhodesian chrome exports to the U.S. puts the ambiguities of sanctions busting into high relief. The country that exports

64. Edgar Lockwood, "An Inside Look at the Sanctions Campaign," *Issue* 4, no. 3 (1974): 74; Tracey, *All for Nothing*, 171; Lake, *The 'Tar Baby' Option*, 256–57.

65. David R. MacDonald, testimony before the House of Representatives, June 19, 1975, Gerald Ford Library, Ann Arbor, Michigan [hereafter GFL]/David R. MacDonald Papers/18.

66. The titanium present in the Rhodesian ore they tested was .04 percent; the titanium in Soviet ore was .03 percent. Richard Knaur, Armco Steel, Statement for the House International Relations Subcommittee, June 19, 1975, GFL/David R. MacDonald Papers/18.

67. When Tracey met Andrew Young, Carter's secretary of state, years later he paid him the "oblique compliment" of telling him how eager he had been "to take him out of the equation." Tracey, *All for Nothing*, 180.

68. DeRoche, *Chrome*, 247–48.

minerals under the label of another country wants it known that its chrome is present in the ore brought into another country, even when it is not. This may not be the same genre as the "phantom tankers" but it asks what is imagined by the imagined community? What is important here is the transnational reach not only of sanctions busting and James Bond and the clever and well-masked exports that stretched beyond South Africa and Gabon; it is the world of Flower's "new friends" and a new, however imaginary, membership in a community of nations that Rhodesia had taken UDI to avoid.

Dealing with Dollars

What could not be relabeled was Rhodesian currency. Even though the dollar had been chosen as its name because it had an international respectability—the U.S., Canada, Hong Kong, Australia, and Taiwan all had dollars—the Rhodesian dollar was polluted. Its very existence outside Rhodesia signaled that illegal trade had taken place: no one wanted it. Throughout the 1970s, as the guerrilla war intensified and as Rhodesia's survival seemed in doubt, individuals sought ways to obtain foreign exchange. There were many stories of small and private currency violations. Rhodesians sometimes bought foreign exchange from visitors or paid their hotel bills so that the equivalent would be deposited in foreign accounts. The press reported two company directors who bought ZAR1,000 from a South African resident in Salisbury, a game warden and his wife who put the unused portion of their travel allowance in a bank account a friend opened for them in Pretoria, and company directors accused of exporting goods to South Africa and not repatriating their earnings from them. There were persistent rumors that leading figures in the Rhodesian Front, perhaps some of the original cowboys, bred Brahmin cattle to export to South Africa: sales took place in Rhodesia for a modest price, and then the full value would be paid in South Africa, in rands.[69] Large currency violations were, like sanctions busting, not reported in the press; the trials of those individuals who were found out were held in camera. The only place I have found detailed descriptions of the export or Rhodesian dollars is in Rhodesian fiction.

In *Ginette* a corrupt businessman gives his lover—an innocent and law-abiding sales manager—instructions on how she can earn foreign

69. Strack, *Sanctions*, 108; Caute, *Under the Skin*, 265–66. One of the largest and most established Brahmin herds in Rhodesia belonged to Lord Graham. Shaw, *Mutoko Madness*, 57.

exchange "by bits of paper." Her task is to bribe the sales agent to produce two invoices, one for the company for the actual purchase price and one for the Ministry of Commerce and Industry at the inflated price. Once the Reserve Bank approved of this figure, the funds were remitted to Europe; the item was purchased for its true price, the sales agent was given 10 percent of the total, and the remainder was deposited in a foreign bank, preferably in Switzerland but anywhere other than Britain would do.[70]

Rhodesian dollars were tagged in a way chrome never was, so identifiable with the rebel regime they could not be used anywhere else. In fiction, however, they were given an international value: one Rhodesian novel begins with a sanctions buster carrying a suitcase of Rhodesian dollars and a cargo bay full of guns to arm the resistance Biafra planned to mount after the formal end of the civil war.[71] In fact, the Rhodesian dollar had a singular and stable market outside the country. Guerrillas seeking to overthrow the regime needed to enter Rhodesia with sufficient local currency to meet their needs. Dealers in Johannesburg bought Rhodesian dollars, smuggled out in the checked baggage of businessmen and savvy tourists, at a discounted rate and smuggled them into Botswana and resold them at a slightly less discounted price. The dollars eventually got to Zambia, where they were issued to the guerrillas operating in Rhodesia.[72] No one in Zambia could purchase Rhodesian dollars because of sanctions and exchange controls; only a small amount of Zambian currency could be taken out of the country without Reserve Bank permission. In *A Time of Madness*, however, a KGB agent stationed in Zambia circumvents this at a casino in Victoria Falls. He buys chips with Zambian kwacha which at the end of the night he converts to Rhodesian dollars. In no other venue in either country could he convert that many kwacha for that much Rhodesian money without arousing suspicion.[73]

Rhodesia's need for foreign exchange was met in very ordinary ways. American Express travelers checks, British postal orders (both left blank), and bankers' drafts and personal checks in any European currency but sterling were all accepted after 1970s.[74] In Rhodesian fiction this need was met in extraordinary ways. In *The Yellow Mountain* a German officer discovered a cache of gold with which the British planned

70. S. B. Smith, *Ginette*, 177–80.
71. Watson, *Conspire to Kill.*
72. S. B. Smith, *Ginette*, 180; Strack, *Sanctions*, 108.
73. Robert Early, *A Time of Madness* (Salisbury: Graham Publishing, 1977), 198–99.
74. Strack, *Sanctions*, 110–11.

to purchase the allegiance of desert nomads during World War II. The cache was located between a guerrilla training camp and an American team drilling for oil. When the officer's niece, married to a farmer in Rhodesia, learns of the gold she encourages her husband to bring it back to Rhodesia. Yes, she admits, it belongs to Britain, but "how many millions worth of Rhodesian funds have the British impounded?" Three Rhodesians, one of them a policeman traveling on his British passport, manage to find the gold, outwit the British treasury and guerrilla commanders and bring it to Rhodesia, where it is to fund the building of a wall along the eastern border.[75]

In the absence of buried treasure, Rhodesian war materials were costly. Sanctions offered the greatest scope for profiteering, kickbacks, currency fraud, and squirreling funds into illegal bank accounts abroad. How Rhodesia acquired planes and mines and guns was the stuff of sanctions-busting lore. There were the Cessnas, there were stories of arms dealers who were happy to barter guns for tobacco or meat, and most of the sanctions-busting heroes in Rhodesian wartime fiction buy at least one plane or helicopter. In nonfiction, Rhodesia paid dearly for arms. According to David Caute, a Belgian-made FN rifle that normally cost US$25 was sold to Rhodesia for US$80.[76] Nevertheless, officials maintained a studied ignorance about how hardware was purchased. When Jack Howman was minister of defence—and in frequent struggles to raise soldiers' pay—he claimed to have no idea how Rhodesia bought helicopters or land mines. The monies came from the treasury, or maybe the Reserve Bank, he said, he did not know where or how they obtained the funds.[77]

The innocence of bureaucrats and the daring sophistication of sanctions busters are a single narrative, the aggrieved Rhodesia rising to the occasion of its exclusion, of managing goods and currencies beyond its borders and beyond the imaginative reach of kith and kin. The plot of *The Yellow Mountain* moved Flower's claim of "new friends" into unchartered territory. Rhodesians accessed foreign exchange across space and time, with the help of the living and the dead.

75. Burton, *Yellow Mountain*. Anthony Chennells has argued that this novel is perhaps the best example of the fantasy of Rhodesians successfully taking on the world. Anthony Chennells, "Rhodesian Discourse, Rhodesian Novels and the Zimbabwe Liberation War," in *Society in Zimbabwe's Liberation War*, v. 2, ed. N. Bhehe and T. Ranger (Harare: University of Zimbabwe Press, 1995), 126–27.

76. Caute, *Under the Skin*, 266.

77. John Hartley Howman, Harare, June and July 1983, NAZ/ORAL/238.

SIX

"Politics as we know the term": Tribes, Chiefs, and the 1969 Constitution

Britain and Rhodesia continued to negotiate after Rhodesia declared UDI. Only the governor could negotiate with the rebel regime, but British envoys could and did hold talks in Salisbury, in London, and on yachts outside territorial waters. Writing from Salisbury in May 1966, Sir Oliver Wright, Wilson's private secretary and a longtime diplomat, did not see any widespread sentiment, let alone pressure, for a settlement. He was, however, optimistic about sanctions, which he predicted would bring about "the day of fiscal reckoning" that would make the Rhodesian Front leadership rethink its rebellion. Wright was disappointed with that same leadership, which he compared not to a midsized British city but to the smallest British county. "One simply must not expect an excess of intellectual agility and speed of mind from an outfit the size of the Rutland County Council."[1]

Even before UDI all negotiations with Britain were organized around Harold Wilson's "five principles" that tallied Rhodesia's right to independence. The actual principles were: (1) There was to be the intention of "unimpeded progress toward majority rule." This meant that the 1961 constitution had to be "maintained and guaranteed," since by

1. Wood, *Matter of Weeks*, 109.

1965 both British and Rhodesian officials insisted that the 1961 constitution promised eventual majority rule. (2) There would be no retrogressive amendments of the 1961 constitution. (3) African access to the franchise would be improved. (4) There would be "progress towards ending racial discrimination." (5) The British government "would need to be satisfied" that any "proposed independence" was "acceptable to the people of Rhodesia as a whole."[2] The five principles were of great importance in Rhodesia, where Rhodesian Front apparatchiks and their critics tended to refer to them by number, and perhaps less important in Britain, where officials tended to use them to bargain with Rhodesia rather than demand they be adopted. Thus, in December 1966 Ian Smith and Harold Wilson met on the HMS *Tiger* on the sea off Gibraltar. Britain proposed very slight changes in the number of seats Africans and Europeans would hold in a new Rhodesian parliament, but Smith rejected these changes. He said he did so because they required the dissolution of the current parliament; he did not say what everyone assumed to be the case, that he rejected the proposals because the right wing of his government would not tolerate them. Almost two years later there were talks on the HMS *Fearless* to discuss the *Tiger* proposals once more, but these too failed. Most discussions centered on how to expand the A and B rolls to include more Africans. No one dared suggest an unfettered course to majority rule, but Britain hinted that they might exchange reserved seats for whites for an increased African electorate.[3]

The 1968 Constitutional Commission

In 1967, a year of no settlement talks, Rhodesia set up a constitutional commission. The country was no closer to majority rule than it had been in 1965, but it was not yet the pariah state it was to become. The new constitution had been promised for years. In an early justification of UDI that was remarkable for its insistence that race was at the core of the decolonization of Africa, Desmond Lardner-Burke complained, "If our skins were black we would have had our Independence—the British could not have cared less, but because we are white they feel they have a duty to impose upon us a system that would bring about the collapse

---

2. There are paraphrases of these principles in many texts. This wording was developed by Harold Wilson and Arthur Bottomley, secretary of state for Commonwealth Relations, in February 1965 and sent to Smith in September. Bottomley to Smith, September 21, 1965, in *Southern Rhodesia: Documents November 1963–November 1965*, 66.

3. Wood, *Matter of Weeks*, 106–8.

of the economy and . . . the country as a whole." Rhodesia had to "remain alone" to solve its own problems, to "find an answer that will not be to the detriment of any race" but would better the country "and all the races who occupy it." "Give us five years to test the genuineness of the European" and to work out a constitution "acceptable to all." Because the kind of democracy practiced in Britain did not work well in Africa, Rhodesia would need to devise a constitution that would be best for its circumstances. A fixed path to majority rule—a clear reference to Wilson's first principle—was "objectionable" to Rhodesian society. In 1961, after all, the Rhodesian electorate had declared its willingness to offer Africans a place in representative government, knowing full well that at some point in the future Africans could exclude Europeans from government. But now, after events in the rest of Africa—and after the boycott of the 1961 referendum and participation in the B roll—"the climate of trust" had become mistrust. Only a new constitution could remove the distrust. Presaging many of the concerns that shaped the debates about the 1969 constitution, Lardner-Burke noted that over 90 percent of government revenue came from the personal and company taxes paid by Europeans, so it was only just that Europeans should write the new constitution.[4]

The constitutional commission was very much a local project: the commissioners were Rhodesians, writing for Rhodesia. There were no British observers, no commissioners who had served in the federal judiciary or who had written a majority rule constitution for another African country, and no representatives of the now-banned African political parties. It was a commission of lesser-known names: William Rae Whaley headed the commission. Whaley was vice chairman of the Rhodesian Broadcasting Corporation and chairman of Rhodesia's Tobacco Corporation. He was a good friend of Ian Smith and a partner in a Salisbury law firm in which Jack Howman, a participant in the *Tiger* talks who held several portfolios in the government, was also a partner. The other European members were Robert Hepburn Cole, a Bulawayo lawyer and RF supporter, and Stanley Morris, who had a long career in the Department of Native Affairs, before it became Internal Affairs in 1962. Morris was what Rhodesians liked to call a "racial biologist"; his critics called him "Bantustan Morris" because of his segregationist views. He had participated in the *Tiger* talks. As chief native commissioner, Morris followed some of the new trends in developmentalist thinking of the 1950s and

4. Desmond Lardner-Burke, *Rhodesia: The Story of a Crisis* (London: Oldbourne, 1966), 68, 86–88.

1960s, insisting that the problems of rural Africa were "human" and resistance was "cultural." This was community development, in which the social fabric of rural Africa was the key to its development, rather than science and technology, and it was to have a peculiar impact on the new constitution.

There were two Africans on the commission. Chief Signola from Matabeleland was as international a figure as the commission had. He had served on the Monckton Commission and accompanied Smith to London for his meetings with Wilson in October 1965. It was generally thought he would support the RF plan to strengthen chiefs at the expense of elected Africans and that he and Morris would emphasize, if not invent, traditions of African leadership. The other African was Charles Mzingeli, former trade unionist and Southern Rhodesia Labour Party stalwart. He had actively opposed universal suffrage and later supported UDI because it promised to curb the violence of African nationalists and because it offered him a political space those same nationalists denied him. In 1967 it was thought that he would support a constitution that limited African aspirations while blunting some of the worst segregationist tendencies of the other commissioners.[5]

The key question of the commission was also its most mechanical: should Rhodesia continue as a monarchy, linked to Britain and the Queen, or should it become a republic? The question was so formulaic that it appeared at the end of the published *Report*, although by the time the *Report* was published in April 1968 the question was irrelevant. In March 1968 Rhodesia hanged three men who had been convicted of political murders in 1964. James Dhlamini and Victor Mlambo were convicted of the murder of Pieter Oberholzer, the first European killed by African nationalists, and Duly Shadrek had been convicted of the murder of a chief in 1964. Their appeal followed the lines of *Madzimbamuto and Baron v. Lardner-Burke* that the RF regime did not have the authority to carry out sentences imposed under the 1961 constitution. The appellate court repeated the judgment in the latter case, that the Rhodesian Front regime was the legal authority of the country. These executions could not be delayed any longer, nor could any stay of execution be granted for the defendants to appeal to the Privy Council, because the

5. Richard Hodder-Williams, "Rhodesia's Search for a Constitution. Or, Whatever Happened to Whaley?" *African Affairs* 69, no. 276 (1970): 217–18, 223–24; Bowman, *Politics in Rhodesia*, 135; Flower, *Serving Secretly*, 40; Jocelyn Alexander, *Unsettled Land*, 65–66; Wood, *Matter of Weeks*, 299; William Hostes H. Nicolle, interview, August 1968, NAZ/OH/308. For Mzingeli's history, see Scarnecchia, *Urban Roots*, 12–28.

chief justice ruled that the Privy Council had no authority to prevent the Rhodesian government from carrying out executions. The defendants, possibly with some encouragement from Commonwealth members or from the Commonwealth Secretariat in London, then petitioned the Queen for the royal prerogative of mercy. The Queen's message commuting the sentences to life in prison was delivered to Ian Smith in the morning. By that afternoon, the chief justice ruled—against the advice of many in the cabinet—that the men would be executed, as "Her Majesty is quite powerless in this matter." Only Rhodesia's government had the authority to exercise mercy or commute a sentence.[6]

Nevertheless, monarchy had its supporters, not the least of which were the high court judges who resigned in protest over the rejection of the authority of the Queen and her Privy Council.[7] Another supporter was Lieutenant Colonel Robert Gayre, laird of the clan of Gayre and Nigg. He had visited Rhodesia once, after he had written a book arguing that Great Zimbabwe was built by Phoenicians. He submitted several memos to the constitutional commission, some of which were read with great care. One of his least-read memos opposed Rhodesian republicanism. In the short term, he wrote, this would disappoint Rhodesia's supporters around the world, who would not approve of such an action. In the long term, however, he was certain that the Commonwealth would fall apart: "Afro-Asian members are only there because of aid." Great changes were coming—Scotland would soon be independent, Britain would join the Common Market, and the Commonwealth would be white. Rhodesia would miss out on all of this if it broke with the Crown.[8] But Rhodesia did ignore the Queen, and all the traditions that were part of the civilization it had taken UDI to uphold. Indeed, the new constitution would keep the Queen and the Commonwealth at arm's length and find a way to govern Africans that did not lead to anything resembling majority rule. As it was worked out in commission and committee by factions in the ruling party, the new constitution changed the dynamic with which Africans were governed in Rhodesia.

6. The chief justice made this ruling the day before the Privy Council ruled on *Madzimbamuto v. Lardner-Burke*. *Africa Report* 13, no. 5 (May 1968): 24–25; "Current Legal Developments," *International and Comparative Law Quarterly* 17, no. 4 (1968): 1049–50; Flower, *Serving Secretly*, 87–88; Goldin, *The Judge*, 102–7; Megahey, *Beleaguered Governor*, 148–51; Wood, *Matter of Weeks*, 420, 423–25.

7. Dendy Young's statement, August 12, 1968, Dendy Young Correspondence, Cabinet Memoranda, 1972, CL/Smith/25.

8. Gayre of Gayre and Nigg, "The Retention of the Monarchy in Rhodesia," n. d., G. H. Hartely Correspondence, 1967–69, NAZ/HA/17/1/3.

A One-Party State in Central Africa

Almost sixty years ago, well before the term became a commonplace descriptor of African states, Colon Leys observed that Southern Rhodesia was a one-party state. Despite the number of European political parties that came and went, both government and opposition parties always had the same characteristics: the government party had a strong parliamentary majority and spoke of, but did not encourage, more African participation in matters of government; the opposition party was too small and too fragile to interfere. Leys argued that this was not a peculiarity of Rhodesia's history or electoral processes, but how the one-party system functioned there. Members of parliament who did not follow the party rank and file, or who were too independent for party discipline, could be forced out to join other parties. Thus the party in power rid itself of dissident members by forcing them to join small segregationist or even smaller integrationist parties.[9] This pattern intensified after UDI. Having won by a small majority in 1962, the Rhodesian Front won by a landslide in 1964; it won all six by-elections starting in 1966. The RF was also a large party: just over 20 percent of the white electorate were members. Party policies were made by two national committees, each of which was made up of an equal number of members of the government and men who did not hold office. Party congresses both at the national and at the branch level were notoriously fractious: the radical American nun Janice McLaughlin said she had "never seen such a rowdy crowd" as the one at an RF meeting in 1976. Party officials and MPs struggled to control the demands of the rank and file at regional and national meetings.[10]

Richard Hodder-Williams noted that the 1969 constitution was in fact the party's constitution.[11] I will link this point to Leys in the following pages, to show how the party's constitution in the one-party state was not just about governing the country, but also about governing the party. The *Report* of the constitutional commission and the debates and fissures that led to the 1969 constitution may have been ways for the Rhodesian government to keep the presentable face of the Rhodesian Front—which may not have been presentable anywhere else—together.

9. Leys, *European Politics*, 173–74.

10. Larry Bowman, "Organization, Power and Decision-Making with the Rhodesian Front," *J. of Commonwealth Political Studies* 7 (1968): 145–65, and "Strains in the Rhodesian Front," *Africa Report* 13, no. 9 (1968): 16–22; Sister Janice McLaughlin, Harare, May 23, 1989, NAZ/ORAL/244; Lancelot Bales Smith interview; Rudland interview; Dupont interview.

11. Hodder-Williams, "Whaley," 228–30.

The Whaley commission sat for four hundred days. It received 650 memoranda from individuals, not all of whom resided in the country, and half as many from interest groups. It authorized posters printed in African languages and invited Africans to give their opinions. The commissioners visited Chiweshe Reserve and were given a guided tour of two townships. It heard testimony from 269 witnesses, in public and in private.[12] Given the wide variety of evidence received, it is not always possible to see the sentiments behind the commission's recommendations, but some questions clearly garnered more interest than others. There were some issues that the *Report* presented as straw men and summarily dismissed, such as secret ballots for lawmakers or compulsory voting for all who had the right to do so. Two issues required lengthy elaboration, however: seven pages were devoted to arguments about whether Rhodesia should have a federal or a unitary system of government, and five to arguments for and against the complete partition of the country along racial lines. The most widely circulated memo about partition came from Colonel Gayre; it had great support within the Rhodesian Front, as we shall see. One MP was so eager to support partition that he gave the commission a brochure that celebrated reservations for Native Americans in the U.S. and Canada.[13] Overall, the *Report* seemed most concerned with arguing with the Tredgold commission, which was quoted more than any other text. That older constitutional order, as we shall see, haunted Rhodesia in its dealings with Britain and in a very few years became a bargaining chip for Smith. By the early 1970s, Smith and his ministers admitted that the 1969 constitution represented the worst of Rhodesian Front racial politics even as they threatened to continue to use it if negotiations with Britain broke down.

What is most important about the Whaley *Report* for my purposes is that it is a Rhodesian Front text. The key words of 1957 and 1961 had been cut loose from their moorings: responsible government became a trope, set apart from its genealogy of disinterest or judgment. Franchise qualifications became "attainments."[14] The gentle euphemisms of federal times, or even the euphemisms of the United Federal Party— "less mature voters," "backwards and illiterate sections of the African population"—gave way to talk of primitive Africans mired in the ways of their tribes. The technologies of the late 1950s of political machinations

---

12. *Report of the Constitutional Commission, 1968* [hereafter Whaley *Report*] (Salisbury, Government Printer, April 1968), 1–3; Wood, *Matter of Weeks*, 448.

13. G. H. Hartley, MP to Constitutional Commission, Re: Political Status of North American Indians, May 18, 1967, G. H. Hartley Correspondence, 1967–69.

14. Whaley *Report*, 51, 53.

to make race insignificant gave way to making race the basis not of governing but of government. Beyond race, there were any number of recommendations that reflected some of the new and increasingly odd ideas within the party. Thus the commission did not want to give education the weight the 1961 constitution had. Schooling alone should not qualify anyone to vote, and higher education often made people "completely ill-equipped to meet and understand the problems of everyday life."[15]

Switzerland, Parity, and a Senate

The constitutional commission was tasked with asking what kind of government was best for the very plural society of Rhodesia. The visions of Rhodesia offered up in response were literally all over the map. Some of the proposals were versions of what had already been proposed on the *Tiger,* but there were new elements that had not been part of official party policies. Many witnesses wanted Rhodesia to be like that plural, multilingual "perfect democracy" Switzerland. The commission agreed that Switzerland was indeed paradise, but that state had been achieved through deep-seated intellectual traditions and the long specific history of the evolution of its cantons. Switzerland could not be reproduced in Rhodesia.[16] Others advocated various forms of partition—often rehearsing some of the earliest proposals for the Central African Federation—which they claimed had solved the problems of plural societies elsewhere in the world.[17] The most audacious proposal came from Colonel Gayre; it proposed partitioning the country. The "three races," Shona, Ndebele, and European, would be separated; populations would be moved and land transferred. This was ridiculous, of course, but it provided an intellectual cover for some of the ideas about race and partition we saw in the testimony before the 1960 constitutional commission. Roger Howman, brother of Jack Howman, had been in the Department of Internal Affairs for forty years; he was a deputy director in 1968. He considered the proposal farcical. The new director of Internal Affairs was an admirer

15. Whaley *Report,* 72.
16. Whaley *Report,* 21–22.
17. Whaley *Report,* 16.

of South Africa's Bantustan policy, however, and he took the proposal seriously.[18]

The Whaley *Report* concluded that Rhodesia was a unitary, indivisible nation. The question was how to govern, which was in fact the question of how many Africans should be allowed to participate in that government. Europeans had "competence and experience" that allowed them to exercise a "more authoritative voice" in national affairs, but they also had to concede that Africans had a place in national politics and that over time they might have "increasing but not limitless power." How long it might take Africans to increase their presence in the legislature allowed for a dig at Wilson's "weeks, not months," as it could not be measured with "clock or calendar." It was therefore "irresponsible" to recommend majority rule or rapid progress thereto at this stage of Rhodesia's history. Nevertheless, the commission would pretend that majority rule was a distinct possibility and thus recommend a solution that ensured that no one race dominated the other.[19]

If one of the rhetorical problems posed by the Whaley commission was how to reject perpetual European domination and prevent ultimate African domination, the solution could be found in the past, specifically a recommendation of the Monckton Commission. That commission had suggested parity as a potential mechanism to reassure whites and Africans about the very questions of racial domination that the federation had avoided, that territorial legislatures move toward an eventual goal of an equal number of seats for African and European representatives. Whaley's parity was a way of imagining party politics in situations where racial cleavages remained unchanged: "The parity principle will produce political balance" because each side would have an equal number of votes so that votes would have to be along party, not racial, lines.[20] Responding to the *Report*, the Forum, a group of lawyers and businessmen formed in 1967 to lobby for an "honorable settlement" for Rhodesia, noted that the Whaley commission's parity was so far in the future that it was a great pity that it had been spelled out with such

18. H. R. G. Howman, *Provincialisation in Rhodesia, 1968–1969 and Rational and Irrational Elements*, ed. G. C. Cashmore (Cambridge, African Studies Centre, 1985), x, 8, 33–34. William Hostes Nicolle, director of internal affairs in 1968, was to spend the next twenty years explaining that everyone confused his complete conviction "that the Land Apportionment Act was the best way of avoiding or reducing racial friction between diverse communities" with support for apartheid. Nicolle, interview, NAZ/OH/308.

19. Whaley *Report*, 12, 38.

20. Whaley *Report*, 12.

precision. It could only be taken as a direct rejection of Wilson's first principle.[21]

The Whaley commission did not recommend parity, however. The problem for Rhodesia was that Africans had not yet advanced "in their political development" so that they could make an "equal contribution to the work of government." And it would take many years before the two races could gain the experience and trust that would come from working together in parliament to allow themselves to put party interests before racial ones. If there was parity today, there would probably be "intermittent or permanent deadlock." Because of this, Europeans would have to "hold the reins of power" by holding the majority of seats; there should also be "a substantial number" of elected African members, who would gain that all-important confidence and experience under European guidance. And here was the crux: because there was a clear need for African members of parliament, a new form of African electorate was required. It would be another temporary measure, the commission admitted: it would last only so long as "sufficient" Africans qualified to vote on the common roll.

The commission recommended two legislative chambers, a legislative assembly elected by three voter rolls, two of which were to be dominated by Europeans, and an upper house to be elected by methods so complicated that the commissioners could not fully describe them. The various electoral rolls for Africans and Europeans, and a new, common roll with the same qualifications as the old A roll, were said to protect Africans. The *Report* argued that if there was a limited number of African members of the legislature, Europeans would not worry about Africans' dominating them and would have no reason to hold back African political progress. The commission wanted some version of the Westminster system, one in which a responsible lower house made laws and an upper house, selected to represent the various racial and political interests in the country, reviewed and occasionally blocked the legislation that the lower house had made in perhaps too great haste. In theory—or as had happened in New Zealand—the upper house could be at odds with the ruling party, so it was necessary to insulate it from party politics. Indeed, echoing the ideas of Harry Reedman several years earlier, members should represent "fields of interest" rather than political parties.

21. The Forum, Comments on the Report, mimeo., April 15, 1968, NAZ/MS811.

And to emulate Rome and the United States, the upper house should be called the senate.[22]

The Sudden Death of the B Roll

The Whaley commission's praise for the principle of parity was matched by its eagerness to dismantle the B roll. The *Report* noted that it was an African roll already, and that even Tredgold understood that it would necessarily remain one for years to come. The *Report* also insisted that it had been a dismal failure. In a particularly contradictory set of explanations, it set out all the reasons why a qualified B roll did not work. First, "the African did not readily understand a sophisticated electoral procedure involving the onus of claiming the vote being placed on himself." Second, the B roll was "a debased form of franchise" which apparently Africans understood made them "second class voters." Third, and sixth and seventh, the fifteen B roll seats did not provide a "satisfactory" measure of African representation but catered to a narrow segment of African interests; it ignored those Africans who lived "under the tribal system." Elected members often failed to stay in contact with their constituents. Fourth, Africans failed to register to vote because of "real or imaginary" intimidation. Fifth, authorities had failed to enlighten Africans as to the "purpose and the value of the vote," which would "offset the sinister influences of the nationalists." As if all this was not reason enough, the unhappy history of the B roll was reason to abolish it. Repeating Whitehead's claim as if it had been a basis for the 1961 constitution, the commission wrote that of the fifty thousand Africans who qualified for the B roll, only ten thousand actually registered in 1962 and of these only one-quarter voted. One-eighth voted in the election of 1965. When B roll voters were required to re-register in 1967, enrollments dropped from over ten thousand to a little more than four thousand.[23]

The commission was not alone in seeking to end the B roll, however. Progressive groups had been unhappy with it for years. The Forum considered the *Tiger* proposals perfectly reasonable. Although its memos and submissions were written by four people, the Forum claimed a membership of over two thousand in Salisbury and Bulawayo in 1968. The Forum asked the constitutional commission to "fade out" the B roll and

22. Whaley *Report*, 29–32. The commission did not want more than two houses, as three would be particularly vulnerable to "an assault by unscrupulous elements."
23. Whaley *Report*, 64.

to consider a legislative assembly made up of reserved seats, seventeen each for Africans and Europeans. This would provide a useful counter to Morris's "foggy thinking" about representing Shona and Ndebele as separate groups. As long as there was a B roll, however, the Forum recommended enfranchising all male and female Africans over thirty, even if they were illiterate, destitute, or unemployed: such voters might have "legitimate observations" on the causes of their illiteracy, destitution, or unemployment. Coloured and Asian voters should be enfranchised on the A roll. Not only did the A roll best represent their interests, but this could be used to satisfy the fifth principle. The senate should be left as it was to provide a constitutional check.[24]

The *Report* recommended doing away with the B roll. It was to be replaced by a common roll and a new scheme of "special African representation," which contained an invention of tradition. Rural Africa, the commission claimed, was not only the site of day-to-day social relations but "a tribal structure" with a "whole set of inherited institutions" that governed politics, religion, economics, and health. According to the *Report*, only a few Africans who lived in the Tribal Trust Lands had any interest in party politics and even fewer understood "sophisticated forms of government." They were preoccupied with crops, livestock, and the weather. Most African men were away for short periods, working for Europeans, and this created its own set of problems which the commission did not identify. Politics "as we know the term" was a matter for discussion first within the family, then in the kraal, and finally in the chief's indaba. "In times of stress" Africans immediately sought out the diviner: "the ways and thoughts of the 'white men' are relatively foreign." The concept of representation could not be applied.[25]

This was 1968. Twenty years earlier there had been a reimagining of rural Africa—especially in British colonies—in which an idealized agrarian society could cure the ills of detribalization through some kind of customary distribution of land and labor. In many places the idea of backward Africans created a space in which the urban "detribalized" Africans could be given a standing in imperial thought; elsewhere it obscured the extent to which African agriculture was shaped by the close cooperation of chiefs and colonial officials.[26] What happened in, and

---

24. Basic Statement, August 4, 1967; submission to constitutional commission by J. H. R. Eastwood, L. K. S. Wilson, and B. W. S. O'Connell, September 13, 1967, the Forum Papers, NAZ/MS 804.

25. Whaley *Report*, 65–66.

26. Colonial debates about how to think about rural Africa in the 1950s were contentious; see Frederick Cooper, *On the African Waterfront: Urban Disorder and the Transformation of Work in*

was imagined for, Rhodesia starting in 1962 was very different. It had originated in agricultural policies and had a very different trajectory, one that J. F. Holleman called somewhat inaccurately "the rediscovery of chiefs." Chiefs were hardly unknown or unrecognized; they had helped various bureaucracies implement agricultural policies for years, and they were not always beloved for having done so. After World War II there were attempts by British and French officials to make chiefs less overtly political, to appoint them much as colonial regimes would appoint civil servants.[27] In Rhodesia the 1969 constitution sought to replace nationalists with chiefs as the spokesmen for African interests. To make such claims, chiefs' authority was said to be ingrained in an imaginary rural society, the values and beliefs of which would allow for villagers' blind allegiance to the office. This fiction depended on concealing the extent to which chiefs worked for the Rhodesian government. Even the chiefs' indaba—which the Rhodesian Front claimed had given African approval to UDI—was a recent and government-inspired innovation in which participation and debate were limited.[28] Fabrications went far beyond who were the real employers of chiefs. The same cabinet ministers who had scoffed at the NDP's referendum and then banned the party only to see ZAPU form eight days later, the same ministers who had feared guerrilla armies being trained in neighboring countries, now claimed that Africans did not understand politics as Europeans did. That it could be repeated with a straight face by the same men who had detained Nkomo and renewed states of emergency and executed men who had killed chiefs was not because it was fictive, but because it fit so well with a hyperbolic notion of community development.

Community development began as a program for colonial administrators in the late 1940s. By the 1960s some version of it was practiced in most of the decolonized world. Its basic premise was that local society—meaning culture, with its specific structures of social organization and patterns of thought—held the key to the development of rural Africa. This was the discourse of "the human factor," of understanding that

---

Colonial Mombasa (New Haven, CT: Yale University Press, 1987), 265–66, and *Decolonization and African Society*, 202–15, 265. David Throup may have oversimplified these debates, but he had a point: "Only romantically inclined Englishmen, escaping from the pressures of industrial Britain, could have failed to realize that this idealized image of African communalism was a delusion and have attempted to foist on the Kikuyu a system of land law that bore little resemblance to their traditions." David W. Throup, *Economic and Social Origins of Mau Mau* (Oxford: James Currey, 1988), 75.

27. Tosh, "Colonial Chiefs"; Cooper, *African Waterfront*, 69, and *Decolonization*, 276.

28. Holleman, *Chief, Council and Commissioner*, 340–45, 349; Alexander, *Unsettled Land*, 71–72, 84–88. For a less charitable view of Holleman than I can muster, see Moore, *Suffering for Territory*, 171–73.

African culture was sometimes a path to progress and sometimes a bar-rier. In community development rights were communal, not individual; solutions centered on "the social organism as a whole" to develop "the collective body." Problems in the Tribal Trust Lands were best addressed by administrators and anthropologists, not by technicians and soil sci-entists. In 1965, however, the detritus of the Native Land Husbandry Act and a shift in policy made chiefs authorities over land and labor. According to the ideas behind community development, the organic, collective nature of rural society—so self-reliant as not to need govern-ment subsidies or development projects—was not something that could transform itself through debate and experimentation, but had to be strengthened and reinforced. By the late 1960s, chiefs stood at the center of the RF's struggles to make their authority over rural areas and arrest their decline. Chiefs provided an imaginary cohesion for rural society; anything more democratic was simply not "natural" for Africans. Chiefs and their subjects were to articulate the limits of state intervention in rural life, and this would, the Rhodesian Front hoped, make chiefs less vulnerable, if not more popular.[29]

According to the *Report*, urban areas, the site of so much African po-litical agitation in the 1950s and 1960s, did not have the institutions of the tribe "to tie the floating population together." The *Report* claimed that most urban Africans were "floating" and "rootless," as eager to de-camp to another town or go on strike as they were to stay in town. Most had no real stake in a "civic structure based on industrial or commercial values." The few who did were the men who lived in town on a "semi-permanent basis." They could be called "emerging or emergent Africans because they leased or owned accommodation for married couples" which "promoted an element of stability" that could create "permanent roots" in urban society and "the gradual severance of tribal affiliation." For this reason the commission proposed the African Urban Areas Voters Roll, qualification for which would be occupying or leasing married ac-commodation in certain designated townships.[30] Again, this was totally made up. Township politics and trade unionism had engaged "industrial values" since the 1930s. Trade unionists (and Capricorns) had argued for property qualifications for African voters so that African workers would remain in towns to acquire the skill levels that earned them higher pay and family housing. The 1961 B roll qualifications had been in large

29. Holleman, *Chief, Council and Commissioner*, 340–41; Alexander, *Unsettled Land*, 66–67, 75–77, 83–84; Munro, *Moral Economy of the State*, 142–49.
30. Whaley *Report*, 66–68.

part shaped by officials' understanding of how skilled the African work-force was and its relationship to township housing. African Purchase Areas—which officials had hoped would have a stabilizing influence on NDP rallies a few years earlier—stood midway between the imagined tribal people of rural Rhodesia and the imagined footloose folk of the townships. In the Purchase Areas, Africans owned land as individuals; this land was often far removed from kin and tribe, whose influence on their lives waned. While these Africans were still concerned with crops and livestock, they were "'on their own' economically" and relied on the European cash economy to succeed. They "gradually" acquired the "pride" of individual ownership and would become "new" Africans.[31]

Between the towns and the Purchase Areas, slightly fewer than 50 per-cent of B roll voters would be eligible to vote on the new common roll. Morris, Mzingeli, and Chief Signola wanted to enfranchise them as well. They argued that these Africans had been encouraged to register by suc-cessive governments and many had risked physical violence to do so: it would be "morally wrong" to deprive these voters of their individual rights because the electoral system was changed. Cole and Whaley ar-gued that the scheme for special representation would more than substi-tute for the B roll. There was no justification for giving the vote to those who did not currently qualify for it: "just laws made for hard cases" and no single law could satisfy the "divergent needs and aspirations" of all Africans. A professor at the University College of Rhodesia in-voked the suburb to explain his dismay: whoever thought it impossible to disenfranchise people who had previously had the vote "never saw a suburb full of whites in Central Africa."[32] The commission retained the disqualifications from the 1961 constitution, which followed those recommended by John Stuart Mill. Voters could be disqualified for men-tal disorders or for having received public assistance for one year; men and women convicted of crimes could not register to vote for five years. Detainees had not been convicted of any crime, however, and should be allowed to vote if they qualified.[33]

The commission was quite specific about how Africans would be rep-resented. The Tribal Trust Lands would elect representatives through an electoral college, to be made up of chiefs, headmen, and the elected members of the African councils proposed in the *Report*. In the Purchase

31. Whaley *Report*, 66–67.
32. Whaley *Report*, 69–70; P. B. Harris, "The Failure of a Constitution: The Whaley Report, Rhodesia, 1968," *International Affairs* 45, no. 2 (1969), 238.
33. Whaley *Report*, 75–76.

Areas Africans would vote on a special African roll, for which they would qualify if they could demonstrate adequate literacy—the ability to fill out and sign the form in English unaided—and could show freehold title, a purchase agreement, or a lease beginning at least three years before the date of enrollment. In town Africans could qualify for the special African roll if they met the minimum income requirements and demonstrated adequate literacy and could show either proof of ownership of a house or other immovable property in town or proof of occupancy of married housing for at least three years before enrollment. The commission estimated that ten thousand Africans, including senior wives in polygynous unions, would qualify to vote in urban areas.[34]

The Slow Death of the A Roll

The A roll was to be abandoned in favor of a common roll. The qualifications were higher than those of the old A roll, but it was not a European roll: Asians and Coloureds could vote if they qualified. The commissioners debated the nature of qualifications but eventually agreed that income was the best method for measuring a person's "capability and responsibility" and that it could provide some measure of his education. They wanted the income qualification raised from that of the 1965 constitution, from £792 to £878. In order to qualify through some combination of education and income, someone who completed primary school would have to earn £528 a year while someone with four years of secondary education would have to earn only £330. Many witnesses suggested that the franchise be based on income tax rather than income. The commission found merit in this idea, but believed it would cause too many anomalies. Rhodesia had a graduated tax, so that a bachelor and a married man with four children might earn the same salary, but the bachelor paid income tax while the father of four did not. Nothing would be gained by not allowing him to vote. The commissioners wanted to raise the property qualification as well so that those "with a substantial stake in the country" would be encouraged to vote. Besides, the A roll qualification bore almost no relationship to present-day property values; it was necessary to establish a new one.[35]

The commissioners did not want to lower the income qualification for those men and women who had a specified standard of education.

34. Whaley *Report*, 78–79.
35. Whaley *Report*, 72–73.

Indeed, it was only when discussing educational standards that the commission allowed itself the language of good judgment and responsibility.
Being well educated, several witnesses pointed out, did not determine a
person's ability to vote. Among the professorate "there is a tendency to
adopt an ideological approach" which was irrelevant to present-day political realities. Educational "attainments" in and of themselves did not
guarantee the "degree of thought and understanding necessary for the
proper exercise of the vote." The commission wanted to make primary
and secondary education one of several factors that would allow a voter
to qualify for the A roll. The commission worried that the old A roll
combination of primary education or four years of secondary school did
not require sufficient income to test a voter's achievements and judgment. The commission, like every franchise commission before it, en-
tertained proposals to raise the voting age to twenty-five, or to maintain
the voting age of twenty-one for persons who had full qualifications
while those with lower "attainments" in income and property would
have to wait until they were twenty-five or even thirty.[36] And just as the
commission rejected any idea of enfranchising everyone over sixty, they
rejected the idea taken from Tredgold's special doorway of enfranchising
anyone who had performed years of loyal service or held high office or
had received honors or awards. There could be no objective assessment
of these awards, the commission believed, and such achievements did
not alone qualify someone to vote. The most contentious debates were
what to do about clergymen (or women, as most of the whites who
voted on the B roll in 1962 were nuns), who had several years of secondary education but limited incomes. The older qualification of four years
of secondary education would have enfranchised most clergymen. Three
of the commissioners wanted to make an exception for clergy, without
bringing back that particular education requirement, but Mzingeli and
Whaley objected. The new criteria of income and education could only
work if there were no exceptions.[37]

In the end, the commission recommended enfranchising clergymen.
Any Rhodesian citizen who had resided in the country for two years and
in a constituency for three months was eligible to apply for the franchise. To qualify, he or she would have to complete and sign the form
in English unaided and have earned an income of not less than £900

36. Whaley *Report*, 70–74. Starting in federal times, Southern Rhodesia had wanted to raise the
voting age to twenty-five for Africans and Europeans alike. This was continually rejected because
of the near-universal standard of twenty-one. Minutes, Inter-governmental committee on federal
franchise qualifications, January 31, 1957, Cabinet Memoranda, CL/Smith/6.

37. Whaley *Report*, 73–74; author's field notes, Grahamstown, June 8, 2008.

per year for the previous two years or owned land or property the net value of which was no less than £3,000. Men and women whose income for the last two years was no less than £600 could qualify if they had completed four years of secondary education. Chiefs and headmen were admitted to the A roll regardless of their qualifications, as were A roll voters even if they did not meet the new qualifications. After considerable debate, the four thousand B roll voters who were registered were also admitted to the common roll.[38] However much the proposed common roll resembled the old A roll, it was to function differently.

The common roll voters were to elect sixty representatives. Special European voters—that is, the Europeans from the common roll—were to elect forty, and the special African voters—split between townsmen, Purchase Area farmers, and the Tribal Trust Lands—were to elect twenty. The senate was to be smaller and more complicated to elect. There were to be twenty-four senators, twelve European and twelve African. Reviving Harry Reedman's Best Man Government, the commissioners proposed that European senators should represent interests rather than political parties, so they could contribute "fresh and valuable" ideas to consideration of laws passed by the legislative assembly. The commission had not determined how these men would be selected, but they should be chosen for "their wisdom and experience" from a wide variety of occupations and fields. Nevertheless, the senate was a national body, and the senators should see themselves as representatives of "all peoples and their interests." The commission thought that senators might best be chosen through some version of a guild system, a combination of occupations and fields of expertise that were selected by their contribution to the gross national product (GNP). To this end, the commission provided a table of different industries—agriculture, mining, wholesale and retail trade—giving the percentage of relative employment and their contributions to the GNP. Secondary industry, for example, employed 15 percent of the workforce but contributed 21 percent to the GNP.

African senators were easier to select. There would be six each from Matabeleland and Mashonaland, and these were to be some combination of chiefs and what the commission called "commoners." The senate was "the natural and proper place for chiefs." Some thought commoners should also serve in the senate, since chiefs might not represent all African interests: the senate could provide an opportunity for chiefs and commoners to air disputes. And of course there would have to be

38. Whaley *Report*, 76–77.

an equal number of chiefs and commoners in the senate: three of each from Matabeleland and Mashonaland.[39] Ian Smith was delighted. Far from rejecting "the possibility of racial harmony in Africa," the new constitution would bring chiefs "into government and administration as the acknowledged leaders of the African people."[40]

The Constitution and the Party

It took five months, until early April 1968, for the *Report* of the Whaley commission to be published. Much was made of the delay—some said that the government waited till the death penalty cases were resolved, while others said it was because the regime was busily negotiating with Britain—but it was irrelevant.[41] Most of the commission's recommendations seem to have been well known before it was published. Indeed, by the time the *Report* appeared in print, the Rhodesian Front had begun to fragment over questions of majority rule and integration, issues that now crystallized around the new meaning of parity. Not only would the senate have an equal number of Africans and Europeans, but the common roll included Asians and Coloureds.

As soon as the *Report* was published, Len Idensohn, the Rhodesian Front's most senior divisional chairman, defected. He announced a new party, the Rhodesia National Party, which would put a stop to the "clandestine integrationist policies" that Ian Smith—whom he called a "white kaffir"—fostered with the new constitution. Idensohn claimed his party could easily attract 75 percent of Rhodesian Front members.[42] This seemed unlikely, especially since its most right-wing elements, including those who had come from the Dominion Party, set about to modify the proposals at once. Lord Graham, minister of agriculture, was one of the most outspoken critics of the *Report*. Party moderates—which included Ian Smith— appeared both angry and anguished. In April and May Smith made speeches throughout the country denouncing the

39. Whaley *Report*, 84–87.
40. Cabinet minutes, May 21, 1968, CL/Smith/22.
41. See Wood, *Matter of Weeks*, 448; Hodder-Williams, "Whaley," 225; Anglo-Rhodesian Negotiations since December 1966, White Paper, 1969, Cabinet Memoranda, CL/Smith/23.
42. Hodder-Williams, "Whaley," 226; *Africa Report* 13, no. 5 (May 1968): 36; Flower, *Serving Secretly*, 96; Wood, *Matter of Weeks*, 448–49. "White kaffir" was well worn in political usage in Rhodesia as a way to show the parallels between compromising whites and African nationalists. A member of the Rhodesia National Party expressed his relief at the failure of the Pearce commission thusly, "The black kaffirs have saved us from the white kaffirs." Quoted in Peter Niesewand, *In Camera: Secret Justice in Rhodesia* (London: Weidenfeld & Nicholson, 1973), 17–18.

"extremists and selfish racialists" in the Rhodesian Front. Reclaiming the sense of a Rhodesian belonging based on history, he went on: "There may be people who indulge this, but the majority of those people are mere birds of passage who have rarely a stake in this country . . . who can, if things go wrong, pack their bags and leave tomorrow."[43] Yet Smith had his own set of objections to the Whaley recommendations, that they would make it even more difficult to reach a settlement with Britain. Even the most sympathetic Conservatives could not support a constitution that offered Africans nothing beyond parity.[44] Groups such as the Forum were even more distressed. The proposed constitution would simply strengthen demands for more and more sanctions. "Rhodesia, puny in physical strength, requires a moral justification for her philosophy."[45]

The Whaley *Report* removed Africans from the institutions of representative government; there did not seem to be much Rhodesian racial biologists could object to. But the struggles between hard-line segregationists and the cabinet were intense. The cabinet broadly accepted Whaley's franchise recommendations, while Len Idensohn, for example, claimed that the inclusion of Asian and Coloured voters on the common roll was tantamount to compulsory integration.[46] Peter Claypole, permanent secretary of the Ministry of Justice, recalled that the Whaley proposals were "unacceptable" to the Rhodesian Front. The increased number of African seats in the house of assembly could only mean that parity would be "reached too soon."[47] Writing from Rhodesia at the time, Larry Bowman saw such debates as part of earlier struggles over the meaning of UDI: was it a grandiose stand for Western civilization—and segregation—as many in the Rhodesian Front claimed, or was it "a family quarrel," an unfortunate rift with Britain that many people in the government wanted resolved as soon as possible?[48] Almost fifty years later this seems too binary: struggles over the Whaley *Report* and the subsequent constitution were at once more layered and more specific. There were deep and abiding struggles over the franchise and what constituted qualification and—now more than ever before—disqualification, and there were newer, forceful struggles over what constituted representation for whom and the extent to which the preservation of tribes

43. *Africa Report* 13, no. 5 (May 1968): 36.

44. Wood, *Matter of Weeks*, 449.

45. The Forum, An Appeal to Statesmanship: The Forum Calls for a Constitution that will Help and not Hinder a Settlement, mimeo., Salisbury, August 5, 1968, NAZ/MS 807.

46. Hodder-Williams, "Whaley," 227–28.

47. Peter Claypole, Harare, October 26, 1988, NAZ/OH/321.

48. Bowman, "Strains in the Rhodesian Front," 17.

and culture could provide a lawful means of political dispossession. The *Report* proposed a constitution based on seats in legislative bodies, not on votes, as Hodder-Williams pointed out years ago: this eroded the entire idea of an African electorate, in whose place the Rhodesian Front substituted a simplistic, reified notion of culture that could lay no claim to the institutions of representative government.

The cabinet approved of the ideas of the common roll and of reserved seats for Africans in the legislative assembly. Its debates were over how many African seats there should be. Some Africans had to be there; they could not be cast out after having had representation for the past six years. The cabinet considered partition impossible but did not want to rule out some form of provincial government that would be subordinate to the national one. "Africans laid great stress on status" and might not be "satisfied" with any solution that did not give some of them "positions of authority and leadership." There was as little chance of parity as there was of majority rule, so Africans had to have some means of achieving the ministerial ranks to which they aspired. The commission had recommended that 25 percent of the seats in the legislative assembly be reserved for Africans, but the cabinet rejected the idea: that percentage would not allow for the workings of a normal party system; there would be no opposition capable of forming a government. Africans would continue to oppose the government but have no real influence. On the other hand, it was critical that the influence of Africans in the legislative assembly be circumscribed so that "they could never be in a position to destroy parliamentary democracy." The cabinet endorsed the idea of a bicameral legislature, but suggested the common roll seats be increased from twenty to twenty-five or even twenty-eight—a few ministers wanted sixty common roll seats—and the special African seats reduced from twenty to fifteen or even twelve. Even so, cabinet members worried that the legislature might be taken over by a left-wing European/ African coalition that would be inimical to European interests. "If such a group were ever able to form a government the way would be open for the imposition of one-party rule in perpetuity."[49]

The Rhodesian Front government did not fully represent the Rhodesian Front party, however. Throughout mid-1968, despite the elaborate and overlapping procedures set up to allow the party, and then the country, to debate the proposed constitution it became clear that the party and the government were rent. By May and June of 1968 the idea

49. Constitutional Commission Report: summary of points raised in discussion, April 23, 1968, Cabinet Minutes 1968, CL/Smith/22.

of partition began to take hold among party members. Smith began to speak out against it, explaining how impossible partition was but how appropriate some form of "separate development" would be if it could be part of the new constitution.[50] Partition was perhaps the most extreme example of issues the new constitution brought to the fore. The idea of parity now made the Rhodesian Front rank and file deeply suspicious, even though this version of parity had nothing to do with governance or the conditions for possible futures but referred to who could sit in how many seats in which legislature. In 1957, the Tredgold commission had struggled with the question of how to define the electorate, of having rules in place that could discern who was qualified to determine how they would be governed. A little over a decade later the idea of "the people"—or at least African people, or the proportion of which was deemed worthy of electing representatives—was replaced by a simplistic notion of tribe that did not require representation. In two RF committees, these debates crystallized into a never-implemented proposal that Africans were tribesmen who needed to adhere to ancient patterns of authority. This was provincialization, a strange combination of partition and the Rhodesian Front's practice of community development.

Provincialization

Two party committees were established to debate the *Report* after it was published. One, headed by Lardner-Burke, assessed parliamentary opinion; the other, headed by divisional chairmen, spoke to party regulars.[51] Provincialization emerged out of the party discussions which recommended that the Rhodesian republic should have separate provincial councils for each of the main ethnic groups, the whites, the Shona, and the Ndebele. These councils would develop into full-fledged parliaments in five years; until then there would be a multiracial national parliament and a senate made up of ten whites, ten chiefs, and ten appointed members. These were confounded by a proposal to do away with a multiracial national parliament and implement the provincial parliaments right away. The proposal was named for its authors, Lord Graham, minister of agriculture, and William Harper, former leader of the Dominion Party and in 1968 minister of internal affairs, and advised by the secretary for internal affairs and designated expert on things African, Hostes Nicolle.

50. Howman, *Provincialisation*, 9.
51. Bowman, "Strains," 18.

Before the Harper-Graham proposals could reach the party congress, the cabinet asked Nicolle and his three deputies to look over the Whaley *Report* to ascertain how it might, or might not, clash with the "tribal system." Roger Howman, one of the deputies, wrote the most extensive memoir written on provincialization. He had been appalled by Gayre's submission, first because it would create "human zoos" and second because it was "taken seriously," although he must have understood that Gayre simply gave academic credibility to some of the ideas about race that had been circulating in and around the Rhodesian Front for years. Howman was "disturbed" by the Harper-Graham proposals. They could only represent a "reasonable and morally defensible hope for the future" for people who believed that Rhodesia was comprised of "irreconcilable, hostile races" who could never live in a unitary state. The proposals were "superficial, narrow and so loosely based on such an exaggeration of selected features of African society as to be unbalanced." Even the Whaley *Report* did not think a government structure could be imposed on rural Africa from above. The other deputies were split, much as the Rhodesian Front was, and could not agree on the role of chiefs in future governments. Howman did not think chiefs were useful administrators, as they tended to take on the characteristics of old men in a home for the aged.[52]

The two RF committees produced a single document of their joint proposals, on which a special party congress voted in September 1968. The final compromise—the yellow paper, so-called because of the color of the paper on which it was printed—was two systems of representation to be introduced over a five-year period. Stage 1, as it was already known, was a multiracial parliament elected from a common roll and a senate with ten African representatives nominated by a council of chiefs; the ten European members would be elected by European MPs. Stage 2 would usher in what became known as provincialization, in which all three "races, European, Matabele, and Mashona" were to have provincial councils responsible for all the governance not handled at the national level. Smith announced that provincialization was the key to political security, the natural progression from community development that provided a way for Africans to manage their own affairs in their own spaces.[53] Various amendments were proposed and voted on; the party congress actually supported the elimination of stage 1 but before the final ballot several government ministers intervened and argued

52. Howman, *Provincialisation*, 33–37, 44.
53. *Africa Report* 13, no. 8 (1988): 30.

that stage 1 should remain. Their arguments rehearsed those of multira-cialists in the 1950s and 1960s, that white prosperity could be achieved only with the cooperation of Africans, who should not be fully disen-franchised. Smith spoke out against the amendment, insisting that the RF he knew was based on merit, not race, and this amendment made it "seem that the colour of one's skin was the deciding factor." In the end, the original yellow paper, with its two stages, was barely approved by the party congress, 217 to 206 with seventy abstentions.[54]

Provincialization was never even begun, but the fact that it had been at the core of RF party politics allowed many in the party, most espe-cially Smith, to become more and more skilled at claiming that they had held the real racialists at bay. Community development—a phrase that was now at least as fluid as parity ever was—was the responsible govern-ment's alternative to separate development. It became commonplace for cabinet ministers to speak of meritocracy. One said that Rhodesia had to recognize Africans' legitimate aspirations to "insure their continued cooperation."[55] Many extremists left the party. Graham resigned five days after he had been elected deputy leader, and Harper resigned a few weeks later. But other factions left as well. Howman retired from Internal Affairs in July 1969.

A Reordering of Party Politics?

There has been a tendency among historians to see the 1969 consti-tution as both an example and evidence of the rightward drift of the Rhodesian Front. At the time, however, there were "hopes or fears" of a deep split in the Rhodesian Front, but instead a standing commit-tee announced it would crackdown on dissidents.[56] Ian Smith however welcomed the defections; he had never liked Harper and considered Graham inept.[57] After the two resignations the cabinet became some-what more moderate and worked out a white paper on the new con-stitution in early 1969. The cabinet maintained that provincialization

54. The Republican Constitution of Rhodesia: Joint Proposals of the Caucus Sub-Committee and the Divisional Chairman's Committee of the Rhodesian Front, June 4, 1968, Cabinet Minutes, CL/Smith/22; *Africa Report* 13, no. 8 (1968): 30; Hodder-Williams, "Whaley," 229–30; Howman, *Provincialisation*, 6–11.
55. N. R. Bertram, Central African Territories, confidential memo, October 1968, the Forum NAZ/MS807.
56. N. R. Bertram, Central African Territories, October 1968.
57. Blake, *Rhodesia*, 401–4; Evans, Rhodesian Front Rule, 141–44.

would happen, but paid careful attention to the new national parliament that would be responsible for national finance, defense, foreign relations, irrigation, and of course telecommunications. The basic franchise qualifications and disqualifications were those recommended by the *Report* for Europeans and Africans: citizenship of Rhodesia, twenty-one or older, and three months' continuous residence in a constituency. A citizen could be disqualified for having a mental disorder or defect, having been convicted of a crime in the last five years, having received public assistance for a year, or having voluntarily acknowledged obedience to a foreign state. Anyone given a suspended sentence could not vote for the period of the suspension. After much debate it was decided that men and women in preventive detention were detained because they imperiled public safety; they should be disqualified even though they had not been convicted of any crime. The cabinet was hesitant to exclude ministers of religion from the common roll as the commission recommended: it seemed unfair to disenfranchise someone because he or she had taken a vow of poverty. Clerics often had better education and greater integrity than the average voter, so they would be "valuable" electors on the common roll.

The European, or common, roll was open to anyone who was not an African. The minimum income qualification was £600 per year for two years and land valued at £1,200. Land values were calculated by deducting the mortgage debt, and women qualified as they had done in the past, by their husbands' income and property. There were no mechanisms by which property and income could be readjusted according to years of schooling. The African roll was subject to more debate by various committees. In the end the minimum qualification for the African roll was an income rate of £200 per year for the previous two years and land or other immovable property valued at £400. The cabinet sought additional mechanisms to enfranchise Africans. It was agreed that Africans could qualify if they were married and owned or leased township property for three years, but the cabinet was unwilling to enfranchise all Purchase Area farmers as the *Report* recommended. It did allow for the use of an educational requirement, that Africans could qualify with a minimum income of £150 for a year and more than two years of secondary education.[58]

58. D. W. Lardner-Burke, Report of the Cabinet Constitutional Committee, February 13, 1969, CL/Smith/22; Revised Report of Working Party No. 3, Electoral Laws and Delimitation, February 20, 1969, Cabinet Memoranda/1, 1969; Report on working party's report, March 5, 1969, Cabinet minutes, 1969, CL/Smith/22.

Representation in this parliament would be determined by the "cal-culated personal income tax" paid by the three provinces. As Africans' income tax contributions increased in relation to the total number of taxpayers, so would their representation in the legislature. The cabinet produced a convoluted system by which the assessed income tax paid by Africans was shown to be "16/66" of the total income tax paid by Europeans and Africans so that the number of Africans in the proposed house of assembly would be sixteen. As Africans paid more income tax, the number of seats would increase by two, split equally between Masho-naland and Matabeleland. The official wording was that this would con-tinue until parity was reached, but the system of linking representation to income tax was designed to limit the number of Africans in the leg-islature.[59] Just to be sure, the new constitution made it clear that at no time would the proportion of African members of the legislature exceed the proportion of European seats justified by the aggregate income tax paid by white people.[60] The use of income tax as a measurement for legislative seats had its roots in Mill, who insisted that only taxpayers should be allowed to elect the representatives who taxed their fellows.[61] In earlier Rhodesian constitutions this had been expressed in terms of disenfranchising tax defaulters and those who had been on "public as-sistance" for a year. A few years later it was obvious that by the intro-duction of tax contributions into the 1969 constitution, parity became impossible; it was a means of preventing parity rather than promoting it. In 1968–1969, African income tax was a 0.6 percent of Rhodesia's total income tax, and African income tax payers were a small fraction of all taxpayers. Of over 71,000 taxpayers in March 1968, 870 were Africans.[62] The average income tax paid by Africans had decreased by 10 percent as the percentage of African tax payers had increased almost two-thirds. This was in part because African wages were low, and in part because Africans tended to have larger families than Europeans did and thus received more tax allowances. Rhodesian economists reckoned that it would be a very long time before Africans paid enough in income tax to reach the 50 percent that was to provide them with parity in the leg-islature. Indeed, the sixteen seats presently occupied by Africans in the

59. D. W. Lardner-Burke, Report of the Cabinet Constitutional Committee; Cabinet Memoranda; White Paper, The New Rhodesian Constitution, n. d. but filed in June 1969, CL/Smith/23; Claypole interview, NAZ/ORAL/321.

60. Handford, *Portrait of an Economy*, 54.

61. John Stuart Mill, *Representative Government*, 176.

62. Central Office of Statistics, *Rhodesia: Income Tax Statistics. Analysis of Assessments and Loss. Statements Issued during the Fiscal Year 1968–69*. Salisbury, mimeo., October 1969, NAZ/RG3/STA551.

house of assembly could not have been achieved if income tax had been the criteria.[63] Tax revenues were in fact not a large enough proportion of total revenues on which to build political institutions, and within a few years economists suggested that Africans' contribution to the gross national product—between 30 and 40 percent—might be a more reasonable basis on which to allocate seats in the assembly.[64]

The cabinet did nothing to simplify how the senate was elected. European senators could not be elected by parliament, various committees explained, because members of the opposition would expect representation in the senate in proportion to that in the lower house. One remedy would be a cumulative vote system in which European members of the lower house would have as many votes as there were vacancies and would vote for more than one candidate, whom they had assessed in advance. African senators were to be elected by tribal trust electoral colleges; the name was taken from the U.S. institution. In Rhodesia, however, the electoral college was designed to achieve representation "based on tribal interests." There would be eight college areas, as they were known, which should be delimited by election law. Each electoral college would consist of chiefs and headmen who would elect one member each. A working party of the cabinet laid out the procedures for the elections to the colleges, meeting with candidates, and for how to proceed in case of a tie.[65]

No sooner was the white paper finished than Britain sent envoys to Rhodesia and arranged another meeting on another yacht to revisit the *Tiger* proposals.[66] Even after Len Idensohn's Rhodesia National Party proved it could not compete in a by-election, the Rhodesian Front campaigned for the new constitution by insisting it was better than its alternatives, especially the 1961 constitution, which the party now maintained would have resulted in a black government in a very few years. In the end 81 percent of the electorate voted for the new constitution, and 72 percent for a republic. Smith called the newspaper accounts that most chiefs opposed the constitution "utter fabrication." In the referenda only one of fifty constituencies voted "no," and that was a periurban constituency in which Africans, Asians, and Coloureds outnumbered Europeans. The most conservative members of the Rhodesian

63. Handford, *Portrait of an Economy*, 54–55.
64. Lardner-Burke, Report of the Cabinet Constitutional Committee.
65. Revised report of Working Party no. 3, Electoral Laws and Delimitation, February 20, 1969, CL/Smith/22; Handford, *Portrait of an Economy*, 54–55.
66. N. R. Bertram, Central African Territories, October 1968; Wood, *Matter of Weeks*, 451–53.

Front who remained in the party were re-elected, which meant the new cabinet would be conservative as well.[67]

The 1969 Constitution

Ian Smith did not mention the Whaley commission and the 1969 constitution in his memoirs, perhaps because a discussion of his response to the debates and fissures in his party would have contradicted his self-presentation of unwavering principle. But Smith's responses, and those of the Rhodesian Front, to the new constitution were agile and expedient. Within a few months the party would claim it was both a meritocracy and segregationist. Rhodesia's republican status did not alarm other countries, although it made citizenship less appealing to Rhodesian residents, as we shall see. Smith used the 1969 constitution as a lure to Britain, proof of the isolation and eccentricity of Rhodesian policies that now endangered the entire region. But the constitution provided such a fantastic vision of African authority and society that the most serious attempt at settlement—the visit of the Pearce Commission in 1972—backfired badly. This fantasy of African politics was such that during the Pearce Commission's visit, the RF would have to create its own African support and opposition.

67. The Forum, Political and Economic Survey: Rhodesia and the Referendum, confidential memo, June 1969, NAZ/MS807; Evans, Rhodesian Front Rule, 145.

SEVEN

"Other people's sons": Conscription, Citizenship, and Families, 1970–1980

When Jack Howman, the law partner of William Whaley and brother of Roger Howman, was minister of defence in 1973, he struggled to raise soldiers' pay.[1] It was traditional, he wrote, "especially in frontier societies" like Rhodesia or South Africa, that citizens had a duty to defend the state. A citizen force should be given "adequate remuneration for comparatively short periods of service" because "young and developing countries" could not afford standing armies. But now Rhodesia mobilized large numbers of young men for rates of pay that had the same purchasing power as they had in 1955. Not only was this too low, but the differential between what men in different regiments were paid was too great for effective service. While the principles that determined policies of different pay and allowances for regular and short-term auxiliary forces were justified, it was time for Rhodesia "to accept the financial and economic consequences of putting the country on a war footing." Raising soldiers' pay was only part of the problem, however. There was also the "X factor": the young men on call-up duty—then not as onerous as it was to become—who had no real

1. An earlier version of this chapter was published as "Civic Virtue, National Service and the Family: The State and Conscription in Rhodesia," *Int. J. African Historical Studies* 37, no. 1 (2004): 105–21. I thank the editors for permission to reprint parts of it.

job mobility and had the emotional upheaval of separation from family and friends should be compensated as well. Howman also sought a gratuity for soldiers of twenty and thirty years' service, almost all of whom were Africans in the Rhodesian African Rifles (RAR). The treasury, however, could see no justification in paying additional allowances to men on call-ups, nor could it justify the extra payment to African troops.[2]

This is as good an introduction to the history of conscription in Rhodesia as I could wish for. What began as a straightforward appeal to citizenship and national defense became an obsession not with the obligations of citizens, but with the fate of white young men called upon to do the work of soldiering, work that had already been done for over a generation by African volunteers. This particular history is not an easy fit with most histories of conscription in which the ability to command the full-time labor of young men, citizens or residents, describes the expanding power of national states. Citizenship was an imprecise category in Rhodesia even in the best of times, and the state's power to command its citizens was at best uneven. Historians of World War I in particular have argued that conscription—and resistance thereto—allowed for the extension of state powers that first impacted citizens (by birth or naturalization) and then loyal resident aliens but almost always impacted poorer residents among them. In the twentieth century, conscription expanded state power not only by drafting young men but also by expanding the apparatus and organizations of surveillance that could distinguish ineligible young men from draft dodgers and conscientious objectors, and could find and prosecute deserters.[3]

Conscription in Rhodesia, especially after 1970, tells a different story, of state power that did not expand beyond the mailing of call-up papers and of a military increasingly frustrated by the state's inability to secure more manpower even as it understood it could not effectively use more soldiers. The questions of whom to conscript and how much to pay them were debated in cabinet offices and the headquarters of Combined Operations (Comops), while national servicemen wrote of

2. J. H. Howman, National Servicemen: Pay and Allowances, March 23, 1973; Extended Service Gratuity Scheme for Security Forces, April 10, 1973, Cabinet Memoranda, CL/Smith/27.

3. Jeanette Keith, *Rich Man's War, Poor Man's Fight: Race, Class, and Power in the Rural South during the First World War* (Chapel Hill: University of North Carolina Press, 2004); Sascha Auerbach, "Negotiating Nationalism: Jewish Conscription and Russian Repatriation in London's East End, 1916–1918," *J. British Studies* 46, no. 3 (2007): 594–620. For resistance to national conscription efforts, see Adrian Cook, *Armies of the Night: The New York City Draft Riots of 1863* (Lexington: University Press of Kentucky, 1974); Iver Bernstein, *The New York City Draft Riots* (New York: Oxford University Press, 1990); Beth Bailey, *America's Army: Making the All-Volunteer Force* (Cambridge, MA: Harvard University Press, 2009).

being pressured by their families to go to war. Family stories—about conscription, foreign soldiers, or the conduct of the war—disclosed the weakness of the coercive power of the state just as they exposed the complexities of belonging in Rhodesia.

National Service for Which Nation?

Rhodesian conscription began before Rhodesian independence. In the last years of the Central African Federation conscription was considered necessary to address the new contingencies of African nationalism. In 1960, the first conscripts were sent to the border Northern Rhodesia shared with the newly independent Congo, where young white Southern Rhodesians were said to have watched in horror as Belgians fled for their lives.[4] At the time of UDI national service for whites, Indians, and Coloureds was four and a half months. Coloureds and Indians served in two units, the Reinforcement Holding Unit and its supplementary Protection Companies, which primarily provided transport and supply. In 1978 these units were combined into the Rhodesia Defence Regiment. Once the guerrilla war began, and certainly by the early 1970s, conscription of white Rhodesian youths intensified. Starting in 1972, all white males ages eighteen to twenty-five were required to undertake nine months "service training" in the army or the police. After their initial service, these men could then be called up over the next three years to serve in the Territorial Army, a force made up of civilians who had completed their military training commanded by regular officers. In mid-1975, after much debate, national service was extended to one year, and all white males ages twenty-five to thirty were liable to call-ups for fifty-nine days; this was extended to eighty-four days almost at once. Men ages thirty to thirty-eight were liable to call-ups for shorter periods. A few months later, in early 1976 conscription was first increased to a year and then to eighteen months by the year's end; the age limit was raised from thirty to thirty-four.[5] The men ages eighteen to thirty-four

4. Geoffrey Bond, *The Incredibles: The Story of the 1st Battalion, The Rhodesian Light Infantry* (Salisbury: Sarum Imprint, 1977), 10–11; Alexandre Binda, *The Saints: The Rhodesian Light Infantry* (Johannesburg: 30 Degrees South, 2007), 22–23, and *The Rhodesia Regiment: From Boer War to Bush War, 1899–1980* (Alberton: Galago, 2012), 148–52. Some conscripts may have first joined the mercenaries and then decamped to South Africa; see Mike Hoare, *Mercenary* (London: Corgi Books, 1978 [1967]), 66–67.

5. J. K. Seirils, "Undoing the United Front? Coloured Soldiers in Rhodesia 1939–1980," *African Studies* 63, no. 1 (2004): 80; Bond, *The Incredibles*, 10–16; Chris Cocks, *Fireforce: One Man's War in the Rhodesian Light Infantry* (Weltevreden Park: South Africa, Covos Day, 1997 [1988]), 111.

who had fulfilled their national service obligation were now placed on "continuous call-up" for the territorial army: they could be redeployed for unspecified intervals. This was so disastrous for morale and complicated to administer that the army sought ways to get men to stay longer or to rationalize reserve duty. In 1977 national servicemen were offered bonuses if they stayed on an extra year. Starting in 1978 territorials and police reservists under the age of thirty-eight were required to serve a maximum of 190 days per year. Men of ages thirty-eight to forty-nine were called up for ten weeks in periods of two to four weeks at a time, but only the most experienced soldiers in that age group were placed on active duty. By then as many as half the men under thirty-eight did not report for reserve duty and the Rhodesian Front was desperate enough to entertain ideas about how to expand the professional army and abolish the call-up altogether, but by January 1979 this was impossible. In preparation for the April election, the manpower requirements were such that men of ages fifty to sixty were called up to serve as guards in urban areas. This last call-up was designed to find those trained former regular soldiers who had avoided call-ups since their retirements; it was not very successful as only 20 percent of the men called up came forward.[6]

All of the above, and every emendation to it, was contested. The question that undergirded conscription was the one that undergirded the nation—who belonged to it and what rights and obligations did they have? In 1966, Lord Graham, then minister of defence, made policy from the longtime practice that national service was based on residency, not citizenship. Rhodesian citizens, South African citizens, and British subjects resident in Rhodesia had to register; all other males had to register after they had resided in the country for three years. Graham cited and dismissed international law, in which citizens of another country could not be conscripted without the consent of that country. This was often abandoned in wartime, he wrote, as Australia had done during World War II. There was such a thing as "national law," which did not limit a state's power to conscript the population that resides within its borders. Under emergency powers draft-age aliens could be directed to

6. Caute, *Under the Skin*, 135–37; Brownell, *Collapse*, 82; Peter Godwin and Ian Hancock, *"Rhodesians Never Die,"* 88, 113, 135, 158–59, 254; Binda, *Rhodesia Regiment*, 192, 228; Anti-Apartheid Movement, *Fireforce Exposed: The Rhodesian Security Forces and Their Role in Defending White Supremacy* (London: Anti-Apartheid Movement, 1979), 8; J. K. Cilliers, *Counter-Insurgency in Rhodesia* (London: Croom Helm, 1985), 43–44; Commanders' Secretariat, Operations Coordinating Committee, Minutes, April 29, 1976, Rhodesian Army Association Papers [hereafter RAA] 2001/086/241/159, British Empire and Commonwealth Museum, Bristol; Joint Operating Command Minutes, June 26, 1978, RAA 2001/086/015/892; Secretary for Law and Order, Usage of 50–60 Age Group, March 9, 1979, RAA 2001/086/147/927.

any industry that was of national importance. Several cabinet ministers opposed this: it might limit further immigration or cause families with young men to go to South Africa or Australia. Of the four thousand aliens in Rhodesia there were only 252 of draft age, Graham reported, so the disadvantages of conscripting aliens clearly outweighed the advantages.[7]

Citizens, Aliens, and Rates of Pay

When Rhodesia became a republic in 1970 the population became one of citizens and aliens and the question of who to conscript became acute, even though citizenship was one of several forms of belonging to Rhodesia. The only group that had routinely invoked the language of citizenship was the Coloured population. "Coloured" was a broad category that denoted peoples of mixed race; in Rhodesia it was a diverse composite that numbered perhaps twenty-four thousand in 1965, or slightly less than 10 percent of the white population.[8] Coloured soldiers, whether volunteers or conscripts, appealed to the rights and obligations of citizenship to describe their service and the benefits that all too often failed to accrue from it. Coloured volunteers in World War II served as drivers in East Africa; they avowed they were "Citizens in the New Order" of the British Empire. After UDI—and after more than a decade of conscription—Coloured activists demanded the "full rights of citizens" in exchange for military service. In 1977 Coloured soldiers petitioned the army that they upheld "the legal and moral duty of all citizens" to defend the country—despite the contempt Rhodesian white soldiers had for them—but they believed the current war was unjust and racist. Nevertheless, they had "no objection" to fighting in it.[9]

When Rhodesia became a republic, the older, federal practice of requiring of South African citizens and British subjects resident in Rhodesia to fulfill the same obligations as citizens became muddled. Although Britain had treaties with many countries that forbid the conscription or service of British nationals in another country's army, Rhodesia had been calling up British subjects for years. By 1970, however, there were

7. Angus Graham, minister of defence, Compulsory Military Service for Aliens, October 28, 1966, and February 15, 1967; Cabinet Memoranda/4, 1966; Cabinet Memoranda/1, 1967, CL/Smith/21.

8. Brownell, *Collapse*, 14–15. There were eleven thousand Indians in 1965.

9. 3 Protection Company, Mt. Darwin to Brig. A. B. Campling, May 20, 1977, Survey of army morale, RAA 2001/086/263/997; Seirlis, "Coloured Soldiers," 84–89. See also Bill Nasson, "Why They Fought: Black Cape Colonists and Imperial Wars, 1899–1918," *Int. J. African Hist. Studies* 37, no. 1 (2004): 55–70.

renewed worries that such a policy would hinder immigration. The larger question, which was never fully resolved, was that of the rights and obligations of citizens relative to those of residents and aliens. This question, the cabinet was told, was all too often conveyed by the "ill-will" national servicemen held toward young aliens, whose families' immigration to Rhodesia had been generously subsidized in the first years of UDI. The cabinet debated how to make national service fair, or at least something that did not "discriminate." It would be simplest to conscript only Rhodesian citizens, but there were not enough of them to meet Rhodesia's manpower needs, and to do so might discourage aliens from becoming Rhodesian citizens. The Ministry of Defence wanted to continue as before, to call up Rhodesian citizens, Irish and South African citizens, and British subjects resident in the country. But this, the cabinet pointed out, would discriminate against the Greek or German or Portuguese citizens who were not called up. Several cabinet ministers proposed a system that was fair to young Rhodesians and did not discriminate within the alien community: all males would be called up regardless of their nationality. Aliens were now required to register after one year's residence in the country or at the age of sixteen, whichever came first. Anxious headmasters and officials complained that well-off parents might send their children to secondary school abroad so they would avoid registration. Anyone, citizen or resident, who was called up could volunteer for a period of service shorter than that for which they would be conscripted. The age for conscription was set at ages eighteen to twenty-three, but because of university deferments the "functional age limit" was twenty-five.[10]

This did not so much make conscription routine as it made belonging to Rhodesia boundless, a perpetual status that carried the same taint Rhodesian chrome did. Karl Greenberg, for example, was a British citizen brought up in Rhodesia. He went to England as soon as he completed high school, in 1976, but he could only get menial jobs, and he found Britons coarse. He decided to join the Royal Navy. He passed the exam to become a trainee officer only to be rejected "when they found out I was from Rhodesia." He then wrote to the BSAP, knowing that it had long recruited from Britain and paid the passage of new recruits. The BSAP wrote back that he had registered at sixteen and would be considered

---

10. The treaties tended to be over a hundred years old and were with "banana republics of no concern to us"; J. H. Howman, minister of defence, Rhodesian Citizens and Aliens, June 11, 1970; Military Training: Age limits, August 13, 1970, Cabinet Memoranda/2, CL/Smith/24; Hancock and Godwin, *"Rhodesians Never Die,"* 160.

a deserter if he did not return at once. Greenberg was baffled: he left Rhodesia as a minor and a British citizen, but now he had to return to join the Rhodesian police.[11]

The question of who was required to serve was joined by the question of how long they were required to do so. Every extended month of service was struggled over by bureaucracies terrified of driving young men out of the country and by a military insistent that national service be increased to two years.[12] Added to the struggle was the elastic nature of Rhodesia's white population. How, and at what point, to call up the sons of emigrating parents was a vexing question throughout the 1970s. If parents were in the process of preparing to emigrate but had not completed all the formalities, sons were liable for national service; if a son had registered for national service and he was called up after his parents completed the paperwork for emigration, he was liable as well.[13] Industries and businesses complained bitterly that the call-up gave the military a monopoly on white youth; they had no access to the labor of young men. The call-up of men between ages thirty-eight and fifty made matters worse. Many of these men occupied critical positions in commerce and industry, and for those businesses that made up the difference between military pay and what a man normally earned, reserve duty was expensive.[14]

Questions about the length of service became questions about soldiers' pay. This was a contentious and expensive issue for whites, Coloureds, and Africans. In 1965 soldiers' pay was based on federal rates, which had been for a small, regular army, but in a few years it was especially complicated by the number of men on reserve duty. Haphazard committees with occasional recommendations to adjust soldiers' pay had created even greater disjunctures, in which conscripts and territorials sometimes earned 40 percent less than regular troops of the same rank. As of 1973 pay rates for conscripts were rationalized across the services. National servicemen earned R$4.50 a day with a R$1 allowance for married men including 75 cents for the first child and 55 cents for each additional one. National servicemen who re-engaged as regulars received a R$150 bonus. African and white soldiers received a bonus for parachute qualifications. The pay of men on reserve duty was raised to

11. Karl Greenberg, *The Gokwe Kid: Dick of the Bushveld* (n.p.: Karl Greenberg, 2012), 7–8.
12. Commanders' Secretariat, Operations Coordinating Committee, Minutes, May 13, 1975, RAA 2001/086/172(A)/146; Ministry of Defence, Memo on Extension of National Service, July 29, 1977, RAA 2001/086/021/1152.
13. Manpower Committee, September 15, 1977, RAA 2001/086/007/882.
14. Caute, *Under the Skin*, 136–37; Godwin and Hancock, *"Rhodesians Never Die,"* 254.

R$1.50 per day in 1973. The marriage allowance was raised to R$3.30 but the allowances for children remained the same as for national servicemen. Reservists received an extra R$1 a day for every day of duty after the first fourteen days. Most reservists had civilian jobs, but there was no legal requirement for employers to make up the difference between the reservists' pay and their salaries: some employers did and some did not. Those who did not found it easier to hire white women or cheaper to hire Africans and this, everyone agreed, intensified the anxiety of white Rhodesian youths.[15]

The army had argued for years that the pay offered African or Coloured, Asian, and Eurasian troops was based on political calculations, not military ones; commanders argued that increasing the pay for Coloured national servicemen was a way to get fewer "layabout types." When it was decided to use a mixed-race unit as riflemen in the northeast the army wanted them paid the same as European troops. It would cost R$3,000 but that was a small price to pay for lessening the burden on the white community. It also turned such men into motivated "front line soldiers who are killing terrorists."[16] In 1977 African regulars—mainly RAR—complained about the wage gap between African and white troops at similar ranks. "If a black officer gets the same pay as a white officer, why then should not an African soldier have the same pay as a white soldier?" The army turned this into an observation about the number of African officers rather than the remuneration for African soldiers. It regretted that the RAR had not been able to commission as many officers as it would have liked—it was too busy making war—but the Africans awarded field commissions were free to use officers' amenities. There could be "no second-class officers" in the Rhodesian army.[17]

Whatever the military wanted, and whoever complained about it, did conscription work? Like much in the history of war, it depends on what you read. Many Rhodesian authors relished the notion of loyal and stoic conscripts: "For white Rhodesia, being male meant armed service

15. J. H. Howman, Minister of Defence, National Servicemen: Pay and Allowances, May 2, 1973; Minister of Finance, Report of the committee set up to examine the question of make-up pay for territorials, August 8, 1973, CL/Smith/26; Paul French, *Shadows of a Forgotten Past: To the Edge with the Rhodesian SAS and Selous Scouts* (Solihull: Helion, 2012), 58; Army Counter Intelligence, Morale throughout the Territorial Army, June 1, 1977, typescript, RAA 2001/086/263/997. Occupations requiring apprenticeships were especially hard hit; see Hancock and Godwin, *"Rhodesians Never Die,"* 159–60.

16. J. H. Howman, National Service: Equal Pay for Coloured, Asian and Eur-Asian (CAE) members of the territorial forces and the reserves, December 5, 1973, CL/Smith/26; Brig. A. B. Campling to 3 Protection Company, Mt Darwin, May 20, 1977, RAA 2001/086/263/997.

17. D. T. Hosking, AS Morale–top secret, typescript, September 7, 1977, RAA 2001/086/263/997; Advancement of Africans in the Defence Forces, Cabinet minutes, May 25, 1976, CL/Smith/37.

without exception: from eighteen years old to sixty-five, everybody served in the army, or the police, or the police reserve."[18] Historians and policy makers took the same sentiment and turned it into a strategic virtue. Arguing that there simply were not enough whites in Rhodesia to fight a war and run a country, they asserted that the army was "mainly the white electorate in arms" and the resulting demographic constraints meant that the war was fought with special forces, small, elite, regular, and often biracial units that gathered the intelligence on which counter-insurgency was based.[19] Many of those units, however, included turned guerrillas, men whose new loyalties were to each other, in a "band of brothers and comrades known as a regiment," a story of new families rather than one of a white-ruled nation claiming its own independence.[20] Other authors, especially those opposed to white rule in Southern Africa, insisted that the war was unpopular among whites, and produced statistics to show how many white males did not serve, that half the eligible three thousand men evaded conscription in 1973, and 6,500 evaded it in 1976.[21]

Whether exaggerated or not, these figures suggest an inflexible binary in which young men either do the state's bidding or resist it. This is not only too simple, it is troubled by the extent that some branches of the service opposed the call-up altogether. The BSAP did not think army reservists could be good policemen, for example, and the air force rejected reservists for anything other than guarding its planes: its work was too specialized for anyone to do occasionally.[22] By 1977, however, conscription was a nightmare to administer. Branches of the service were at least as worried about the size of the call-up as they were about the number of draft dodgers. The police had transport, weapons, ammunition, or radios for only half the number of men they could call

18. Alan Thrush, *Of Land and Spirits* (Guernsey, Transition Publishing, 1997), 242. A deserter echoed this in 1979: when he arrived in England, the first things that struck him were "the lack of army trucks and people in camo." Anonymous, letter to the editor, *Zimbabwe Democrat* 2, no. 1 (January 1979): 6; Terence Ranger papers, Rhodes House, Oxford.

19. Lewis H. Gann, "From Ox Wagon to Armored Car in Rhodesia," *Military Review* 48, no. 4 (1968): 63–72; Bruce Hoffman, Jennifer M. Tauw, and David Arnold, *Lessons for Contemporary Counter-insurgencies: Lessons from Rhodesia* (Santa Monica: RAND, 1991), 47.

20. Reid-Daly, *Selous Scouts*, 176–79.

21. *"Rhodesians Never Die,"* 113–14, 136, 160; *Fire Force Exposed*, 7–8.

22. Interim debriefing, Joint Planning Staff, Operation Hurricane, February 12, 1974, RAA 2001/086/222/147; Joint Operating Command [hereafter JOC] Minutes, April 6, 1978, RAA 2001/086/007/082. A former RAF pilot, now a professor of law at the University College of Rhodesia, told Jan Morris he loved spending one week in four piloting younger troopies to remote areas. It was a "renewal of youth for him." Jan Morris, *Destinations. Essays from Rolling Stone* (New York: Oxford University Press, 1982 [1980]), 127–28.

up at any one time. Any "increase in call-up levels would therefore be quite meaningless and serve no useful purpose." The number of protection companies increased faster than there were officers available to command them, and the Guard Force did not have enough staff to administer a call-up every thirty days.[23] A common complaint was that more time was spent administering the call-up than fighting the war.[24] National servicemen were horrified by the inefficiency of a war fought with a reserve army. One was "filled with dread" at "actually having to serve in a demoralized, half-baked territorial outfit."[25] Reservists did not like it either. A man on patrol with Dan Wylie complained that he had often had to rewrite orders. "No sanity. No pragmatism. But is it really surprising? We're part-timers. Chemists. Editors. Musicians. We have to make this transition, become aggressive, tactical. . . . How can we cope with that?"[26]

Family Stories

Perhaps the most intense struggle over the fate of young men took place in their families where the homilies about citizenship and obligation were coupled with anger and disappointment, at sons and at the regime. If Rhodesians were ambivalent about conscription, they were equally ambivalent about evading it. As is fairly common in war memoirs, many young men could not fully articulate their reasons for volunteering.[27] When young Rhodesian men recalled their being called up, however, their writings took a very specific form. Conscription seemed to be an issue of family membership rather than one of national membership, although that family membership constituted a notion of the rights and obligations of citizenship. Parents expected their sons to do their

23. Major Mike Williams as told to Robin Moore, *Major Mike* (New York: Ace, 1981 [1978]), 16; British South Africa Police, HQ, Salisbury, to Comops, Utilization of Manpower, August 22, 1977; Guard Force HQ, Salisbury to Comops HQ, Re: Sixty Days In-Thirty Days Out Call-up, August 23, 1977, RAA 2001/086/147/927.

24. Operations Coordinating Committee [hereafter OCC] Minutes, September 7, 1977, RAA Papers, 2001/086/233/245.

25. Chris Cocks, *Survival Course* (Weltevreden Park; Covos Day, 1999), 6.

26. Dan Wylie, *Dead Leaves: Two Years in the Rhodesia War* (Scottsville: University of Natal Press, 2000), 128.

27. Samuel Hynes, *The Soldiers' Tale: Bearing Witness to Modern War* (New York: Penguin, 1998), 45–51; Charlie Warren, *Stick Leader RLI* (Durban: Just Done Productions, 2007), 1–2; Stu Taylor, *Lost in Africa* (Johannesburg: 30 Degrees South, 2007), 16–19; Jake Harper-Ronald as told to Greg Budd, *Sunday, Bloody Sunday: A Soldier's War in Northern Ireland, Rhodesia, Mozambique, and Iraq* (Alberton: Galago, 2009), 23.

national service; the consequences of draft dodging were grave, and they were articulated in the home. Graham Doke was a national serviceman who later wrote a novel in which the protagonist had been accepted at Oxford shortly before he got his call-up papers. He desperately wanted to go to Oxford, but it was too late to postpone his admission. His father was adamant that he stay and fight. "You'll never be able to come back, you know. You've got your call-up papers—you can't go now." This was a "recurring theme for everyone," Doke noted, although his father added that national service was "what a man should do."[28] Progressive families were no less adamant that their sons do their national service. Peter Godwin wanted to leave the country when he was drafted, but his father lectured him on how "dishonorable" that would be. "The way I see it, Pete," his father said, "we've been kept safe all these years by other peoples' sons, yet when it comes our turn you're a scarper. It's not really on, is it?" Godwin's father explained that the war was neither about patriotism nor the Rhodesian way of life: it was about strategy. If his son were to serve, he'd "only be holding the line while the politicians negotiate. We have to keep the war under control while they hammer out a settlement. We can't let the future of the country be dictated on the battlefield." Godwin's mother took another, more inclusive line: "You'll be serving for blacks as well as for whites, just keeping people safe," she said. Besides, "it'll stand you good in later life."[29] Chris Cocks planned to leave the country when he was called up. He didn't really believe in the Rhodesian cause, either: his parents voted against the Rhodesian Front and he had gone to a multiracial private school and had African friends. He had organized the necessary visas to leave the country, but when he said goodbye to his sisters, they were shocked— "not so much for national honor but for the shame it would bring to our parents"—and so through "pleading, cajoling and sound 'common sense'" they persuaded him to stay. Or, as he put it years later, "I got cold feet, succumbing to a fear of the system and my parents more than anything else." Cocks fought for Rhodesia, but he never got over his doubts, "and I was certainly no patriot."[30]

When sons did emigrate, fathers took it personally. In one wartime novel, the son of a Rhodesian bureaucrat—a district commissioner— has emigrated to the peaceful suburbia of Connecticut, "where the last

---

28. Graham Doke, *First Born* (Cape Town: Book, 2000), 75; Conrad K., *In the Shadow of the Tokolosh* (Chelmsford: Silverling Inspired Publishing, 2010), 200.

29. Peter Godwin, *Mukiwa: A White Boy in Africa* (London: Macmillan, 1996), 208; Doke, *First Born*, 75.

30. Cocks, *Fireforce*, 7; Chris Cocks, *Survival Course* (Weltevreden Park: Covos Day, 1999), 54.

dangerous Redskin had been attended to a hundred years ago." He had "turned his back on the country that bred him, to lead a normal life and rear his family in a less troubled environment. 'And who can blame him?'" his father asks himself, knowing that his son's departure "was a personal hurt, a rejection to all he had worked for and believed in. If young men weren't prepared to fight when things got tough, then it was a pretty poor look-out for the world."[31] Nonfictional parents—or at least the nonfictional parents who complained about their sons' service assignment—were not so judicious, nor did they all think that national service was simply about protecting other families. Neil Jackson's father was delighted when his son was called up, hoping the Rhodesian Light Infantry (RLI) would teach him discipline and cleanliness. Stu Taylor's parents wanted him to enlist in the BSAP or the more exclusive SAS, "socially stable" units with fewer misfits than the RLI in which he enlisted.[32] Other parents wanted their sons in glamorous regiments, misfits and all. In 1979 parents of sons called up in the most recent intake complained that their sons were sent to the Guard Force. The minister of manpower promised he would look into it, but families should rest assured that these young men "would not be taking a 'back seat' in the war and that their role would be active, important, responsible and open to initiative as their counterparts in the SAS or RLI."[33]

National service was not enforced. It was not illegal to ignore a call-up notice nor was there the will or the manpower to track down men who did not report for duty.[34] Less than one hundred Jehovah's Witnesses were prosecuted for failing to register between 1968 and 1975, but they were fined, not put to other work.[35] Young men thought it "unthinkable" to become a conscientious objector, but many left the country. Of these, many went to South Africa and at least as many went to the United Kingdom, where they could get asylum or a place at a university after a lengthy process. There was an occasional draft resisters' newsletter

31. C. E. Dibb, *Spotted Soldiers* (Salisbury: Leo Publications, 1978), 51–52.
32. Jackson was immediately seconded to his unit's rugby team. Binda, *Rhodesia Regiment*, 220; Taylor, *Lost*, 19.
33. JOC Minutes, January 18, 1979; RAA 2001/086/004/895. The SAS and the RLI were two of Rhodesia's three all-white units.
34. Compos HQ, Salisbury, Exemptions, December 15, 1978, RAA 2001/086/017/919.
35. J. R. Howman, Minister of Defence, Military Service: Jehovah's Witnesses, May 18, 1971, Cabinet Memoranda, CL/Smith/25. Proposals that Jehovah's Witnesses be put to work in the tobacco industry were dismissed because smoking was against their religion, but this turned out not to be true. D. W. Lardner-Burke, minister of law and order, Jehovah's Witnesses, May 3, 1974; Cabinet Memoranda, CL/Smith/27.

published in London in the late 1970s, the *Zimbabwe Democrat*.[36] By 1979 men went absent without leave from the elite regiments of the SAS or the Selous Scouts, and from all ranks of the RAR.[37]

Familial articulations of citizenship did not seem to extend beyond the period of the call-up, however. Cocks was flattered by the camaraderie the regulars offered him; he enlisted—"perversely," he later wrote—for another three years rather than serve the additional six months now required of conscripts. His parents "were utterly mortified that I had forsaken a university degree for the doubtful privilege of another two years in the army." It was "a transitory fad," they said, and they blamed his "dubious mates" who had talked him into joining a commando battalion.[38] Godwin, on the other hand, had no interest in extended service, either for the state or to shock his parents. He was devastated when his national service commitment was increased by six months: he had been accepted to Cambridge for the coming year only; if he could not come, he would have to reapply. He secured his demobilization by signing a document that promised he would go back into the security forces "whenever, and as soon as, I returned. . . . They were that desperate for manpower." Godwin was called up when he returned a year later for his sister's funeral. She had been killed when she and her fiancé drove into a Rhodesian army ambush, so Godwin was especially furious: "I was particularly disinclined to return to uniform under the circumstances."[39] For parents, and for a few sons, conscription was fine. It defined a national loyalty that was socially and legally limited; it mapped a space in which families did some of the work of states, briefly, and it put limits on the bonds of soldiering that might have an allure for young men. The professional soldier, the volunteers, the unorthodox regiments were in practice less appealing to Rhodesian families in need of protection. Rhodesians who belonged to the nation whether or not they believed in its project would fight for it as required, after which they would—as Cocks's, Godwin's, and Doke's parents planned—send their sons abroad for university.

Conscription may be a legal relationship between citizens and states, but its practice in Rhodesia was in part shaped by relations between conscripts and regular soldiers. Young conscripts, particularly those in the RLI—the all-white regiment of Cocks and Taylor, and a few men we

36. Author's field notes, Harare, July 29, 1995; Anthony Trethowan, *Delta Scout: Ground Coverage Operator* (Johannesburg: 30 Degrees South, 2008), 35.

37. Caute, *Under the Skin*, 363; author's field notes, Durban, August 21, 2006.

38. Cocks, *Fireforce*, 110–12, and *Survival Course*, 54; see also Taylor, *Lost*, 47, 50–51.

39. Godwin, *Mukiwa*, 261–62.

will meet later—recalled their exclusion by regular soldiers.[40] Regular soldiers in almost all branches of the security forces complained bitterly of the preferential treatment given to the young men who were released early so they could begin their studies at university.[41] Men in elite regiments complained about how much time was lost on the drill national servicemen required. In Angus Shaw's novel Peter Walls, the nonfictional commander-in-chief of the Rhodesian army whom we will meet again, addressed a group of RLI national servicemen. "The general wanted us to know it was a fallacy that the regulars sneered at conscripts like us. To prove it, he adopted an air of confidentiality and began telling us about the latest intelligence reports. . . . He was letting us in on something big . . . he trusted us, he valued us. . . . We weren't just cannon fodder."[42]

The call-ups of older men made the obligations of citizenship and resistance thereto less familial and more economic. In mid-1978, for example, 85 percent of men in the thirty-eight to forty-nine age group registered, but only 25 percent of retired regulars—a small group to begin with—who were over fifty did so.[43] Men over forty, David Caute wrote, had very little morale and very short tempers. They complained about having to bring their own torches and batteries; those who used their own vehicles while on duty were furious that they were not reimbursed for petrol. Rhodesia's attempts to increase what it demanded of its citizens, in terms of age and time served, miscarried badly: businessmen left their offices only to be given menial tasks in the lower ranks of the armed forces, and the sheer number of older men called up caused many people to believe the war was already lost.[44] The idea that the state's claim on adult males should have limits, and those limits, as Godwin's family firmly believed, could and should be set by personal considerations. When a demobilized Chris Cocks was called up for service in the Police Anti-Terrorist United (PATU), his wife complained; he had "done enough fighting for this bloody country." And indeed, as a PATU stick leader, Cocks soon learned that while "on paper" each stick should have

40. See also Binda, *The Saints*, 187.

41. Army Counter-Intelligence, Morale throughout the Rhodesian Army, June 1, 1977, typescript, RAA 2001/086/263/997.

42. Dennis Croukamp, *Only My Friends Call Me "Crouks"* (Cape Town: Pseudo Publishing, 2006), 172–76; Angus Shaw, *Kandaya: Another Time, Another Place* (Harare: Baobab Books, 1993), 3–4.

43. National Joint Operating Command [JOC] Minutes, June 28, 1978, RAA 2001/086/015/892; Secretary for Law and Order to National Manpower Board, Usage of 50–60 Age Group, March 9, 1979, RAA 2001/086/147/927.

44. Caute, *Under the Skin*, 362–63; Anti-Apartheid Movement, *Fireforce Exposed*, 7–9; Thrush, *Land and Spirits*, 242, 286–87.

six to eight members, in practice it was five at the most: some were away, or sick, or "just plain didn't feel like it."[45]

National Service and National Bureaucracies

How do we explain this? That national service was anything but national and that the obligations of citizenship were an extension of the nagging and moral authority of families and the ability of older men to control, and contain, their sons at a specific moment? The Rhodesian army might not have put it quite this way, but they were aware of the tension; they repeated a saying among young men, "We don't mind dying for Rhodesia, but not for the RF."[46] The full persuasive authority of fathers was applied to the army and manpower boards as men tried to get their sons exemptions from national service or to arrange a call-up so a young man could get into one of "the four crack regiments" of the army, or barring that, find him a desk job.[47] Not only did everyone lobby on behalf of sons and nephews, but relevant government departments and ministries took these entreaties very seriously. The question of how to call up farmers, and what to do with farmers' families when they were away from their homes, was never fully resolved. Men who were the sole proprietors of businesses were the subject of much debate; it was only in 1977 that they were required to do short periods of duty in the police reserve.[48] Admission to university, particularly to those in South Africa or England, bedeviled Rhodesian manpower administrators. Some young men were released from national service to study abroad; others were not. When an angry father pointed out that young men going to universities in South Africa had to do six months more national service than those going to the University College of Rhodesia, the policy was changed. All students, wherever they were going to university, had to complete two years of national service before starting their studies, but

45. Chris Cocks, *Survival Course*, 11, 13. PATU training usually consisted of a day's lectures on how to handle road blocks, shooting, and some target practice; see David Craven, *Mapolisa: Some Reminiscences of a Rhodesian Policeman* (Weltevreden Park: Covos Day, 1998), 126–27.
46. Commanders' Secretariat, Operations Coordinating Committee [OCC] Minutes, August 18, 1976, RAA 2001/0086/241/159.
47. Doke, *First Born*, 5–6; B. H. Mussett, Joint Minister of Lands, Natural Resources, and Rural Development to Secretary for Defence, January 27, 1979; RAA 2001/086/147/927.
48. 3rd draft, Statement by the Minister of Combined Operations (Comops), May 24, 1977, Manpower Committee Minutes, April 29, 1977, to March 29, 1978, RAA 2001/086/007/882.

students going to overseas universities could be released after twenty-one months so they could be there at the start of term.[49]

Personal situations received more sympathy than the rhetoric of massive white mobilization would suggest. Rob Wells, a garage owner, had evaded the draft until 1978. When he was called up he was advised to go into the police reserve as that would give him the most flexible schedule.[50] Thomas Bassett was twenty-five when he was called up. He wrote that he had a wife, two children, and a job in South Africa; the expense and inconvenience of national service would be too great for him to serve at this time, but he would like to do so at a later, more suitable time. If he did not return now, he asked, would he be blacklisted? Not at all, wrote Combined Operations: he showed his willingness to serve and that was what counted. The Department of Security Manpower was outraged that the army had so casually released a man from his service obligations: "we are told that there is a crying need for manpower in the services and that we are too lenient with our exceptions" and this young man should serve. Comops did not immediately call him up, however; they asked him to write directly to the department.[51]

This anecdote maps the fault line of Rhodesian conscription. Repeated conflict between the army and civilian authorities meant that conscription and continual call-ups generated an uneven and often diffident expansion of state power. We have already seen that families did some of the work of conscription, but by 1978 the weakness of the state's coercive power was of great concern to security forces. The military complained about lax government bodies in charge of manpower and defense exemptions, both of which complained that the army was unable to use manpower efficiently. In finger-pointing correspondence from December 1978, when both the army and the government understood that the April 1979 election would require an increase in manpower, Comops's frustration and disappointment with government agencies was obvious. In the last year, defense exemption boards had given exemptions and deferments to over 2,400 men without consulting the security forces. They gave into pressure from individuals or groups; anyone who could claim they provided an essential economic service was exempted. They

49. Caute, *Under the Skin*, 136–37; H. W. Markham, Midlands, to Comops HQ, Salisbury, August 19, 1977; Comops HQ, Early Release of University Students, September 30, 1977, RAA 2001/086/147/927; Manpower Committee, Minutes, October 25, 1977, RAA 2001/086/007/882.

50. Rob Wells, *The Part-Time War* (Cambridge: Fern House, 2011), 5.

51. Thomas W. Bassett to Army HQ, Salisbury, September 27, 1978; Comops to Bassett, October 27, 1978; Dept. of Security Manpower to Comops, January 24, 1979; Secretary, Comops to Bassett, February 2, 1979, RAA 2001/086/147/927.

did not send the police after men who did not report for duty. Comops recommended that both the national boards tasked with granting exemptions be abolished so that the security forces could take sole responsibility for deferments and exemptions. The government should make it illegal to ignore a call-up notice, and the military and BSAP should be allowed to arrest anyone who did not report for duty: unit commanders could issue arrest warrants. Immigrants should only be exempt from conscription for eighteen months. Banks should stop external payments for those who left the country to evade their duty. The working hours in private business and government offices should be extended as well.

The minister of manpower was outraged. The real problem was not the conflicting demands of the economy and security, but that the army did not make the best use of the manpower it had called up. It was his finding that security forces gave far more exemptions than the manpower board did. The army had already been offered at least a dozen manpower plans, none of which had been utilized. What was needed was an investigation of army practices to understand why manpower was used so badly, but of course that would require more manpower. The final compromise was that the civilian exemption boards would be given a better appreciation of the needs of security forces, which meant they were asked to include retired military officers on each board.[52]

National Service and Nationality

So who was willing to fight, or even register to fight, for the Rhodesian Front, for the idea of white privilege maintained against majority rule? Many Rhodesians believed that it was the new arrivals—recent immigrants who had benefited from the assistance packages of the first years of UDI—who would risk life and limb for the privileges Rhodesia offered. Rhodesian-born Angus Shaw was scathing: the men who had exchanged council housing in the East End of London for a house in the sun with servants were willing to pay the price, even if it meant "burning down the odd village" when they were called up. This was a wartime version of ideas that circulated in the country well before UDI in which new immigrants were worthy of contempt. After UDI recent immigrants were often considered too quick to become racist or too complacent about

52. Comops Headquarters, Salisbury, Manpower, December 7, 1978; Exemptions, December 15, 1978, RAA 2001/086/017/919.

racist policies because they themselves were now prospering.[53] It was also an overstatement. An annual average of more than thirteen thousand people left Rhodesia and moved to Britain or Australia or South Africa beginning in 1973.[54] These were the people, Rhodesian politicians across the political spectrum complained, who did not put down roots: they came for the servants and swimming pools and left when they had to defend them, because, as van der Byl put it, it was "inconvenient" to serve Rhodesia in her time of need.[55]

Outside the country, the issue of new immigrants was eclipsed by that of foreign soldiers. These men were, according to most writings on the war, professional soldiers from Great Britain and significant numbers of Vietnam veterans from the U.S., Australia, and New Zealand, plus a few ex-legionnaires from continental Europe, who came to fight for Rhodesia. Some came because they wanted adventure; others found it the best career option available to them.[56] Jake Harper-Ronald, SAS, thought foreign soldiers "had come along for the ride." Some clearly did: Angus Shaw thought otherwise. If these men "went around looking for other people's nasty little wars to fight in" they were the same as mercenaries: "it wasn't their war."[57]

Whose war was it? The actual number of foreign soldiers is almost impossible to ascertain, since almost everyone who provided a number had a reason to distort it. Most sources claim there were 1,500 foreign soldiers, of whom perhaps 400 were American; the Rhodesian army thought there were perhaps 1,000 foreign soldiers, of whom 100 were American.[58] Even within the disputed figures, there was little attempt to distinguish what "foreign" actually meant: it is not clear if the figure of

53. Shaw, *Kandaya*, 26. He was repeating the conventional wisdom of social science and journalists. One study found that after five years new immigrants were as opposed to social contact between Africans and Europeans as were Rhodesians who had lived there thirty years. Charles Frantz and Cyril A. Rogers, "Length of Residence and Race Attitudes in Southern Rhodesia," *Race* 3 (1962): 46–54. In 1963 a journalist claimed that the Rhodesian electorate included people who would have voted Labour at home but were now "the miners in their Jaguars, the thousands of households where cheap black labour makes living so easy, the take-home pay thirty to fifty per cent higher than Britain." Patrick Keatley, *The Politics of Partnership* (Baltimore: Penguin, 1963), 226, 328.

54. Brownell, *Collapse*, 75–79.

55. Quoted in Paul A. Moorcraft, *A Short Thousand Years: The End of Rhodesia's Rebellion* (Salisbury: Galaxie, 1980), 3; Hills, *Rebel People*, 204–5.

56. J. R. T. Wood, *The War Diaries of Andre Dennison* (Gibralter: Ashanti Publishing, 1989), 4–5; Peter McAleese, *No Mean Soldier: The Story of the Ultimate Professional Soldier in the SAS and Other Forces* (London: Cassell, 2000 [1993]), 76.

57. Harper-Ronald, *Bloody Sunday*, 82; Shaw, *Kandaya*, 182.

58. Richard Lobban, "American Mercenaries in Rhodesia, *J. of Southern African Affairs* 3 (1978): 319–25; Operations Coordinating Committee, Minutes, August 30, 1977, September 7, 1977, RAA 2001/086/233/1245.

1,500 includes South African nationals resident in Rhodesia. Nor was there any concerted effort to distinguish who was foreign and who was mercenary, a term used most often for political effect. The British press, progressive and not so progressive, loved the idea of Rhodesia's mercenary force. The *Sunday Times* claimed that 40 percent of Rhodesian army regulars were foreign-born, a figure that seems perfectly accurate, if meaningless, given that more than 40 percent of white Rhodesian males had been born in another country.[59]

The Rhodesian army—which had every reason to dissemble—seemed baffled that anyone would accuse it of using mercenaries. It made light of news reports about recruiting mercenaries, but it rejected any idea that might look mercenary as well. In 1976 the Operations Coordinating Committee rejected Portugal's offer to send them two hundred white soldiers who had fought in Angola. Another one hundred white Portuguese were in South Africa, but would be willing to fight for Rhodesia if Rhodesia could pay their passage.[60] A month later Colonel Mike Hoare, who had raised Moise Tshombe's mercenary force in Katanga fifteen years before, proposed an international brigade that would counter Russians or Cubans invading Rhodesia. This would be the Rhodesian Foreign Legion, which would have a "mystique similar to that of the French Foreign Legion" and would be multiracial, recruited from Europe and Africa (but not Rhodesia or South Africa), have French as its official language, and "be motivated by a genuine anti-Communist conviction." They would have to be single men, paid in Rhodesian currency, who could be granted Rhodesian citizenship after a year's service. Hoare had worked out the two phases of recruitment and had chosen the color of the uniforms. The army's joint planning staff all but laughed: any international brigade would be called a mercenary force, and this one sounded expensive and ineffective.[61] Commanders were slightly more gracious to the exiled King Zog of Albania. As Prince Lekka he had been to Sandhurst with several Rhodesian officers, all of whom declined his offer of five hundred men who would come and fight for Rhodesia while being trained as an expeditionary force to liberate his kingdom.[62]

59. *Sunday Times* [London] quoted in Jonathan Bloch, Britain's Contribution to Rhodesia's War Effort, typescript London, August 29, 1979, NAZ/IDAF/MS 589/9.

60. Commander's Secretariat, Operations Coordinating Committee, March 12 and 25, 1976, RAA 2001/086/241/159.

61. International Brigade, Joint Planning Staff, Ministry of Defence, Salisbury, April 13, 1976, RAA 2001/086/227/122.

62. Minutes, OCC, September 16, 1977, RAA 2001/086/223/248; author's field notes, Pretoria, May 22, 2008.

With the exception of a group of French paratroopers who formed the incompetent 7th Company of the Rhodesia Regiment, most foreign soldiers came as individuals. Most learned of opportunities in Rhodesia through ads in military magazines or recruitment meetings.[63] All foreign (as opposed to foreign-born) soldiers fought under decidedly unmercenary conditions: they were, at the military's insistence, paid at local rates, in Rhodesian currency, which were substantially higher for enlisted men than for conscript soldiers. They were taxed at local rates as well.[64] Foreign soldiers in the RLI and the SAS complained bitterly about the way they were treated; European nationals in the SAS deserted in large numbers, usually leaving the country.[65] In Rhodesia, talk of foreign soldiers seemed to be a way to talk about Rhodesians and the difference between Rhodesians and foreigners, or at least Britons. Citizenship did not itself make good soldiers, but belonging to the country—a claim on place and history—did. Jake Harper-Ronald joined the SAS after returning to Rhodesia after years in Britain's parachute regiment. His new commanding officer was certain he could learn new tactics and techniques "without any problems as he knew I was Rhodesian born."[66] David Lemon, a British-born BSAP, had been in Rhodesia nine years when his superintendent called him "lily-livered. . . . When you've been here for five years, Sonny—if you last that long—your views will change."[67]

Some foreign soldiers just happened to pitch up in Rhodesia in wartime. Timothy Bax was a British subject. He was born in Tanganyika; he grew up there and in Canada. He took a job in South Africa after finishing school. In 1970 he drove to Rhodesia for a holiday; his car broke down but he could not afford the repairs. Drinking in a bar with RLI, he asked if anyone knew of a job he could get on a tourist visa. An RLI called the recruiting officer over: he could easily arrange a permanent residence permit if he was willing to join "a fighting man's army." Others had stories that recalled the depth and breadth of the British Empire. A few were linked to Rhodesia, as was the great-grandson of Lord Salisbury, for whom Rhodesia's capital was named. He came because he

---

63. Caute, *Under the Skin*, 107, 137–40; Wood, *Andre Dennison*, 5; McAleese, *No Mean Soldier*, 76–77.

64. Joint Planning Staff, Ministry of Defence, International Brigade, April 12, 1976, RAA 2001/086/227/122; Cocks, *Fireforce*, 87–88; Caute, *Under the Skin*, 107; Barry Cohen, "The War in Rhodesia: A Dissenter's View," *African Affairs* 76 (1977): 492–93.

65. Army Counterintelligence, Morale survey conducted with RLI, July 19, 1977, RAA 2001/086/263/997; McAleese, *No Mean Soldier*, 158; French, *Forgotten Past*, 37–38. The SAS hierarchy was mortified: "In no other SAS unit in the world did soldiers desert . . . in such numbers."

66. Harper-Ronald, *Bloody Sunday*, 81.

67. David Lemon, *Never Quite a Soldier*, 67.

was frustrated with British counter-insurgency in Ulster, where he had been an officer in the Grenadier Guards. In Rhodesia he wrote for the *Daily Telegraph* and went on patrol with the RLI.[68]

Nowhere were family bonds richer and more racially entangled than in fiction. In Richard Gledhill's novel about the RLI, the hero, like the author, was born in Kenya and arrived in Rhodesia via England and Australia. The novel begins with the hero-as-a-child hiding in the attic while a Mau Mau gang, led by the house servant, rapes his mother and kills his father. As the novel progresses, the hero learns that the ZANLA he is hunting is the grandson of a man who, years before, worked in Kenya and married a local woman; he fathered a son who grew up to become the very house servant who led the attack on the hero's parents. These two soldiers, black and white, are locked in a struggle that is as familial as it is transnational. Why did Gledhill's hero join the RLI, someone asks. Regimental or national loyalty, let alone a sense of place, had nothing to do with it. "My parents were killed by Mau Mau when I was a kid. It has nothing to do with politics. It's a personal thing."[69]

But if fighting for Rhodesia was such a personal thing, how could it serve a nation, even a renegade one that was not fully served by its citizens' belief in national service? How do we understand the will to go to war if young men were not willing to die for their country but were willing to delay going to Oxford for it? How do we understand parents insisting their sons report for national service because it was a way to manage defeat, not to ensure victory?[70] Rhodesian officials were well aware of their citizens' desire for limited participation in the war, but they were far more uneasy about the number of foreign soldiers—however small or large it was—who fought for the cause. On the one hand, foreign soldiers proved that "kith and kin" was real, that the world was full of people who agreed with them, who could "feel more like a Rhodesian" than members of the countries they came from.[71] On the other hand, it made being Rhodesia little more than a default nationality, thinking oneself Rhodesian because no other country fit the bill: the state that imagined its own independence now had soldiers who imagined themselves to

68. Tim Bax, *Three Sips of Gin: Dominating the Battlespace with Rhodesia's Elite Selous Scouts* (Solihull: Helion, 2012), 105–13. Caute, *Under the Skin*, 49–52; Wood, *Andre Dennison*, 3–5; Anti-Apartheid Movement, *Fireforce Exposed*, 28; Reid-Daly, *Selous Scouts, passim*; Cocks, *Fireforce*, 86–87; Wessels, *PK*, 239.

69. Gledhill, *One Commando*, 1–16, 38, 58–59, 73.

70. I take this point from Michael Geyer, "Insurrectionary Warfare: The German Debate about *Levée en Masse* in October 1918," *J. Modern History* 73, no. 3 (2001): 459–527.

71. Robin Moore, *The White Tribe* (Publishers Encampment, WY: Affiliated Writers of America, 1991), 23, 187.

be Rhodesian. Rhodesia's struggle against African nationalists—politely called the bush war in Rhodesia—encouraged some men to come who had no real interest in the country they defended. Robin Moore, an American novelist and the amanuensis of the Green Berets, arrived in Rhodesia in the early 1970s and often called himself the unofficial American ambassador. He founded an organization called the Crippled Eagles, so named because they were crippled by U.S. government harassment. Some of the younger Americans were happy to explain why they came to the journalists Moore invited to Sunday afternoons by the swimming pool in 1977. One told David Caute that he had answered an ad in *Soldier of Fortune* because after Vietnam and Angola "we can't afford to lose any more countries." Another cheerfully informed Christopher Hitchens that he didn't care "about the rich white guys and their farms and their dough. But I'm fighting for them because they're white, and the white man is running out all over."[72] In a book published in 1977 specifically to inform the American public of the situation in Rhodesia and the importance of ending sanctions, Moore presented eight vignettes about individual Crippled Eagles. One man explained why he came to Rhodesia with a question about Angola, which seems to have had all the power for these young men that Sparta had for a generation of Rhodesian Front party hacks. Others said they came out of loyalty to "other Anglo-Saxons" or because they feared the direction in which the United States was heading.[73]

These statements problematized the notion of nationality beyond all recognition, and they threw citizenship into high relief. What did it mean to be willing to die for Rhodesia while thinking about Angola? If one's obligation to a nation could be based on white men "running out" or an almost laughable kith and kin in the "we" that mourned the loss of Vietnam, how meaningful could belonging be, and how important were the constitutional guarantees of citizenship? Foreign soldiers raise questions that are beyond citizenship, questions about what might link place and warfare: patria is not the issue; politics is. And the politics are queerly utopian: *somewhere* communism had to be stopped; *somewhere* men had to stand up against terrorism; *somewhere* the western world had to stand fast against the eastern hordes. All these tropes, of course, meant race: it was a black government that these men came to

72. Caute, *Under the Skin*, 138. See also interview with David Crowley, Marine, Vietnam Center, Texas Tech University, Lubbock, Texas, who claimed that many Americans were attracted by the romance of the Rhodesian army: it had a cavalry.

73. Robin Moore, *Rhodesia* (New York; Condor, 1977), 201, 208, 217, 232.

fight against. And race, as Benedict Anderson pointed out years ago, is decidedly un-national: the various terminology used to disparage the guerrillas—gooks, or terrorists, or CTs—*"erases nation-ness"* from the enemy, who became a racial or political embodiment.[74]

Rhodesia suggests that the opposite is also true, that fighting for all the tropes that meant white rule was also without any loyalty to a nation, without any historical specificity or any reference to place. Rhodesia just happened to be in the right place at the right time for these soldiers. For white national servicemen, whether Rhodesian citizens or residents, the question of nation-ness was inverted. However much Rhodesia was imagined as Thermopylae, however much independence was to give its transient white population a bogus place in history, the cause for which young men fought was most often depicted as intimate and familial; when it was not it was without reference to the continent or its history. The struggle over national service took place in the vocabularies of "other people's sons," of belonging, of community, of something separate from political histories or dying for the Rhodesian Front. And that belonging was even vaguer than Rhodesian puffery. In 1977 Jan Morris wrote an eerie observation of young Rhodesian soldiers on leave around the hotel pool where she took her lunch. "Stripped to their trunks and sun-bleached hair, they seem to have lost all ethnic identity. They might have been moon men." She guessed some were mercenaries from Europe but all of them were "subtly changed in posture and physique; all seemed to me specific not simply to the place, but to the time, to the prospect."[75]

What made Rhodesian conscripts so rooted in time and space was the same thing that made national service so contradictory for whites: Rhodesia was an African country ruled by its white minority. The rhetoric

74. Benedict Anderson, *Imagined Communities: Reflections on the Origin and Spread of Nationalism* (London: Verso, 1983), 135; italics in the original.

75. Morris, *Destinations*, 136. Morris could not hear them over the hubbub of the terrace, but she would not have been surprised "to hear them conversing in some unintelligible tongue, an ad hoc vernacular evolved especially for white Rhodesia, 1977." She must have already known about Taal, the RLI slang that was originally Coloured slang—hence its Afrikaans elements—and that became a patois that national servicemen were supposed to use. A regimental history of the RLI has a glossary with examples of how to use Taal in a variety of situations and sentences, from seeing a crocodile to wanting to have dinner; Bond, *Incredibles*, 151–53. There are several glossaries of Taal; see Shaw, *Kandaya*, 206–9; Binda, *The Saints*, 124; Bax, *Three Sips*, 111. One war novel is written entirely in Taal; see Paul Hotz, *Muzukuru: A Guerrilla's Story* (Johannesburg: Ravan, 1990), while in another the heroine comments on the way the war has changed language (Sylvia Bond-Smith, *Ginette* [Bulawayo: Black Eagle Press, 1980], 120–21). According to Stu Taylor, speaking in Taal could keep a man out of the SAS however well he had done on the selection course. The SAS wanted men "with a bit more finesse"; see Taylor, *Lost*, 63–65.

of responsible government, a way of life, of standards, of civilization, or even of a negotiated settlement meant, as Peter Godwin's mother had stressed, that young white conscripts fought for white and black alike. This was as national as conscription got, and it was the source of constant, and imaginative, tension. If familial rhetoric defined the nation as biracial, the mixing of races and the entangled, convoluted impossibilities thereof, were addressed in Rhodesian wartime novels. Several portrayed the war as a struggle within families where racial boundaries were already breached. All of these ended in death, but these deaths were the result of racial conflict, not the bonds between races that the fictional characters established. In Michael Hartmann's *Game for Vultures*, a reservist has married a Coloured woman, much to the consternation of friends and family. On patrol with a "puffing quintet of businessmen," he is wounded by a guerrilla who turns out to be his brother-in-law. The guerrilla is captured and interrogated, which brackets the larger plot, in which the reservists' sanction-busting brother double-crosses ZAPU in its purchase of small aircraft. Before the newly purchased planes are destroyed by Rhodesian operatives the Coloured guerrilla escapes, breaks into the reservist's flat, kills his sister, and is killed by the reservist himself.[76]

William Rayner's *The Day of Chaminuka* begins with the death of a Rhodesian man who has lived in England for years; he had gone there as much to escape his domineering father as to evade the draft. The woman he lived with is bereft and goes to Rhodesia possibly to tell his father of his death or to confront him about how much he harmed his son. Once on the family farm she learns that the father has not been so terrible or ungenerous after all; he had supported his son in Britain for years. She finds herself attracted to the father but before anything can be consummated, or resolved, guerrillas break into the house and hold her and the farmer at gunpoint. The leader of the guerrilla gang is particularly enraged: years ago his pregnant mother, a servant in that house, had been sent away by the master. The farmer is stunned. The servant was the love of his life. He did not know she was pregnant, and the master who sent her away was not him but his son: the guerrilla who holds a gun to his head is also his son. The farmer is thrilled that he has a son and embraces the guerrilla, who is horrified he got things so wrong. The farmer and his servant are reunited and with their son try to fight off guerrillas attacking the farm, but the farmer is shot and dies.[77]

76. Michael Hartmann, *Game for Vultures* (London: Pan Books 1976 [1975]).
77. William Rayner, *The Day of Chaminuka* (New York: Athenaeum, 1977 [1976]).

National Service for Africans?

The imaginary that produced the entanglements of these novels, even if no character lived long enough to resolve them, imagined Rhodesia's African volunteer regiment as a kind of parallel to all-white ones. The Rhodesian African Rifles were not entirely black, however. They were what was called an *askari* regiment, in which black soldiers were commanded by white officers.[78] The RAR was also far and away the most experienced infantry unit in the country, having done storied service in World War II and Malaysia.[79] 1RAR was the most effective fighting force in Rhodesia throughout the 1970s.[80] As white Rhodesians told it, however, the RAR was a regiment shaped by familial concerns. The "black Rhodesian army," one wrote, was "patriarchal in that a man will probably join the army to follow his father's footsteps; there's a lot of pride involved."[81] David Caute claimed that RAR volunteers came from the same areas the hardcore guerrillas came from.[82] Later, police superintendents claimed many RAR supported Mugabe's election because of pressure from their wives, who wanted an end to the long war.[83]

The idea of national service for Africans had been the source of disheartened debates in the ministries and cabinet rooms for years, but it was considered "fraught with danger." Growing unemployment in 1977 increased the number of Africans enlisting in the RAR: "one should never refuse volunteers." There was not enough equipment for these new soldiers, but African troops were a bargain for the army: 3,200 African soldiers cost only as much as 640 white territorials and fought at least as well.[84] By 1977 repeated call-ups had led any number of civilian firms to employ only Africans or white women, and this added to general anxiety about white emigration: in a survey of army morale,

---

78. This generated a variety of intimate jokes: a woman says her boyfriend is in the RAR. Is he an African, someone asks. No, she replies, but he has African privates. See Shaw, *Kandaya*, 90.

79. Alexandre Binda, *Masodja: The History of the Rhodesian African Rifles and Its Forerunner, the Rhodesia Native Regiment* (Johannesburg: 30 Degrees South, 2007), 64–81, 126–68; Timothy Stapleton, *African Police and Soldiers in Colonial Zimbabwe, 1913–80* (Rochester, NY: University of Rochester Press, 2011), 183–97.

80. Author's field notes, Harare, August 2, 2006; Stapleton, *African Police and Soldiers*, 201.

81. Cohen, "Dissenter's View," 484.

82. Caute, *Under the Skin*, 190.

83. Stapleton, *African Police and Soldiers*, 181. The superintendent claimed that Mugabe ran in the 1979 election, which he did not.

84. Comops to Ministry of Defence, Case for Additional African Soldiers, November 27, 1977, RAA 2001/086/263/997.

one-third of those interviewed said they would leave the country when they had completed their national service.[85]

Everyone agreed that in theory African university students and articled clerks and apprentices should be conscripted, and on the same basis that white young men served—more than half the white male students at the university had completed their national service—but almost everyone agreed it was impossible. The army took several positions on the conscription of African university students. It had assessed that 12 percent of students backed Nkomo and the rest Muzorewa, and "if a package deal could be sold on the basis of a white plus Muzorewa fight against Nkomo/Mugabe" perhaps there would be "no major problems." Rhodesian officials disagreed. Local whites might see this as the last gasp of Rhodesia and it would lower morale and increase emigration even further. African students—unlike Indian or Coloured ones—would react with outrage: "they were all nationalists to a man."[86] Army intelligence officers admitted that any group of young, educated Africans would include the government's "most virulent enemies," who should not serve: there was the inevitable security problem of conscripting men sympathetic to guerrillas, and the more important possibility that they would undermine the morale of other African soldiers "whenever possible" by discrediting African officers and overstating "tribal differences." Such men would "exaggerate each and every grievance." Some army officers suggested that African conscripts, like white ones, could be reformed by special training and Spartan conditions, but the army refused to devote any specific funds for this as "it would be a great folly to risk the Army's good race relations, high morale and fighting efficiency and the security of the country, for the sake of having to employ 560 unwilling malcontents who are most unlikely to make useful soldiers."[87]

The internal settlement of 1978, and the election of a Muzorewa-headed government in 1979, brought these issues to a head. The gradual conscription of Africans—not university students—did not relieve whites from continual call-ups, however, as the army now considered it necessary to have access to the experience of older men (ages thirty-eight

85. Army Counterintelligence, Morale throughout the Rhodesian Army, typescript, June 1, 1977, RAA 2001/086/263/997.

86. So were white students, apparently. In 1976 the BSAP was called to the university to look at graffiti: "Close this Ter camp"; "Let RLI loose, we'll clean the country"; "Join the army, Mt. Pleasant Kaffir High School"; "We want control, let us loose, RLI." BSAP liaised with Special Branch, May 1976, RAA 2001/086/050/1001.

87. Carbon of paper, labeled "secret," Training of African University Aspirants and African Apprentices, n.d. but filed with late 1977 papers. RAA 2001/086/263/997.

to fifty) because "this leadership element is essential."[88] Graham Atkins of the Rhodesia Regiment, the most integrated of national service regiments, was pleased that the army "had fully embraced non-racialism" although Rhodesian civilian life lagged far behind. One Saturday afternoon he and some friends were out on a rare day pass. Dressed in jackets and ties, they came upon a wedding reception and wanted to join in, to drink and meet young women. The problem was Moses "our good humored comrade-in-arms" who was African. It would be impossible to sneak him into the wedding, and while Moses was willing to wait outside, Atkins went to the bar and returned with a silver tray and white napkin. "Your ticket in," he told Moses. "Just do your best impersonation of a waiter, and you'll blend in perfectly." Moses did, but not without occasional jests from his comrades, "six beers. *Checha!* Quick."[89]

Aside from turning national servicemen into domestic workers, there was the larger question of how young white men saw their still-extended national service for a government that had blacks at its head, even if it was a figurehead. Was fighting for an African government within the domain of familial authority? Did fathers' ability to control their sons make them willing to do what African families did not do? White soldiers, especially those ambivalent about the Rhodesian Front, had every reason to want Africans to serve alongside them and in other regiments. Chris Cocks, for example, found the racial exclusivity of elite regiments laughable. The SAS did not admit black soldiers into its ranks, he wrote. "There were no black soldiers in the Long Range Desert Group, the forerunner of the SAS, during World War II. There had been no black soldiers in Malaya, so for what sane reason would anyone think it necessary to have black troops in an African SAS?"[90] After the internal settlement of 1978, national servicemen complained that they did not know what they were fighting for if there was going to be majority rule.[91] A fictional RLI, coming off patrol, went to his commanding officer and removed

88. OCC Minutes, August 23, 1977, RAA 2001/086/223/245; JOC Minutes, April 6, 1978, RAA 2001 branch to see if this was an attempt to discredit the RLI. Intelligence reports: casual sources, May 27, 1976, RAA 2001/086/007/882.

89. Atkins, *White Man*, 79–80. He was not alone. In the second version of his memoirs, Ron Reid-Daly recalled a visit from a South African general in his quarters. When Reid-Daly sent his major-domo for more ice, the general asked if he could "really trust these black soldiers of yours?" Reid-Daly was indignant: the man he sent for ice was a high-ranking insurgent. "He is now my butler and he could off me at any time if he chose to do so. If I can trust him I can sure as hell trust my own soldiers." Ron Reid-Daly, *Pamwe Chete: The Legend of the Selous Scouts* (Weltevreden Park: Covos-Day, 1998), 472.

90. Cocks, *Survival Course*, 104.

91. Consolidated report from the Main JOCs on the state of morale in the Rhodesian Army, June 1, 1977, RAA 2001/086/263/997.

the strap that held his 12kg Belgian-made machine gun. "If you're going to give it to the kaffirs, get the kaffirs to carry this."[92] The young Dan Wylie wrote in his diary, "A lot of guys are ratty about serving a black government, but in the last resort they'll fight because they're told to. Personally, I'm fighting for a way of life; if the government starts wrecking those standards, I'll fight the government instead. Or go to Spain."[93]

Rhodesia or Spain? Lead a rebellion or relax in a warm climate? There is clearly not much patriotism here, and even less sense of loyalty to a specific place, but by then the place had changed its name to Zimbabwe-Rhodesia. There were papers and reports about how to remake national service so as to involve both black and white. These reports contained dire warnings to an unspecified audience. "The white population will no longer accept the main burden. Any imbalance . . . will lead to further emigration of whites." There was nothing left to do but call up Africans.[94] Questions of citizens and residents gave way to broad racial terminologies, and vocabularies of leadership and discipline were expressed in numbers and ratios. There were 2,300 whites available for national service and 470,000 Africans, but the new army could not have a ratio of 2,300 to 470,000, of course. The generals thought a ratio of 20:1 as "acceptable to whites." That ratio, however, could not provide enough leadership or specialists, and so they recommended a "realistic ratio" of 15:1. This too was a fantasy and was never implemented. The older men who made up Comops instead wrote that they hoped that the Africans and whites currently doing national service would sign on as regulars, and that five thousand Africans and whites might be called up for protection duties. The increase in manpower was not necessarily for the waning war effort, but another performance for a specific audience: it would have a "favourable effect" on the white population "who will be aware of the greater participation of Africans in national service."[95] White citizenry were to become spectators.

Such an army never came into being because Zimbabwe-Rhodesia gave way to Zimbabwe in the election of late February 1980. Soldiers supporting Muzorewa, ill-disciplined as they were, came as close to being a loyalist African army as the country had ever had. The Joint Op-

92. Shaw, *Kandaya*, 81–82.

93. Wylie, *Dead Leaves*, 39.

94. JOC Minutes, Movement of African Security Forces from African Areas to European Areas, August 25, 1978, RAA 2001/086/015/892; Comops Headquarters, The Future of National Service, mimeo., March 26, 1979, RAA 2001/086/147/927.

95. Comops HQ, Salisbury, The Future of National Service, mimeo., March 26, 1979, RAA 2001/086/147/927.

erating Command had several plans ready to revise national service, of course, and to discontinue the call-ups which now seemed meaningless and expensive. They were surprised when the prime minister–elect, Robert Mugabe, asked to keep the call-up at least "until the outstanding dissident element had been rounded up."[96] By then, however, The call-up was no longer about disciplining young men, but about disciplining a population.

The linear political narrative and the false starts around the inclusion of Africans before 1980 do not tell the entire story, which is one of the uneven expansion of state power and the frequency with which military and civilian authorities were at odds with each other. Much of my evidence for the conflict between them seems almost amusing—who allowed for more exemptions, who should be working longer hours, who had the wherewithal to arrest deserters—but taken together, this evidence provides a window into the very real antagonism between the Rhodesian security forces and the Rhodesian Front government. As the following chapters show, that antagonism was never resolved and would end in the security forces literally capturing the role of the state in early 1980.

96. JOC Minutes, March 7, 1980, March 10, 1980, March 14, 1980, RAA 2001/086/101/159.

EIGHT

"Why come now and ask us for our opinion?": The 1972 Pearce Commission and the African National Council

There were two immediate effects of the 1969 constitution.[1] First, Ian Smith and other Rhodesian Front politicians were able to present themselves as moderates, insisting their party put merit above considerations of race. Second, the British government panicked. Rhodesia now had a constitution that all but stripped Africans of access to the institutions of representative government. It had also become a republic, and while no one thought that would change its renegade status in any way, this intensified the sense that Rhodesia was now a nation adrift in its own ideologies. After years of fruitless and sometimes farcical negotiations, the new Conservative government in Britain thought a new relationship to Rhodesia would prevent the country from becoming "an armed frontier on the Zambezi," involved in

1. An earlier version of this chapter was published as "'Normal Political Activities': Rhodesia, the Pearce Commission, and the African National Council," in *J. of African History* 52, no. 3 (2011): 321–40. I thank Cambridge University Press for permission to reprint parts of it.

"a bloody war."[2] By 1971 the Conservative government was willing to water down the five principles in order to achieve a settlement.

Proposals and Principles

Shortly after Conservatives came to power in Britain in July 1970, Alec Douglas-Home, the Conservative Foreign and Commonwealth secretary, began negotiations with Ian Smith in Salisbury. Douglas-Home, as foreign secretary, had failed to contain Smith and the Rhodesian Front in 1964; in 1970, the basis for negotiations was not at all clear: Rhodesia was clearly not going to give up minority rule and Britain had no actual say in its government. The white paper Smith and Douglas-Home eventually produced, called *Proposals for a Settlement,* revealed Britain's weak bargaining position: it agreed to legitimate Rhodesia in exchange for the promise of eventual majority rule. Although the details represented major concessions both for the Rhodesian Front and the Foreign Office, the settlement allowed for independence under the 1961 constitution, the very thing Smith had demanded from Wilson six years earlier.[3] Why did Britain now agree to this? The 1969 constitution. As the proposals were worked through and debated, Smith promised that if Britain recognized an independent Rhodesia he would void the 1969 constitution. If there was no recognition of Rhodesia, however, he had no choice but to continue to use it.

Whether or not the proposals would be accepted would depend on Wilson's fifth principle that Britain "would need to be satisfied" that any settlement was "acceptable to the population of Rhodesia as a whole." This was the most problematic of the five principles. The Rhodesian Front negotiators in London in October 1965 tried desperately to explain that they had already implemented the first four principles, but the fifth caused consternation and accusations. They agreed that Britain had the right to seek such satisfaction; it was the phrase "as a whole" that was—and would continue to be—challenging. Indeed, before there were any principles at all, in 1964, Smith had actively sought a way around a referendum on the question of independence. He approached chiefs and social scientists to recommend the best mechanism for testing

---

2. Alec Douglas-Home, *The Way the Wind Blows* (New York: Quadrangle, 1976), 251–53.
3. Robert Blake insisted that the Anglo-Rhodesian proposals were "only just within" the five principles. Blake, *Rhodesia,* 404.

African opinion. The chiefs were eager to have a greater say in government, but the social scientists responded with a letter to *The Herald*. They were unwilling to be part of any political test, and they reminded government that while all male Africans were involved in decision making in rural areas, African society was no longer purely tribal but increasingly oriented toward western values. Thus the most valid test would be one in which every man could vote.[4] The chiefs' indaba was Smith's only other option. Even as it was planned—by Stanley Morris, then permanent secretary in the Department of Internal Affairs—the Conservative government refused to send observers. When it did take place, Labour was in power in Britain; Arthur Bottomley, the secretary of state for Commonwealth Relations, refused to attend, but he asked that he be allowed to meet with Nkomo and Sithole, both of whom were in detention. Smith found this hard to fathom and fell back on what he called the chiefs' claim "that the British government was conniving with terrorists in their campaign of intimidation, arson, and murder."[5]

A year later, when the five principles were in place and Rhodesian Front negotiators met with Wilson and Bottomley in London, Smith was only slightly less reproachful. The Labour government had suggested "a four race referendum"—Europeans, Asians, Coloureds, and Africans—to satisfy the fifth principle, but the Rhodesian delegation objected. Such a referendum would involve the "invidious business" of assigning people to racial groups, one of which, the Asians, constituted only 1 percent of the population and should not be allowed veto power. While Africans were a large percentage of the population, they were "not as advanced as Europeans." Ian Smith opposed any kind of inclusive referendum. Constitutional issues were far more complex than voting for a candidate, he said, and Africans simply did not understand how to make sophisticated judgments.[6] Seven years later, however, Douglas-Home told Smith that the settlement proposals would require African support before they could be approved by parliament.[7] There had to be an independent way to ascertain if the proposals were acceptable to the "population as a whole," and this was the task of the Pearce Commission.

4. Holleman, *Chief, Council, and Commissioner*, 347–48.
5. Blake, *Rhodesia*, 367–68; Smith, *Betrayal*, 82; Wood, *So Far*, 241–48.
6. Record of meetings held at 10 Downing Street, October 7, 1965, and October 19, 1965, in *Southern Rhodesia*, 77–79, 120; Wood, *So Far*, 375–76.
7. Quoted in Meredith, *Another Country*, 92.

Normal for Rhodesia

The Pearce Commission's visit to Rhodesia is generally considered a major event in the struggle against Rhodesian independence, yet there is very little secondary literature about it. African responses to the commission have been described as a critical step toward majority rule, the first time rural masses were allowed to speak out against the regime, when "Africans themselves" slammed the door to settlement. The Pearce Commission was a moment of African empowerment epitomized by Judith Todd's title *The Right to Say No.*[8] Todd's account is not the exception, but the rule. The Pearce Commission has been the stuff of memoirs rather than of historical inquiry. In large part, this is because the Pearce Commission fits so neatly into the grand narrative of Rhodesia-into-Zimbabwe: it was the end of Britain's willingness to negotiate; it was "a benchmark in race relations," a turning point after which white reaction could never fully contain the resurgence of African aspirations.[9] In this narrative, Rhodesia's racism was absolute; it was attacked by the African masses but not fragmented by anything the Rhodesian Front might have done. Indeed, shortly after Africans' rejection of the proposals, white moderates began to sound just like the RF.[10] In this way, David Martin and Phyllis Johnson's *The Struggle for Zimbabwe*—almost an official history of the 1980s state—mentions the Pearce Commission only as background to the squalid story of Bishop Abel Muzorewa, a story that will become even more seedy in subsequent chapters.[11] The Rhodesia-into-Zimbabwe narrative omits the cynicism with which the proposals were written and the near disinterest with which they were met in Rhodesia. Lord Goodman, one of Douglas-Home's negotiators in Salisbury, later said the goal of settlement was to prevent apartheid,

---

8. Moorcraft, *Short Thousand Years*, 27; Good, *U. D. I.*, 316; Diana Auret, *Reaching for Justice: The Catholic Commission for Justice and Peace* (Gweru: Mambo, 1992), 23; Judith Todd, *The Right to Say No* (London: Sedgwick & Johnson, 1972); Jocelyn Alexander, JoAnn McGregor, and Terence Ranger, *Violence and Memory: One Hundred Years in the 'Dark Forests' of Matabeleland* (Oxford: James Currey, 2000), 123–27.

9. Blake, *Rhodesia*, 405; Raftopoulos and Mlambo, *Becoming Zimbabwe*, 141–42. This was the consensus of journalists; see Peter Niesewand, "Settlement brings about a nationalist rebirth," *Africa Report* 17, no. 2 (1972): 8–10; Meredith, *Another Country*, 98–103; Caute, *Under the Skin*, 198. The political scientist Larry Bowman thought it "too early to tell" if the African successes of the Pearce Commission would impact African politics in Rhodesia and the guerrilla armies outside the country. Bowman, *Politics in Rhodesia*, 128–29.

10. Ian Hancock, *White Liberals*, 163–64.

11. Martin and Johnson, *Struggle for Zimbabwe*, 98–99.

not to permit majority rule. When asked if the proposals sold out the Africans, he replied, "The African has been sold out long ago."[12] An unidentified African told a Rhodesian newspaper that white men had long insisted that Africans did not understand enough to vote. "Why come now and ask us for our opinion?"[13]

In the grand narrative Rhodesian reaction intensified in the late 1960s, after which time there were brief openings for different factions of the state. Between 1971 and 1973 Africans and their political parties were able to exploit theses openings for their first open, grassroots movement in Rhodesia in over a decade, even as the Rhodesian Front and a few multiracial parties also sought to maneuver within these openings. If I add the cynicism and disinterest to this narrative, it becomes more nuanced and layered: it becomes possible to see the extent to which these openings and closings were shaped by the very political forces that were encumbered by recent history. Thus the Rhodesian Front, having made African politics in Rhodesia all but illegal, had to construct its own African support and in very short time its own African opposition. African politicians, in exile or in detention, also arranged for new political parties to do their bidding; for the most part this worked well. The Pearce Commission had asked that Rhodesia allow "normal political activities" during their visit, much to the derision of progressives around the world. By normal, the commission did not mean what was legal in Rhodesia—no public meetings and political activists denied access to rural areas—but a loosening of restrictions that would allow "some reasonable political activity" throughout the country.[14] This normal was accompanied by another kind of normal political activity altogether, in which political parties past and present created new organizations to promote their respective goals.

White Paper, Black Politics

The White Paper of November 1971 renounced Britain's claim to rule Rhodesia; it promised to legalize Rhodesian independence so long as Rhodesia made efforts to conform to the conditions of the post-decolonized

---

12. Brian Brivati, *Lord Goodman* (London: Richard Cohen, 1999), 203–4; Bowman, *Politics in Rhodesia*, 124.

13. Quoted in Mervyn Jones, *Rhodesia: The White Judge's Burden* (London: International Defence and Aid Fund, 1972), 5.

14. *Report of the Commission on Rhodesian Opinion under the Chairmanship of the Right Honourable Lord Pearce* [hereafter *Pearce Report*], Cmd. 4964 (London, HMSO, 1972), 32, 37.

world: increasing African access to the franchise, ending forced labor, limiting detention without charges to six weeks. This would require gutting the 1969 constitution or returning to the 1961 constitution, which had held a distant possibility of majority rule or of an equal number of African and European seats in the legislature.[15] The proposals for settlement contained some distinctly postcolonial elements as well: amnesty for actions committed by disciplined security forces, and £5 million in matched funds from Britain and Rhodesia to develop African areas.[16] However much these proposals might have seemed commonplace in 1971, they represented a significant compromise on the part of the Rhodesian Front government. As a cabinet committee put it, it was now time to exchange "some of our social and political achievement in return for release from the economic effects of sanctions."[17] The proposals did not specifically guarantee recognition, but instead used the language of legitimacy. In the late 1960s and during the Pearce Commission's visit, "recognition" became a synecdoche, the part of the larger whole of settlement that came to represent the whole.

Douglas-Home extolled the economic advantages of settlement in Parliament and boardrooms: it would provide jobs for Africans and this, more than majority rule, was what everyone in Rhodesia wanted.[18] Moderates and the white business community were cautious but they actively supported the proposals; they had long wanted some kind of settlement with Britain. Their goals were fairly narrow; they were less concerned with recognition than they were with the lifting of sanctions. Overall, they saw the idea of settlement as something that would make Rhodesia compromise and have a "conventional constitution" with appropriate safeguards, and generally become less reactionary, less like South Africa.[19] Moderates in the multiracial movement praised the economic advantages. The Centre Party, perhaps the most successful of a long line of multiracial organizations in that it stood African candidates for B roll seats, supported the proposals. Pat Bashford, the party's head,

15. Claire Palley had criticized the White Paper by calculating just how far in the future majority rule was under the 1961 constitution: at least thirty-three years. Palley, "The Time-Scale for Majority Rule," *Issue: A J. of Opinion* 2, no. 2 (1972), 52–64.

16. Government of Rhodesia, *Proposals for a Settlement*, Cmd. R. R. 46–1971, November 25, 1971 (Salisbury: Government Printer, 1971).

17. United Kingdom Committee, February 22, 1971, CL/Smith/4/003(M).

18. Douglas-Home, *Wind Blows*, 302–4.

19. The Forum, Sanctions: an Appreciation, n. d., but filed in April 1969, NAZ/MS807. The idea that Rhodesians should struggle to differentiate themselves from white South Africans predated UDI; see Holderness, *Lost Chance*, 227. The fact of isolationism and calcified attitudes was a constant theme in visitors' writings after UDI; see Denis Hills, *Rebel People*, 199.

tried to establish himself as the bridge between white moderates and African nationalism much as Michael Blundell had done in late colonial Kenya. But as Ian Hancock has pointed out, what may have worked for Kenya in the late 1950s seemed quaint for Rhodesia in 1972, especially when the Centre Party's African members failed to support the proposals or the party's line on them. Percy Mkudu was a former MP and successful businessman in the eastern highlands who was a strong supporter of the Centre Party. After two of his businesses were attacked in January 1972 he denounced the proposals. Ronnie Sadomba, MP from Nemakonde, had originally approved of the proposals; he told the Centre Party executive that he would leave the country at once if there was majority rule. By mid-February he understood that he was "an obvious target" and resigned from the Centre Party—"a surprise to us all and a personal. blow to some"—and campaigned against settlement.[20] These were painful defections, but the Centre Party continued to support the proposals. Party leaders began to praise the possibilities of an independent Rhodesia, one that would have no use for the strident nationalisms that had "been overtaken by history," especially the "latter-day pioneers and pseudo frontiersmen who are forever bobbing up on the right." Centre Party speakers loved to quote the latest threat from Lord Graham: "We will eat sadza rather than agree with Britain."[21]

African politicians drew battle lines even before the Pearce Commission arrived in Rhodesia. In a letter from prison Rev. Ndabaningi Sithole told Edward Heath that "Nazis must be smiling in their graves" over these proposals.[22] When a group of African clergymen met with Douglas-Home in Rhodesia to discuss the proposals, Bishop Abel Muzorewa thought the meeting a waste of time. The proposals were inconsequential; disputes between Rhodesian leaders and the British had nothing to do with African goals, especially majority rule.[23] Muzorewa, consecrated United Methodist Bishop of Rhodesia in 1968, had long been an outspoken critic of racial oppression in Rhodesia. He led the

20. Hancock, *White Liberals*, 152–53, 161–62; "What Happened to Ronnie Sadomba," *Centre Point* 2, no. 4 (February 1972): 1; Jane Parpart, "Silenced Visions of Citizenship, Democracy and Nation: African MPs in Rhodesian Parliaments, 1963–1978," in *Redemptive or Grotesque Nationalism? Rethinking Contemporary Politics in Zimbabwe*, ed. Sabelo J. Ndlovu-Gatsheni and James Muzondidya (Bern: Peter Lang, 2011), 187–216.

21. Sadza is the African staple starch. T. B. P. Bashford, speech at Rhodes Hall, Bulawayo; N. J. McNally, speech at Rhodes Hall, Bulawayo, February 15,1972; Diana Mitchell Papers, Herbert Hoover Institution, Stanford University; Hancock, *White Liberals*, 151–56.

22. Rev. Ndabaningi Sithole, Salisbury Prison, letter to Edward Heath, November 1971, in Nyangoni and Nyandoro, eds., *Zimbabwe Independence Movements*, 201–5.

23. Bishop Abel Muzorewa, *Rise Up and Walk: An Autobiography* (Johannesburg: Jonathan Ball, 1978), 92.

African organization that was to successfully oppose the settlement proposals in 1972, and a year later—the same year he was awarded the United Nations Prize for Human Rights—he began his own negotiations with the Rhodesian Front government. He was often ridiculed. Julius Nyerere charitably said that Muzorewa should have returned to the pulpit in 1972; almost everyone else denounced him as a puppet, a weak and vain man.[24] Muzorewa's political party maintained some credibility with the political parties and armies in exile until he became the figurehead president of the short-lived Zimbabwe-Rhodesia and his guerrillas became a private army. Muzorewa's willingness to be stage-managed by a truly wide variety of political interests is part of my argument, in this and subsequent chapters, that Rhodesia had sediment upon sediment of political affiliations that participants all understood as normal, if not everyday politics. Each layer of affiliation complicated the labyrinth of political belonging, but no single layer closed down possibilities or openings.

Even without Muzorewa and Sithole, Africans understood that the proposals would once and for all end their access to legal protections from Britain.[25] Property qualification would still determine the franchise, and race would determine representation in the legislature. The proposals actually offered less than the 1961 constitution had done, although they reversed the most regressive aspect of the 1969 constitution, that African representation would increase proportional to Africans' contribution to the national income taxes.[26] The few African MPs elected to parliament on the African roll objected to proposals negotiated without their participation. They complained that consulting chiefs was "a very lame and wrong interpretation" of African politics and made it clear that without African involvement in negotiating the proposals there was no one to persuade "our people" to accept them.[27] In mid-December 1971, Muzorewa announced the formation of the ANC, the African National Council—the acronym, which took hold at once, had a profound national and international meaning, as it referenced the party that preceded the NDP and South Africa's banned political party—to oppose settlement. Shortly thereafter, several African groups were formed to promote the case for settlement and a few white groups

24. Martin and Johnson, *Struggle for Zimbabwe*, 217; Meredith, *Another Country*, 85–87; Caute, *Under the Skin*, 184, 269–70.

25. See, for example, Todd, *Say No*, 54.

26. Emmet V. Mittlebeeler, "The Settlement," *Africa Report* 17, no. 2 (1972): 11–13.

27. House of Assembly, *Parliamentary Debates*, November 24, 1971, 2nd session, 12th parliament, vol. 80 (Salisbury, 1972), cols. 1034, 1038–39, 1042–43; Hancock, *White Liberals*, 152–54.

were formed to encourage both white Rhodesians and their African employees to support the proposals.

When Muzorewa met with the Pearce Commission he told them that the ANC had been formed in December 1971 "as a spontaneous grassroots reaction to the announcement of the terms of the Anglo-Rhodesian proposals."[28] Yet it was common knowledge that the ANC was an invention of the banned political parties. In his autobiography, Muzorewa described how the ANC had been created by a joint ZAPU and ZANU committee. He had been selected as a "neutral leader"; he was promised the full support of the two leaders still in detention, Ndabaningi Sithole and Joshua Nkomo. The ANC's executive committee would be equally divided between the two parties.[29] Years later, Nkomo claimed that he and Garfield Todd had looked for someone they could trust to coordinate African opposition in the terms they themselves would have used. They initially wanted Bishop Abel Muzorewa to be treasurer of the new organization—"if a bishop cannot raise money, who can?"—with Josiah Chinamaso, of ZAPU, its chairman, but they decided that the ANC would have a broader appeal with Muzorewa as chairman.[30] By the time the commission arrived in Rhodesia, Chinamaso was detained; some said this was when ZANU came to dominate the ANC.[31]

Within a few days of the publication of the proposals African prosettlement groups emerged, seemingly from nowhere. Some, like the Congress National Union, existed only on paper. Others, like the Rhodesia Settlement Forum (RSF), for example, were formed right after the ANC was formed. The RSF had almost no credibility among Africans. It was an African organization that spoke only to white businessmen. Its chairman was a former ZAPU, who had been arrested when he returned from Tanzania but was released the next day. For many observers this proved he was either a police informer or had been turned into one. To add to the suspicion, the RSF had its offices in a building owned by a Rhodesian Front MP and its published materials spoke to the needs of the business community, not those of former guerrillas. The RSF insisted that the settlement would bring an end to sanctions; its brochures calcu-

28. *Pearce Report*, 121.

29. Martin and Johnson, *Struggle for Zimbabwe*, 98; Muzorewa, *Rise Up*, 94–95; Eliakim M. Sibanda, *The Zimbabwe African People's Union* (Trenton, NJ: Red Sea Press, 2005), 205–6.

30. Nkomo, *My Life*, 141. A biography of Garfield Todd claimed the ANC was created on the instructions of detained ZANU leadership; Todd's connection to the new party was through its vice president, the Rev. Canaan Banana; see Ruth Weiss with Jane Parpart, *Sir Garfield Todd and the Making of Zimbabwe* (London: British Academic Press, 1999), 174.

31. T. H. P. Bashford, Confidential: The African National Council and Settlement, typescript, February 17, 1972. Borthwick Historical Institute, University of York, Centre Party Papers, CE/1.

lated the interest-free loans that would have been available to Rhodesia's public sector if only it had been as legal as other African nations. If there was a settlement, the RSF assured its audience, then Rhodesia could draw on loans from the World Bank, Canada, and West Germany.[32]

Pearce had asked the government not to interfere with the commission's work and not to campaign for either a "yes" or "no" vote. This did not stop Smith from making speeches threatening Britain—and Africans—with the 1969 constitution. If Africans were to reject the proposals, he broadcast to the nation ten days after the commission arrived, it would be "a clear indication of their preference for our present 1969 constitution," which he personally would find "a pleasant surprise."[33] At the same time, both the Rhodesian Front government and party supported and funded African pro-settlement groups; the Ministry of Information reprinted newspaper editorials that argued that however flawed the proposals were they would keep Rhodesia from drifting toward apartheid[34]—the same position white moderate groups had. Two white pro-settlement groups founded and funded by the remnants of the multiracial movement were formed in January and February of 1972: People against Racial Discrimination (PARD) was headed by former Capricorns. It supported settlement but wanted to appear apolitical, and so took no stands on anything else. The all-white Committee to Organize Support for Settlement (COSS) included former members of Garfield Todd's United Rhodesia Party. COSS was very well funded, possibly by the Rhodesian Front and definitely by Lonrho. It sent letters to the two hundred African telephone subscribers in Salisbury and the four thousand African teachers and headmasters throughout the country, and it distributed two thousand pamphlets and thirty thousand broadsheets with cartoon images showing how Africans would reap material benefits from a settlement.[35]

32. Muzorewa, *Rise Up*, 106; Tony Kirk, "Rhodesia's 'Pro-Settlement Groups' and the Anglo-Rhodesian Constitutional Dispute," *Issue: A J. of Opinion* 3, no. 1 (1973): 2–5; Rhodesia Settlement Forum, Why Settlement Is Vital for Rhodesia, Salisbury, November 21, 1971, in Nyangoni and Nyandoro, *Independence Movements*, 187–201.

33. Jones, *Judge's Burden*, 7. By the time of the Pearce Commission's visit Conservative party researchers knew enough to call Smith "a very political animal," who nevertheless was suspected of having "the essential inferiority complex" of colonials. Hudson, *Triumph or Tragedy*, 95.

34. Ministry of Information, Immigration, and Tourism, *Rhodesia Settlement Proposals: Courage and Faith Needed* (Salisbury, 1972).

35. Ruben Jamela, former leader of the Trade Union Congress, refused to be associated with PARD. See Kirk, "Pro-Settlement Groups," 4–5; Rowland Fothergill, *Laboratory for Peace: The Story of Ken and Lilian Mew and of Ranche House College, Salisbury* (Bulawayo: Louis Bolze Publishing, 1984), 136–49; Diana Mitchell, "PARD on Me 'COSS I'm Non-Political," *Centre Point* 2, no. 5 (March 1972): 4; Hancock, *White Liberals*, 156–58. Lonrho also gave funds to Joshua Nkomo; see *Nkomo*, 182–84.

The Test of Acceptability

The royal commission was headed by Lord Pearce; two of the commissioners had been colonial governors, and many more had been in the colonial service. This worried any number of Rhodesian officials, who feared that these men "hated our guts." They were "colonial office types," with an "inbred hostility" to Europeans in Rhodesia. Several commissioners had been in the administration of Northern Rhodesia and Nyasaland, which Rhodesian administrators thought of as a kind of second-class administration. Rhodesians administered their own country. "Our fellows went home at night."[36] To counter the Colonial Office types Rhodesia offered to send Stanley Morris to London to advise the commission on how to proceed. The commission rejected Morris and arrived in Salisbury in January 1972 to test the acceptability of the Anglo-Rhodesian proposals.

Even the choice of dates made Rhodesians suspicious. Ian Smith later wrote that Rhodesians had expected the commission to come in December and be gone by Christmas. Otherwise "dilly-dallying would play into the hands of mischief makers bent on sabotaging the agreement." When the commission announced it would come after the holiday season, in January, Smith's lieutenants saw the heavy hand of the Foreign Office, long out of step with the new Conservative government on the Rhodesian question.[37] The commission, however, did not see the problem as one of when it came but of how long it stayed in Rhodesia: it understood that it was the source of "rioting and tension"—especially after the riots during the first week of its visit—and that there would be no "calming down" until the proposals were either accepted or rejected.[38]

More important than the timing was the question of how "the population of Rhodesia as a whole" was constituted and how it might be tested. Everyone understood that the "population" was subdivided into Europeans, Asians, Coloureds, and Africans, but as the test was discussed, designed, leaked, and countered, a new set of categories were deployed by the government. There was "the silent majority," "responsible opinion," "expert opinion," "ex-detainees," and the people Ian Smith

---

36. Rt. Hon. Sir Hugh Beadle, Bulawayo, February 5, 1972, NAZ/ORAL/BE2; Hon. H. J. Quinton Salisbury, May 1977 and May 1978, NAZ/ORAL/QU2. The sympathies of the former colonial governors are a minor trope in Pearce Commission writings; see Judith Todd's account of her meeting with Sir Glyn Jones, in her *Say No*, 115–16.

37. Smith, *Betrayal*, 154–55.

38. Nyagumbo, *With the People*, 214; *Pearce Report*, 12–13, 97; Meredith, *Another Country*, 93.

frequently called "the happiest Africans in the world."[39] Most of the happy Africans lived in the Tribal Trust Lands, but there was no way most rural Africans could be polled: as Smith kept telling everyone, "the vast majority of them had never exercised a vote in their lives."[40] By January 1972 the government did not oppose the idea of a test, however, although by then a number of white moderate groups did. COSS in particular relied on arguments Smith would later use, that there was too much intimidation in the Tribal Trust Lands for a test to yield reliable results, and that tribal Africans always shouted "no" to ideas they did not wholeheartedly support.[41]

How the commission would ascertain the opinion of those Africans with whom it could meet became an issue of great importance. The proposals had to be translated into local languages. They were to be simplified, perhaps even dumbed down, "for persons not used to official documents." The translation began by stressing the importance of the people of Rhodesia making a decision, which reduced the issue of settlement to that of legalizing UDI: Rhodesia would become an independent nation, and Britain would give up its claim to make Rhodesia's laws.[42]

The practice of the test was another question altogether. The commission initially believed that scientific sampling could overcome any challenges. Social scientists had assured them that a representative sample of 1,200 Africans could be devised and sampled by twenty local assessors. These 1,200 Africans would be "completely representative" of the population; they would not know in advance they were being sampled. If someone refused to talk to the assessors it would not show evidence of fear or intimidation; instead it would demonstrate the resilience of scientific method. People who refused to talk would give the commission the opinion of the "silent majority."[43] Once on the ground, even

---

39. Smith, *Betrayal*, 151–58.

40. Smith, *Betrayal*, 153.

41. Meredith, *Another County*, 97; Hancock, *White Liberals*, 159.

42. *Pearce Report*, 6.

43. Record of Meeting between Harold Smedly and J. F. Gaylard, January 17, 1972, Pearce Commission, Sundry Meetings, CL/Smith/4/003(M). In the U.S., random, or probability, sampling had become increasingly inclusive and scientific in the 1940s and 1950s; by 1955 there was a shift in scientific sampling to develop ways to recognize the variety of minority opinions. See Sarah Igo, *The Averaged American: Surveys, Citizens, and the Making of a Mass Public* (Cambridge: Harvard University Press, 2007), 126–34, 148–49. Southern Rhodesia had been exposed to survey research since the late 1950s, and researchers prided themselves on the rigorous methods they brought to survey research and the census; see Cyril A. Rogers and C. Frantz, *Racial Themes in Southern Rhodesia: The Attitudes and Behavior of the White Population* (New Haven, CT: Yale University Press, 1962), 42–86; Barry M. Shutz, "European Population Patterns, Cultural Persistence, and Political Change in Rhodesia," *Canadian J. of African Studies* 7, no. 2 (1975): 3–25.

with experienced survey research teams and more than enough data from which to construct a sampling frame, the best scientific methods proved impossible. Local experts in survey research withdrew their offers to help, urban officials refused to allow the commissioners into several African townships, and African interviewers became less and less willing to be associated with the project. The commission then decided to keep the survey to a minimum; in the end it followed the fiction of the 1969 constitution, that all African politics were conducted in their tribes by their chiefs. There were to be meetings—wherever possible and as large as possible—in the Tribal Trust Lands, with chiefs present. There would be two translators at every meeting: a native English speaker who could translate Shona or Sindebele into English and someone whose native language was Shona or Sindebele who could translate English into one of those languages. The two translators may have set an uneasy tone for these meetings, since it was promoted as a way for one interpreter to check the other both for "correct translation and for possible distortion through conscious or unconscious bias."[44] Even so, Judith Todd claimed that she once heard "normal" translated as "no more."[45]

Political setbacks followed methodological setbacks. For every planned large township meeting there was one canceled, and smaller meetings had to be held in courtrooms. The commission struggled with how to balance the need for public debate with the "existing restrictions" on rural African political meetings. The minister for internal affairs believed public meetings should take place but warned the commission that "the tribal system" did not permit individual Africans to "undermine established authority." The commission did not seek to undermine established authority either, stating simply that all witnesses before the commission were to be given immunity for their statements and that canvassing for a "yes" or "no" vote was permitted but "violence and intimidation were not." Wearing the insignia of any political party or displaying its banners was also banned.[46] Rhodesia had released fifty-seven detainees in accordance with the settlement proposals, which Smith considered an enormous risk: "the tribal Africans were a simple and primitive people who were highly susceptible to intimidation,"

44. *Pearce Report*, 6.
45. Todd, *Say No*, 72.
46. *Pearce Report*, 31–32, 38. In a few urban areas, public meetings had to be postponed because of demonstrations and riots. Subsequent meetings were held in the magistrate's court and went smoothly, 172.

which the ex-detainees would certainly attempt.[47] There were over sixty African politicians still in detention. By the time the commission arrived the former prime minister Sir Garfield Todd and his daughter, Judith, and some well-established African nationalists, most especially Josiah and Ruth Chinamaso, had been detained as well. The commissioners were taken aback by these recent detentions: they assumed these people had been jailed to stifle their political influence.[48] Commissioners met with these and many other detainees; they noted that as a group, political prisoners seemed exceptionally well informed.[49]

The fiction that Africans would offer their opinions in large public meetings in full view of a variety of authorities was conducted in the language of the ballot. Africans—and everyone else—were told to vote "yes" or "no." The commission was adamant that the vote was to be quantitative rather than qualitative. If the test had asked some version of "*ought* the proposals to be accepted" in all or in part, then the opinions of ten wise men would outweigh those of "10,000 foolish men." But the test was about whether to accept the proposals as a package. If someone—perhaps an African—approved of some parts of the proposals and did not agree with other parts, he would make a personal choice to support or reject them with his vote, "as an individual," rather than as part of a larger group of "people." This is why the vote had to be quantitative: it did not matter if Africans rejected the proposals because they rejected the current government or if they rejected the proposals because of the conditions of the settlement. The commission took written evidence from the European, Asian, and Coloured communities, and from some Africans. In written submissions almost 97 percent of Europeans favored the proposals and 96 percent of Asian respondents did. African submissions opposed the proposals, but there were enough concerns about signatures or the privacy in which the petitions were signed that the commission decided to reject all the African petitions. Nevertheless, it was estimated that well over three-quarters of the eleven thousand submissions opposed the proposals.[50] The bulk of the African votes came from public meetings in rural communities.

47. Record of Meeting held in Prime Minister's Office, January 12, 1972, 4PM, Pearce Commission, Sundry Meetings, CL/Smith/4/003(M).

48. *Pearce Report*, 39–40.

49. *Pearce Report*, 70; Todd, *Say No*, 114–18; Didymus Mutasa, *Rhodesian Black behind Bars* (London: Mowbrays, 1974), 75–76.

50. *Pearce Report*, 11–12, 58–59, 72–73. The Asian community—0.2 percent of the population, the *Report* insisted—was divided. In Bulawayo and Salisbury prominent members of the community met with commissioners and were critical of the proposals but were willing to accept them "by default."

Politics and Intimidation, Politics of Intimidation

Everyone agreed that these meetings were tumultuous. Commissioners found them "boisterous" but "friendly and good-natured if sometimes noisy." Nowhere did commissioners feel threatened. In Matabeleland South the team saw an efficient "ANC machine" using persuasion, propaganda, catchphrases, and emotional appeals, but saw no evidence of threats or intimidation. The team assigned to Matabeleland North found crowds "dominated by a few politically active cheerleaders"—men who had been released from detention and restriction and rejoined a well-organized ZAPU underground—who were vocal in expressing their political views. Most districts voted "no"; in the one that did not the team disregarded the results of public meetings—"minds were clearly made up beforehand"—and summarized their meetings with individuals and small groups.[51] Phillipa Berlyn traveled with a team of commissioners as one of the native English-speaking Shona translators. She described large crowds, sometimes "tense" and sometimes "touching." Commissioners were annoyed by those Africans who spoke in riddles and were often baffled by long and complicated questions. Once commissioners were asked why Britain had to loan Rhodesia £5 million a year for the Tribal Trust Lands. Did the Rhodesian government not have sufficient funds? The commissioners patiently explained that even a country as rich as Britain had to borrow money to build roads and railways. This made the crowd suspicious: if Britain had to borrow money, why was it promising to give money away? What motivated the sudden funding of the Tribal Trust Lands? Berlyn only once saw a crowd refuse to hear the commissioners; they destroyed the pamphlets that were dutifully handed out explaining the proposals in three languages. Berlyn knew the crowds were intimidated to a certain degree. The ANC had been formed at the behest of ZAPU and ZANU, she wrote, and the bishop was a figurehead, no more than a messenger for the leaders in detention whose "message had gone out and the 'no' vote was an echo of that message."[52]

Muzorewa claimed that chiefs and headmen had been bribed with beer and meat to support the proposals; he seemed to agree with the commission that this added to the festive atmosphere of the meetings.

51. *Pearce Report*, 106, 165, 178–79; Alexander, *Dark Forests*, 126.
52. Phillipa Berlyn, *The Quiet Man: A Biography of Ian Douglas Smith, I. D. Prime Minister of Rhodesia* (Salisbury: M. O. Collins, 1978), 205–6. Berlyn met men in remote villages who asked her what UDI was, and why Britain and Rhodesia were quarreling.

Crowds estimated at four thousand or so shouted and danced when a speaker rejected the proposals; men and women waved placards—some "handmade and mis-spelt," some printed—all saying "no" when asked their opinions. There were "stentorian cries" of "kwete" (no) or "big big no," or "no to the proposals." Chiefs who had supported the proposals scrambled to announce they now rejected them. "I am chief of my people," one said. "If my people reject these proposals, I also say 'kwete.'"[53] Security forces, however, felt an "undercurrent of tension" in the crowds Muzorewa described as "jubilant." A young policeman noticed the youths in jeans and sunglasses who walked through the crowds at rural meetings, haranguing the crowd as they tried to listen to some version of the proposals read in Shona. His superior officer explained that these young men made sure the vote went "their way" by making it clear that anyone who voted "yes" would be beaten, or worse. There was no point in arresting these youths. "This is Africa," his superior said, "and any vote here hinges on threats and intimidation."[54] The combination of beer and noise, of easily bullied chiefs, and of young men in their urban best and implicit threats shows how popular—in the sense of "people as a whole"—these meetings were.

It is tempting to see the meetings as similar to the carnival of voting in Britain and the United States in the eighteenth and nineteenth centuries, where the franchised and the disenfranchised came together amidst drink, bribes, and men armed with clubs to determine the outcome of an election. Such gatherings, however, like those of the Pearce Commission, were scenes of implicit if not actual violence.[55] Historians of Zimbabwe have tried to walk a fine line between historicizing political violence and dismissing it as a Rhodesian imaginary that intensified in the early 1970s. But political violence was also a fact of African politics that had emerged in the early 1960s, flattening class and gender divisions in order to ensure participation in protests and strikes.[56] More recently, Lloyd Sachikonye has argued that what appears to be endemic violence in Zimbabwe's political culture is in fact a deep history of small groups tasked with coercion and acting with impunity.[57] Certainly these

53. *Pearce Report*, 17; Muzorewa, *Rise Up*, 99–101.

54. Lemon, *Never Quite a Soldier*, 55.

55. See Morgan, *Inventing the People*, 183–89; Frank O'Gorman, "The Secret Ballot in Nineteenth-Century Britain," in *The Hidden History of the Secret Ballot*, ed. Romain Bertrand et al. (Bloomington: Indiana University Press, 2006), 16–42.

56. Norma Kriger, "ZANU (PF) Strategies in General Elections, 1980–2000: Discourse and Coercion," *African Affairs* 104, no. 414 (2005): 1–6; Scarnecchia, *Urban Roots*, 94–99, 158–59.

57. Lloyd Sachikonye, *When a State Turns on Its Citizens: Instrumentalized Violence and Political Culture* (Harare: Weaver, 2011).

ideas were in play in the first months of 1972. In confidential memos, the Centre Party blamed ZAPU supporters for township violence and university students for rural violence in and out of meetings: these students had been sent home when the government closed the university to keep Salisbury quiet during the commission's visit.[58] But the young men haranguing the crowds at public meetings, not unlike the cartoon broadsheets extolling the virtues of settlement, may have been engaged in drumming up interest instead of—or as well as—coercion.

During the Pearce Commission's time in Rhodesia, however, the issue of intimidation was by no means straightforward. Africans rejected the proposals openly and with great vigor. If there had been an attempt to pressure them to accept the proposals, it was a dismal failure. If Africans had been pressured into rejecting the proposals, however, they seemed eager to do so, which the commission thought unlikely if people had been forced to vote a certain way.[59] Yet accusations of intimidation were widespread and applied to everyone. The idea of widespread government coercion strengthened the grand narrative and made Africans' rejection of the proposals part of the renewed nationalist politics the Pearce Commission came to represent. For the government, and for many Rhodesian businessmen, the idea of widespread African intimidation explained why Africans rejected proposals that had so much white support.

The *Report* of the Pearce Commission devoted more than twenty pages to intimidation, most of which discounted the most frequent complaints. Thus, teams in Victoria and Manicaland, for example, saw no evidence of government pressure in public meetings. The ANC made vague accusations—that this or that chief had been reprimanded, or had his salary withheld, for opposing the proposals—that the commission was unable to confirm or deny: commissioners assumed they were exaggerated somewhat. The commission did take particular exception to the practice of thirty-day detentions which it firmly believed suppressed support for the ANC, although it believed the detentions resulting from the riots of January 1972 to be lawful and reasonable.[60] Years later, Rhodesian officials said the commissioners were naïve. They had not wanted district commissioners present at meetings and so did not realize that they were taking evidence from "the same crowd" at each meeting. The men who gave evidence "used to go around in buses, three busloads at a time" and take turns giving evidence so it was not the same men all the

58. Bashford, The African National Council and Settlement.
59. *Pearce Report*, 104–5.
60. *Pearce Report*, 88–98. For survey of detentions, see Jones, *Judge's Burden*, 16–22.

time. These "agitators" followed commissioners as they traveled from district to district.[61]

The commission knew about the fate of African members of the Centre Party, and it reported the vague and anonymous letters written to Africans who openly praised the proposals: sometimes these threatened individuals; sometimes they threatened crops. It was the intimidation of Africans by their white employers that was to prove a gray area: there were powerful anecdotes that no one could verify. Workers told of being given letters supporting the proposals from their employers which they were instructed to sign. Employees at Bernstein Manufacturing Company alleged that they were told "the security of your job" depended on saying "yes." Farmworkers told one commissioner that they were told they would lose their jobs if they voted "no." They were told to vote "yes," not merely to refrain from voting "no."[62] The commission could find no definitive proof that any employee was dismissed for rejecting the proposals, although they found many coincidences. A typical example was that of a tractor driver at Wankie Colliery who appeared before the commissioners along with two colliery officials. He rejected the proposals and was dismissed ten days later. When the commissioners enquired, they were told he had proven himself to be a "dangerous" driver and had to be let go.[63]

Many employers claimed that their employees opposed the proposals because they had been threatened by the ANC; many of those employees said they were not threatened, but that they read the proposals and did not like them. A nursing sister in Salisbury told the commission that no one was intimidated into voting "no." "When we first heard of the settlement we were full of joy" but after reading them "we realized they were not for us."[64] The commission also recorded intimidation, threats, and general pressures imposed by district officers, police, and security forces. Some told chiefs that the proposals had already been accepted; others took great care to make sure chiefs instructed their people to vote "yes." There was an exchange of dossiers: the one provided by the government consisted of newspaper clippings; the one provided by independent journalists detailed administrative abuses.[65] Smith used

---

61. Quinton interview, NAZ/ORAL/QU2. Smith repeated this in his memoirs. "Leading agitators traveled in advance of the commission, from meeting to meeting, orchestrating the opposition." Smith, *Betrayal*, 155.

62. Jones, *Judge's Burden*, 10.

63. *Pearce Report*, 96.

64. *Pearce Report*, 108.

65. *Pearce Report*, 104–7; Hancock, *White Liberals*, 152–53; Peter Niesewand, "Settlement," 8–10.

the occasion to tell journalists how unfortunate it was that Africans were so susceptible to intimidation. It was "incredible" to him and probably most Europeans just how susceptible they were; it was "the African psychology." If someone came to his house and told him not to vote "yes" he would vote "yes" the next day, even if he had planned to vote "no," just to prove he could not bullied. "Regrettably, the African reacts in the very reverse manner." Rhodesians had known this for years, which is why they had to prevent intimidation with a system of restriction and preventative detention.[66]

The ANC, ZAPU, and ZANU

In the end, the commission was convinced that the overwhelming majority of Africans rejected the proposals. It insisted that most Africans had voted "no" on the proposals and that "no" meant "no": there was no silent majority in the "no" votes, no unspoken "yes" in the "no" votes, and no culturally specific way that this "no" could mean "yes."[67] Furthermore, the commission gave little credit to the activities of Muzorewa's ANC; it thought the group itself was surprised at its success: it could not have expanded as quickly as it did if there had been widespread support for the proposals.

It was not the ANC that expanded, however: it was an underground ZAPU that was reanimated by detainees coming home. It seems unlikely that the commission did not know the genealogy of the ANC. If nothing else, Phillipa Berlyn, who traveled with a team for weeks, had written newspaper articles explaining at whose behest the ANC was formed.[68] Pat Bashford of the Centre Party wrote newspaper articles and circulated memos detailing how ZAPU was behind almost every ANC move. African members of the Centre Party blamed the township violence on ZAPU youths; the largely ZANU leadership of the ANC was unable to contain it: "the old ZAPU/ZANU split is still very real."[69] The Pearce Commission reported none of this, even as Muzorewa boasted that the ANC had superseded ZANU and ZAPU whenever he was out of the country. On a visit to the United States in February to protest the Byrd Amendment, Muzorewa told everyone he met that "we no longer

66. Niesewand, *In Camera*, 67.
67. *Pearce Report*, 40, 11.
68. Berlyn, *Quiet Man*, 206.
69. Bashford, The African National Council and Settlement.

have ZANU and ZAPU" and the question of "'where do you belong?' This division was one of our worst enemies in these last years."[70] The Pearce Commission did not trace the various genealogies of some of the groups formed shortly after the ANC, either, especially the RSF, PARD, and COSS, all of which actively opposed the ANC.

But if the ANC was really ZAPU (or ZANU and ZAPU), and if the African pro-settlement groups were really RF and the white pro-settlement groups were really Capricorns and the Centre Party or Garfield Todd's old party, how do we understand politics in Rhodesia? Were political organizations a matter of substitutions and stand-ins, a careful and deliberate layering of names and interests that almost all Rhodesians, black and white, understood, but visiting commissioners chose to ignore? Were "normal political activities" evident in these genealogies of parties and organizations? In the absence of legal political activity, of commonplace rallies and demonstrations and political meetings, did older parties, even those as decrepit as the Capricorns, found and fund proxies to carry out their goals? The political activities the Pearce Commission described, and those they failed to describe, were frequently multiracial and always deeply rooted in Rhodesian political history.

When "No" Means "No"

The *Report* of the Pearce Commission was to be published in May 1972. In March and April, representatives of the ANC and the Rhodesian government, among others, traveled to London to make the cases they had not been able to make in Rhodesia. There Muzorewa alluded to the ANC's origins so as to make it clear that he had broken with his party's past. The new ANC would recruit organizations, not individuals. At a press conference at the House of Commons Muzorewa announced to everyone who knew the ANC's history that he had diluted the ZANU and ZAPU influence in the ANC by expanding the executive committee from nine (in which ZANU and ZAPU each had three representatives) to fifty-five.[71] For whom was such an announcement intended? There were many other venues from which Muzorewa could have spoken to Rhodesians in exile. Was he speaking to the Pearce Commission and the

---

70. Nancy McKeon, "Rhodesia's Fighting Bishop," *Africa Report* 17, no. 3 (1972): 9.

71. Among the groups that now made up the ANC were the African Christian Council (founded 1906), the African Farmers Union (founded 1936), and the African Teachers Association (founded 1944). "Rhodesia: ANC and Others," *Africa Confidential* 13, no. 10 (May 19, 1972): 6–7; Muzorewa, *Rise Up*, 106–11.

Foreign Office then drafting the report? Was Muzorewa telling the commission that what it had heard in Rhodesia was no longer accurate, that the ANC was now disentangled from its origins the previous December?

In April, J. F. Gaylard, secretary to the Rhodesian cabinet, arrived in London to meet with Douglas-Home and others in the Conservative government. Ian Smith, he reported, expected the proposals to be accepted; the very idea that they might not be made his message shrill. A "no" vote would indicate that the test was flawed. Had it not been the responsibility of the British government to "ensure the right answer because this was the best solution for all in Rhodesia?" Given all the advantages of the proposals, the proper evaluation of Rhodesian opinion would give a "yes" answer. Everyone but Africans—European, Asian, Coloured—had accepted the proposals "and the Africans with little understanding of the proposals should not be allowed to cast a veto."[72] The commission had not talked to enough Africans, he said. The "silent majority" had accepted the proposals through their chiefs. The Centre Party, which had African members, recommended a "yes" vote, and when industrialists polled their employees they found that 85 percent of them supported the proposals.[73] Douglas-Home was uneasy about the silent majority and the figures supporting it. He had been told these figures six months earlier and assumed that most Africans favored a settlement.[74]

Douglas-Home wondered if the proposals could remain on the table. If there was an expansion of the franchise, for example, perhaps moderate Africans and Europeans might work together, especially if they thought the only alternative was the 1969 constitution. Gaylard responded that Africans had already vetoed moderate opinion; Smith had no other choice than to restore the position of the governing party. If

72. Meetings, Dorneywood, April 17, 1972, 11 a.m., and 1 p.m., CL/Smith/4003(M).
73. Meeting, Dorneywood, April 17, 1972, 11 a.m., CL/Smith/4/003(M). A Centre Party delegation had also come to London in March to ask that the proposals be implemented so as to develop rural areas; they had only been vetoed, they argued, because of intimidation. See Hancock, *White Liberals*, 160; "Rhodesia: ANC and Others," *Africa Confidential* 13, no. 10 (May 19, 1972): 7. Six months later, the Centre Party congress rejected a motion that it disconnect its phones and close its offices. Diana Mitchell, Paper for circulation at Centre Party Congress, October 28, 1972, Borthwick Historical Institute, CE/5.
74. For much of 1972 Douglas-Home and his negotiators claimed to have been misled by Rhodesians and their fictions. Lord Goodman said Smith had assured him that chiefs could deliver the African vote: "No one warned me that the idea that chiefs could control tribes was wrong. The tribes controlled the chiefs." Quoted in Brivati, *Lord Goodman*, 204. Even before the White Paper was published, Douglas-Home wrote memos about what to do if the proposals were rejected; Alec Douglas-Home, Rhodesia: Options in the Event of a Failure to Achieve a Settlement, November 5, 1971, The National Archives of the United Kingdom, Kew [hereafter TNA]/CAB/129/159/128.

the proposals were rejected, white Rhodesians would feel let down by the British government and by Africans and "there would be a reaction against Africans."[75] It took Denis Greenhill from the Foreign Office to remind Gaylard that if the vote was "no" the only way to keep Britain involved was to keep some of the proposals on the table: if Rhodesia went back to the 1969 constitution it would get no sympathy from Britain, and no peace from the United Nations.[76]

Smith was bitterly disappointed when Greenhill arrived in Salisbury in May to tell him the *Report* said "no." By then, Greenhill was impatient. The commission had created political difficulties for all concerned, but the negative vote was "a political fact" and the British could not now implement any of the proposals. However much Britain wanted to recognize Rhodesia and lift sanctions, this was not possible because the vote was "no."[77] Smith called the report "irresponsible." The commissioners had done their jobs badly: they associated "with people like university academics" and sought the views of "loafers." Their real problem, according to Smith, was the interpretation of evidence, implicit and explicit. The *Report* "indicated a lack of understanding of the African and how very susceptible they were to intimidation." The release of detainees set loose "known intimidators" who "could put fear into a mass of people by merely appearing in their midst . . . they had a magic effect on crowds of Africans." The *Report* had justified intimidation as a way nationalists could further their aims. Smith insisted that traditional leaders spoke for Africans. "Tribesmen never spoke unless they wished to object." Thus there was a silent majority which, properly counted, had voted "yes." Such a count would have shown that Africans accepted the proposals. The *Report* condemned government and chiefs and went out of its way to praise the ANC, at one point calling it "tolerant." Such a "jolt law and order wise" meant that his government had no choice but to continue under the 1969 constitution.[78]

When the Rhodesian House of Assembly debated the *Report* in June, Smith complained that the proposals had been negotiated between governments; the people should never have been asked to approve or

75. Some Rhodesian cabinet committees were more flexible than Smith was. A fraction of the United Kingdom committee, for example, suggested that Rhodesia implement some of the proposals anyway and wait for Britain to react. United Kingdom Committee, April 26, 1972, CL /Smith/4/300(M).

76. Meeting, Dorneywood; Second meeting, Carlton Terrace, April 19, 1972, CL/Smith/4/300(M).

77. Meeting with Prime Minister and Sir Denis Greenhill, May 17, 1972, Test of Acceptability Discussions and meetings with British file, CL/Smith/ 4/003(M).

78. Notes on third meeting between Prime Minister and Sir Denis Greenhill, May 19, 1972, 8:30 a.m., CL/Smith/4/003(M).

reject them. The settlement failed because of African intransigence and British incompetence. The commission had been "deceived" by "the loud roar of the mobs." This must have been the only time in history "when the least responsible elements in a country were able to influence the future . . . simply by shouting 'No' sufficiently loudly and often." Rhodesians would compromise no more, Smith said. For the first time in months, he invoked the tropes of the first years of UDI: there would be no "abandoning of our standards of civilization." Rhodesian Front MPs expanded on Smith's rhetoric, complaining that the commission seemed to believe "that the mass of people in this country were intelligent enough to know what this is about." Another blamed Africans: they were ignorant of the import of the proposals or they "permitted unruly numbers" to reject the proposals and all that they offered. A "no" vote from illiterate tribesmen had vetoed the "yes" of responsible elements. MPs recited the mantra of numbers, of how many Africans were polled and where the commission found them. There was the question of voters. The British had a franchise based on age; Rhodesians had one based on qualifications: how then could the British commission ascertain a "majority" of the people? African MPs—even those who had left the Centre Party over the issue of settlement—were trapped by the confines of the 1969 constitution. The tiny number of Africans enfranchised under the new voter qualifications left them all but illegitimate. One African MP's question admitted as much: what was the role of African MPs, he asked, if the government maintained that chiefs were the real spokesmen of African peoples? When another African MP said his constituents supported the commission's findings, a white MP shouted out, "all fifteen of them."[79]

Smith's reply to the debate added deception to the theme of the commission's incompetence. It was now clear, he said, that the commission itself may have misled Africans about the true purpose of their visit. The "charade" that was the constant use of the Union Jack, the reprise of "God Save the Queen" that preceded every radio announcement may have made many Africans believe that British authority had been reinstated in Rhodesia, and it was to this that they voted "no." Smith criticized the African MPs for "adhering slavishly" to the commission's findings. Did they believe there were any Africans happier than those in Rhodesia? "Are they any happier in Zambia or Burundi, or Uganda . . . ?" Even as there were widespread arrests of rural ANC members, even as

79. *Parliamentary Debates*, June 8, 1972 (Salisbury, 1972), cols. 18, 22, 28, 32, 42, 85–86, 102, 130, 146, 148, 170, 176, 189.

British diplomats in the region were "pleased" that there was no white backlash and "a peaceful" security situation, Smith announced it was now up "to the African people of Rhodesia" to show that the verdict of the Pearce Commission was incorrect.[80]

The Many Meanings of "No"

In July 1972 Muzorewa spoke to a multiracial audience in Salisbury. He denounced the proposals again, but announced that because the present situation was so dire—a condition he described in the same terms of isolation and impasse that white moderates had used for years—"our people" would work for an orderly transition to democratic rule that guaranteed peace and prosperity for all Rhodesians.[81] Such open support for something like the 1971 proposals seems to have encouraged Douglas-Home to suggest that he could return to Rhodesia in September to see if further talks were possible. Rhodesian officials said "no": all talks should be between governments, not individual ministers. But by September there was greater interest in, and lobbying for, settlement in Rhodesia than there had been in January. Several white groups— the Rhodesia Progressive Liberal Forum, the Settlement Council, the National Democratic Convention—that had sprung up after the publication of the Pearce *Report* were all meeting and seeking ways of getting the proposals accepted, Special Branch told the cabinet. There were a few African pro-settlement groups as well, either too small to merit police surveillance or already controlled by the RF. The most prominent groups were the African Settlement Council and the Rhodesian Youth Association; all had ties to white businesses and Rhodesian Front MPs, as had the restructured Rhodesia Settlement Forum.[82]

80. *Parliamentary Debates*, June 8, 1972, cols. 207, 209–10, 213; "Rhodesia: Distant Prospects," *Africa Confidential* 13, no. 16 (August 11, 1972): 7; Flower, *Serving Secretly*, 100–101. A government pamphlet published that month concluded that the British should amend the proposals to earn "the respect and gratitude of those Rhodesians whose interests Britain claims to represent." Ministry of Information, *Where Did Pearce Go Wrong? A Brief Appreciation of the Pearce Report* (Salisbury, 1972), 5.
81. Return to Legality, address by Bishop Abel Muzorewa, ANC, Henry Margolis Hall, Salisbury, July 20, 1972, in Nyangoni and Nyandoro, *Independence Movements*, 242–49; Muzorewa, *Rise Up*, 118, 123. The Centre Party suggested the proposals be revisited as well; see "An Open Letter to the Minister of Internal Affairs," *Centre Point* 2, no. 9 (July 1972): 1.
82. Kirk, "Pro-Settlement Groups," 4–5. Muzorewa noted that these African groups were funded by the Rhodesian government at the same time it denounced the ANC as "rabble-rousers." Nevertheless, he boasted that the ANC was not banned because the Rhodesian government could not establish a link between it and the banned political parties now in Lusaka. Muzorewa, *Rise Up*, 120–21, 124–25.

Nevertheless, Special Branch thought it necessary to have an established African political group support settlement. They had already asked a Centre Party lawyer to approach Nkomo to see if he would support the 1971 proposals. When this failed, Special Branch recommended releasing Garfield Todd, to show a more magnanimous side of the Rhodesian Front. The real issue seemed the ANC, however. The government had begun "a complete dissolution" of the ANC: by October it had R$62 in the bank and its leaders' passports had been withdrawn. Special Branch now recommended that it would be "more politic" to find a way to pressure its leaders into thinking that supporting settlement would be in their best interests. "The bait of international recognition as an official opposition in any new parliament might be enough to persuade the ANC to rethink their opposition to the proposals." It was suggested that Special Branch drop hints of proposed legislation to well-placed ANC leaders, so as to find a way for them "to have a credible change of heart." There were some worries about restoring the ANC to its full force, although most thought the risk acceptable in the short run. Besides, once the ANC was recognized by the government it could never regain its credibility.[83]

In the first months of 1973, the Foreign Office had met with ANC leaders in London, their passports having been reinstated. Rhodesia's Special Branch had been kept well informed of the planned meeting. The Foreign Office was relieved to hear that the ANC did not demand majority rule and that there were conditions under which the ANC would support a settlement. The ANC also told the Foreign Office it was involved in the guerrilla struggle, which it did not appear to believe. Based on these meetings, Douglas-Home suggested new proposals that the Rhodesian government and "responsible Africans," including the ANC, could review in advance of any public test. But the Rhodesian government did not want new proposals; the old ones had been part of a package deal that had already granted far-reaching concessions to Africans. Douglas-Home then asked if it might be possible for the government and "responsible Africans" to meet privately and reframe the issue for Africans, as a choice between the 1971 proposals and the 1969 constitution. That would amount to reversing the Pearce Commission's verdict. Douglas-Home was not willing to go ahead unless there was

83. "Rhodesia: Distant Prospects," 6–7; Minutes, Working Committee of the United Kingdom Committee, October 11, 1972. Within a few months there were concerns that if the government worked with the ANC it would weaken the position of the chiefs who had expressed private support for the proposals. Working Party of the United Kingdom Committee, December 8, 1972, CL/Smith/4/003(M).

significant support for this in Rhodesia. Should he go through the effort of steering this through Parliament and "arrange for sanctions to be lifted by the UN," something would have to save the face of African opinion in Rhodesia. The face saving would be Muzorewa's task. RF cabinet ministers wondered if there was a way to enhance his reputation as a world leader of African opinion. Special Branch did not think so; Muzorewa lacked leadership qualities and largely did whatever senior ANC officials told him to do.[84]

Did Special Branch not know who these ANC leaders were or who constituted the rural ANC? This seems unlikely, however flawed Rhodesian intelligence might have been; Special Branch may have been hesitant to have such information written down. Perhaps it thought the ANC was now so detached from African politics that such information was irrelevant? Perhaps it considered Muzorewa too cynically ambitious to worry about the party's origins? In any case, it appeared that the ANC listened carefully to Douglas-Home. In July 1973 Smith had heard reports that Muzorewa now thought his opposition to settlement was a "mistake," while Muzorewa said the ANC had received information "in private" that the government had softened somewhat. The two held meetings that seem to have been arranged by some combination of Greenfield, Gaylard, and Rhodesia's Special Branch. The meetings accomplished nothing in terms of policy but a great deal in terms of posture. Muzorewa called the talks "a meaningless exercise," but he continued to meet with Smith well into 1974, even as he struggled against an increasingly critical executive committee. By mid-1974, however, Smith was quite pleased: he had received a personal message from Douglas-Home "commiserating" him for the misfortunes and setbacks of negotiations that suggested that the best way forward was to make an agreement with "responsible black leaders" within the country.[85]

The talks between Smith and Muzorewa, however, had great meaning to African nationalists. ZANU denounced them as soon as they began. A letter from Salisbury Prison signed by Ndabaningi Sithole, Robert Mugabe, and four other members of ZANU's central committee not only denounced the ANC for meeting with Smith but went to great lengths to disassociate ZANU from Muzorewa's party. "ZANU had always been

84. United Kingdom Committee, Memoranda, December 8, 1972, and Minutes, May 31, 1973, CL/Smith/ 4/003(M). Special Branch had at first considered Muzorewa a stepping-stone with which to get to Canaan Banana, whom they considered the "most outspoken" of the two. He should be in detention, Special Branch noted, but perhaps he would be easier to manipulate if he was not detained. Working Party of the United Kingdom Committee, December 8, 1972, CL/Smith/4/003(M).
85. Muzorewa, *Rise Up*, 131–33; Smith, *Betrayal*, 157–58.

231

an organisation apart from and independent from any other . . . and no organisation has authority to speak on ZANU's behalf."[86] However many reinventions and dilutions the ANC had undergone in the last year, its founders still acknowledged their ties to the organization, if only to sever them.

Conclusion

The Pearce Commission never managed to reach the level of a discursive turning point. Supposedly moderate Rhodesian Front officials tried in vain to make the rejection of the 1971 proposals the equivalent of the rejection of the 1961 constitution, but such assertions, even when made within earshot of the commission, never gained traction. "Twice in ten years the white man has held out the possibilities of progress to Africans," proclaimed Des Frost, the party chairman, "and twice the hand of friendship has been rejected. The African must realise that there are limits to how far the tolerance of whites will stretch."[87] The Centre Party, however, seemed reborn. Once Smith began meeting with Muzorewa, it could again claim that because the RF had no credibility with Africans and the ANC had failed to earn the confidence of whites, "we are the only people to influence the credibility gap both ways."[88] The ANC carried on, despite its history and its associations, severed or visible, with ZANU, ZAPU, Smith, Special Branch, and the Foreign Office in London. By the end of 1974 it was a significant political presence in détente exercises and even became the umbrella under which ZANU and ZAPU operated in the difficult years 1975–1977. The greatest impact of the Pearce Commission was the extent of African mobilization that now seemed possible in the county, but a close second was that the rejection of the proposals called Smith's bluff. Having tried to use the 1969 constitution as a way to bludgeon Rhodesia's way to legality, he found his government alone with a constitution it did not want and that could not be implemented, and with a weaker bargaining position than it had had before.

86. Quoted in Martin and Johnson, *Struggle for Zimbabwe*, 101.
87. Quoted in Meredith, *Another Country*, 96.
88. Diana Mitchell, Paper for circulation at the Centre Party Congress, October 28, 1972; Minutes, special meeting, March 31, 1974, Centre Party Papers CE/5.

NINE

"Your vote means peace": The Making and Unmaking of the Internal Settlement, 1975–1979

The debris of the Pearce Commission washed up on many shores. Once it became clear that Rhodesia would compromise, and that there were African politicians willing to negotiate with the Smith regime, South Africa, Britain, and the United States became interested—at different times with different degrees of enthusiasm—in some kind of peaceful settlement to the Rhodesian problem.[1] There was détente, followed so shortly by the collapse of ZANLA in Zambia that the guerrilla war seemed to wane for a few years. In August 1975, South Africa pressured the Rhodesian government into a constitutional conference that was to take place on neutral ground, in this case a South Africa Railways car parked on the bridge over Victoria Falls, between Zambia and Rhodesia. The negotiations broke down, but not before Ian Smith realized that South Africa was ready to sacrifice Rhodesia for security on its northern border: in his memoirs, Smith reflected: "When the crunch comes, blacks will stand together, but with the white people dog starts eating dog."[2] Nevertheless, the lure of recognition and a promise

1. But see Blake, *Rhodesia*, 405: after the Pearce Commission report "Rhodesia became a non-subject" in Britain.
2. Smith, *Betrayal*, 182.

of an end to sanctions were great: whatever the Rhodesian Front said privately about other white people, they participated in any number of negotiations they did not want.

The All-Party Conference in Geneva, 1976

Early in 1976, Henry Kissinger toured East and Southern Africa to seek some kind of settlement that would ensure that Rhodesia would not become "another Angola," that there would not be Cuban troops there. In two trips Kissinger met with everyone from Nyerere of Tanzania to Vorster of South Africa. He promised that the United States would continue to uphold UN sanctions and that it would work to ensure negotiations that would lead to majority rule. Everyone he spoke to made it clear that they too wanted a peaceful solution, without foreign soldiers of any kind, which could be worked out in an all-party conference held in Europe.[3] In private meetings, such as one in Germany with Vorster and several of his ministers, Kissinger was easily convinced that South Africa could control Ian Smith and that promoting Joshua Nkomo to a position in an interim government would keep Soviet and Cuban troops out.[4] These ideas and assertions became the Kissinger proposals, in which Rhodesia would have majority rule in two years. The details of how this might transpire were vaguely left to South Africa to work out with Smith, after which they would be debated in Geneva in October 1976. Smith made no attempt to hide his disappointment: he told Kissinger the proposals were "his own suicide note" and he told his countrymen they did not represent the best solution for Rhodesia.[5]

Another critical audience for the Kissinger proposals was the frontline presidents. These were the men who led the states that bordered on Rhodesia and hosted parties and armies in exile. Julius Nyerere of Tanzania, Samora Machel of Mozambique, and Kenneth Kaunda of Zambia all housed the armies of ZANU and ZAPU; Botswana accommodated

3. Fact Sheet, September 27, 1976, GFL/ David Gergen/1, Office of the Press Secretary; Kissinger speech at luncheon in Lusaka, April 27, 1976, Election Campaign Papers, GFL/Gergen/16; Brent Scowcroft, National Security Adviser, to Ford, cables from Henry Kissinger, September 1976, GFL/ Trip Briefing Book/42, 1974–76.

4. When Kissinger wondered if it would be best if Britain assumed control over Rhodesia, Vorster said "Amen to that!" Memorandum of Conversation, June 23, 1976, Bodenmais, Federal Republic of Germany, GFL/National Security Adviser Memoranda of Conversation Collection.

5. Caute, *Under the Skin*, 65–66; Memorandum of Conversation, Ford, Kissinger, and Scowcroft, September 11, 1976, GFL/NSA Memoranda of Conversation Collection.

refugees in various states of moving into guerrilla camps in Zambia or Tanzania. For all their steadfast loyalty to the guerrillas' cause, Kaunda and Machel had uneasy relations with the foreign armies on their soil. Kaunda's opponents claimed he made Zambia into an "occupied country," and Machel never fully trusted ZANLA.[6] All the frontline presidents had some leverage over ZANU and ZAPU, and they shared a keen interest in a peaceful transition to majority rule. These men were critical actors in the events of the next two chapters. In 1976, however, perhaps under pressure from Britain, the frontline presidents managed to convince ZANU and ZAPU to form a Patriotic Front (PF) to intensify the armed struggle and to send a joint delegation to Geneva, to distinguish themselves from the acronyms of umbrella and breakaway organizations, and to distance themselves from Muzorewa.[7]

The Geneva talks had gone on for a few unproductive weeks when Kissinger became part of a lame duck administration in the United States. The conference unraveled soon after that, but a newly revitalized ZANU in the Patriotic Front was able to establish itself in Geneva. Robert Mugabe, who was not fully in control of ZANU in 1976, rejected the Kissinger proposals: by the time he arrived in Geneva he demanded a transfer of power in a few months. Nyerere and Kaunda, however much they had inspired Kissinger a few months before, wanted even shorter timetables to majority rule.[8] By December most participants postured and many shouted at each other, with neither British nor U.S. representatives keeping order. P. K. van der Byl, heading the Rhodesian Front delegation after Smith returned to Salisbury, complained that the Patriotic Front had kept everyone waiting at every session of the conference, sometimes for half a day. Mugabe hit back: "It did not matter keeping those people waiting who had kept Zimbabwe waiting eleven years for independence."[9] Even so, hardly anyone in the Patriotic Front delegation wanted the conference to succeed, let alone bring about a speedy transition to majority rule. As a ZANU lawyer later told Stephen Stedman, the party had not done "the political work" to win an election:

6. Author's field notes, Lusaka, August 9, 2006.
7. Martin and Johnson, *Struggle for Zimbabwe*, 268–70; Caute, *Under the Skin*, 66–68; Nkomo claimed this was his idea, *My Life*, 160.
8. See M. Tamarkin, *The Making of Zimbabwe: Decolonization in Regional and International Politics* (London: Frank Cass, 1990), 152–53, for a description of who was moderate and who was a "hot head."
9. Van der Byl, Geneva, to Prime Minister, December 2, 1976. Rhodesia: official communications, CL/4/006(M).

"Muzorewa might have won but not us." ZANU was best served by intensifying the war effort before negotiating again.[10]

The conference adjourned in mid-December and was never reconvened. It accomplished nothing; its importance was how it was structured, as Smith clearly understood. The British had brought Zambia's foreign minister as an observer: it was his insights into nationalists' goals, rather than those of the Rhodesian Front regime, on which they relied. Moreover, Smith wrote in late December, had he known that his delegation would not be treated as the government of Rhodesia he never would have agreed to come. He was not asking the British to recognize the de jure status of the government as Rhodesian courts had, but he did expect that Britain accept the de facto existence and status of the RF government as the "only authority" capable of implementing a constitutional agreement in the country. This had never been a problem in previous negotiations with Britain—indeed, the 1971 settlement proposals had been negotiated and signed in the cabinet rooms in Salisbury—but now his government was given the status equivalent to a party.[11]

The Anglo-American Proposals of 1977

In May 1977 Britain formed the joint Anglo-American Consultative Group. This was actually two officials, John Graham, of the Foreign and Commonwealth Office (FCO), who had been Douglas-Home's private secretary when he negotiated the 1971 proposals in Salisbury, and Stephen Low, U.S. ambassador to Zambia. Graham and Low were to work out the constitutional means by which a transition to majority rule might be achieved. South Africa pressured the Rhodesian Front into attending these meetings, which it did with limited enthusiasm. The main concern of the Rhodesian Front government was not whether there would be majority rule elections or not, but what role the U.S. and Britain envisioned for white Rhodesians after the election. What would happen to Rhodesian citizens in and out of the African-ruled country? The RF had specific recommendations. Rhodesian citizenship, whether by birth or naturalization, would be legally transferred to that of the new state. No future government could alter that. Anyone with dual citizenship

10. Simba Mubako quoted in Stephen John Stedman, *Peacemaking in Civil War: International Mediation in Zimbabwe, 1974–1980* (Boulder, CO: Lynne Reiner, 1988), 108–9.

11. L. O. Fletcher, Pretoria, to Flower, Salisbury, information obtained from a reliable source from personal interview with Mark Chona, November 9, 1976; Smith to Anthony Crossland, confidential, December 22, 1976, Cory/Smith/4/006(M).

in Britain and Rhodesia could continue to have both; this was a standard practice in former British colonies. Europeans whose only citizenship was Rhodesian and who feared they might be victimized in some way could be granted British citizenship if they did not already have it, but Africans who had Rhodesian citizenship could not be granted British citizenship. Finally, anyone who had "voluntarily acquired" citizenship in a country other than Britain would be required to renounce their Rhodesian citizenship. This too was standard practice.[12]

In their initial meetings, Rhodesian ministers made impassioned, if formulaic, pleas for a qualified franchise, noting as they had for years that the introduction of one man, one vote in Africa had not led to democratic systems. J. F. Gaylard was more instrumental: franchise qualifications would instill "confidence" in white Rhodesians; it would encourage them to stay. Without franchise qualifications how could the Anglo-American group guarantee that there would be a mechanism by which a proportion of the parliament could block laws that were contrary to the public good? This was the "blocking mechanism," the Rhodesian fantasy of how to manage African legislative aspirations that had been bandied about since the early 1960s. A blocking mechanism required having enough legislators sympathetic to European interests to safeguard those interests, although this was always expressed as a protection against arbitrary and exclusionary laws.[13] Even though universal adult suffrage could not produce a blocking proportion of white representatives, and even though no one in the U.S. or Britain was willing to even consider a qualified franchise, debates about the blocking mechanism went on for months. Finally an exasperated John Graham pointed out that Rhodesia's elections had to demonstrate to the world at large that Rhodesia now practiced universal suffrage; lunatics could be denied the vote but illiterates could not. He recommended reserved seats for whites as the only way to safeguard whites under one man, one vote. It would not be popular in London or Washington, but in an assembly of one hundred members it might be possible to reserve ten seats for whites and ten for blacks without risking accusations of racism. This would only be a psychological prop for whites, since ten seats out of a hundred in an assembly where they might have three or four more seats was not really a safeguard, but it had worked well in several African

12. Notes on discussions between British consultative group and Rhodesian government officials, July 10, 1977, Prime Minister's file, CL/Smith/4/005(M).

13. Even as fewer Africans were allowed representation in Rhodesia's constitutions, proposed blocking mechanisms became more and more formidable. See The Forum, Comments on the Report of the Reconciliation Commission, April 15, 1968, NAZ/MS811.

countries in their pre-independence elections, and was promoted by those governments, as we shall see. Gaylard however doubted that this would maintain white confidence. He continued to ask for one-third of the seats in the assembly reserved for whites, while Ian Smith returned to the need for a qualified franchise. An exasperated Graham reminded him that they had made a deal: Britain would guarantee civil servants' pensions in exchange for Rhodesia giving up the qualified franchise.[14]

In their private conversations Graham and Low brought other messages to Rhodesian officials. They had been to Lusaka and Maputo, they had met with Nkomo and Mugabe. In Salisbury they tried to convince whoever they could that these men were not nearly as extreme as Rhodesians had been led to believe. Both men were socialists, and both hoped that a socialist state would be established in a majority-ruled Rhodesia "eventually," but they had every intention of maintaining, if not expanding, their "links to the west." Communist countries, Graham and Low explained, were very generous with arms and ammunition but did not provide the kind of aid that the majority-ruled nation would need. White fears were not entirely justified: "The sort of state that would come about if the two nationalists took over would still be the sort of place where the whites could live in comfort and security."[15]

Not everyone was reassured. Smith called for an election in August 1977, as much to quell a right-wing revolt in his party as to placate anyone outside of it. In his campaign Smith returned to the exaggerations of the first years of UDI: Rhodesia was fighting "the battle for Africa" on behalf of a western civilization that was now too decadent to defend itself, "asking the white man to commit suicide."[16] The Rhodesian Front won all the European seats: such a show of unity and commitment, Smith told the nation, would tell the U.S. and Britain that Rhodesians would not negotiate their own destruction. A few weeks later he announced he would abandon the Anglo-American settlement plan. This brought about a new round of meetings in Pretoria, Lusaka, and London, during which Smith realized that Muzorewa, not the Rhodesian Front, had the support of South Africa. If there was a moment in which Rhodesia became categorically different from the other African territories whose self-determination was delayed—Algeria or Spanish Sahara—it was this:

14. Notes of discussions between Anglo-American Consultative Group and Rhodesian government officials, May 25, 1977, July 8, 1977; Notes on meeting with Rhodesian officials, Salisbury, November 7, 1977, Cory/Smith/4/005(M). The pensions were guaranteed even if the civil servants left the country; see Caute, *Under the Skin*, 242.

15. Peter Claypole, interview, NAZ/ORAL/OH/321.

16. Evans, Rhodesian Front Rule, 331.

Rhodesia became the former possession no one else wanted. There seemed no alternative but to design an internal settlement for themselves. "We had enough trouble dealing with some of these local chaps without our friends to the south adding fuel to the fire."[17]

In November, a few days after Rhodesian generals held frustrating meetings with the Commonwealth peacekeeping force in which it was made clear that any cease-fire had to involve security forces as well as ZANLA and ZIPRA, Smith announced his acceptance of the principle of majority rule.[18] He began negotiations with the African nationalist parties that were legal in Rhodesia: the UANC (Muzorewa had added the "United" after Ndabaningi Sithole called his party the ANC), Sithole's ANC, and Chief Chirau's Zimbabwe United People's Organization (ZUPO). It took several weeks before all three parties were willing to meet together. Once they met, there were arguments about the name of the newly governed country—Muzorewa and Sithole both wanted Zimbabwe—and arguments about the voting age, which Graham insisted be lowered to eighteen because that was the age of conscription. The critical issue remained that of how many reserved seats for whites would constitute a safeguard, which the three parties debated for weeks. Smith said he would accept universal suffrage "in exchange" for safeguards for white Rhodesians. Smith was concerned that British diplomats recommended that "adequate representation for minority groups" was one-fifth of parliamentary seats. Was 20 percent adequate? He suggested one-third. The UANC was at first against one-third white representation in parliament, but then argued that if there was to be one-third representation, it should be elected by the common roll. Sithole objected. By definition seats reserved specifically for whites had to represent white interests and thus must be elected by white voters. He insisted there should only be twenty such representatives: he was certain Asians and Coloureds would not want special representation. There were arguments and accusations: Muzorewa walked out on several meetings. Finally there was a compromise, attributed to the UANC but fully supported by the Rhodesian Front government, that there would be twenty reserved seats elected by a separate roll and eight "special seats" elected by a common roll.[19] Over a year later, when late colonial constitutions were

17. Smith, *Betrayal*, 231–34.

18. Notes of meeting with Commonwealth peacekeeping force, Officers Mess, BSAP Depot, November 2, 1977, CL/Smith/4/005(M).

19. Notes of meeting with Rhodesian government officials, Salisbury, November 7, 1977, CL/Smith/4/005(M); Muzorewa, *Rise Up*, 229–36; Official record of meeting between representatives of the Rhodesian Government, the African National Council (Sithole), the United African

deployed as models in all discussions of settlement, Muzorewa would insist that this was standard constitutional practice, that Tanganyika's first election had even more generous voting rights for minorities than Zimbabwe-Rhodesia had. The Foreign Office was at pains to explain that it did not: the twenty-one reserved seats (ten for Europeans, eleven for Asians) out of seventy-one were all elected from a common roll. Zimbabwe-Rhodesia not only had reserved seats elected by a white voters' roll; it required the votes of at least seventy-eight members of the assembly to amend the constitution.[20]

Reserved seats, or special electorates, were a tried-and-true late colonial practice: they protected the rights of minority or vulnerable groups from the overwhelming weight of universal suffrage, which many colonialists and members of minority groups believed would only perpetuate inequalities. The question for Rhodesia from 1977 to 1979 was how to justify seats for a minority that had held great and repressive power for fourteen years. British diplomats assumed that African nations would condemn the idea of reserved seats, but no one in Southern Africa or in the frontline states seemed to worry. Even the Patriotic Front approved of the principle, but wanted to make sure there were constraints in its practice.

As a late colonial and early postcolonial practice, reserved seats for whites were imagined as a gentle social engineering, a way to ease tensions in what we would now call post-conflict societies. All of this begs the question of what kind of nation-state was imagined by the social engineers who devised separate electoral rolls? The question is not one of how many selves can self-determine a nation's future, but of the registers in which self-determination can take place. If self-determination was a matter of constitutional guarantees, who wrote the constitution and who guaranteed its rights? The promise of Woodrow Wilson's self-determination offered international organizations as a vehicle to secure colonial freedom, but in practice this was considered too risky: only established states who could join these international organizations— who could make treaties and write constitutions—could determine their own governance. Newer states, in some shape or form, would have

---

National Council, and the Zimbabwe United People's Organization, February 7, 1978. Kent B. Crane papers, Hoover Institution Archives, Stanford, California; Harold Hawkins, Acknowledged Diplomatic Representative (ADR), Cape Town to Gaylard, January 30 and 31, 1978, Prime Minister files, CL/Smith/4/006(M); Hudson, *Triumph or Tragedy?*, 135–36.

20. Note on the Prime Minister's Discussion with Bishop Abel Muzorewa, London, July 13, 1979; Muzorewa to Thatcher, July 25, 1979; J. S. Wall, FCO, Representation of Minorities in the Tanzanian Constitution, July 26, 1979, TNA/PREM/19/108.

constitutions written for them. These different registers seem to have given many nations a colonial ambivalence, a built-in instability about who was allowed to represent whom. The instability and its ability to fracture, historians of South Asia remind us, is not a coincidence: the making of special electorates and the reserved seats for which they vote are ways for politicians to create constituencies that would vanish in one man, one vote elections. Reserved seats are not simply a way to protect minorities; they are a way to perpetuate political parties.[21]

The Internal Settlement of 1978

In February 1978 Smith and Muzorewa announced an interim government that would be a combination of the Rhodesian Front and the UANC. This troubled the Anglo-American group, which toured the region to discuss whether the Patriotic Front should be included or not, and whether that inclusion or exclusion would lead to Soviet intervention.[22] More worrisome to the United Kingdom and the United States, however, was that the new government and the proposals on which it was based required a referendum, which brought the question of the franchise, and how Rhodesia had understood the franchise, to the fore. The Rhodesian Front government wanted to have the referendum voted on by Rhodesia's legal voters. This was the common roll of the 1969 constitution, which included Asian and Coloured voters but no Africans. The government argued that such a referendum would be simple to organize, fulfill parliamentary requirements, and make the internal settlement internally legitimate. In interviews with foreign newspapers, Smith insisted that this had nothing to do with race. He did not believe in majority rule—"in Britain, Germany or anywhere"—but he feared that world pressure wanted Rhodesia to enfranchise "nitwits."[23] The U.S. and Britain were taken aback: they insisted on an African election. The Rhodesian Front government protested that this would be time consuming and would make the electoral process unduly complicated, as there

21. I take this paragraph from several sources: Partha Chatterjee, *The Politics of the Governed: Reflections on Popular Politics in Most of the World* (New York: Columbia University Press, 2004); Sinha, *Specters of Mother India*; Andrew Reynolds, "Reserved Seats in National Legislatures: A Research Note," *Legislative Studies Quarterly* 30, no. 2 (2005): 301–10; John Kelly and Martha Kaplan, "Legal Fictions after Empire."
22. No one imagined a Cuban invasion in 1978. Discussions with Anglo-American Envoys, April 10, 1978, CL/Smith/4/005(M).
23. Evans, Rhodesian Front Rule, 342.

would be a referendum and a general election. If the white referendum vote was held first, a later African vote could veto it, and that would be disastrous. And, of course, a general election would invite intimidation.[24]

What was not overtly addressed in Rhodesian Front objections to an African election and what the Anglo-American group seemed oblivious to was the question of migrant labor. For almost eighty years many of the labor requirements of Rhodesian agriculture and industry were met by men and women from neighboring territories, especially Mozambique, Nyasaland, and Northern Rhodesia. Men in the mining sector and in industrial work in towns tended to stay in Rhodesia for years, but they eventually returned home. Farmworkers did not, however, and by the 1970s there were second- and even third-generation Malawians and Mozambiquans working and living on white-owned farms.[25] Whether or not these people could be enfranchised put the question of self-determination into high relief. Was the self the people living in the country at the time of the election, or was it a group whose belonging was guaranteed by law? Could men and women vote if history and economy had placed them in Rhodesia for years, or could they only vote if they belonged to Rhodesia through fathers and grandfathers?

This was something late colonial elections had addressed elsewhere. In Nyasaland in 1961 and Northern Rhodesia in 1962 it was understood that a high proportion of the population worked outside the territory. The normal requirement of continuous residence in a district for a specified period before the election would have disenfranchised too many people. In Nyasaland electoral laws were amended so that a voter could register if he or she had lived in a district for two years at any time in the past. In Northern Rhodesia men and women could register if they lived in a district for the three months prior to the election or maintained a home there. In Kenya absentee ballots allowed migrant laborers to vote where they worked, not where they lived.[26] In Rhodesia, where very few Africans had been enfranchised in the previous fourteen years the question of who could vote was a question of who the electorate was imagined to be. In Zanzibar in the late 1950s, for example, the

24. Hawkins to Gaylard, February 24, 1978, March 15, 1978, April 5, 1978, April 25, 1978, Prime Minister Files, CL/Smith/4/006(M).
25. A few examples include I. R. Phimister and C. van Onselen, *Studies in the History of African Mine Labour in Colonial Zimbabwe* (Salisbury: Mambo Press, 1978); Phimister, *Zimbabwe*, passim; Rubert, *Promising Weed*, 42–52, 89–120; Blair Rutherford, *Working on the Margins: Black Workers, White Farmers in Postcolonial Zimbabwe* (Harare: Weaver, 2001).
26. Mair, *Nyasaland Election*, 16; Mulford, *Northern Rhodesia General Election*, 54; Bennett and Rosberg, *Kenyatta Election*, 56–58.

question of where an African registrant was born was a question of the nature of their belonging to the island: was a registrant of slave or free-born origin? In Spanish Sahara twenty years later, allowing a population of settlers from Morocco to vote effectively disenfranchised a nomadic people who were not in the territory at the time of the census.[27] Many in the Rhodesian Front government envisioned the 1979 election as a procedure that would provide the regime with a figurehead, nothing more. There was no electorate to be educated or built; instead African voters were caricatured as they had been since the early 1960s. It was only necessary to avoid the problem of the Pearce Commission, in which Africans responded to complex questions by voting "no" but "the one-man-one-vote election envisioned by the US and the UK took care of all that." Parties and candidates could say "vote for me" or "vote for us," which would be "something Africans understood."[28]

Rhodesia set about holding this election and legitimating the internal settlement with great fanfare. The plan for one man, one vote election followed the contours of the Anglo-American proposals: dual citizenship was allowed, the voting age was eighteen, and each polling station served a ten-mile radius. There would be no constituencies since, as Rhodesian officials had been saying for years, most Africans had never voted before. In January 71 percent of eligible common roll voters cast their ballots; an overwhelming percentage—85 percent—approved the internal settlement.[29] This was virtually meaningless to anyone in the United States or the United Kingdom; it was the April election that was a cause of great concern. As the African election approached, various diplomats sought ways to get it postponed, going so far as to hint that sanctions might be lifted if the election was delayed.

In February 1979 the FCO dispatched the head of its Rhodesia department, Robin Renwick, and Stephen Low to visit the region and try to talk everyone out of holding the election. In Salisbury, they met with Muzorewa, who was to become head of government: he wanted the election to go on as scheduled. Once there was an African prime minister, he said, guerrillas would lay down their arms. They met with General Peter Walls, who assured them that he was "not a Smith man" and that

27. Glassman, *War of Words*, 155–57; Toby Shelley, *Endgame in the Western Sahara: What Future for Africa's Last Colony* (London: Zed, 2004), 139–40, 150.

28. Accredited Diplomatic Representative, Cape Town, to J. F. Gaylard February 24, 1978, Communications with ADR (SA), January 1, 1978–May 31, 1978, Gaylard file v. 2. CL/Smith/4/006(M).

29. Notes on discussions between British consultative group and Rhodesian government officials, July 10, 1977, CL/Smith/4/005(M). Journalists suggested that whites voted to end the war, not to live under black rule; see Moorcraft, *Short Thousand Years*, 126–27.

the April election was necessary. He had no doubt his troops could keep both guerrilla armies at bay during the voting period. Ian Smith refused to meet with them, but David Smith, minister of finance, did. Within a few months the British would come to think of David Smith as the intellectual heart of the Rhodesian Front, and a man eager to find a settlement. At this meeting he argued that the only way to protect the rural population was to end the war, so the April election was necessary. In Lusaka they met with Nkomo, who complained more about ZANU than he did about the Rhodesian Front. In Maputo, they met with Mugabe and his high command. Mugabe said he believed in elections, but not this one. ZANU would not risk losing politically what they had won militarily, nor would they cede power to those who had not done the fighting. Mugabe assured the diplomats that ZANU would "persuade" people not to vote in the April election; his goal was elections held after a new government could be established with ZANU in control. Renwick despaired that he could not convince Mugabe to negotiate. He turned to the young embassy officer who was the British liaison to ZANU. This young man spent a great deal of time eating and drinking with the leadership; he reported "They will not take you seriously until they get to Lancaster House. They know that it is there that the independence constitutions for other British colonies were decided."[30]

The April 1979 Election

It seemed as if nothing could postpone the April 1979 elections. The previous August Ian Smith met secretly with Joshua Nkomo and Kenneth Kaunda in Zambia, possibly to secure agreement on the remnants of the Anglo-American proposals, or possibly to negotiate an eventual three-way coalition between himself, Muzorewa, and Nkomo.[31] Whatever happened or did not happen at the meetings hardly mattered, however. Negotiations ceased after ZIPRA shot down two civilian Rhodesian aircraft, one in September 1978 and another in February 1979. Rhodesia responded to both attacks with swift, airborne violence—the villa in

---

30. Robin Renwick, *Unconventional Diplomacy in Southern Africa* (New York: St. Martin's Press, 1997), 6–12.

31. Smith, *Betrayal*, 261–64; Nkomo, *My Life*, 157–58. P. K. van der Byl said these meetings were arranged by Tiny Rowland of Lonrho, who funded Nkomo's travel. See Wessels, *PK*, 231; and Nkomo, *My Life*, 182–84.

which Renwick met Nkomo was destroyed a week after his visit—but even then there was no talk of postponing the elections.[32]

In many ways, the April election was farcical: a one man, one vote in a party-list election for a government for which no African had previously voted. As if the 1969 constitution or the protestations around the Pearce Commission had never happened, the 1979 election was conceived as a voters' free-for-all. The Rhodesian Front and the parties of the transitional government all wanted this settlement to be the one that worked. They all wanted recognition and the withdrawal of sanctions and argued, even before the poll, that if turnout was high enough, this election would satisfy Wilson's fifth principle. The entire Directorate of Elections, industrialists, and members of the transitional government entreated employers to make sure their employees voted. The minister of mines explained why. "The higher percentage poll we get, the easier it will be for our friends overseas to help gain recognition and the removal of sanctions." The government took out full-page ads, "Your vote means peace" and "Your vote will help bring better job opportunities." The Rhodesian director of elections dispensed with voter rolls, voter qualifications and registration, and citizenship. Letters were sent to anyone who employed more than ten Africans asking them to do all they could to help their African workers vote. Domestic servants were tutored in the ways of the secret ballot and taken to vote in their employers' cars, urban factory workers were brought in batches in company trucks, and farmworkers were brought by trucks and farm vehicles. Traffic laws were amended to allow tractors on roads so long as they were carrying people to or from a polling station. Most observers were taken aback by such amendments: between one-half and one-third of farmworkers were from neighboring countries, they had never before had the rights of citizens. The amended law that allowed anyone who was over eighteen who had lived in the country two years to vote was seen as a proof of the cynicism of the regime.[33]

32. Moorcraft suggests that Kaunda colluded with the first of these raids, so as to weaken ZIPRA in Zambia; see *Short Thousand Years*, 116–18. These two incidents, often collapsed into one—called "Viscount," after one of the planes—figure in Rhodesian fiction, a template of African brutality and white retaliation. See Peter Armstrong, *Operation Zambezi: The Raid into Zambia* (Salisbury: Welston Press, 1979); Sylvia Bond Smith, *Ginette*, 241–43.

33. Caute, *Under the Skin*, 324–27; Claire Palley, The Rhodesian Election Campaign: On Whether Elections Were Fair and Free and Whether Principles Required for Rhodesian Independence Have Been Satisfied (London: Catholic Institute for Race Relations, mimeo., April 1979), 16, 18; Masipula Sithole, "The General Elections, 1979–85," in *Zimbabwe: The Political Economy of Transition 1980–1986*, ed. Ibbo Mandaza (Dakar: Codesria Books, 1986), 75–98; Parliamentary Human Rights Group, Free and Fair? The 1979 Rhodesian Election, mimeo., London, May 1979, 30–31. The author of the

There were four sets of observers in the 1979 election, three British and one American. Margaret Thatcher, then leader of the opposition, had sent Viscount Boyd (Alan Lennox-Boyd) to report on the elections, the Parliamentary Human Rights Group sent Lord Chitnis, and the Catholic Institute for International Relations sent Claire Palley, and New York City's Freedom House sent a delegation that included Bayard Rustin and Max Yeargan. Freedom House produced one of the longest reports, rich in background, which declared the election "credible" given the presence of security forces, the threat of guerrilla intimidation, and how little most of the population knew about voting or elections.[34] Neither the Freedom House report nor the Boyd report was ever published. Boyd's team had almost unlimited access to the Directorate of Elections and its thorough but out-of-date demographic data; the team was not troubled by how little care was taken to ascertain citizenship and proof of eligibility. Indeed, the Boyd team thought this made the election fair. There was no need to prove citizenship because there were so many reasons, "not the least of which was the unacceptability to most countries of a Rhodesian passport," that most Rhodesian residents "of all races" were not citizens, and this did not seem sufficient reason to disenfranchise them.

Viscount Boyd surveyed the African continent and announced that the absence of an electoral roll should not invalidate any election. The first elections in Gabon and Mozambique were carried out without the registration of voters, and in Swaziland voters were registered but they were not required to show proof of citizenship when they did so. The war had sent many Africans into neighboring countries in search of some security. Even though very few seemed to have returned from Zambia or Mozambique to vote, the experience of Equatorial Guinea in 1968—where refugees who returned to vote had not registered and were turned away from polling stations—should serve as a good enough reason to dispense with registration. People would not understand why they were disenfranchised and would be frustrated with the electoral process. It was better to dispense with registration altogether. In the end,

---

report, Lord Chitnis, was the son of Asian immigrants and a prominent member of the Liberal Party; he was made a life peer in 1977.

34. Report of the Freedom House Mission to Observe the Elections in Zimbabwe Rhodesia—April 1979, mimeo., New York City, Freedom House, May 20, 1979, George Loft Papers 10/19, Hoover Institution Archives; Jervis Anderson, *Bayard Rustin: Troubles I've Seen* (New York: Harper Collins, 1997), 342–42. David Caute asked Rustin if he had seen any indication of an Ndebele boycott in Bulawayo. "Who are they?" Rustin asked. Caute, *Under the Skin*, 337.

the report concluded, the turnout was impressive. No one really knew how many Africans of voting age there were, but even if the observers accepted the highest estimate, extrapolated from 1969 figures, of 3.5 million, turnout was over 50 percent.[35] Boyd admitted that in the early days of campaigning the private armies of Muzorewa and Sithole, recast as security force auxiliaries, were unrestrained in rural areas, but soon they "helped counteract" the intimidation of the Patriotic Front. The electoral machinery ran with an efficiency comparable to those of western European democracies, and the conduct of the election was "above serious reproach." The election was free insofar as nothing in the pressures of the current situation curtailed voters' freedom.[36]

The two reports that found the elections unfree and unfair were published. Lord Chitnis and his assistant—seconded from the Catholic Institute of Race Relations—spent two weeks in the country; he relied heavily on an International Red Cross document from the previous month which described a climate "of wanton and persistent cruelty" in which security forces had virtually unlimited power of arrest and detention. He noted, as did Internal Affairs, that turnout was highest in the areas with the most intense security force presence, and that security force auxiliaries were given ample opportunities to vote more than once. No one seemed to pay much attention to voters who appeared too young to cast a ballot, and it was common practice for poll workers to fill out ballots for illiterate voters. The election was "nothing more than a gigantic confidence trick" that forced on a "cowed and indoctrinated black population" a settlement and a constitution on which they had not been consulted and could not reject. He concluded that the frenzy about turnout, the propaganda, and the "callous" intimidation meant that the election was "not a valid test of opinion, and its results are meaningless."[37]

35. Viscount Boyd of Merton, Report to the Prime Minister on the Election Held in Zimbabwe/Rhodesia in April 1979, TNA/PREM/19/106. Peter Lord Carrington, *Reflecting on Things Past* (New York: Harper & Row, 1988), 291–93. Thatcher at first found the Boyd Report "thorough and convincing" and hoped to see it published. Thatcher to FCO, May 18, 1979, TNA/PREM/19/106.

36. Boyd Report. Not every member of his team agreed. In what amounted to a brief minority report, John Drinkwater wrote that security force auxiliaries used physical violence to intimidate voters; see John Drinkwater, Q. C., Report on the General Election held in April 1979 in Zimbabwe-Rhodesia, May 3, 1973, Archibald Campbell papers, RH Mss Afr s. 1761.

37. Lord Chitnis, Free or Fair? 16–18, 20, 46, 50, 52. Internal Affairs was relieved that even in those places where security force auxiliaries were "electioneering," a high turnout was anticipated. Ministry of Internal Affairs, Salisbury, Intelligence reports, February 1979. Rhodesian Army Association papers, 2001/086/026B/157, British Empire and Commonwealth Museum, Bristol.

Claire Palley spent the most time in the country, having arrived a few weeks before the election as a visitor. She wrote two reports, the first of which was written about the campaign. She was keenly aware of the issues of turnout, the explicit and implicit intimidation, including Muzorewa's use of spirit mediums to encourage voters' support, but she was alone among the observers to focus on the new electoral law. The most important change was that of citizenship requirements. For the past thirty years, Rhodesian governments had been unwilling to grant citizenship to alien Africans, mainly farmworkers who were born in Mozambique and Malawi, and did not allow them the rights and obligations that residents had. In this election only, 250,000 alien farmworkers, totaling 8 or 9 percent of the electorate, were allowed to vote. As a group, they were "highly susceptible" to pressure from their employers. Employers had been asked to take their employees to polling stations; for this election political parties were allowed to do so as well, but employers were expected to keep their workers safe from such intimidation. Also for this election, Rhodesia jettisoned the registration of voters and all the documentation required to prove eligibility. Africans were to present themselves at polling stations with some document showing their names; if African women had no such documents, they should be accompanied by a male relative.[38] Palley had been told the same comparisons that Viscount Boyd had. Fair enough, she wrote: Zambia, Angola, Mozambique, Tanzania, and Swaziland all had elections without voters' registration, but in those cases the number of votes cast had not been a political issue nor was the outcome in any of those countries likely to have been determined by aliens.[39] By her second report, published after the election, she turned the example of other countries on its head. Could free and fair elections have been held in Ethiopia, Uganda, Vietnam, and Lebanon during their civil wars? What had happened in Zimbabwe-Rhodesia instead was that Muzorewa invoked the precedent of Lebanon to justify the need for private armies. Palley's second report concluded that the election would bring only "change without change," that the 1979 constitution and the Muzorewa government,

---

38. Mick Delap, "The April 1979 Elections in Zimbabwe-Rhodesia," *African Affairs* 78, no. 313 (1979): 431–38.

39. Palley, Election Campaign, 14, 21–22. The list went on: African candidates were not required to show receipts for their expenditures, which seemed excessive to Palley, 22–23.

elected by the constant breach of electoral law, would not bring about genuine majority rule.[40]

The Frontline States and Zimbabwe-Rhodesia, 1979

No one was willing to call the 1979 election an unqualified success either in its organization or its conduct. Nevertheless, very many Africans had voted, most of them for the first time, and while they had not been consulted about the need for a transitional government or who should run it, it was possible to see in the percentage of Africans participating in the poll the desire to end the war and accept a resolution within the framework of the Rhodesian government. Most important—especially to the rest of Africa—was that there was a government in Rhodesia, or in Zimbabwe-Rhodesia, elected by somewhere between 45 and 65 percent of all eligible voters. The actual figure was disputed by everyone, but everyone acknowledged that it was well in excess of the 20 percent that both Mugabe and Nkomo predicted would turn out.[41] The actual details of voting had a great impact—certainly greater than the conduct of the war—on the Patriotic Front and its host countries, but for everyone else the fact of the vote had either to be reckoned with or replaced with another mode of legitimation.[42] In Britain there were not unexpected Conservative speeches about the need to now recognize the new nation. The new prime minister, Margaret Thatcher, suggested as much but she was outflanked by Foreign Office and backed down almost at once. Instead, the FCO sent envoys to Africa.[43]

Lord Harlech, who had been with the Pearce Commission, arrived at the end of May. The reports of his visit with Nyerere were instructive. Nyerere had been proposing an all-party conference on Rhodesia to a select few for years, and this seemed to him the right moment for both

---

40. Claire Palley, Zimbabwe-Rhodesia: Should the Present Government be Recognised? (London: Minority Rights Group and the Catholic Institute for Race Relations, 1979), 9, 28–30, 36.

41. "Zimbabwe Rhodesia: Conference Calculations," 1–2; "Zimbabwe: The Election Conundrum," Africa Confidential 20, no. 25 (December 12, 1979): 2.

42. Mathew Preston, "Stalemate and the Termination of Civil War: Rhodesia Reassessed," J. Peace Research 41, no. 1 (2004): 65–83.

43. There was a tension between Thatcher and the Foreign Office—she believed it "didn't stick up for Britain and was softly conciliatory when the reverse was needed"—which Carrington seems to have negotiated successfully; see Carrington, Things Past, 285–86. Julian Amery, also of the FCO, thought differently, that Carrington preferred diplomacy, or negotiating settlements, to foreign policy, which meant protecting British interests; see Charlton, Last Colony, 27.

Muzorewa and the Patriotic Front to make concessions. While he did not suggest a cease-fire, he acknowledged that the vote in Zimbabwe-Rhodesia could not be denied. As long as no other nation recognized Zimbabwe-Rhodesia the Patriotic Front and the frontline states would consider negotiating a new constitution and new elections. It was critical that the Patriotic Front have a say in framing any new constitution that might merit diplomatic recognition. The question of entrenched guarantees for minority groups was not in itself a stumbling block, he said; it was a matter of degree.[44]

When Kaunda met with Harlech, he suggested that the 1979 election provided Britain with an ideal moment to support the aspirations of African nationalists and counter Soviet influence. If Britain refused to recognize Muzorewa's regime, there would be a "realistic basis" on which to arrange a cease-fire. Harlech offered to rid the constitution of reserved seats for whites and the blocking mechanism so that the elected government might merit recognition. Kaunda had no objection to the principle of reserved seats for whites for a limited period. Both Tanzania and Zambia had such provisions in their original constitutions. He did not object to the constitution itself but to the circumstance of its negotiation. Although he never used the term all-party conference, he urged Britain to draw up a new constitution that they could put to Muzorewa, Smith, Nkomo, and Mugabe.[45] Invocations of Communist threats may have been untimely: in May 1979 the U.S. State Department reversed course and said there was little reason to worry that Kaunda would be driven into Cuban or Soviet arms; his major difficulty seemed to be "Nkomo's ego."[46] British intelligence had long ceased to concern itself with the Soviet Union and understood the extent to which Kaunda was not wholly independent of ZAPU and would "not dare withdraw his support for Mr. Nkomo." Perhaps for this reason Kaunda insisted that any new constitutional negotiations had to be put forward by the British, not by Zimbabwe-Rhodesia or the frontline states.[47]

44. Brent Scowcroft to Gerald Ford, Henry Kissinger's visit to Julius Nyerere, September 15, 1976, GFL/NSA Trip briefing books and cables for Henry Kissinger 1974–76, Box 42; Sir Peter Moon, Dar es Salaam to FCO, May 15, 1979, and May 29, 1979, TNA/PREM/19/106.

45. Harlech, Lusaka, to FCO, June 14, 1979, TNA/PFREM19/107.

46. Assistant to Cyrus Vance to FCO, May 15, 1979, TNA/PREM/19/106.

47. Record of a meeting between the Prime Minister and the Prime Minister of Australia, the Rt. Hon. Malcolm Fraser, Canberra, June 30, 1979; FCO, summary of Lord Harlech's telegrams, June 25, 1979, TNA/PREM/119/107.

The Frontline States, the Commonwealth, and
Zimbabwe-Rhodesia, 1979

Although Lord Carrington wrote that the Lancaster House conference was "born in Lusaka,"[48] by the time the Commonwealth heads of government held their annual meeting there in August 1979,[49] an all-party conference had already been agreed to and to a large extent shaped. For most of July African officials were lobbied by British diplomats and British diplomats were lobbied by African officials to establish the parameters within which a constitutional conference could take place. Harlech returned to the region to meet with Muzorewa and several others, including Ian Smith and David Smith. Muzorewa brought Gaylard and his deputy, Dr. Silas Mundawarara, to the meeting, in which Muzorewa did little more than point out that his government was a legal one. He claimed that all that was keeping African nations from recognizing his regime was that Britain had not yet done so. Harlech seemed almost bored with the meeting and thought Muzorewa's tone was a performance for his deputies. Harlech hoped that if Muzorewa were to come to an all-party confernce in London he would be much more responsive to the issues at hand. That afternoon Harlech met with Chief Ndiweni (of the small United National Federal Party), Ian Smith and David Smith. Sithole, Harlech cabled, "was a dead loss" who did not come to the meeting and Ian Smith "a nonentity" who did come for no reason Harlech could discern. David Smith wanted to know what kind of constitutional changes Britain had in mind. Harlech replied that thus far the major complaint in Africa had focused on the reserved seats for whites, although no one seriously questioned the principle of special representation for whites. Whites were "jittery," David Smith said; they might react badly to a reduction in the number of reserved seats. Why not increase the number of black seats? The real problem, he went on, was the civil service and the need to maintain standards; how could even a black-ruled nation Africanize for the sake of Africanization? There should be an independent commission to appoint civil servants; it should not be left to the ministries themselves. David Smith wanted to make sure Harlech knew that the Rhodesian Front elements in the

---

48. Carrington, *Things Past*, 295–96.

49. The Commonwealth Heads of Government Annual Meetings are called CHOGAMs, pronounced as a word, not as initials, in a way that seems to join schoolboy cleverness and decolonization.

government restrained their African counterparts, who would otherwise be waging war on Zambia.[50]

These meetings were straightforward compared to those in Mozambique. Pronouncements and mediations of pronouncements required translation and interpretation, so that Machel's adviser met with the British ambassador to discuss what the foreign minister, Joaquim Chissano, had said to Harlech. What was made clear was that FRELIMO would support the Patriotic Front, just as Tanzania had sheltered FRELIMO through a decade of war. The British had to understand that no changes could have occurred in Rhodesia or even Zimbabwe-Rhodesia had it not been for the guerrilla war; Muzorewa had reaped the rewards of the Patriotic Front's struggles and sacrifices. It was unreasonable to expect the Patriotic Front, Mozambique, or anyone else to accept the current government. The ambassador returned to the British point, but with a threat. Muzorewa's election had brought black majority rule to Rhodesia; there were now fears that Muzorewa would be keen to demonstrate his newfound strength and escalate the war to stay in power. FRELIMO was aware of this. The British had to understand that harsh words, either in Maputo or when the Organization of African Unity met, did not mean a refusal to negotiate, although any negotiated settlement had to include the Patriotic Front. Mozambique would be guided by ZANU, but in certain circumstances might seek to influence them.[51] This kind of promise, of support and influence, will shape many of the events in the next two chapters.

All this was reported in meetings with various Commonwealth prime ministers, especially those of Australia, Canada, Kenya, and Nigeria.[52] All agreed that the April election had created what Thatcher's government repeatedly called a "new situation" in Rhodesia that Britain could use to construct a constitutional settlement. What was not discussed but was the topic of copious cable traffic was the extent to which Muzorewa's authority had begun to fray by July 1979. Sithole still refused to concede the election; both his private army and Muzorewa's had become increasingly violent after the election. Once in office, Muzorewa seemed

50. Harlech to FCO, July 3, 1979, TNA/PREM/19/107.
51. Doble, Maputo, to FCO, July 3, 1979, TNA/PREM/19/107.
52. Note of a tête-á-tête discussion between the Prime Minister and Daniel Arap Moi of Kenya, London, June 13, 1979; Harlech, Lagos, to FCO, June 21, 1979; Prime Minister's bilateral meeting with Premier Clark of Canada, Tokyo, June 29, 1979; Record of a meeting between the Prime Minister and the prime minister of Australia, Canberra, June 30, 1979, TNA/PREM19/107.

increasingly under the control of the Rhodesian military.[53] Muzorewa was banned from the OAU meeting in Monrovia, and all but dismissed in London. Thatcher reassured him "that he and his colleagues had come a tremendously long way" but made it clear that Britain could not legally recognize any country that did not have a constitution similar to those British colonies had had at independence.[54] By the time the Commonwealth heads of state met, there seemed little interest in preserving whatever legitimacy the Salisbury regime might have. Instead there were discussions, in gardens and hallways, about which parts of the current constitution, or of the Anglo-American proposals, should be kept and which should be abandoned altogether.

Negotiations in Lusaka both continued the conversations of the cable traffic and at the same time honed them. Hastings Banda of Malawi, for example, told Thatcher that his views had not changed since the 1960s: Rhodesia was a British problem, and the British had to solve it. Britain should force Muzorewa to make his constitution acceptable. Thatcher however wanted to talk about the major criticism of the constitution, reserved seats and the blocking mechanism. Banda was not concerned. No independence constitution had a blocking mechanism, but there were many precedents for reserved parliamentary seats for minorities, including one in Malawi's independence constitution.

Thatcher met with Nyerere. Speaking for the frontline states, he said Zimbabwe-Rhodesia could not be recognized. The problem was not just the April election, but the constitution. He had no objection to a public service commission, which could in fact be a check on interference by the executive. He believed in reserving seats for minorities, at least at first. Tanganyika had done this, and eventually minorities saw that there was no need for such an arrangement and the constitution was amended. This constitution, however, entrenched the particular powers of the white minority, and this was unacceptable. Should there be a proposed constitution that he and other Commonwealth heads of state found "democratic," and if there were free and fair supervised elections, he could not guarantee that the Patriotic Front would stop fighting, but

---

53. Flower, *Serving Secretly*, 204–5. Wilson, Salisbury to FCO, Zimbabwe Rhodesia Press Roundup, July 18, 1979; Patrick Allison, Lusaka, to FCO, July 26, 1979, TNA/PREM/19/108; Renwick, *Unconventional Diplomacy*, 25.

54. Note on the Prime Minister's discussion with Bishop Abel Muzorewa, London, July 13, 1979, TNA/PREM/19/108; Charlton, *Last Colony*, 31–32; Alois S. Mlambo, "Discordant Voices: The Organization of African Unity's Responses to the Unilateral Declaration of Independence, 1965–1975," *Afriche e Orienti* 2 (2011): 122–34.

he could promise that if ZANU or ZAPU continued the war they would do so without the support of the frontline states.[55] In contrast, Kaunda's comments were constrained, either because he was host of the meeting or because of his relations with ZAPU, but in conversation with the Canadian prime minister's secretary he said Zambia would support a democratic constitution even if the Patriotic Front did not. To this end he headed what journalists called "the tight little group" that drafted the Lusaka communiqué and the all-party conference it proposed that would be held at Lancaster House in September.[56]

55. Note of the Prime Minister's discussion with Life President Banda, Lusaka, July 31, 1979; notes of a meeting between the Prime Minister and President Nyerere, July 31, 1979, TNA/PREM/19/109.

56. Note on the Prime Minister's conversation with the prime minister of Canada, Lusaka, August 2, 1979, TNA/PREM/19/109. The other members were Malcolm Fraser of Australia; Michael Manley of Jamaica; Nyerere of Tanzania; General Adefope of Nigeria, who nationalized British Petroleum during the meetings; Lord Carrington; Sir Shridath Ramphal, secretary-general of the Commonwealth; and Anthony Duff, Lusaka, to FCO, August 5, 1979, TNA/PREM19/109.

TEN

"Lancaster House was redundant": Constitutions, Citizens, and the Frontline Presidents

The independence constitutions for British territories were all negotiated in a building within walking distance of Buckingham Palace that was managed by the Foreign and Commonwealth Office. This was Lancaster House. In many African nations the name became a shorthand for the compromises that became the constitution, for who was there and who agreed to what under which circumstances. In Zimbabwe in recent years Lancaster House has been cast as the event that created Zimbabwe and in doing so hindered all the advances of the guerrilla struggle. The settlement negotiated there easily became a political weapon available to all who participated in the conference. Political studies of Zimbabwe agree that it was at Lancaster House that the seeds of Zimbabwe's recent weakness were sown; it was at Lancaster House that the Patriotic Front and especially Mugabe's ZANU were cheated and lied to. Mugabe later claimed that the "rushed" Patriotic Front had given up its demands for land in exchange for one man, one vote elections.[1]

---

1. Charlton, *Last Colony*, 79–80; Patrick Bond and Masimba Manyanya, *Zimbabwe's Plunge: Exhausted Nationalism, Neoliberalism and the Search for Social Justice* (Pietermaritzburg: University of Natal Press, 2002), 77; Norma Kriger, *Guerrilla*

This chapter argues the opposite: that despite the enormous meanings invested in the constitutional conference before, during, and after 1980, there was little in the way of bargaining or even room to maneuver by all parties. The constitutional conference established the Lusaka Agreement of August, based as it was on the Anglo-American proposals of 1977, as a law: one man, one vote elections were not in question. How the parties got there, and what they were able to negotiate when they did, was constrained. The Lancaster House conference was stage-managed by the Commonwealth heads of states in their meetings in Lusaka and orchestrated by the presidents of Mozambique, Zambia, and Tanzania, and by a Conservative FCO that was not concerned with how much help it had in reaching a settlement. The constitution and many of the cease-fire arrangements were fashioned by the Commonwealth heads of state in Zambia in August and worked out in London a few weeks later. A ZAPU delegate told Stephen Stedman as much in 1987: "Lancaster House was redundant, no real negotiations took place, the real negotiations were done in Lusaka."[2]

No one from the Patriotic Front or Muzorewa's government was present in Lusaka. Nevertheless, Muzorewa accepted the invitation to Lancaster House without a moment's hesitation, whereas the Patriotic Front agreed to come only after issuing statements that were to constitute its bargaining position at the conference: that there be no special seats for minorities, that Britain take responsibility for the elections, and that the liberation forces control the army during the interim period.[3] The Patriotic Front continued its bluster after it accepted the invitation. At the Non-Aligned Movement meeting in Havana a few weeks before Lancaster House, Samora Machel took both Mugabe and Nkomo to task for their public disdain for a constitutional conference. The Patriotic Front should go to London without preconditions, he said. When Mugabe insisted he would not negotiate until the Rhodesian army had been dismantled, Machel reacted sharply: Muzorewa was not a black puppet, whatever he might be called in public; he had popular support and an army. Although the OAU recognized the Patriotic Front as

Veterans in Post-War Zimbabwe: Symbolic and Violent Politics, 1980–1987 (Cambridge: Cambridge University Press, 2003), 33, 39–40; Daniel Compagnon, *A Predictable Tragedy: Robert Mugabe and the Collapse of Zimbabwe* (Philadelphia: University of Pennsylvania Press, 2011), 167. As I wrote this, it took three keystrokes to find an article about the 2002 elections in Zimbabwe entitled "The trail from Lancaster House." www.guardian.com/world/2002/jan16/zimbabwe.chrismcgeal

2. Quoted in Stedman, *Peacemaking*, 173–74.

3. Prime Minister, Rhodesia: Constitutional Conference, August 31, 1979, TNA/PREM/19/111.

the legitimate representatives of the Zimbabwean people, many African countries were thinking of recognizing Muzorewa's government: the time to negotiate was now. When Mugabe bristled and pointed out that a revolutionary army had taken over in Mozambique, Machel snapped at him: FRELIMO had defeated a foreign army in war. Although he made no mention of the recent Rhodesian raids into Mozambique, he urged the Patriotic Front to go to London as a unified body. Mozambique, he said, would support the outcome of free and fair elections, whoever won.[4]

The Constitutional Conference

Lancaster House was great theater.[5] All the suspense of negotiations, of who would walk out and who would compromise, was not only anticipated but understood to be part of the process. Peter Lord Carrington, the foreign secretary, later wrote, "I thought it likely that the invited parties would come, and then create trouble at the moment they decided most favorable, break off the proceedings, walk out" and leave Thatcher's government, secure in the knowledge that it had tried but was regretfully forced to recognize the government in Salisbury.[6] At the time, however, Carrington had read the cables coming into the FCO and knew full well the pressures under which the Patriotic Front would be negotiating: he knew that neither Nkomo nor Mugabe could walk out. He must have known how unlikely it was for the conference to completely break down, just as he had known for months how disappointed Thatcher's government was with Muzorewa, a man "without any political skills at all."[7] Given how much the FCO knew, and how tense the situation was however much anyone knew, the conference was carefully choreographed. The most obvious choreography was Carrington's, that

4. United Kingdom Mission to UN [hereafter UKMIS] to Rhodesia Desk, FCO, London, September 11, 1979, summarizing verbal report from the foreign minister of Botswana. TNA/PREM19/111. Both Joacquim Chissano, Machel's successor, and Robert Mugabe recalled condensed versions of this encounter; see Charlton, *Last Colony*, 69, 124. There is more than a suggestion that Machel doubted ZANLA's military effectiveness. Months earlier he had begun to send his own troops on reconnaissance with ZANLA so as to receive trustworthy reports on the state of the war in Rhodesia. "Zimbabwe Rhodesia: Conference Calculations," *Africa Confidential* 20, no. 17 (August 22, 1979): 1–2.
5. Years later it had its own BBC Radio 4 program; see Charlton, *Last Colony*.
6. Carrington, *Things Past*, 297.
7. The quote is from Ian Gow, Thatcher's parliamentary secretary, quoted in Charlton, *Last Colony*, 33.

CHAPTER TEN

each segment of the settlement—the constitution, the transitional arrangements, and the cease-fire—be negotiated and resolved before the
conference could go onto the next. The less obvious choreography was
that of the frontline presidents, who, as this section shows, took a firm
hand in shaping the conduct of the Patriotic Front at the conference.
This chapter will not be a history of the Lancaster House conference in
its entirety. I concentrate instead on issues of citizenship and voting that
have informed earlier chapters of this book—although at this time, at
the war's end, the questions of citizenship were less complicated by race
than they were by place and by the two hundred thousand Zimbabwean
refugees living outside the country.

There were three delegations: Muzorewa's government, usually called
the Salisbury delegation, including David Smith and an increasingly
marginal Ian Smith; the British delegation, chaired either by Carrington
or the somewhat more conservative Ian Gilmour, lord privy seal; and
the Patriotic Front delegation, which was in fact two delegations, one
for ZANU and one for ZAPU. The PF delegation rarely spoke as one.
There was also an audience, in and out of Lancaster House. There were
U.S. and Commonwealth observers at the conference. Sir Shridath Ramphal, secretary-general of the Commonwealth, organized meetings of
Commonwealth heads of state during the conference to "make sure" the
British government and the Patriotic Front "got it right." He spent many
evenings in the London apartments of Nkomo and Mugabe advising
them.[8] There were Mozambiquan and Zambian envoys in London ready
to offer counsel and convey messages. Laurens van der Post claimed he
was carrying vital messages from South Africa to Thatcher.[9]

There are several participants' accounts—by Carrington, Davidow,
Flower, Nkomo, Renwick, and Smith—all of which made much of the
drama, the cleverness, and the betrayals, so much so that they tend to
be unhelpful as historical accounts.[10] This compounds the difficulty of
working with the published and archival materials about the conference,
in which so much of what anyone might call negotiations went on in
bilateral meetings, where an increasingly frustrated Carrington worked
out agreements with one delegation at a time, in private. There are no

8. Quoted in Charlton, *Last Colony*, 109.
9. Note of a conversation (on the telephone) between the prime minister and Mr. Laurens van
der Post, August 31, 1979, TNA/PREM/19/111. Van der Post often took credit for preventing the collapse of the talks; see Jones, *Storyteller*, 337–38. Nyerere did not seem to have any intermediaries in
London during the conference.
10. Nkomo barely described the conference, let alone the drama. Instead he detailed ZIPRA's
plans for land and air invasion of Rhodesia; Nkomo, *My Life*, 196–98.

summaries of these meetings I have found, but it is clear that much of what was said in the conference room was in response to what had been said in private, or what had been said in the press, or what transpired between a frontline president and a member of the Patriotic Front. These are probably fairly typical of the dynamic and coercive working of power maintained outside archival surveillance, but they present historians with a challenge. Rather than see these practices as secret secret, charged information the importance of which is in part the way it reveals the presence of bureaucracies of surveillance, they show the fits and starts and false starts of political thinking and political talk.[11] There is a back-and-forth quality to my use of archives for this section, largely because a chronological reading of the plenary sessions or diplomatic cables does not, in and of itself, show how the work of negotiation was carried out, let alone the anxieties and strategies in play. In the following sections I argue that the Lancaster House settlement was shaped in large parts by the frontline presidents, while the debates at Lancaster House were shaped by the Patriotic Front's fears that the corrupt electoral practices of the 1979 election would be repeated when its candidates stood for office.

The Independence Constitution

The proposed independence constitution was published on August 14, the same day invitations were issued to the conference. It had a justiciable declaration of rights with a typical list of rights and protections and freedoms. It had the standard features of an independent judiciary, of defense forces acting under the law, of constitutional guarantees of the pension rights of civil servants, and a public service commission that would maintain high standards of efficiency while recognizing the legitimate claims of the majority of the population. The fluidity of Rhodesian citizenship was recognized by law. Every citizen of Rhodesia, whether by birth or naturalized, would automatically become a citizen of Zimbabwe. Anyone qualified to be a citizen but who was not had five years in which to apply for citizenship. Every person born in Zimbabwe after independence (which meant 1980, not 1965), unless the child of a diplomat or enemy alien, would become a citizen of Zimbabwe by birth.

11. Luise White, "Telling More: Secrets, Lies and History," *History and Theory* 39 (2000): 11–22; Ann Laura Stoler, *Along the Archival Grain: Epistemic Anxieties and Colonial Common Sense* (Princeton, NJ: Princeton University Press, 2009), 25–28.

Every child born outside the country to a father who was a Zimbabwean citizen by birth (or, in the case of illegitimate children, a mother who was a Zimbabwean by birth) would become a citizen of Zimbabwe. Any woman married to a Zimbabwean citizen was automatically a citizen; a divorced or widowed woman who had been married to a Zimbabwean man who was a citizen at the time of the marriage could apply for citizenship. Dual citizenship was to be permitted. Parliament was to be elected by all citizens who were over eighteen. So long as there was a limit set on special minority representation—this was soon to be set at seven years—white citizens over eighteen could either be enrolled on the white voters' roll or the common one. The constitution did not specify how many parliamentarians there would be or if they would be divided between upper and lower houses. The lower house was presented as algebraic, Y members elected by the common roll from Y constituencies and Z white members elected from the white roll for Z white constituencies. A delimitation commission would establish the Y and Z constituencies. The constitution proposed a senate selected by even more cumbersome electoral practices than in the 1969 constitution.[12]

The constitution was sent to the frontline presidents for comment in mid-August. Nyerere was pleased with most of it. His only concern was to make the constitution resemble those of decolonization. Late in August he wrote to Thatcher explaining that while he understood the principle behind reserved seats, it was a mistake to let the minority community elect them by a separate roll. Instead, Zimbabwe should follow the original Tanganyika constitution of 1961 in which candidates for European seats would be Europeans nominated by Europeans, but "the entire multi-racial electorate" elected them. Such a system had two advantages: European candidates had to consider the interest of African voters "and in particular avoid provocative racial statements," and African voters had to think of European candidates as potential political allies, rather than "as people automatically hostile to their interests." In Tanganyika this program broke down racial stereotypes and assisted political integration, Nyerere wrote, so that some Europeans originally elected to reserved seats had been elected to parliament "on their own

---

12. Rhodesia: Outline of Proposals for an Independence Constitution (Annex A), August 14, 1979, TNA/PREM/19/111. In the House of Lords there was considerable objection to dual citizenship, "which landed us in such trouble with Ugandan Asians"; see W. Arnold, to FCO, September 12, 1979, TNA/PREM/19/112.

merits" in competition with African candidates."[13] No one thought this a serious option for an independent Zimbabwe.

The ideas of citizenship in the proposed constitution were similar to those developed at the end of federation, a legalization of belonging either by birth or personal history. In 1963 this only referred to white people, but in 1979 the inclusion of birthright citizenship was critical to the idea of a developmentalist state, able to lay claim to whoever rightfully belonged within its borders. The Patriot Front was outraged about the specificity of race in the British proposals, which, Mugabe complained, "call this minority 'European' or 'white.'" His delegation certainly wanted to see everyone in Zimbabwe represented in the legislature, but it opposed the British obsession with dividing everyone by race. All the people who live in Zimbabwe should be citizens of the country. "Is it possible to call a section of the community European? Surely there can be no such thing as a European in Africa?" When Carrington replied that the "political realities of the past cannot be ignored," nor could "the hopes and fears" of the people, Mugabe claimed the high ground. The liberation war had been waged to destroy the racial basis of Rhodesian society, and now the British "want us to retain such a system." Ian Gilmour reminded him that it had been agreed in Lusaka that the new constitution had to contain provisions that encouraged whites to stay. Mugabe was not convinced. Why give pensions to Rhodesian civil servants, he asked. Why not state that they would be rewarded for treason?[14]

Weeks of bilateral meetings followed. The Patriotic Front presented its own proposed constitution on September 17. It did not refer to pensions and it called the minority white. It proposed a ninety-six-seat national assembly, with twenty-four seats reserved for white members: fifteen would be elected by a white voters' roll, and nine elected on the common roll. If this was not acceptable to the conference, the Patriotic Front would accept twenty-four seats of a ninety-six-seat assembly reserved for whites, all elected by a white voters' roll. All amendments to the constitution would require a two-thirds vote of both the national assembly and the senate, which had to act within three months. If the senate did not act, the amendment would be presented to the president

13. Nyerere to Thatcher, August 25, 1979, TNA/PREM/19/110; Hinchcliffe, Dar es Salaam, to FCO, September 1, 1979, TNA/PREM/19/111. Nyerere opposed this kind of voting when the Colonial Office first proposed it in Tanganyika, but he was able to turn it to his considerable advantage by the election of 1958; see John Iliffe, "Breaking the Chain," 168–97.

14. Stedman, *Peacemaking*, 178–79.

anyway. The senate was to be expanded to sixty members, forty-eight of whom would be elected by members of the lower house and twelve of whom would be elected by the white members. The senate could not delay legislation as it had in the past; it was allowed one month to consider ordinary bills and three months to consider constitutional changes.

The PF's proposals for citizenship in the new constitution were contentious. Anyone deprived of their citizenship after 1965 should be allowed to resume it, but dual citizenship was not allowed. Any Zimbabwean with dual citizenship would have to renounce the other one within a year of independence, or at the age of eighteen. With very careful wording, the Patriotic Front sought to make it impossible for anyone not already a citizen of Rhodesia before November 11, 1965, to become a citizen of Zimbabwe; anyone who immigrated to Rhodesia during UDI and became a citizen would not be automatically granted citizenship in Zimbabwe either.[15] This bore no relation to earlier constitutions or ideas about citizenship therein; this was membership pure and simple, citizenship as an exclusionary category that was to extract a political price for the exclusions of UDI.[16] It was also far more grounded in the politics of exile and liberation support groups than anything that had gone on in Rhodesia between 1965 and 1979.[17] Anyone who had been in Rhodesia, or even read letters to the editor in Rhodesian newspapers, would have known the extent to which new immigrants eschewed Rhodesian citizenship, that many did not stay long enough to fulfill the residency requirement and that many of those who did waited until they were past conscription age to take out citizenship papers.[18]

On October 3 Carrington tabled a revised constitution that addressed the disputed points. This version had already been accepted by the Salisbury delegation; only Ian Smith opposed it, but his attempt to rally support for his position in London and Salisbury failed and isolated him further from the conference. The rest of the delegation, including some

15. Patriotic Front, Brief summary of proposals for an independence constitution for Zimbabwe, mimeo., TNA/PREM/19/112.

16. I take this point from Linda Bozniak, *The Citizen and the Alien: Dilemmas of Contemporary Membership* (Princeton, NJ: Princeton University Press, 2012). I am grateful to Elizabeth Dale for this reference.

17. Liberation support movements, particularly in Europe, were irate because of the ease with which white European citizens could take up residence in and benefit from the racist regimes in southern Africa. See Comité Angola (Amsterdam), Anti-Apartheid Movement (London), Anti-Apartheid Movement (Dublin), et al.; *White Migration to Southern Africa*, mimeo., Geneva, Centre Europe-Tiers Monde, 1975.

18. Brownell, *Collapse*, 72–84; see also Caute, *Under the Skin*, 113–14, 155; Lewis, *Too Bright the Vision*, 246.

from the Rhodesian Front, argued that pensions were more important to white Rhodesians than were reserved seats in perpetuity.[19] The first issue Carrington brought to the entire conference was citizenship. In the revised constitution, anyone who had citizenship before independence would be confirmed as citizens thereafter. Carrington had rejected the Patriotic Front's proposals out of hand. They would leave many thousands of people either stateless or with insecure status as they awaited investigations into whether or not they could become citizens of Zimbabwe. These proposals retained dual citizenship. Pensions were not only guaranteed but could be remitted overseas. The draft constitution noted that the PF might find it unreasonable for the new state to pay for service to the illegal one, but the United Kingdom had never taken on such a burden before and would not do so now. As for parliament and the question of reserved seats, the British proposals provided for 20 percent of seats in the house of assembly to be reserved for whites for seven years. During that time, it could only be amended by a unanimous vote in the chamber. After that it would be carried forward and subject to the normal procedures by which the constitution could be amended, a 70 percent majority. The senate was made larger, to make it more representative, but its delaying power was reduced.[20]

The frontline presidents responded. Nyerere found the Patriotic Front's citizenship proposals fully justified. It was the British who were of two minds about Zimbabwean citizenship, making it automatic while at the same time demanding the right to dual citizenship. He did not see pensions, however, as an impediment to the PF accepting the constitution.[21] Kaunda telephoned Thatcher, after which he sent a long cable that suggested he had already spoken to Nkomo. Citizenship, he wrote, "had given the Patriotic Front great cause for concern but this may no longer be a crucial issue." He was, however, concerned about reserved seats for whites, not that there would be too many, but that their role in parliament would be too great. In his view, the 20 percent of the seats reserved

19. Stedman, *Peacemaking*, 180–81; Renwick, *Unconventional Diplomacy*, 38–39; Carrington, *Things Past*, 300; R. C. Byatt, Salisbury, to FCO, October 1, 1979, TNA/PREM/19/112. Ian Smith called the constitution's supporters "quislings" and wrote that it was accepted because the vote was taken in a secret ballot to hide the "treachery" and "treason" of the others. Evans, Rhodesian Front Rule, 342; Smith, *Betrayal*, 319–20. Ken Flower was equally dramatic, telling Muzorewa "that he was being martyred and that the choice he had to make was agonizingly unfair"; Flower, *Serving Secretly*, 238.

20. FCO, Rhodesia: The Independence Constitution, October 3, 1979, TNA/PREM/19/112.

21. Sir Peter Moon, British High Commissioner, Dar es Salaam, to FCO, October 1, 1979, TNA/PREM/19/112.

for whites "should be exclusively designed to represent white interests." Given that this constitution gave 20 percent of the seats to 3 percent of the population, this 20 percent should not be allowed "to form a coalition with any of the black groups" which would, obviously, amount to "a new blocking mechanism." Indeed, the unanimity rule was yet another form of blocking mechanism, which he urged the British delegation to reconsider. Kaunda also assured Thatcher that if the PF was willing to accept the 70 percent provision for amending the constitution, instead of the two-thirds they had demanded previously, "this should be accepted as a reasonable compromise to cover all clauses."[22]

What made the Patriotic Front apprehensive about Carrington's revised constitution was not its content but the fact that the Salisbury delegation had agreed to it in bilateral meetings away from the conference. The Patriotic Front believed that now they had no choice but to accept it as well. It took Chissano to translate the anxieties of the PF to the British. The Patriotic Front believed that Muzorewa's government was now free to implement the new constitution and be recognized as legitimate. Although the transitional arrangements and the cease-fire were still to be negotiated with the Patriotic Front, Chissano explained to the British ambassador that any suggestion of a privileged role for the Salisbury delegation or any hint of deals made in secret caused the PF "psychological problems."[23] Whatever the Patriotic Front knew of such conversations—Mozambique had observers at Lancaster House—it was not reassured in any way. Apprehension gave way to empty threats. A few days later, when Carrington went off to the Conservative Party conference to do battle with his right wing and the Monday Club, Mugabe went to the press in grand style. If the conference were to deadlock, he said, the Patriotic Front would send its military men back to Africa. "We can win without Lancaster House." The PF welcomed a settlement, he said, but "we can achieve peace and justice for our people through the barrel of a gun."[24] After a few days of futile negotiations, Carrington gave the Patriotic Front a deadline and hinted at what the PF feared most, that he would continue bilateral talks with the Salisbury delegation. This was the moment of great theatrical suspense. Journalists announced

22. Kaunda to Thatcher, October 10, 1979. Had Kaunda brought up the question of pensions, Thatcher's briefing document instructed her to explain these were an "essential and common element" in any solution to the Rhodesia problem. Points President Kaunda is likely to raise with the prime minister, typescript, October 9, 1979, TNA/PREM/19/112.

23. Parsons, Maputo, to FCO, October 4, 1979, TNA/PREM/19/112.

24. Quoted in Jeffrey Davidow, *A Peace in Southern Africa: The Lancaster House Conference on Rhodesia, 1979* (Boulder, CO: Westview Press, 1984), 62–63; Carrington, *Things Past*, 298–300.

that Carrington would either make a deal without the Patriotic Front or threaten to do so as a way to bargain with it.[25] But again, Carrington had to know the pressures the PF was under. He reassured the United States—and presumably many in London—that he would do no such thing. The FCO had always thought there was a "reasonable prospect" that the PF would in the end accept the constitution.[26]

The Patriotic Front accepted the constitution a few days later. Jeffrey Davidow of the U.S. delegation thought this was due to Carrington's well-informed brinksmanship, aided by wiretaps and bugs in the hotel rooms of the PF (and presumably Salisbury) leaders.[27] Cadres in the struggle thought otherwise. In a story told by the African National Congress in Lusaka Kenneth Kaunda came to see Nkomo off when he left for the Lancaster House conference. When Nkomo casually said "See you when we get back," Kaunda just shook his head. This was when Nkomo realized the war was over, that ZAPU had to reach a settlement this time because it lost its Zambian base. Stephen Stedman's interviews with ZAPU delegates described the intense debates within the PF delegation and the hollow threats of returning to war. In the midst of these meetings Josiah Tongogara, commander of ZANLA forces, arrived from Mozambique to inform his comrades what ZAPU already knew: if they walked out of negotiations, their frontline patrons would take away their bases.[28]

The Transition

Even as Carrington was reassuring Americans that the PF would sign the constitution, he briefed them on the plans for the transition. The purpose of the transition was free and fair elections by which the people of Rhodesia would choose their future government. The British wanted a brief, uncomplicated transitional period with a transitional government

25. Meredith, *Another Country*, 380–85.
26. Carrington to Washington, D.C., Rhodesia: Consultations with the Americans, October 10, 1979, TNA/PREM/19/112.
27. Davidow, *Peace in Southern Africa*, 128n; Smith, *Betrayal*, 316.
28. Stedman, *Peacekeeping*, 182; Charlton, *Last Colony*, 130–31. Gillian Slovo, *Every Secret Thing: My Family, My Country* (London: Little, Brown, 1997), 132. Carrington was well aware that Nkomo was likely to compromise; see Carrington to OAU heads of state, October 11, 1979, TNA/PREM/19/113. Years later he wrote that the constitution was accepted because "everybody (including Mugabe) began to prefer the idea of settlement to the alternatives"; *Things Past*, 300–301. Nkomo however wrote in his memoirs that the PF only agreed to the constitution because it did not want to give Britain reason "to wash their hands of the whole affair"; Nkomo, *My Life*, 192.

or a transitional constitution for which they would take full responsibility. This period should not last more than three months—as British diplomats said at the time and as Commonwealth observers said years later, no one thought a cease-fire could hold much longer.[29]

However reasonable these points seemed to the U.S., they were explosive to both the Salisbury and PF delegations. The questions of the interim, of who would govern, who would police, who could campaign, and, above all, who could vote and where they might do so were freighted with the recent past; the counterfeit practices by which Muzorewa was elected cast a long and monotonous shadow over the conference well into November. The British decided against an interim government in favor of a colonial one. As Ian Gilmour patiently explained, rather than allow one side—in this case Muzorewa's elected government—to run the country, it was better to give the task to neither side, the British.[30] Muzorewa, who constantly reminded the conference that his government was already the legally elected government of the country, backed down on the issue of the British governor.[31] The Patriotic Front accepted the governor, but repeatedly asked that his powers be clarified. The issue was one of trust, Carrington said. Anyone who wanted free and fair elections would have to trust the British. Mugabe seized the moment: Wilson had asked Africans to trust the British in 1965: why should they trust the British now? It would be better, as the Patriotic Front had said before, that an interim government be formed right away. The British delegation remained firm that there could be no interim government before the elections. Muzorewa's ministers would remain in their posts; it took days for the conference to be reassured that they would not enact any legislation during the transition. There were no reassurances regarding Rhodesian forces, however. There was no case in the history of decolonization in which an existing government or security forces had been dismantled before independence. The Patriotic Front delegation

29. Carrington to Washington October 10, 1979, TNA/PREM/112; Stedman, *Peacemaking*, 183; author's field notes, London, June 12, 1911.

30. Statement delivered by Ian Gilmour, 21st plenary, October 31, 1979. These notes were generously loaned to me by Stephen Stedman.

31. This "bitter pill" has been attributed to Carrington's skillful persuasion or to General Peter Walls's more direct influence and the unwillingness of many whites in Muzorewa's delegation to sacrifice any constitutional gains for his leadership; see Davidow, *Peace in Southern Africa*, 69–70; and Tamarkin, *Making of Zimbabwe*, 266. The only people who seemed to want Muzorewa to stay in office, even as a figurehead, were those white Rhodesians who called themselves moderate, including Sir Robert Tredgold's sister, who feared that if Muzorewa stepped down it would create a realignment of African politics in the country; see Byatt, Salisbury, to FCO, October 22, 1979, TNA/PREM/19/113.

interrupted: this was not decolonization. Only a new government and new security forces could prevent another UDI.

The PF was especially concerned that the police—Rhodesia's BSAP— would be charged with keeping order during the transition. How could any agency of the illegal regime that had participated in the war be trusted to protect Patriotic Front candidates, let alone allow them to campaign? Edison Zvobgo of the PF delegation, under whose name various death lists were issued from Mozambique prior to the 1979 election, went to the press. "Does Britain really expect Mugabe and Nkomo to sleep in Salisbury guarded by Muzorewa's men? We might not even see the end of an election." Carrington understood the Patriotic Front's reservations, but he noted that the BSAP were the only police force available, that there was simply no such thing as a civil police force in Rhodesia. Ian Smith defended the police: they had only become involved in the war because of guerrilla attacks on civilians. Mugabe did not disagree; instead he pointed out that this underscored the extent to which the police were part of the Rhodesian war effort. Such arguments went on for days. How exactly would the governor supervise the police; how could the PF be sure the BSAP would not follow the punitive laws of the Rhodesian state? So long as Patriotic Front forces were not part of the governing apparatus, they could not provide any kind of check on the excesses of existing forces. Leo Solomon Baron, a ZAPU lawyer and defendant in *Madzimbamuto and Baron vs. Lardner-Burke,* observed that in any postwar situation the police were feared; the use of the BSAP could intimidate voters. Josiah Tongogara thought his forces would object, perhaps violently, to the use of the police.[32] The PF went on at length about the abuse of police power in decolonization. Only an international police force could guarantee that Rhodesia would not endure the instability and suffering that Cyprus and Palestine had experienced.[33] Such historical examples seem to have made Carrington and Gilmour uneasy, not because they were inaccurate, but because they so contradicted the idea of orderly, electoral path to decolonization that was so critical to Lancaster House.

32. Zvobgo quoted in Stedman, *Peacemaking,* 190. Tongogara joined the PF delegation for the sessions on October 30 and November 1. Summary of the 20th plenary, October 30, 1979; 21st plenary, October 31, 1979; 24th plenary, November 1, 1979; 27th plenary, November 6, 1979. For one of Zvobgo's death lists, see Hudson, *Triumph or Tragedy?,* 226–33.

33. Summary of 24th plenary, November 1, 1979; "Patriotic Front Analysis of British Proposals for the Interim Period," November 12, 1979; see Stedman, *Peacemaking,* 188.

The Transition and the Frontline Presidents

While Carrington met with the Salisbury delegation, he sent his minister for African affairs, Richard Luce, to the frontline states. Officially, this was to inform these presidents of the British proposals; unofficially, it seemed to be the most reliable way to find out what kinds of objections and demands the Patriotic Front would have. Kaunda expressed concerns about the timescale for the elections and the registration of voters. Registration, to which Zambia attached the utmost importance, could be done in three months; that was how long it took in Zambia, and Rhodesia had much better roads and communication systems. Kaunda was "insistent" that the Patriotic Front be allowed adequate time to campaign. The PF was competing against parties already established in the country; six months would be the "fairer" period to give them an equal chance. Less time would be considered a "trick."[34] In Mozambique, however, Chissano found the imposition of British control an excellent idea. He wanted Muzorewa to step down, and he did not think it was necessary to dismantle the security forces, although the rest of the world might not approve. The security forces would have to be watched, however. He supported Carrington in thinking the interim period should be as short as possible, although he was sure the PF would demand adequate time to campaign. Neither the Patriotic Front nor the Salisbury delegation could be expected to agree to peace at any price.[35] The foreign minister of Botswana—the man who had told the British about Machel's bullying the PF in Havana—chided Luce for not involving the frontline states more often in the negotiations. His government did not object to a two- or three-month interim period. Botswana understood the difficulties of registering voters and delimiting constituencies, and he hoped there would be some sympathy for the Patriotic Front's request for a longer interim period. He had no sympathy, however, for any demands to integrate guerrilla forces into the security forces before the election. Indeed, he repeated what Chissano had said, that the frontline presidents had already told the Patriotic Front that a new government had to be elected before a new military was put in place.[36]

For the frontline presidents, the concerns about the length of the interim period were concerns about refugees: whether or not they could

---

34. Richard Luce to FCO, October 20, 1979, TNA/PREM/19/113.
35. Luce to FCO, October 22, 1979, TNA/PREM/19/113.
36. Luce to FCO, October 22, 1979, TNA/PREM/19/113.

return to Zimbabwe and how long that might take. The question of armed men involved in any degree in an election on foreign soil made front-line presidents extremely uneasy, as the next chapter shows. The foreign minister of Angola, for example, worried about the definition of refugees. Did it include freedom fighters? Were they to lay down their arms and return to Rhodesia or would they travel home armed, through the Angolan countryside? Was it possible to have an interim period long enough for these men to go home and explain their political goals to what he assumed was an illiterate peasantry?[37] While I do not want to draw a straight line between how guerrillas were imagined as partici-pants in the election of 1980 and ideas about war veterans in Zimbabwe in recent years, frontline presidents' fears of guerrillas in electoral poli-tics in their respective countries are worth noting. Months before ma-jority rule no one seemed able to imagine a place for these men and women in everyday politics.

Nyerere met with Luce and then clarified certain points with the British high commissioner. He understood why the British wanted such a short interim period, but two months was too short a time and he could not recommend the PF accept it. The PF wanted six months, to "go home" and establish themselves before the elections.[38] A few days later Luce met with Kaunda. Kaunda then wrote to Thatcher, not so much to elaborate on what he said to Luce, but to lay the groundwork for the arguments Nkomo would make in London. The interim period the British proposed was too short. There were hundreds of thousands of refugees who would have to return home to vote, and the Patriotic Front would need time to organize themselves into a political party. Both par-ties had been banned for over fifteen years; the leadership had been in detention or exile for almost as long: they would require a reasonable period to campaign. The major requirement for holding free and fair elections was the registration of voters. Kaunda was alarmed that the British did not think this could be done in the interim period; the regis-tration of voters, he insisted, could be accomplished in three months.[39] The goals of voter registration and of sufficient time to mount an effec-tive campaign were the other side of the imaginary of orderly electoral decolonization, about which Kaunda and Nyerere seemed nostalgic. The demands the Patriotic Front brought to the conference at the end of October imagined elections as anything but orderly, however. The PF

37. Luce to FCO, October 24, 1979, TNA/PREM/19/113.
38. Sir Peter Moon, Dar es Salaam, to FCO, October 28, 1979, TNA/PREM/19/113.
39. Kaunda to Thatcher, October 26, 1979, TNA/PREM/19/113.

demanded not only the registration of voters but the banning of mobile polling stations.

The Election

However much information the FCO had gathered about the Patriotic Front's anxieties and concerns, and however well versed the British delegation was in the PF's objections, Carrington did not seem prepared for the intense repetitive bickering about the arrangements for the new election and how they threatened to split the Patriotic Front delegation. Once it had been agreed that the governor would take full control, the Salisbury delegation accepted the British proposals for the interim. Muzorewa's deputy, Silas Mundawarara, issued a statement to the entire conference but presumably for the benefit of the Patriotic Front, explaining why it had done so and why registering voters was impossible. He agreed that constituencies were the best basis for free and fair elections, but in this case speed was of the essence. There was no way that 2.8 million people, including thousands displaced by war, could be registered in their home areas; thus there could be no fair delimitation of constituencies. People had been living with insecurity too long to delay elections.[40] Mugabe was not impressed. Why was there no new election law? The old election law, the one ignored in 1979, was that of an illegal regime. Among its provisions was one that disenfranchised anyone who had been in detention for six months or more. Surely those laws could no longer stand. What of the election observers? Was their job just to look, to observe and to register the results once the votes were tallied? Or did they have some authority to supervise, to make sure the elections were free and fair? As for the registration of voters, the British delegation had used the example of Botswana to argue that it would take a long time, but Mugabe countered with the examples of Zambia and Kenya. Zambia had registered seven hundred voters a day in every constituency in the 1960s. That should be the model for the conference.[41]

40. Statement by Dr. Mundawarara, 21st plenary, October 31, 1979.

41. Summary, 21st plenary, October 31, 1979. Zambia, and its various figures for voter registration, figures prominently in these debates. ZAPU was based in Lusaka, and ZANU had been until 1975, so both parties would have been familiar with Kaunda's account of early voter registration. The seven hundred a week may not be an accurate figure, however. In the eleven weeks allowed for voter registration, lower roll registration was less than half of the government's goal. Even when UNIP received an extension, the party may have managed only as many as five hundred lower and upper roll registrations per week. Mulford, *Northern Rhodesia General Election*, 52–58.

In the lengthy and acrimonious debates that followed, the Patriotic Front asked that the interim period be long enough to bring refugees back to vote. Would the British pay for their transport to go home? Gilmour and Renwick asked if these refugees included cadres detained by ZANU in Mozambique. Mugabe said there were no such detainees but that many ZANU members were in detention and restriction in Zimbabwe-Rhodesia. Gilmour asked the Salisbury delegation if they would release detainees. Mundawarara responded that there were no political detainees in the country. The Patriotic Front wanted the electoral law changed, to dispense with the elaborate legal procedures by which parties scheduled meetings and advertised in the news media. Gilmour assured the PF that the British governor would make sure campaigns and elections were fair. After that, the Patriotic Front began to make a series of demands that had little to do with how decolonizing elections were imagined and everything to do with how the 1979 election was conducted. The PF opposed mobile polling stations. The British delegation could not fathom why. Because, Leo Baron explained, mobile polling stations could lead to all kinds of abuses when there was no registration of voters. If all voters were registered there would be no problem, but without registration what was to prevent people from going from one polling station to another and voting twice? Mundawarara was taken aback: in 1979 no one reported any problems at mobile polling stations; they were indispensable for people in remote areas. The Patriotic Front wanted one day of voting instead of two or the three of 1979. Nkomo explained why: if the election took place over three days, there were more opportunities to bus people from one polling station to another, as they could travel at night. This could not happen, Gilmour said. There were indelible dyes that lasted longer than the polling period and this should serve as a way to prevent people voting more than once wherever they voted.[42]

Gilmour issued a statement that evening. He answered most of the PF's questions by underscoring the extent of the governor's control over security forces and the running of the government. There could be no new electoral law until a new government was in place. For the forthcoming election, there would be a British electoral commissioner who would make sure no one could vote twice. Moreover, each party would have a representative at each polling station. But there could not be voter registration. It would take too long. The Patriotic Front's demands

42. Summary, 22nd plenary, October 31, 1979.

for officials to register voters and then delimit constituencies were tasks for a post-independence election, not an interim one.[43]

The next day Nkomo asked for a longer interim period. If it was only two months and failed, the British would be held responsible, whereas if it were six months, there could be power sharing. Carrington was impatient. The interim was to last two months, he said. This would be ample time to campaign while the cease-fire was in place; the British firmly believed that the shorter the interim period the better it would be for all concerned. Nkomo wanted four months; then he asked for five or six months. Simon Muzenda, from Mugabe's delegation, explained that it would take five months to remove all the land mines, so people could travel safely to polling stations. Carrington said the cease-fire would begin as soon as the governor arrived; no one could wait for land mines to be dug up. Nkomo was undeterred: some things, like voter registration, could not be done until there was a cease-fire. And there was the matter of delimiting constituencies. It was important to learn the size of the electorate. He produced a mathematical formula to tell the conference how this might best be done: if the cease-fire period was X and the registration/delimitation period was Y, then the total period of the interim was $X + Y + 2$.[44]

On November 2, Carrington brought revised proposals before the conference. These repeated that the governor would be responsible for the conduct of the elections but there would be freedom of assembly and freedom of movement. All parties would be legal and free to campaign. The Commonwealth observers would serve as an additional guarantee that the election was free and fair. The British fully understood that the thousands of refugees living outside Rhodesia wanted to return to vote in the election. It would be difficult to organize the return of all refugees, but the governor would begin the task of bringing everyone home, although the task would have to be completed by the independent government and the neighboring states. The numbers were daunting. There were perhaps as many as 200,000 refugees altogether: between 50,000 and 60,000 in Zambia, 20,000 and 30,000 in Botswana, and the rest in Mozambique. The interim period would be two months; this had been accepted by the Salisbury delegation but the Patriotic Front continued to object.[45] Over the next few days, the PF continued their objections,

43. Statement by Lord Privy Seal [Ian Gilmour], 22nd plenary, October 31, 1979.

44. Summary 23rd plenary, November 1, 1979.

45. Conference paper, November 2, 1979; Carrington's statement, 25th plenary, November 2, 1979; Kaunda to Thatcher, November 7, 1979, TNA/PREM/19/114.

often returning to issues that Carrington thought had been resolved. There were concerns about the security forces and the judiciary. Several Patriotic Front delegates demanded that the interim arrangements be negotiated again.[46]

The repetitive debates of the first half of November were generally thought to be a delaying tactic by the PF, although what it might have gained beyond a clarification of what the frontline presidents would support is not clear. But however impatient Carrington and Gilmour were, this delay gave the British delegation an enormous advantage, as high commissioners and ambassadors assessed the mood of the front-line presidents. They found newly articulated concerns and openings. Kaunda asked for an interim period of five months. The Patriotic Front needed time to return and "to get adjusted." How could they return, set up offices, and campaign in just two months? He was adamant that as many refugees as possible return to Zimbabwe before the election. Could Britain airlift them out? He did not want them voting in the Zimbabwean election from Zambia: this would be a grave threat, he wrote to Thatcher. At the same time he was concerned about armed men traveling through Zambia to return home.[47]

Elsewhere in the region there was talk, for the first time since the conference began, of an inevitable split between ZANU and ZAPU. In Mozambique, several ambassadors from Eastern bloc countries—countries that funded the guerrilla armies—complained to British diplomats that there was no hope for socialism in a free Zimbabwe, and even less hope of Nkomo and Mugabe uniting. "Everybody, but everybody," the East German ambassador said with emphasis, is "fed up" with Rhodesia and "fervently" wants a solution.[48] In South Africa the prime minister, P. W. Botha, seemed willing to abandon Muzorewa altogether. South African diplomats in London believed the conference had fallen into a trap laid by Nkomo's "Soviet instigators," but Botha blamed Muzorewa. He looked "more and more like a patient with a terminal illness" than a politician worthy of the ZAR270 million he had been

46. Summary, 26th plenary, November 5, 1979; Statement by Gilmour, 27th plenary, November 6, 1979; summary, 27th plenary, November 6, 1979.

47. Sir Leonard Allison, British high commissioner, Lusaka, to FCO, November 1, 1979; Kaunda to FCO, November 1, 1979; Allison, Lusaka, to FCO, November 3, 1979; Allison, Lusaka, to FCO, November 6, 1979; Kaunda to Thatcher, November 7, 1979, TNA/PREM/19/114.

48. Achilles Papadopoulos, British ambassador, Maputo, to FCO, November 2, 1979, TNA/PREM/19/114. Obviously there were disagreements about this. The next day at a social occasion Papadopoulos was told by someone close to the president that if the conference broke down, Mozambique would support renewed war, which would require military equipment and military personal from "a number of countries." Papadopoulos to FCO, November 3, 1979, TNA/PREM/19/114.

given by South Africa. Rhodesia seemed to be a lost cause. If the British really believed that the stalemate would end soon, Botha hoped they would take over the funding of Muzorewa, "without which he would be lost."[49]

A few days after Zimbabwe-Rhodesia security forces raided eastern Zambia, Kaunda traveled to London. He had already told Thatcher that he accepted all but two of the British proposals: he still insisted that the interim period was too short and the refugees must return home. Once he had left Lusaka, his cabinet ministers were only too eager to tell the British high commissioner that a settlement was near. The problem now was creating a level playing field for the election, so the Patriotic Front could not cry "foul" if they lost the election.[50] In London, Mark Chona, Zambia's foreign minister, briefed Thatcher and Carrington in the morning and Kaunda met with them in the evening of November 8.[51] Thatcher and Carrington clearly wanted Kaunda to use his influence on Nkomo to resolve the PF's objections to the issues of the transition. To their surprise, Kaunda did not dwell on the length of the interim but on what advantages Muzorewa as even a figurehead prime minister might have in the election. Carrington did not think this was necessarily a problem, that perhaps a coalition government could create stability in the early years of independence. Kaunda disagreed. A coalition government would be too weak; only a government elected by a strong majority could give the country the direction it required. Carrington and Thatcher agreed and then shamelessly praised Nkomo as "the most charismatic" figure among Zimbabwean nationalists.[52]

The British delegation seemed to be emboldened by this meeting and quickly gave up flattering Nkomo. Thanks to Kaunda, they had already seen the Patriotic Front's proposals. In a statement the next morning, Carrington complained that the PF often said it had the support of 80 percent of the population. Why then did it need two months to put

49. John Leahy, British ambassador, Pretoria, to FCO, November 3. 1979, TNA/PREM/19/114. Factions in Nigeria actively supported Muzorewa and offered to send troops to monitor the cease-fire and protect him. Sir Mervyn Brown, Lagos, to FCO, November 7, 1979, TNA/PREM/19/114.

50. Kaunda to Thatcher, November 7, 1979, TNA/PREM/19/114. A "maize squeeze" was announced in Salisbury the same day, presumably as a warning against Zambian retaliation, but November was immediately after the maize harvest so it was unlikely that this intensified Kaunda's eagerness to help with a settlement, but see Tamarkin, *Making of Zimbabwe*, 266; Allison to FCO, November 8, 1979, TNA/PREM/19/114.

51. Ian Gow, Note of a meeting held at the residence of the Zambian high commissioner, London, November 7, 1979, TNA/PREM/19/114; author's field notes, Lusaka, August 12, 2006.

52. Richard Alexander, Thatcher's private secretary, to FCO, President Kaunda's visit, November 8, 1979, TNA/PREM/19/114.

it to a test?[53] When the Patriotic Front finally presented its proposals on November 12, they generated very little excitement and even less discussion. There was very little to discuss. Much of the document was devoted to parsing the exact meaning of "elections under British supervision" and "the whole electoral process" the Commonwealth was supposed to observe. It repeated questions about the role of the judiciary and the powers of the governor. It demanded a longer interim, because "military experience" showed how difficult it was to keep the peace in the first two or three months of a cease-fire. After that it was easy. A longer interim would allow for the registration of voters, which would prevent voting by nonresidents "such as tourists and people coming across the borders," voting by people younger than the voting age, and fraudulent voting, such as putting marked ballots in ballot boxes before the election. Without registering voters it was impossible to figure out the voting population or create constituencies of any accuracy. If there were no constituencies people could vote in districts other than the ones in which they lived. Registration was necessary for party list elections to be free and fair. Britain was wrong to say that registration would take too long. If there was a large enough staff, registration could be completed in three months. Zambia was once again the example. The document repeated what was by now the old saw that prior to independence Zambia had registered seven hundred voters per day in every constituency. If the same rate was achieved in Zimbabwe it would be possible to register 3 million voters in sixty days.[54]

Although Mugabe and Nkomo wanted more discussions and bilateral meetings, there were neither. The Salisbury delegation must have known—as did Carrington—how much the loose practices of the 1979 election lurked behind the demand for voter registration and stationary polling booths, just as the Salisbury delegation also must have understood that their own precarious position in the next election rendered these concerns to the point. On November 14, Kaunda's proposals were tabled. These proposed some compromises: an interim period of at least four months, an electoral commission that represented both the Patriotic Front and Muzorewa's government, and no less than three hundred Commonwealth observers chosen by the Commonwealth Secretariat from a minimum of ten countries. Carrington replied with a few clarifications—the governor would have complete control over all

53. Carrington statement, 30th plenary, November 10, 1979.
54. PF delegation document, circulated to conference, November 12, 1979; Carrington's statement, 32nd plenary, November 14, 1979.

forces; all electoral misconduct would be dealt with at once, and he made the slightest of compromises about the interim period. Knowing full well that this was more of a posture than a position for Kaunda, Carrington said that the British had initially envisioned elections to be held four to six weeks after the cease-fire began, but taking into account the views of the Patriotic Front they now believed elections should take place eight or nine weeks, or two months, after the cease-fire.[55] It was the slightest of sleights of hand, but it worked. Even though the Salisbury delegation objected to Kaunda's proposals on the grounds that he was not one of the parties of the all-party conference, the PF agreed that their forces would be under the governor's control and signed the transitional agreement.[56]

Conclusion

Throughout the Lancaster House meetings, no one in Julius Nyerere's government was willing to compromise on the length of the interim period. Nyerere accepted all the other British proposals, but this one was "unreasonable." As late as November 12 he assured the British high commissioner in Tanzania that he and the other frontline presidents would make sure that the Patriotic Front kept its part of a cease-fire, but that cease-fire had to be six months. He had, after all, not hesitated to ask the PF to accept terms it did not like, but now he wanted an additional Commonwealth meeting to assess the length of the interim period.[57] On November 14, presumably aware of Kaunda's proposals, Nyerere wrote to Thatcher with perhaps his most ominous defense of the six-month interim period. Two months was simply not enough time for the Patriotic Front to have a fair chance in the polling booths. The parties of the PF had been in exile too long; they had organized themselves for war, not political campaigning. They had no political organization, no candidates ready, and no means of moving around the countryside. If the British insisted on a two-month cease-fire, "there will not be a cease fire at all."[58] As the next chapter argues, he was not far wrong.

55. Proposals by President Kaunda; statement by Carrington, 32nd plenary, November 14, 1979.

56. Summary and Carrington's statement, 33rd plenary, November 15, 1979.

57. Moon, Dar es Salaam, to FCO, November 9, 1979; Moon to FCO, November 12, 1979, TNA/PREM/19/114. For a different view of Nyerere's role in the events in this chapter, see Arrigo Palloti, "Tanzania and the Decolonization of Rhodesia," *Afriche e Orienti* 2 (2011): 215–31.

58. Nyerere to Thatcher, November 14, 1979, TNA/PREM/19/114.

ELEVEN

"Adequate and acceptable": The 1980 Election and the Idea of Decolonization

The historiography of Zimbabwe, the independent majority-ruled nation, usually begins at Lancaster House.[1] The 1980 election is almost an afterthought in this chronology, a harbinger of state practices rather than a point of origin for one nation or the moment of demise for another. When Rhodesia ended is not at all clear. Did it end in April 1979, with the government of Zimbabwe-Rhodesia, or in December 1979, when it came, for the first time, under the direct control of Great Britain? This chapter argues that decisions made and unmade at Lancaster House did not found Zimbabwe or end Rhodesia; instead, the elections brought about the new nation. Rhodesia, however, underwent a quiet military takeover before the 1979 constitutional conference was over.

General Walls and Mrs. Thatcher, Part 1

It took until mid-December for the Lancaster House conference to work out the details of the cease-fire, especially the question of how many assembly points were required for returning guerrillas and how and when they would

---

1. See Tamarkin, *Making of Zimbabwe*; and Stedman, *Peacemaking*.

gather in them. As these debates were taking place, there was a revision, if not subversion, of the agreement and its sensibilities. In October and November there was a shift in FCO communications about the parties in the all-party elections. The near-disdain with which Muzorewa had been described gave way to subtle but consistent support, especially for his ability to win the forthcoming election. To this end, Britain and South Africa wanted to lift sanctions before the 1980 poll; if sanctions remained in place, no one thought Muzorewa would have a chance of winning.[2] Once the cease-fire officially began there seemed to be a complete turn-around regarding ZAPU. The often-contemptuous view of Nkomo—one observer at Lancaster House told me "everyone knew Joshua couldn't run a country"[3]—gave way to praise for him and his army. His soldiers were disciplined and their commanders an elite group.

In early December General Peter Walls, Rhodesia's commander of Combined Operations, met privately with Margaret Thatcher. They congratulated each other on the success of the conference and the final agreement which was a foregone conclusion: they and the rest of the world could give a well-earned sigh of relief. Walls nevertheless worried that he would not be able to fulfill his responsibilities to the people of Zimbabwe-Rhodesia if, as under the British proposals, he could not consult with Muzorewa or the governor, Lord Christopher Soames. Could he be guaranteed access to the governor without having to go through others to obtain it? Thatcher assured him that Soames was free to seek advice on how to maintain law and order from anyone at any time, but to be safe she would instruct the governor, orally and in writing, that Walls should have direct access to him "just as the chiefs of staff had direct access to her in this country." She would also make sure that Walls would be present when the governor met with Muzorewa. Nevertheless, Walls worried, as white Rhodesians had done for decades, that Britain would bow to domestic and international pressures and not defend the country from the violence of African insurgents. He knew for a fact that the Patriotic Front would not implement the cease-fire, but would threaten and intimidate whoever they could. What if guerrilla forces in a neighboring country acted in such a way as to threaten the elections? If diplomatic solutions failed, would the governor allow the security forces to strike across the border? The British proposals put

2. Byatt, ADR Salisbury, to FCO, Rhodesia: Discussions with the National Joint Operations Committee, October 1, 1979; Allinson, Lusaka to FCO, November 24, 1979; Sir Anthony Parsons, UKMIS to FCO, November 24, 1979; Record of a conversation between Lord Carrington and the South African Foreign Minister, November 28, 1979, TNA/PREM19/115.
3. Author's field notes, London, June 15, 2011.

the Commonwealth Monitoring Force in charge of assembly points and allowed the Rhodesian security forces to maintain peace and make free and fair elections possible. Could this be interpreted to allow security forces "to deal with the terrorists"? Thatcher was "confident" that Walls and Lord Soames would find a way to guarantee law and order in the land.[4] With this conversation the Rhodesian Front, and its claims to power and privilege, was evacuated from the interim period.

Ending the War

Lord Soames arrived in Salisbury on December 12. He kept emergency powers and martial law in place, as attacks on white farmers had increased in December, albeit by cadres acting against orders.[5] For the next few days the parties of the Patriotic Front continued to object to the final cease-fire agreement, but, under pressure from the frontline presidents, Nkomo and Mugabe initialed it on December 17.[6] This was a day after Carrington's deadline and five days after Britain had lifted sanctions. Nine days after that Josiah Tongogara, commander of ZANLA forces, was killed in a car crash in Mozambique. This death, with its question of whether or not it was really an accident, took on a powerful meaning to all parties before and after the 1980 election. His death troubled the British, who had found him easiest to work with at Lancaster House, and worried ZANLA, many of whom saw this as an intimation of the future.[7] As if to signal a new kind of politics, and to limit ZAPU's national aspirations, at the start of the election campaign ZANU broke the Patriotic

4. Record of a conversation between the Prime Minister and General Peter Walls, December 6, 1979. When this was sent to the FCO, Thatcher's secretary requested that no copies be made, TNA/PREM19/116.

5. Caute, *Under the Skin*, 384–86. Only a few whites were killed, but many farms were attacked and ransacked. George Houser of the American Committee on Africa described security force harassment whenever he traveled with ZANU(PF): they clearly thought his companions were his captors. George M. Houser, *No One Can Stop the Rain: Glimpses of Africa's Liberation Struggle* (New York: Pilgrim Press, 1989), 337–43.

6. Machel was said to have delivered a message to Mugabe saying he should stop quibbling: an electoral victory was theirs. The war was over, and if he did not sign the agreement he would be welcomed back to Mozambique, where he would be given a beach villa where he could write his memoirs. Davidow, *Peace in Southern Africa*, 89. In private, Machel was the only frontline president who thought it logical that Soames should arrive in Salisbury before the agreement was signed; it would be best if he was there to oversee the start of the cease-fire, Papadopoulos, Maputo, to FCO, December 11, 1979, TNA/PREM19/116.

7. Renwick, *Unconventional Diplomacy*, 68–69; see also Stiff, *See You in November*, 338–40; White, *Herbert Chitepo*, 90–92.

Front but used the acronym as a new parenthetical suffix, ZANU(PF).[8] ZAPU campaigned as the Patriotic Front although many observers did not use the term.

Was there really a cease-fire? According to the agreement, hostilities were to cease on December 28, and by January 4 all guerrillas were to be at rendezvous points from which they would be transported to sixteen assembly points. The number and location of assembly points and the timetable had been worked out in London with great care. In the end, there was very little dispute about how many guerrillas came to the assembly points: official estimates were between 19,000 and 20,000 out of total force levels probably over-estimated at Lancaster House to be 35,000. What was disputed, and what immediately took on great political importance, was the rate at which guerrillas assembled. ZANLA was slow to do so: there were incidents and near-incidents in the eastern region, which the Commonwealth Monitoring Force diffused, but not before Muzorewa demanded that ZANU(PF) be banned from the election because it did not send fighters to the assembly points on time.[9]

ZANU(PF) and the governor's staff provided widely different estimates of how many ZANLA had assembled by January 5. A week later Soames estimated fifteen thousand ZANLA, including youths, at assembly points and another three thousand who had infiltrated the country at the start of the assembly process.[10] These figures do not do justice to the difficulty of the entire enterprise, in which monitoring forces waited days in the summer heat for ZANLA who arrived armed, fearing a trap, and who had to be convinced that it was safe to be marched or bused to assembly points where they would be vulnerable to attacks from the air. That it worked as well as it did, despite the adventurism of some Rhodesian army detachments, explains why it was considered such an unqualified success.[11] ZIPRA was credited with sending men to the rendezvous points almost at once. Events in 1981 did not bear this out, but at the time this made a good impression on Soames and most of the Commonwealth

8. Kriger, *Guerrilla Veterans*, 29.

9. Soames, Salisbury, to FCO, December 31, 1979; Soames, Salisbury, to FCO, January 7, 1980, TNA/PREM19/342. For banning political parties, see Soames, Salisbury, to FCO, December 18, 1979, TNA/PREM/19/116.

10. Martin and Johnson, *Struggle for Zimbabwe*, 321; Renwick, *Unconventional Diplomacy*, 74–75; Gilmour, FCO to Salisbury, January 3, 1980, TNA/PREM19/342; Soames, Salisbury, to FCO, ZANLA; Observance of Ceasefire, January 12, 1980, TNA/PREM19/343.

11. For descriptions see Alexander, McGregor, and Ranger, *Violence and Memory*, 181–84; Caute, *Under the Skin*, 387–91; Martin and Johnson, *Struggle for Zimbabwe*, 321.

Monitoring Force.[12] The ZIPRA assembly points "were like a breath of fresh air," and ZIPRA officers were "smart, efficient and courteous."[13] A journalist joked that the British regarded ZIPRA commanders with awe, "as if the entire physics faculty of MIT had walked out of the bush."[14]

In a contrast that began before any ZIPRA reached any assembly points, ZANLA were seen as ill-disciplined and unreliable soldiers with a leadership that would not honor the cease-fire. This was more than an echo of Walls's threatening prediction. ZANLA's procrastination was only part of the continued theatrics of Lancaster House; it was a response to Soames's continued use of the Rhodesian army, rather than the police as specified in the agreement, as a peacekeeping force. Soames insisted that the security situation necessitated this. He interpreted the Lancaster House agreement to mean that he could not rely on external forces; the Rhodesian army was internal, as were the security force auxiliaries. These auxiliaries were young men, originally without formal military training, who had been Muzorewa's private army, called without much imagination *Pfumo reVanhu,* or spear of the people. Some had been trained in Libya, some hastily in the country, but all were made auxiliaries of the security forces in 1979.[15] Soames also allowed South African troops to remain on the Rhodesian side of Beitbridge, to protect the bridge and themselves.[16]

All this outraged the parties that had been the Patriotic Front and the frontline presidents.[17] Nyerere and Machel said they could only ensure that their "clients" carried out their part of the bargain if the British carried out theirs.[18] But Kaunda was alarmed at the broader trend of casting ZAPU as "goodies" and ZANU as "baddies." Whatever the speed with which these armies assembled, "pillorying" ZANU would harm any

12. For who and what ZIPRA left outside the camps, see Alexander, McGregor, and Ranger, *Violence and Memory,* 182–84; and Luise White, "'Whoever saw a country with four armies?' The Battle of Bulawayo Revisited," *J. of Southern African Studies* 33, no. 3 (2007): 619–31; for praise for ZIPRA, see Kriger, *Guerrilla Veterans,* 48–50.

13. P. H. J. Petter-Bowyer, *Winds of Destruction* (Victoria, BC: Tafford, 2003), 539, 548.

14. Renwick, *Unconventional Diplomacy,* 75–76; Stephen Chan, *The Commonwealth Observer Group in Zimbabwe* (Gweru: Mambo Press, 1985), 78.

15. McAleese, *No Mean Soldier,* 162–63. Muzorewa also had a security force, with the menacing name of *Zizo reVanhu,* "eyes of the people." Sithole too had a private army to go with his own particular ZANU. These men were trained in Uganda; they were considered too difficult to work with and were eliminated by security forces in 1979; see Flower, *Serving Secretly,* 204.

16. South African commanders did want their men stationed on the bridge itself in case it was attacked. Leahy, Pretoria, to FCO, January 11, 1980, TNA/PREM19/342.

17. Mugabe to Thatcher, January 8, 1980; Neilson, Lusaka, to FCO, January 9, 1980; Moon, Dar es Salaam, to FCO January 12, 1980, TNA/PREM19/342.

18. Moon, Dar es Salaam, to FCO, January 11, 1980; Papadopoulos, Maputo, to FCO, January 19, 1980, TNA/PREM19/342.

chance for a lasting peace in the region.[19] Whatever anyone knew, or surmised, about Walls's unfettered access to the governor, everyone in the region assumed that the security forces had Soames's full support. In the first days of the assembly phrase, Soames tended to rely on Walls for an understanding of the relationship between assembled forces and the election. Soames repeated Walls's assertion that most of the ZANLA at assembly points were youths, sent there in numbers sufficient to make sure their party would not be excluded from the election.[20] By mid-January Soames claimed that Tongogara had exaggerated the number of ZANLA in Rhodesia so as to justify the movement of guerrillas into the country during the cease-fire.[21]

General Walls and Lord Soames

Did Soames take his cues from Walls? Soames certainly did not know local politics or culture—he did not know that Zambia's minister of home affairs was Rhodesian-born, for example—but he clearly had grave doubts about the Rhodesian commander, whatever facts and fictions he took from him. He complained to the FCO about Walls and his "exaggeration" of the security situation. As early as January 3 Soames wrote that his major task was to "keep the Rhodesian military in hand." Otherwise he feared they would continue to cause "bloody incidents" that would lead to an emptying out of assembly areas and give Rhodesians an excuse to restart the war. He desperately wanted to contain the auxiliaries.[22] The FCO's recommendation was that Soames should arrange an "accommodation" between Nkomo and Walls. This would provide a new level of international acceptance for the elections and, it was hoped, keep Rhodesian commanders from doing anything "stupid."[23]

19. Neilson, Lusaka, to Soames, Salisbury, January 9, 1980; Neilson, Lusaka, to FCO, January 10, 1980, TNA/PREM19/342.

20. Walls assured the governor's staff that most of these were teenage *mujibas* who carried only stick grenades or obsolete weapons. These were not the real ZANLA: "Every self-respecting terrorist has an AK-47," and these men remained outside the cease-fire process "for purposes of political intimidation." Quoted in Renwick, *Unconventional Diplomacy*, 78; see also Kriger, *Guerrilla Veterans*, 47; Soames, Salisbury, to FCO, January 9, 1980, TNA/PREM19/342.

21. Soames, Salisbury, to FCO, ZANLA: Observance of Ceasefire, January 12, 1980, TNAK/PREM19/343.

22. Soames, Salisbury, to FCO, Nkomo's Return, January 3, 1980; Record of a call by Bishop Muzorewa, January 9, 1980, TNAK/PREM19/342; Ramphal to Thatcher, January 12, 1980; Soames to FCO, January 12 and 14, 1980, TNA/PREM19/343.

23. Robin Renwick, FCO, memo, January 14, 1980, TNA/PREM19/343.

Walls, however, had already tested the limits of international acceptance by insisting on the token contingent of South African troops at Beitbridge. This was condemned with growing urgency by Mugabe and the frontline presidents and by the OAU. [24] Even Thatcher wanted them gone; the number was too small to be worth the international censure.[25] It was not the censure that worried Soames, however, but that Walls had no interest in world opinion. Should South Africans leave Beitbridge because of international pressure, Soames feared Walls and "how far his anger would take him." If Rhodesian forces "got out of control," the agreement would break down.

By mid-January Walls began to take credit for persuading the Salisbury delegation to accept the Lancaster House agreement; Soames now feared he would call a press conference and say he had done so only because he had been told that Rhodesian forces would be allowed to maintain security and be allowed to do whatever could be done to make sure Muzorewa won the election.[26] There was no press conference. Instead, there was another meeting with Soames in which Walls complained that he was under intense pressure from his own forces and from the white community because the governor was not even trying to "preserve" Muzorewa's authority. In fact, the British seemed to be doing all they could to make Muzorewa seem irrelevant to Africans. "The whole psychology" was in favor of the parties of the Patriotic Front: there were daily tributes to their role in maintaining the cease-fire. Walls was willing to bring Nkomo in, but only if ZANU(PF) was dealt with for violations of the cease-fire. If Soames was not going to ban ZANU(PF) outright, and if the South Africans were withdrawn from Beitbridge, would he then allow Rhodesian forces "a selective response" to breaches of the agreement?[27] South Africa agreed to withdraw its troops from Beitbridge in late January; the fact of their presence nevertheless triggered emotional debates in the OAU and the UN, which prompted Carrington to

24. Monrovia to FCO, January 10, 1980; Dar es Salaam, to FCO, Text of President Nyerere's message, January 13; Papadopoulos, Maputo, to FCO, January 14, 1980, TNA/PREM19/343.

25. Prime Minister's conversation with the Lord Privy Seal [Ian Gilmour], January 13, 1980, TNA/PREM19/343.

26. Soames to FCO, South African Forces, January 15, 1980, TNA/PREM19/343. Walls was repeating, or perhaps had influenced, South Africa's position, that the struggle was between the forces of moderation (Muzorewa) and the communist Patriotic Front parties, of which Nkomo's was less communist than Mugabe's. While many in the government thought it would have been best if they removed their troops from Beitbridge, South Africans were dismayed at the objections to their small and innocuous contingent when it was ZANLA perpetuating the most serious breaches of the cease-fire. Leahy, Cape Town, to FCO, South African Forces in Rhodesia, January 16, 1980, TNA/PREM19/343.

27. Soames, Salisbury, to FCO, January 19, 1980, TNA/PREM19/343.

complain about being lectured on free and fair elections by Liberia and East Germany.[28]

The Postwar Situation

Even as there were widespread fears that the cease-fire would not hold, even as talk of banning ZANU(PF) from the election continued, there was a sense that the guerrilla war was over. White holiday makers returned to Matopos resorts in January, while ZANLA held "victory parades" in villages in the eastern highlands as they returned to the country from Mozambique. Rhodesian commanders complained that these parades were a new form of political intimidation and indoctrination,[29] but the peopling of the assembly points and the holiday chalets marked a definite change in the constitution of the war. Denis Hills, normally sympathetic to African aspirations from his teaching post in the eastern highlands, had not believed a cease-fire was possible. Almost grudgingly he noted that the rate of Africans killed daily had dropped dramatically.[30] I submit that whether or not violence continued was not the issue: the context had changed. Because there was now a cease-fire agreement, and because armed men had returned to the country—according to the agreement, refugees were men and women who returned unarmed—and were put in specific spaces governed by that agreement, this was now a postwar world. If there was continued violence it was by definition carried out by armed men "still out"—in the countryside or even in another country, not in assembly points—and from the Rhodesian security forces.[31]

Rhodesia in early 1980 was in some ways a precursor of the post-conflict societies of the early 1990s, especially the former Yugoslav republics that, however independent, required continual international

28. Leahy, Cape Town, to FCO, Rhodesia: South African Troops, January 23, 1980, TNA/ PREM19/344. For OAU and UN, see Doubleday, Monrovia, to FCO, Rhodesia, January 17, 1980; UKMIS, New York, to FCO, Rhodesia, January 17, 1980, TNA/PREM19/343, and UKMIS, New York, to FCO, Rhodesia and the Security Situation, January 31, 1980, UKMIS to FCO, Rhodesia and the Security Council, January 31, 1980, UKMIS to FCO, February 1, 1980, TNA/PREM19/344.

29. Terence Ranger, *Voices from the Rocks: Nature, Culture & History in the Matopos Hills of Zimbabwe* (Oxford, James Currey, 1999), 342; Soames, Salisbury to FCO, January 3, 1980, TNAK/PREM19/342; Renwick, *Unconventional Diplomacy*, 72; Caute, *Under the Skin*, 389–90.

30. Hills, *Last Days*, 159.

31. Renwick, *Unconventional Diplomacy*, 78–79. Men in assembly points, especially ZIPRA in Matabeleland, routinely left the camps to cache weapons and ammunition nearby; see Alexander, McGregor, and Ranger, *Violence and Memory*, 181.

surveillance.[32] In other ways, however, Rhodesia's postwar was something temporary, a stepping-stone that was to be a progression that was also a place holder, moving not necessarily toward peace but something called, with no irony whatsoever, independence. This was achieved by one critical ritual, for which there was a large and attentive audience: elections. This was decolonization, the independence that had to be given to someone who had been freely chosen by the self that would self-govern. Because this was decolonization in 1980 and not 1960, the mantra of free and fair elections was repeated everywhere. Free and fair did not necessarily describe a practice—and certainly not one with which Rhodesian voters, black or white, were familiar—but a dogma: if someone could vote without legal or physical impediments, the election demonstrated democratic participation. The extension of the franchise, rather than the outcome of an election, was essential to the creation of a citizenry who could choose its own rulers. For observers of African elections in the 1970s and 1980s the right to vote legitimated the election's results. Carrington said as much in 1990, "I don't think I ever thought it was going to be the *ideal*. After all, one was not *blind*."[33]

There was postwar violence, of course, but it was violence that had been anticipated. As soon as the agreement was signed, Soames predicted "the amount of intimidation and general skullduggery will no doubt increase on both sides" and Carrington reminded an optimistic Jimmy Carter that intimidation would continue.[34] A few weeks later Muzorewa and Mundawarara called on Margaret Thatcher to assure her that they did not worry as much about intimidation as they did about campaigning during the rainy season.[35] Were these statements based on events on the ground or ways of talking about African politics there? Did they differ because the situation changed or because officials said different things to different audiences? There were rapid shifts in the complexity of local politics, but at the same time accusations of intimidation form part of a larger narrative that itself was shaped by the genealogy of the term. Intimidation, and the categories undergirding it, had a long shelf life in the politics in the country. But for all the beatings and petrol

32. Aida Hozic, "The Origins of 'Post-Conflict,'" in *Post-Conflict Studies: An Interdisciplinary Approach*, ed. Chip Gagnon and Keith Brown (New York: Routledge, 2014), 19–38.

33. Tom Young, "Elections and Electoral Politics in Africa," *Africa*, 63, no. 3 (1993): 299–312; see also Toby Shelley, *Endgame in the Western Sahara* (London: Zed Books, 2004). Carrington quoted in Charlton, *Last Colony*, 24.

34. Soames, Salisbury, to FCO, December 18, 1979; extract of a meeting between Thatcher, Carter, Carrington, and Ahmed Salim, New York, December 18, 1979, TNA/PREM19/116.

35. Record of a call by Bishop Muzorewa, January 9, 1980, TNA/PREM19/342.

bombs of urban African politics of the 1950s and 1960s, African political parties tried to police their own excesses or at least the excesses practiced by their youth leagues. When they were unable, or sometimes able, to do so they were banned, first by the United Federal Party and then by the Rhodesian Front. Under the Rhodesian Front, however, intimidation became an African cultural trait that made African participation in political processes almost impossible; it was the grounds for repression. As we saw in chapter 8, Africans could be protected from their natural susceptibility to intimidation only by the preventative detention of "intimidators."

No one doubted that there was widespread intimidation before the 1980 election. Eight parties—all but one of which were descended in some way from ZANU or ZAPU—contested the common roll election. ZANU(PF) won by a little more than 1 million votes. The historiography has been divided on why this happened. Articles researched shortly before or after the election concluded that people voted for ZANU(PF) or ZAPU because they promised to end the war, and "only they *could* end the war." Muzorewa had little credibility, and the excesses of his auxiliaries made many people see former guerrillas, especially those outside the assembly points, as their protectors.[36] Martin and Johnson, who had every reason to find the election uncomplicated, maintained that the real problem was the violence of security forces. Beyond that, everything was fine, once Soames overcame his original dislike of Mugabe.[37] Masipula Sithole noted that the accusations and counter-accusations of intimidation involved at least four political parties complaining to Soames.[38] Norma Kriger argued that ZANU(PF) won the election through excessive threats and violence. Observers had gone out of their way to ignore this evidence and pronounce the election and the victors legitimate.[39] Daniel Compagnon agreed: the "outside world was quite happy to uphold the fiction of a multiparty democracy in the making."[40]

---

36. Lionel Cliffe, Joshua Mpofu, and Barry Munslow, "Nationalist Politics in Zimbabwe: The 1980 Election and Beyond," *Rev. African Pol. Economy* 18 (1980): 44–67; Tony Rich, "Legacies of the Past? The Results of the 1980 Election in Midlands Province, Zimbabwe," *Africa* 52, no. 3 (1982): 42–55. Rich conducted interviews in May and June 1980, when many people might have thought it wise to speak well of ZANU(PF).

37. Martin and Johnson, *Struggle for Zimbabwe*, 322–23, 326.

38. Masipula Sithole, "The General Elections 1979–1980," in *Zimbabwe: The Political Economy of Transition, 1980–1986,* ed. Ibbo Mandaza (Dakar: Codesria Books, 1986), 81–85.

39. Norma Kriger, "ZANU(PF) Strategies in General Elections, 1980–2000: Discourse and Coercion," *African Affairs* 104, no. 414 (2009): 1–6.

40. Compagnon, *Predictable Tragedy*, 37.

The 1980 Election Observed

Who were these observers who represented the outside world? There were 125 members of the Commonwealth Observers Group (COG) mandated in Lusaka, the British Electoral Commission, headed by a local government official, Sir John Boynton, and an additional 230 observers. The FCO rejected a mission from the OAU; it was thought the COG already favored the Patriotic Front parties and there was no need for more observers to do so. Most observers represented governments, but some represented independent groups and some were "registered unofficial observers," including a few British academics and several observers from the 1979 election—Lord Chitnis, the Freedom House delegation from New York—and Jeffrey Davidow, who had been with the U.S. delegation at Lancaster House. Most delegations produced reports, and one official observer wrote a novel.[41] The 1980 election was a "founding" election, critical to the imagined orderly transfer of power: such elections would not only legitimate a new nation but would make free and fair voting practices routine.[42] It was also an election in which the campaign was observed for weeks before the poll. The COG, for example, arrived a month before the poll.[43] There were two official reports, that of the British electoral commission and that of the COG. I will discuss these at length below, but both admitted that intimidation was widespread, and both concluded that intimidation was not in and of itself sufficient to determine the results of the election.

41. Commonwealth Secretariat, *Southern Rhodesia Elections, February 1980: Report of the Commonwealth Observer Group on Elections Leading to Independent Zimbabwe* (London, Commonwealth Secretariat, 1980); Parsons, UKMIS to FCO, OAU and Rhodesia, February 8, 1980; Soames to FCO, Rhodesia and the OAU, February 10, 1980, TNA/PREM19/344. Typical of the country reports was that of Australia, which devoted four pages to the election; see Joint Committee on Foreign Affairs and Defence, *Zimbabwe (May 1980)* (Canberra: Australian Government Printing Service, 1980), 124–29. Peter Wilkinson led the New Zealand election observer team in 1980 and returned often in the 1980s. His novel was published posthumously. Peter Wilkinson, *Msasa* (Workworth: C. E. Wilkinson, 1992).

42. Michael Cowen and Liisa Laakso, "An Overview of Election Studies in Africa," *J. Modern African Studies* 35, no. 4 (1997): 717–44; Lindberg, *Democracy and Elections*, 72–74.

43. By the 1990s Commonwealth observers were known mainly for pronouncing elections free and fair before the victor was announced. Gisela Geisler, "Fair? What has fairness got to do with it? Vagaries of election observation and democratic standards," *J. of Modern African Studies* 31, no. 4 (1993): 613–67; Douglas G. Anglin, "International Election Monitoring: The African Experience," *African Affairs* 97, no. 389 (1998): 471–95. A member of the Commonwealth Observers Group later pointed out the dangers of seeing the Zimbabwe observers as a model for any other election. Each election was unique; each observation team had to be "extemporaneous." When at the end of 1980 the Commonwealth Secretariat sent observers to Uganda, the group did little more than to validate a rigged election. See Chan, *Commonwealth Observers*, 39–40.

Intimidation Observed

How much intimidation was there in January and February 1980, and who was responsible for it? The answers varied over time and by audience, but for the representatives of most political parties what was important about intimidation was not the assaults on individual candidates or groups of supporters, but whether their party could safely hold rallies and display their publicity in a given area. Thus, for most of January, almost everyone complained that auxiliaries and the security forces campaigned for the UANC, often with great violence. In "friendly" meetings with Soames, Nkomo condemned the auxiliaries, as did his representatives in New York.[44] In a written statement to the COG, the central committee of ZAPU (which did not call itself the Patriotic Front) denounced the governor's implicit support for the UANC and the auxiliaries that were once its army. But the "devastating fact" was that the UANC civil service would manage polling stations. "The advertising about the secrecy of the vote, the 100 British supervisors, the Election Commissioners, etc. is totally theoretical and unconvincing when compared with the credibility of the UANC bully-boy who says that he will know how anyone voted because *HIS* people are running the election."[45]

In his meeting with the COG in January, a day after he had spoken to Soames, Nkomo offered an analysis of ZANU(PF) intimidation. The party was not as strong as its army, Nkomo explained, which is why it now resorted to violence to keep ZAPU from campaigning in the eastern region: "if ZANU(PF) was so confident of its political strength, why was it using the gun to get people to vote in its favour?"[46] When Ian Smith, now a candidate for parliament on the white voters' roll, called on Soames at the end of January he showed no interest in analyzing ZANU(PF) or anyone else. Indeed, the governor assumed he was looking for an issue on which to stake a political comeback. Speaking for "the entire white community," Smith complained that unchecked ZANLA intimidation would allow Mugabe to win the election. Soames disagreed. He thought a Muzorewa-Nkomo coalition would win instead;

44. Soames, Salisbury, to FCO, January 17, 1980, TNA/PREM19/343; Parsons, UKMIS to FCO, January 31 and February 2, 1980, Rhodesian Auxiliaries, TNA/PREM19/344.

45. PF Central Committee, memorandum to COG, February 28, 1980. COG Operations in Rhodesia, Correspondence with Patriotic Front, Commonwealth Secretariat, London [hereafter CWSec]/COG/51–6B.

46. Meeting with Joshua Nkomo, January 18, 1980, COG, Operations in Rhodesia: Correspondence with the Patriotic Front, CWSec/COG/51/B-6B.

the British were "satisfied" with Nkomo's "attitude" and with ZIPRA's "compliance." This did not seem to relieve Smith as much as give him new fodder for his campaign; he could now say that he had met with the governor, who would "meekly" accept a PF government.[47]

Is it possible to see ZANU(PF)'s intimidation as both real and as an invention of the Rhodesian security forces? Were the indeterminate plans for an Nkomo-Muzorewa (or Nkomo-Muzorewa-RF) coalition on the table or were they a sop offered to distressed white politicians? These questions do not prove or deny the extent of anyone's violence or devious plotting, but suggest the different political uses of violence and proposed coalitions. Talk of intimidation and coalitions were both descriptions of political events and discursive strategies, ways of making points and ways of bargaining.

At the end of January Nkomo began to complain vocally to Soames about ZANLA's intimidation throughout the eastern provinces.[48] Did this mean that ZANU(PF) intimidation increased or that Nkomo saw an opportunity in condemning it? Was he privy to talk of coalitions or did he simply want it known that ZANLA made it impossible for his party to hold meetings safely in the eastern part of the country? In any case, Nkomo claimed that ZANU(PF) intimidation was now more dangerous than that of the security forces. Soames said "the vibes were good" during this meeting, during which he tried to convince Nkomo to tell the frontline presidents about ZANLA's excesses.[49] Nkomo knew that such communication would be problematic. He had long had a difficult relationship with Nyerere—he wrote that what Nyerere liked about Mugabe was that he was not Nkomo—which was made worse by his complaints about ZANLA. Indeed, Nyerere had strongly urged Nkomo to state his case in private messages to the frontline presidents, rather than to the governor and at press conferences.[50]

By February it seemed that only veteran politicians with small parties or marginal futures complained about the UANC and the auxiliaries, and then only to the COG. James Chikerema of the Zimbabwe Democratic Party, Ndabaningi Sithole, representing what was by then his almost private ZANU, and a gloomy Garfield Todd all complained that the UANC made it almost impossible for other parties to campaign or even

47. Soames, Salisbury, to FCO, Rhodesia: Security Situation, January 29, 1980, TNA/PREM19/344.
48. Soames, Salisbury, to FCO, January 30, 1980, Rhodesia: ZANLA Activity, TNA/PREM19/344.
49. Soames, Salisbury, to FCO, Rhodesia: Nkomo's views, February 5, 1980, TNA/PREM19/344.
50. Nkomo, *My Life*, 208–9; Soames, Salisbury, to FCO, Rhodesia: Nkomo's views, February 12, 1980; Moon, Dar es Salaam, to FCO, Rhodesia, February 8, 1980, TNA/PREM19/344.

display posters.[51] Muzorewa, however, expressed nothing but bitterness in his February meeting with Soames. He regretted signing the Lancaster House agreement, claiming it permitted the violence that now made it impossible for the UANC to campaign in areas dominated by ZANU(PF). Soames reminded him that as governor he had legal powers to ban a party from competing in a district. This did not mollify Muzorewa, who wanted ZANU(PF) banned outright; only then could there be free and fair elections.[52] The next day Mugabe presented Soames with a list of abuses and atrocities committed by the security forces and the auxiliaries. Soames dismissed this out of hand; the problem was that ZANLA was violent: that if only Mugabe's men behaved like Nkomo's "there would have been no real problems." Soames asked for, and received, a formulaic renunciation of violence in the form of a broadcast ordering all ZANLA not in assembly places to go to them and stay there. "We are compelled not to interfere with meetings of other parties. . . . Our people should vote nicely and without fighting."[53] Soames was not impressed. He admitted to the FCO how conflicted he was about ZANU(PF). On the one hand, he was looking for a way "of cutting Mugabe down to size without—if possible—excluding him from the election." On the other, he was convinced no African country, nor Nkomo, and especially not the white community would accept results based on intimidation.[54]

When Mugabe first met with the COG he was the voice of reason. He objected to Soames's continued use of security forces and auxiliaries to campaign for Muzorewa, but also to Soames's misplaced complaints about ZANU(PF). Mugabe knew there were some excesses by ZANLA outside the assembly points, but he could not control every cadre who wanted to continue fighting a war that had, after all, spread over a large area. Ten days later he met with the COG to report on his meeting with

51. Record of meeting with James Chikerema, Salisbury, February 1, 1980, COG Operations in Rhodesia: Correspondence with ZDP, CWSec/COG/51/B-6C; Meeting with Rev. N. Sithole (ZANU), February 2, 1980, COG Operations in Rhodesia, Zimbabwe African National Union, CWSec/COG/51/B-6D; Conversation with Garfield Todd, February 12, 1980, CWSec/COG/51/B-6-A.

52. Soames, Salisbury, to FCO, Rhodesia: Bishop Muzorewa, February 5, 1980, TNA/PREM19/344. This shocked Kaunda, who wrote to Thatcher and Ramphal to voice his concern. He knew that ZANLA and ZIPRA were "not blameless," but Soames allowed Muzorewa's auxiliaries to roam the countryside campaigning for Muzorewa. Kaunda to Ramphal, February 15, 1980; Sir Shridath S. Ramphal [SSR] Papers, CWSec/SG/Corr/HC/1980: Zambia.

53. Meeting with Christopher Soames, February 13, 1980, CWSec/COG/51/B-6A. Soames, Salisbury, to FCO, Text of broadcast, February 9, 1980. For content of meeting with Mugabe, see Soames to FCO, Rhodesia: Elections, February 7, 1980; Rhodesia: Intimidation, February 8, 1980; Rhodesia: Conduct of Auxiliaries, February 10, 1980; TNA/PREM19/344.

54. Soames to FCO, Rhodesia: Elections, February 7, 1980; Rhodesia: Intimidation, February 8, 1980; Rhodesia: Conduct of Auxiliaries, February 10, 1980; TNA/PREM19/344.

Soames. This time he was aggrieved that the governor wanted to ban ZANU(PF) from some areas. Once again, the governor failed to understand the history of the war. ZANU(PF) had "created liberated zones" of educated, politicized people who were now loyal to the party and "shunned" other parties, but this was not the same as intimidation. Mugabe felt certain the UANC could hold rallies in the central region; Sithole had been able to do so just a few days ago.[55]

Was Mugabe right? Was ZANLA violence and intimidation simply misplaced warfare? It is obvious that the postwar, pre-election violence served to intimidate politicians and populations, but the violent acts were those of the guerrilla war: abductions, targeted assassinations, commandeering food and young women from villages, and the all-night *pungwe*, the meetings in which villagers were forced to sing and chant slogans. More to the point was that the guerrilla war had become particularly brutal—some said "anarchic"—after the private armies became involved in 1978. The struggle was not necessarily more violent, but in many places—especially the eastern region—it was carried out by poorly trained but well-armed young men.[56] Did some of these cadres continue these practices weeks after the cease-fire?

The COG met with Soames in February. He readily admitted that the security forces were often violent, but they could not be "turned around" overnight. He was, however, surprised to hear that there were almost constant complaints about the activities of Muzorewa's auxiliaries in Mashonaland. Outside of the western region, where Nkomo's party had long been in control, violence and intimidation were commonplace. In some places only ZANU(PF) could hold meetings, and in others the violence and intimidation were directed at ZANU(PF). UANC supporters made it almost impossible for candidates from Chikerema's Zimbabwe Democratic Party to campaign in parts of the central region. Should this pattern continue, the COG warned Soames, eight of the nine competing parties—the exception was the Rhodesian Front—would have grounds to contest the election results. Soames was taken aback: he said this was

---

55. Record of meetings with Robert Mugabe, February 2 and February 12, 1980, COG operations in Rhodesia, Correspondence with ZANU(PF), CWSec/COG/51/B-6A. Sithole was a former comrade, a bond that may have served him well in some districts.

56. Ian Linden, *Church and State in Rhodesia, 1959–1979* (Munich: Kaiser Verlag, 1979), 272–74; R. S. Roberts, "The Armed Forces and Chimurenga: Ideology and Historiography," *Heritage of Zimbabwe* 7 (1987): 31–47; Norma J. Kriger, *Zimbabwe's Guerrilla War: Peasant Voices* (Cambridge: Cambridge University Press, 1992), 116–32; Schmidt, *Colonialism and Violence*, 155–56, 160–64; Luise White, "'Heading for the Gun': Skills and Sophistication in an African Guerrilla War," *Comp. Studies in Soc. and History* 51, no. 2 (2009): 247–48.

the first he had heard of any party other than ZANU(PF) obstructing meetings.[57]

Political violence intensified in February. Mugabe accused Soames of disrupting his campaign because he feared a ZANU(PF) victory. Muzorewa first blamed the parties that had been the Patriotic Front for the increasing violence, but then blamed the guerrillas neither Nkomo nor Mugabe could control.[58] Kaunda and Nyerere both condemned Soames's condemnations of ZANU(PF), while General Walls sought opportunities to visit assembly points with Nkomo.[59] Despite the violence of the week before the election—in a three-day period there were twenty-seven contacts involving security forces, thirteen shootings, three murders, an abduction, and one attack on a homestead—the COG saw the situation as improving. ZANLA were "trickling back" to assembly points, and some districts appeared to be on the cusp of free and fair elections. Soames agreed. However many attacks there were on individuals, all parties seemed able to campaign. Soames did not think "free and fair" was appropriate terminology in these circumstances but there were now "chances for a reasonably democratic election."[60]

The 1980 Election

In the end, ZANU(PF) won fifty-seven seats with 1,668,992 votes, over 1 million more votes than ZAPU's 638,879 votes and twenty seats. The UANC won three seats with 219,307 votes.[61] Nkomo and Muzorewa quickly denounced the results as illegitimate, but all groups of observers

57. Meeting with Christopher Soames, February 13, 1980, CWSec/COG/51/B-6A. Situation Report, Gwelo, February 11–15, 1980; Fort Victoria Weekly Report, week beginning February 10, 1980, Rhodesia: COG in Rhodesia, CWSec/COG/51/B-3. In Gwelo the COG heard many complaints from ZANU(PF) that Rhodesian countergangs were impersonating them to intimidate people.

58. UKMIS to FCO, Nyerere's letter to Waldheim, February 13, 1980; Soames, Salisbury to FCO, Rhodesia: Situation Reports, February 9–11; February 12, 1980; February 13, 1980, TNA/PREM19/344; Soames, Salisbury, to FCO, Rhodesia: ZANLA activity, February 17, 1980, TNA/PREM19/345.

59. Soames, Salisbury, to FCO, February 21, 1980; Carrington to Salisbury, February 22, 1980; Soames, Salisbury to FCO, February 21, 1980; TNA/PREM19/345.

60. S. G. Ikoku, summary of discussion with governor, February 15, 1980; Rajeshwar Dayal, Chairman COG, meeting with Soames, February 20, 1980. COG operations in Rhodesia, Correspondence with Governor, CWSec/51/B-8; Soames, Salisbury, to FCO, Rhodesia: Sitrep, 15, 23, and 24 February, 1980, TNA/PREM19/345.

61. There is anecdotal evidence that Walls and Carrington both expected a UANC victory, but that seems unlikely. See Lemon, *Never Quite a Soldier*, 256–57; author's field notes, London, June 13, 2011. Special Branch had predicted that Muzorewa and ZANU(PF) would divide the Shona votes so that Nkomo would win. See Renwick, *Unconventional Diplomacy*, 93.

did not: they pronounced the election if not free, then "adequate and acceptable" to the democratic nations of the world.[62] Was this because the observers were pro-ZANU(PF), anti-UANC, or just relieved that the process had come to an end?

Such questions tend to flatten our understandings both of intimidation and of the election. Both the British and COG reports acknowledged the brutality and the extent of the intimidation, and both provided equations showing why intimidation was not a factor in the final vote. The British report did not mention intimidation by ZAPU and claimed—as did Soames—that all reports of security force intimidation proved unfounded. It argued that there was no significant intimidation in urban areas but these voted as strongly for ZANU(PF) as rural areas outside Matabeleland did, hence intimidation did not "materially distort" the vote. Indeed, the high turnout indicated that people were not afraid to vote. To be safe, the report concluded with brief summaries from other teams of observers: all thought the election was well-run, a technical marvel in trying times, without misconduct sufficient to affect the result.[63] The COG report was four times as long as the British one. It included press releases, correspondence—including letters from Muzorewa demanding "proof" of their "impartiality"—and research on African literacy. The COG documented widespread intimidation, mainly by security forces and auxiliaries but also by ZANLA and ZIPRA. Thus, the Commonwealth Observers Group understood the resounding victory of ZANU(PF) as evidence that intimidation did not determine the vote. The election was "adequate and acceptable" because it revealed the will of the people in the high turnout and the "orderly and relaxed manner" in which people went to the polls.[64] This echoed the Pearce Commission *Report*, in which widespread enthusiasm was said to disavow widespread intimidation, but in this case "orderly" may have had many meanings. Writing from the eastern highlands, an unusually cynical Denis Hills thought the three days of voting were orderly and "scrupulously fair" because no African had any doubt that Mugabe would win.[65]

What kind of questions would allow for another kind of analysis of this election? I suggest two linked questions. First, how did the observers

---

62. *Report of the COG*, 144–46; Nkomo, *My Life*, 208–10; Kriger, *Guerrilla Veterans*, 51–53.

63. Sir John Boynton, *Southern Rhodesia, Independence Elections 1980: Report of the Electoral Commissioner, Salisbury, March 1980* (London: HMSO, 1980), 59, 95, 99. The American Committee on Africa visited "many" polling stations in Salisbury and saw "no infractions worth mentioning." Houser, *No One Can Stop the Rain*, 342.

64. *Report of the COG*, 132–33, 144–46, 173–84.

65. Hills, *Last Days*, 172–74.

define intimidation, and second, how did they imagine an electoral process that could correct for that? The COG believed that the greatest violence was due to the security forces and suggested that much of the intimidation attributed to ZIPRA and ZANLA were in fact acts of banditry by men accustomed to living comfortably off the land.[66] The British electoral commission was crystal clear: intimidation was violence, abductions, and murder, most of it done by ZANLA. What it did not consider intimidation was what it called the "T-shirt test." If someone felt safe enough to demonstrate his or her party affiliation in a public place this would discount allegations of "general intimidation."[67] Who might wear a party T-shirt or what history that person or that party might bring to an area was not the issue; that the shirt could be "freely worn" was.

The British Electoral Commission understood the history but firmly believed that it could be remedied by an impartial electoral process. A properly organized election could offer an antidote for the abuses of the previous months. Reason, evidence, and experience would carry the day. David Caute caricatured this electoral imaginary—which was that of the frontline presidents a few months before—as one in which "fine old colonial servants" believed they were witnessing "another of those impartial operations that were the glory of the Empire in its sunset."[68] The election was to be like those in western, democratic nations—that was precisely the point. There were three days of voting. There were 656 polling stations, 335 fixed and another 321 mobile. This way there would be no reason to transport voters across district boundaries. Since census figures were outdated, it was assumed some districts would have more voters than had been estimated. Citizens over eighteen could vote, as could anyone who had been resident in the country for two years.[69] Men

66. Operations in Rhodesia, sub-committee 4 on political freedom, CWSec/COG/51/B-4D.

67. *Boynton Report*, 10, 11–13.

68. Caute, *Under the Skin*, 411.

69. Although this was a regulation left over from the 1979 election, in 1980 it was in place to accommodate refugees who were citizens but who had not been resident in the country for several years. As the election was being planned there was some anxiety about how to arrange voting by some two hundred thousand refugees, most of whom might be in camps. This turned out to be unnecessary. Despite protests by the OAU internationally and by the COG within Rhodesia, only 33,430 refugees returned and these could be given temporary identity documents that allowed them to vote. Almost twice as many refugees returned from Botswana as did from Mozambique, much to the chagrin of the COG: each day half the number of refugees admitted to Rhodesia were sent back, presumably because they were armed. A week before the election Soames asked Mozambique to "restrict" the number of "young men of military age" who could enter Rhodesia. See *Boynton Report*, 74; *Report of the COG*, 166–67, 172–73; UKMIS to FCO, Rhodesia and the Security Council, Janu-

were required to produce a document that gave their name and place of residence; women who did not have such documents could have a male relative vouch for them. There was no agreed-upon way to assess a voter's age; challenges were time consuming and thus infrequent; it was assumed that underage voting occurred. Both hands of each voter were dipped in an indelible dye that was visible under a fluorescent light for four or five days; it could not be washed off and thus would prevent people voting twice. There were private voting booths in which each person marked his or her ballot. Ballots were printed in Rhodesia under security designed and maintained by the royal printer in London. Each marked ballot was placed in a specially made ballot box, reinforced with metal edges and sealed at the top. As this was a party-list election, ballots were in English with party symbols displayed prominently next to party names. At the end of each day's voting each box was sealed by a British supervisor, and at the end of the poll the sealed boxes were sent to provincial headquarters to be counted, a measure adopted to protect districts from reprisals.[70] There was a massive publicity campaign to combat the stories that a "black box" had been invented that could tell how a person voted, or that spirit mediums would reveal how a person voted. Rumors could be, and were, proven false. During the first days of voting, there were stories that Coca-Cola or special creams could erase the indelible dye. The COG experimented with Coca-Cola and with various creams in front of television crews to reveal that the dye was indeed indelible.[71]

Two weeks after the ZAPU central committee had complained, the Boynton commission agreed that it was too "intimidatory" to allow civil servants to supervise polling stations, at least in the countryside. Boynton had initially thought that having agents from all parties at the polling stations would prevent abuses by any single party, but Soames firmly believed that the presence of a ZANU(PF) agent at a polling station would intimidate "an unsophisticated voter." Anxieties about what party agents might do at polling stations had reached the level of

ary 24, 1980, TNA/PREM19/343; UKMIS to FCO, Nyerere's letter to Waldheim, February 13, 1980, TNA/PREM19/344; Rajeshwar Dayal to Soames, problem of repatriation of refugees, February 18, 1980, CWSec/COG/51/B-8.

70. *Boynton Report*, 20, 45–46, 71–73, 75, 93; Soames, Salisbury to FCO, Election, March 2, 1980, TNA/PREM19/346.

71. Meeting with Robert Mugabe and Rex Nhongo, February 26, 1990, COG Operations in Rhodesia, Correspondence with ZANU(PF), CWSec/COG/51/B-6A; *Boynton Report*, 62, 68, 93–94; *Report of the COG*, 324.

**You are the only
one who will ever know
for whom you voted.
Your vote is completely secret.
But it is vital that you use your vote to
choose a black majority Government.**

DO NOT BE AFRAID TO VOTE.

3   Poster placed on behalf of Election Directorates

"psychosis." It was not possible to ban them, nor could the monitoring force spare the manpower to keep them in check, so Soames requested 581 British policemen to arrive February 25 and stay for one week, to serve as supervisors at each polling station.[72] Not everyone loved the Bobbies, but everyone sympathized with their cautious efforts to ascertain if voters were indeed over eighteen. What no one was sure of was if their presence canceled out that of the party agents who stared at voters or wrote down their names with great flourish.[73]

72. Soames, Salisbury to FCO. Election Supervision, February 9, 1980, TNA/PREM19/344; *Boynton Report*, 49, 65–67; *Report of the COG*, 298–99. There was no police presence in Bulawayo or Salisbury because anyone who feared a specific party agent at one polling station could go to another one.

73. *Boynton Report*, 50, 69, 93; Hills, *Last Days*, 173; Lemon, *Never Quite a Soldier*, 260–61.

Even before they entered the polling stations, however, African voters were prepared for this election through texts, advertisements, and films. The directorate of elections produced a film, narrated in local languages, about where to vote, how to mark the ballot, and how secret it was. It ran full-page ads in newspapers proclaiming "1980 is the year of the new Zimbabwe" and "Your vote is secret" followed by only slightly smaller print that said "don't be afraid to use it." Written on the diagonal of both ads was "Your vote is your right. *Use* it." There were leaflets with cartoon characters. In one, a man reassured a friend that his vote would be secret; in another, one woman told another that she should

4   Original caption reads: "Those who are supported by Communist Russia claim they will give you all the things you want. But they are evil because the State will own all the things that are yours. Your land . . . your cattle . . . your home . . . even your children will belong to the State. The State will give you only what it says you need—you will have only the poorest things in life . . . and your neighbor will have only the same. This form of Socialism is a trick. This form of Socialism will rob you of your own property."

5   Original caption reads: "The true freedom of a democratic government means you will have
    your own home and your own cattle. Your children will be free to choose their own jobs and
    their own education. All the things you own now will remain yours to do with exactly as you
    wish. True freedom lets you work and save for the things you want."

not leave voting to her husband. Both she and her husband belonged to
Zimbabwe, "both of you have the right to vote in your land."[74]

The terminologies of civil society seeped into the practices of the war.
In January and February ZANU(PF) described the all-night meetings—
the pungwe—of the guerrilla war as "voter education."[75] There were

---

74. *Report of the COG*, 284–97.
75. As one ZANU(PF) cadre told a researcher, "we weren't doing anything but teaching people
how to vote." Rich, "Legacies of the Past," 47.

parody texts and desperate texts. Anti-Marxist pamphlets dropped from airplanes—often near COG teams—contrasted "Marxism Socialism" with "True Freedom." Designed by the man who illustrated UANC posters, the socialist side of the page showed war, Kalashnikov rifles, forced labor, angry commissars, and sad people. On the freedom side there was peace, schools, and farms available for purchase.[76]

A few days before the election, a forged issue of *Moto*—a progressive, often pro-ZANU(PF), Catholic publication—was left in newsstands and stores in Bulawayo and Salisbury by white men rumored to be policemen. The front page offered "a psychological analysis" of Mugabe. He had been attached to his mother as a child, and now his friends believed that the sexual deprivation and experiences he endured "with other convicts" in prison accounted for "his effeminate appearance and gestures." A week before the election it was apparently difficult to find loyal typesetters, however: the issue was dated February 32, 1980.[77]

The Secret Ballot, Reified

If decolonization required a founding election first to reveal to whom independence would be given and second to establish a habit of electing a government, then the secret ballot was key to the freeness and fairness of that election. Long considered a cornerstone of democracy, the secret ballot was first proposed to protect voters following the Terror of the French Revolution; it was finally enshrined in the universal declaration of human rights in 1948. Since 1948, however, the secret ballot in and of itself has become an absolute, something that stands alone as a mark of a free and fair election. It occupies a space that spans the global and universal to the personal and individual (as in the closed-off voting booth) and has little to do with local political culture.[78] That is precisely the point: the secret ballot was to allow someone, alone in the voting booth,

76. *Report of the COG*, 210–19; Chan, *Observers Group*, 77; Renwick, *Unconventional Diplomacy*, 90. Caute found these more subtle than the UANC advertisements from late February; *Under the Skin*, 415–16.

77. COG, Correspondence with Governor, February 23, 1980, CWSec/COG/51/B-8; Hills, *Last Days*, 168–69; Caute, *Under the Skin*, 418. The police investigated and found no evidence that police were involved in the forgery. N. K. Macaulay, Superintendent, Moto Newspaper: Pirate edition, February 24, 1980, in *Report of the COG*, 221–24.

78. Bruce L. Kinzer, "The Un-Englishness of the Secret Ballot," *Albion, A Quarterly J. Concerned with British Studies* 10, no. 3 (1978): 237–56; Guy S. Goodwin-Gill, *Free and Fair Elections: International Law and Practice* (Geneva: Inter-Parliamentary Union, 1994), 73–74; Frank O'Gorman, "The Secret Ballot in Nineteenth-Century Britain," and John Crowley, "The Uses and Abuses of the Secret Ballot in the American Age of Reform," in Bertrand et. al., *Secret Ballot*, 16–42, 43–68.

to make a decision about how he or she would be governed. Making this decision away from the pressures of tradition or local politics was to transform the voter: members of communities would join nations, and tribesmen would become citizens. The men and women who emerged from the private booth, who marked their ballots in secret, were ready for democratic government.[79] In 1980, however, after many elections in Africa, the transformation was not so much of individuals as it was of the polity itself. The secret ballot was not understood to change individuals but was part of a set of practices—sealed ballot boxes, fixed polling places, party representatives kept at bay—that was to change the state itself, to make it democratic.[80] This is why so many observers found the 1980 election to be something akin to free and fair: because it was conducted with the practices that were necessary for democratic elections, not because of history and certainly not because of current events. And this is why the demand to nullify the 1980 election because of violence and intimidation could do nothing more than demand a return to the rule of whites.

The secret ballot contained a range of practices that were both protective and coercive, however. It made literacy essential to the vote, as voters were alone in the booth.[81] As historians of Europe and North America have begun to elaborate on the importance of the secret ballot as a colonial phenomenon—its first modern use was in Australia in 1856—historians of former colonies have begun to suggest that the deployment of the secret ballot followed local ideas about political participation and the place of the individual therein.[82] In Tanganyika's election of 1958 the government produced colorful ballots for illiterates and aggressively policed who could enter a polling station. There were private voting booths through which voters circulated quickly, as they were required only to make a mark on the ballot paper. In the last colonial election in Kenya, shortly after the end of the state of emergency, the government maintained a secret ballot by swearing everyone to an oath

79. Lindberg, *Democracy and Elections*, 19–20; Young, "Elections in Africa"; Malcolm Crook and Tom Crook, "Reforming Voting Practices in a Global Age: The Making and Remaking of the Modern Secret Ballot in Britain, France, and the United States, c.1600–c.1950," *Past and Present* 212 (2011): 200; Peter Pels, "Imagining Elections: Modernity, Mediation and the Secret Ballot in Late-Colonial Tanganyika," in Bertrand et. al., *Hidden History*. 105; Justin Willis and Atta el Battahani, "'We Changed the Laws': Electoral Practice and Malpractice in Sudan since 1953," *African Affairs* 109, no. 435: 195–212; Gilmartin, "Global History of Voting," 407–23.

80. Young, "Elections in Africa," 299–313.

81. Keyssar, *The Right to Vote*, 114–15.

82. Crook and Crook, "Making and Remaking of the Modern Secret Ballot," 200; Peter Pels, "Imagining Elections," 100–113; Gilmartin, "Global History of Voting," 407–23.

of secrecy upon entering the polling station. In Sudan under military rule, the secret ballot was used alongside ballot boxes marked for specific parties or for a "yes" or "no" on referenda. The government called both practices democratic.[83] In the case of Zimbabwe's—or Rhodesia's—1980 election, the secret ballot was given the power to correct for the abuses of the campaign: if no one could know how someone voted, it did not matter if he or she had been threatened or intimidated.

How then do we assess the import of the secret ballot to Africans in 1980? In the universalist narrative the secret ballot sits astride local practices; the local narrative is more difficult to discern, especially since most African voters had voted only once before, if that. African ideas about the secret ballot had been part of the discourse of minority and majority rule for almost twenty-five years. It is possible to read in the early chapters of this book that Africans' "desire" for a secret ballot, as noted by federal franchise committees, became demands for private voting booths—or at least ones with doors on them—in the NDP referendum of 1961.[84] It took the politics of the 1969 constitution for the Rhodesian Front to imagine that Africans never ventured a political opinion, unless they did so in public to dispute their chiefs. By February 1980, after months of leaflets and films, there was no question that Africans understood the import of the secret ballot to election officials. "Almost everyone" told the election commissioners that they themselves were satisfied that their vote would be secret but that they knew "many" who worried that their vote could become known.[85] Election observers in 1980, intent on showing a new democracy at work, may have lost sight of the ways in which the secret ballot operated alongside the importance of public statements of affiliation and fidelity that were the cultural logic of the ordeal, the boisterous meetings of the Pearce Commission and the pungwe. I do not want to draw a straight line between 1908 and 1980, or even between 1972 and 1980, but was Africans' use of the secret ballot their eager participation in universal democratic processes, the only way they expressed political choices?

83. Crook and Crook, "Reforming Voting Practices," 199–201, 208; Pels, "Imagining Elections," 108; Bennett and Rosberg, *The Kenyatta Election*, 75; Willis and el Battahani, "'We Changed the Laws,'" 195–96, 204–6.

84. In 1961 voters did not object to the ballots left lying around in some polling stations. "Heavy Polling in NDP Referendum Reported: Firm 'No' Vote Expected," *Central African Daily News*, July 24, 1961, 2–4.

85. Women assured the commissioners that they would make up their own minds about how to vote, however their husbands might instruct them. *Boynton Report*, 14.

CHAPTER ELEVEN

General Walls and Mrs. Thatcher, Part 2

Even before the voting began, there were pleas and attempts to postpone it, and once voting was underway, attempts to disregard the vote. In early February, when Nkomo first asked Soames to postpone the elections, he said no. Two weeks later the idea appealed to the governor, at least for the specific areas in which Nkomo's party could not campaign.[86] By then Soames knew of Walls's latest threatening scenario, in which a demoralized Muzorewa would quit the race and his men, the auxiliaries, would join ZANU(PF). This would guarantee a "Mugabe government," Walls said, which would leave the security forces with no choice other than to resume the fighting. Sir Anthony Duff, the deputy governor, seems to have taken this seriously, but he proposed another strategy. There could be "some comparatively minor action" that would either postpone the election or abrogate the results in one or two areas. He hoped this would prevent Walls from denouncing the elections as unfree and unfair. And if Mugabe were deprived of a few seats it might improve the "political/psychological atmosphere after the election."[87]

For whom was the "political/psychological atmosphere" an issue in February? The Rhodesian Front had already won all twenty seats in the white voters' roll election on February 14, and Walls was, more often than not, given the political status of head of the white community. It was Walls, not David Smith or Muzorewa—and certainly not Ian Smith—who was invited to Mozambique in February to consult with Machel, who arranged for him to meet with Mugabe.[88] Upon his return, Walls, along with Ken Flower of the CIO, was summoned to a meeting by Muzorewa and Ian Smith, who wanted to discuss the possibility of declaring the Lancaster House agreement null and void. If that was not possible, Smith and Muzorewa wanted to know if there was a way to postpone the elections; if that was not possible was there a means to reinstate Muzorewa's government, perhaps by involving Nkomo in it. Much to the relief of Soames and his staff, Walls wanted to go ahead with the elections, possibly in response to the optimistic report by the CIO that Muzorewa had great support in the townships and among workers on

---

86. Soames, Salisbury to FCO, Rhodesia: Nkomo's views, February 5, 1980; Soames, Salisbury, to FCO, Rhodesia: Nkomo's views, February 19, 1980; TNA/PREM19/345.

87. Soames, Salisbury, to FCO, February 21, 1980, TNA/PREM19/345.

88. Machel was eager to tell Walls that Mugabe was not a Marxist. Soames, Salisbury, to FCO, Rhodesia/Mozambique January 18, 1980, TNA/PREM19/343; Doble, Maputo to FCO, February 21, 1980, TNA/PREM19/345.

European-owned farms. Muzorewa and Smith knew they could do nothing without the support of the army.[89] Even as the voting took place, Mugabe had a "constructive" meeting with Soames to discuss plans creating a new national army out of three that existed now. He was relieved that Soames would not void election results in any area, despite the intimidation. Almost in passing, Mugabe said a "natural coalition" government would be with Nkomo but that he was "perfectly ready" to include Muzorewa.[90] The next day, the last day of voting, Mugabe told Soames that most of the intimidation was done by Muzorewa's men, his men second, and Nkomo's a close third.[91] Also on that day Nkomo met with Soames's staff to talk about possible coalitions. Nkomo was adamant that he would reject any coalition with Mugabe, who had broken an alliance with him and prevented his party from campaigning. Nkomo was confident he had the support of the twenty white members of parliament, and he had already scheduled meetings with the most fervent Muzorewa supporters among them, including David Smith. He personally would welcome a coalition with the UANC; the problem was Muzorewa, who "was not acceptable elsewhere in Africa."[92]

On March 1, the day before the results were announced, Walls wrote to Thatcher. The broadly genial tone of their conversation in December was replaced by angry specifics. Lord Soames had been "inadequate" as governor, unwilling to "rely on us for advice" or even to treat Rhodesian commanders—by which he meant himself—as if they had a special status, as if their firepower had not driven the Patriotic Front to Lancaster House. Soames's failure to act in the best interests of "a moderate, freedom-loving and anti-marxist society" allowed hundreds of left-wing and "definitely anti-Muzorewa" observers into the country, all of whom contributed to the "emotional and hysterical wave" of propaganda leveled against the security forces. Because of "the sheer terror accepted pathetically by your representatives," a Mugabe victory was very likely. Walls could provide evidence of intimidation, but he wished Thatcher could see "the sullen hurt and misery in the eyes and faces of our black

---

89. Hudson, *Triumph or Tragedy*, 188–89; Renwick, *Unconventional Diplomacy*, 93–94.

90. Soames, Salisbury, to FCO, Meeting with Mugabe, February 27, 1980, TNA/PREM19/345. The decision to count all votes from all districts was not made easily, Soames told the FCO, but he did not want to give "external critics," especially the frontline states, any excuse not to pronounce elections free and fair; Soames, Salisbury to FCO, Rhodesian elections, February 25, 1980, TNA/PREM19/345.

91. Soames, Salisbury, to FCO, Meeting with Mugabe, February 27, 1980, TNA/PREM19/345.

92. Soames, Salisbury, to FCO, Rhodesia, February 28, 1980, TNA/PREM19/345. Nyerere at least had told the British high commissioner that he would accept a Muzorewa government if it was elected freely and fairly. Moon, Dar es Salaam, to FCO, February 23, 1980, TNA/PREM19/345.

people, who are normally so cheerful, good natured, and full of good will."

Walls proposed three scenarios. First, if ZANU(PF) won a simple majority of seats—fifty-one or more—or if enough defectors from other parties joined it to make a majority, then in order for "a free nation" to survive Thatcher should declare the election null and void because of the massive intimidation that frustrated the free choice of the people. Second, if ZANU(PF) got fewer than fifty seats the British should support a coalition government with Mugabe, Muzorewa, Nkomo, and Smith, which would be encouraged to use every effort, "overt or devious," to oust Mugabe and his supporters. Third, if the election were declared null and void, or if moderate parties were not able to form a working coalition, the British should remain to run the country—as a council of ministers, perhaps—and allow the security forces to provide safe passage for "people of all races" who wished to take "refuge" in South Africa or elsewhere. This third scenario contained a threat. Walls wrote that the continued British presence would be preferable to his taking "unconstitutional action," which would not only be dangerous but was "loathsome" to the professional soldier. However, if Thatcher was unable to honor the bond between them, Walls reserved the right to take whatever action necessary to protect the interests of the people he had pledged to serve.[93]

Here, perhaps, is where Rhodesian independence ended. Did Walls imagine that a coup would be possible, let alone plausible in 1980? Did he think his fawning conversation with Thatcher the previous December meant that there was any support for the remnants of the Rhodesian Front, or that majority rule could be delayed? The politics imagined by Walls were not even wholly supported within Rhodesia, but his sense of the range of possibilities available to a military in Africa in the first months of 1980 revealed the true extremes of Rhodesian independence and how impossible they had become.

As if to underscore this point, Thatcher did not directly reply. Instead she and Carrington drafted instructions on how Soames and Duff should respond. The first drafts defended Soames and did not hesitate to call the elections free and fair. Thatcher presented two possible outcomes of the election. First, ZANU(PF) got fewer than forty seats and a moderate coalition was possible. In the second, ZANU(PF) won an absolute majority, in which case Mugabe would head a national government in which

93. Walls, Salisbury, to Thatcher, March 1, 1980, TNA/PREM19/346.

all parties were represented. In the first and second drafts, Thatcher responded to Walls's threat. Any action that overturned the election results would have grave consequences, and Walls should not claim South African support he might not have. She had heard of various plans that security forces would attack ZANLA in the assembly places in the event of a Mugabe landslide, but she did not think this would actually happen.[94] The second draft became the final version of Thatcher's response, delivered orally by Duff and Renwick after the election results were known. It did not initially calm Walls. He seemed unconcerned by the judgment of the electoral commission or that the prime minister categorically refused to invalidate the election results, arguing that the British had allowed the intimidation that brought about Muzorewa's defeat. When some of his commanders said they thought Muzorewa could not have won in any event, Walls changed tactics at once. He told Renwick and Duff that there was a danger of a white exodus if ZANU(PF) formed a government, and civil servants, including Africans, feared for their pensions. Could Soames stay on? This was a time for calm and "reconciliation," Duff said; he assured Walls that the British would help with pensions and that the governor would stay as long as Mugabe requested.

On March 4, when the election results were announced, Walls requested a meeting with Renwick. He now claimed that he had rejected pressure from elements of the security forces and the Rhodesian Front to prevent a Mugabe-led government, but he needed to be confident that the British intended to make sure Mugabe formed a broadly based government. Otherwise many whites would leave right away. If there were the proper assurances from the governor Walls was sure he could convince most whites to do what he was planning to do, to stay on for six months and then evaluate the situation. Renwick did not argue with him: the governor was already working to exert his influence to make sure Nkomo was given a senior position in the government. Walls hoped that a senior white politician, perhaps David Smith, could be in the government. Renwick could not speak to that issue, but asked if Walls would oversee the integration of the forces. Walls was pleased; he did not ask that Soames stay on after the independence ceremonies.[95]

94. Carrington, FCO, to Soames, Salisbury, Rhodesia: Message from General Walls, March 2, 1980; R. M. J. Lyme, prime minister's secretary, to FCO, March 3, 1980, TNA/PREM19/346.

95. Soames, Salisbury, to FCO, Rhodesia: formation of the government, March 4, 1980, TNA/PREM19/346.

Nkomo's first response to learning the vote was to telephone Soames, who found him "severely shaken," threatening to leave the country. Soames scheduled a meeting with him the next day to do all he could to encourage him to join Mugabe's government.[96] And indeed, a few days later Mugabe met with Nkomo to decide which ministries would go to ZAPU, which had stopped calling itself the Patriotic Front. Mugabe was committed to bringing Europeans into the cabinet as well, although "not necessarily from the Rhodesian Front."[97] In the first government of Zimbabwe Nkomo became minister for home affairs. Mugabe appointed two Rhodesian Front stalwarts to the cabinet: Dennis Norman minister for agriculture and David Smith, already negotiating loans with Britain, minister of finance.[98] Was Mugabe pressured by the governor and his staff? Was he eager to establish a national government to rule with a party that remained weaker than its army? Certainly he borrowed liberally from the FCO: "reconciliation," for example, was a favorite term in the cable traffic from London in early March. On more than one occasion Soames called for "calm, reconciliation, and the like."[99]

The Postwar and the Postelection

There are many accounts of white Rhodesians' shock and chagrin when they learned of Mugabe's victory.[100] These stories turned out not to have much traction, however, as whites in the 1980s learned to speak well, or at least to speak well when in the presence of foreigners, of the man they had hated. Farmers who had said they would leave if ZANU(PF) came to power now said they would leave if Mugabe left; others said it was the best government they had ever known.[101] The stories that carried weight and were perhaps more commonly told are those of Walls's unrealized

96. FCO to Soames, Salisbury, Rhodesia: Message from General Walls, March 3, 1980, TNA/PREM19/346.

97. Soames, Salisbury, to FCO, Rhodesia: press, March 7, 1980, TNA/PREM19/346.

98. Nkomo, *My Life*, 212–13; FCO to Soames, Salisbury, Aid for Zimbabwe and Rhodesian Debt, February 7, 1980, TNA/PREM19/344; Privy Council Office, London, Rhodesia, March 17, 1980, TNA/PREM19/346.

99. Soames, Salisbury, to FCO, Rhodesia: formation of the government, March 3, 1980, TNA/PREM19/346.

100. See, for example, Hills, *Last Days*, 175–77; Caute, *Under the Skin*, 424–25.

101. Robin Palmer, "Land Reform in Zimbabwe, 1980–1990," *African Affairs* 89, no. 355 (1990): 163–81; Michael Kandiah and Sue Onslow, eds., *Britain and Rhodesia: The Route to Settlement* (London: Centre for Contemporary British History, 2008), 107–8. By 1990, the monthly magazine of the National Farmers Union counseled its members to be "positive and optimistic" when speaking with journalists. See Pilossof, *Unbearable Whiteness*, 89.

and unrealistic threat, the coup or the attack that would keep Mugabe from ever taking office. There are accounts of assassination plots called off.[102] There were rumors of contingency plans drawn up in January to protect Muzorewa and Nkomo should they win enough seats to form a coalition. There may or may not have been an Operation Quartz, the supposed coup planned for March 4 in which security forces would take over the country and attack ZANLA in their assembly places. Certainly many police and soldiers thought there was a coup planned. "All day, we cleaned our weapons and waited for the code word 'quartz' to be transmitted on the radio" but in vain.[103] And there was the story of the South African plot to assassinate Mugabe—and Soames, Carrington, and Prince Charles should they be in the motorcade—as he went to the independence ceremonies. Uncovered by the same CIO that predicted a Muzorewa victory, it never happened.[104]

The confusion about whether a coup was planned or not was intensified in August 1980 when Walls gave two speeches in South Africa. In one he said that as a professional soldier he would never consider a coup, and in the other that as an individual citizen he would exercise his right to say or do anything to halt the advance of Marxism. The British press and Zimbabwe parliamentarians announced details of this possible coup and then denounced each other for announcing those details, but Walls was banned from Zimbabwe in September.[105] These stories are of a piece with a literature about brilliant Rhodesian strategies curtailed by international politics, but they also serve as a reminder of the military takeover of what was left of Rhodesia.

102. Stiff, *See You*, 347–49.
103. Lemon, *Never Quite a Soldier*, 261; Peter Claypole, Harare, October 26, 1988, NAZ/OH/321.
104. Jim Parker, *Assignment Selous Scouts: Inside Story of a Rhodesian Special Branch Officer* (Alberton: Galago, 2006), 213–18.
105. Pat Scully, *Exit Rhodesia* (Ladysmith: Cotswold Press, 1984), 189–93.

TWELVE

"People such as ourselves": Rhodesia, Rhonasia, and the History of Zimbabwe

Announcing UDI to the nation, Ian Smith made all sorts of complaints and predictions. He attacked decolonization, which created "the absurd situation" in which "people such as ourselves, who have ruled ourselves with an impressive record for over forty years" were not given the independence so casually given to countries that had not even had self-government for a year. Rhodesians might "be a small country but we are a determined people who have been called upon to play a role of world-wide significance." This was standard fare for announcements of independence, except for the curious construction of just what a vague category the newly independent people were. The people who called themselves Rhodesians in the mid-1960s also called themselves pioneers, Britons, the only true Britons left, Britons' kith and kin, Spartans, the last good white man left, and as African as any black man. Aside from "belongers"— people who were born there or were the children of men who were—almost none of these people were eager to become citizens of Rhodesia if it meant giving up any other citizenship. Earlier in the speech, Smith declared that "the mantle of the pioneers has fallen on our shoulders" to preserve civilization, as if "people such as ourselves" just had to be in residence to be up to the task. And for political purposes, "people such as ourselves" included Africans, not only the chiefs and disgruntled trade unionists who supported UDI but the men who campaigned for settlement in 1972. I do not want to belabor a point I have made many times in this book, but without Africans to participate, however superficially, in the Rhodesian Front regime there were simply not enough whites to claim any significance at all, as the continual references to Aberdeen and Portsmouth make clear.

Any good nationalist speech would make grand claims, of course, and by the standards of Rhodesian Front apparatchiks' speeches in 1965, this one was modest. The claims to heroic roles and worldwide significance were those of standing firm against "appeasement," of being "the first Western nation in the last twenty years to have the determination and fortitude to say: So far and no further."[1] Rhodesia's responsible government and civilization—Christianity, working phones, the qualified franchise—did not give Rhodesia a place in the world as much as they underscored the absurdity of their situation: Rhodesia was unlike anywhere else in British Africa in the mid-1960s. Rhodesia was the suburb masquerading as a nation, the country whose agents would soon pretend their reconnaissance planes belonged to the Malagasy Fisheries Surveillance Team. Rhodesia mattered because it was so literally reactionary, so firmly located in past ideas that no one in the Rhodesian Front fully interrogated, and because it lasted as long as it did. Rhodesia did not survive because of its ideology or its friends abroad, and in all likelihood not because of the strength of its military; it survived because it was something close to pragmatic. Rhodesia's policies, particularly in regard to Africans and the entire question of race, were situational; they were worked out in order to better segregate parks and swimming pools and as a way to make sure white children with one "creole" grandparent could attend a whites-only government school. Rhodesia's policies about the inclusion of Africans into political and social life were not made off the cuff, so to speak, but they were made up as the country went along. If there was an ideology it was a hodgepodge, of John Stuart Mill and Harry Reedman and Henry Kissinger and the man who told the 1960 constitutional commission that Africans could not draw a straight line. When it was strategic, as in the 1979 election, the Rhodesian Front promoted one man, one vote.

1. Smith, *Betrayal*, 104–6.

Rhodesia and Rhonasia

I began this book writing against the linear Rhodesia-into-Zimbabwe story, the narrative of progress in which the past racial practices were defeated and an independent country ruled by its African majority came into being, a state that was finally a nation. It is not just that the many names of Rhodesia complicate this, but that the entire history of 1965 to 1980, with negotiations and settlement plans that were sometimes insincere and sometimes desperate, suggests that no straight line is possible, that there were tendrils and fissures and openings and closings (many, many closings). The significance of Rhodesia lay only partly in its increasingly harsh racial policies. These cannot be separated from its years of painstaking honing of the franchise so that it could articulate Africans' difference to the point that in 1969 Africans were removed from the institutions of representative government altogether. Rhodesia's history is one of an army enough at odds with the state that it eventually took over the state, but so late in the processes of dismantling Rhodesia that it misjudged its own significance, local or worldwide. Rhodesia's history of white privilege was not simply privileging ordinary white people but rather privileging their ordinary lives: the civil servants who could best be encouraged by attractive women at home and at work, the schoolgirls in Umtali, and the schoolboys willing to do national service until they could go abroad for university. It is the history, short as it was, of Rhonasia, of ideas about place and belonging that were thought to transcend race.

Rhonasia, we should recall, was an effort to save the Central African Federation. There is no plausible story of the federation-to-Zimbabwe, and no possible story of Rhonasia-to-Zimbabwe. The story of Rhonasia to Rhodesia, however, would have told us just how literally reactionary Rhodesian Front rule was, how strenuously it rejected ideas of multi-racialism and nonracialism in order to govern the people they called "themselves" as they had never done in the past—even those who had been in Rhodesia in the past—with constitutional guarantees that not only limited African participation in politics but limited African political aspirations. What makes Rhonasia so important, and why I have chosen to bracket this book with it, is that it marks the early history of decolonization, a failed experiment in territories and the place of races therein that gave way to majority rule and to Rhodesia's UDI. Smith's speech was clear on this point: It was Britain, not Rhodesia, that "rejected the possibility of racial harmony in Africa. The responsibility for the break-up of the Central African Federation was Great Britain's alone. Their experiment failed," and now Britain demanded that Africans rule Rhodesia.[2] In Rhodesia, as in Northern Rhodesia and Nyasaland, expanding the African franchise would have meant majority rule. The breakup of the federation forced the hand of the white-ruled nation-state.[3]

The History of Zimbabwe

The history of Zimbabwe is Rhodesia. This has produced its own historiography, which is that of colonial Zimbabwe, a history of Rhodesia written with the concerns and questions of what was done to Africans in that time and place and how Africans struggled against it. In this historiography the coming of majority rule in 1980 was the same as decolonization.[4] In much of this literature, the history of Zimbabwe begins at Lancaster House, where good deals were exchanged for bad deals for which modern Zimbabwe paid the price. One of the things that distressed me as I wrote this book was that several scholars seemed to believe Robert Mugabe's boast that he secured one man, one vote democracy instead of getting a guarantee on land redistribution.[5] The very notion that the Patriotic Front delegation or anyone else in 1979 bargained in order to bring one man, one vote to postwar Zimbabwe should alert us that something is seriously wrong, that the scholarly world of Zimbabwean history is almost completely cut off from that of late colonialism. Central to the exploding demands for citizenship among Africans after World War II was the right to vote, and the right to be elected. Colonial officials were often in favor of this: they saw in an expanded franchise party politics that could provide a pathway around politics that were essentially racial or ethnic. This gave rise to the "clever fancy franchise" Nkomo decried, one of many elaborate reckonings of income and literacy to make sure some Africans could be elected

---

2. Smith, *Betrayal*, 105.

3. For a very important discussion of how un-inevitable the nation-state was in decolonizing Africa, see Cooper, *Africa and the World*, 66–89.

4. Terence Ranger has expressed concern about the invention of new histories of Zimbabwe. In one of these tendencies the liberation war and the ruling party are the wellspring of national history; another proposes a deeper history in which African culture is rich with deep ancestral memories and a made-up period of Portuguese rule. See "Nationalist Historiography, Patriotic History and the History of the Nation: The Struggle over the Past in Zimbabwe," *J. Southern African Studies* 30, no. 2 (2004): 215–34.

5. Charlton, *Last Colony*, 79–80; Bond, *Zimbabwe's Plunge*, 77; Compagnon, *Predictable Tragedy*, 79, 167.

to represent Africans in colonial assemblies. By the mid-1960s an expanded franchise became the natural logic of decolonization, promoted by former colonial powers and the UN as the foundation of democracy. It was also hoped that an expanded franchise would, if there was a large enough turnout, marginalize extremists, the very boast Whitehead made so mistakenly after the referendum on the 1961 constitution. The expanded franchise was to allow for other restrictive practices to come to the fore—two voting rolls, multiple preference voting, fractional voting—but the idea of universal suffrage was firmly in place years before anyone from the Patriotic Front set foot in Lancaster House.

Can we imagine a history of Zimbabwe that includes Rhodesia beyond the catalog of racial affronts and assaults on rights? Can we imagine a history of Zimbabwe that predates Lancaster House? As Zimbabwe has spiraled downward, as what seemed so special and heroic came to look like any other sad and impoverished African country, scholars have looked to the conduct of the guerrilla war or Rhodesian Front to see the origins of decline and the source of misrule. Whoever is blamed in this either/or narrative, it seems to be a fairly insidious example of what Frederick Cooper has called "leapfrogging," a writing of colonial history in broad and casually ahistorical brushstrokes, in which scholars link two processes without paying attention to what happened in the twenty or thirty years between them.[6] In Zimbabwean historiography the frog seems to have leapt in a very straight line. To use a commonplace example, ZANU(PF) won the 1980 election by coercion and intimidation and won the 2008 election by coercion and intimidation.[7] I do not necessarily disagree with this assertion, but I fear that it simplifies the past in order to establish a line of argument that is, by the very process by which it came into being, a simplification.

Is another kind of history possible? Can the history of Rhodesian independence, abhorrent racial policies included, encourage a complication of Zimbabwe's past? Can the history of independent Zimbabwe begin with the decolonization of the rest of Africa, the very politics that generated Rhodesian independence and that had been over long enough for Carrington and the FCO to doubt that whatever happened at Lancaster House would be "ideal"? There are several ways to approach this—the role of the party in the civil service and the making of "uncivil

---

6. Frederick Cooper, *Colonialism in Question: Theory, Knowledge, History* (Berkeley: University of California Press, 2005), 17–18.

7. For a thorough study of the 2008 election, see the aptly titled *Defying the Winds of Change: Zimbabwe's 2008 Elections*, ed. E. V. Masunungure (Harare: Weaver Press, 2009).

society" come to mind—but none may be as important as beginning the history of Zimbabwe with the constitutions of late colonialism and the many times they were revised. The franchise commissions that sought to do away with racial politics imagined, or imagined someone believed they imagined, that they could allocate rights based on differences that were historically constituted but were not really about race. None of these commissions or conferences or constitutions managed to make race irrelevant, of course, but they ushered in a kind of constitution writing that shaped politics in the region for at least fourteen years and probably more. The constitutions that succeeded the 1961 constitution were drafted with the idea that constitutions were themselves expedients, a way to use rights for Africans to bargain with or mollify an international audience to achieve a specific end. Each of these constitutions had carefully worked out rights for Africans and when and how often these could be exercised, and each one contained the means to constrain Africans' ability to exercise those rights.

Bibliography

Government and Other Official Reports

Advisory Committee on the Review of the Constitution of the
    Federation and Nyasaland. *Report and Appendix VIII. Evidence.*
    Vol. IV. Cmnd. 1151-III. London: HMSO, 1960.
Boynton, Sir John. *Southern Rhodesia Independence Elections 1980:
    Report of the Electoral Commissioner,* London: HMSO, 1980.
Commonwealth Secretariat. *Southern Rhodesia Elections, February
    1980: The Report of the Commonwealth Observer Group on the
    Elections Leading to Independent Zimbabwe.* London: Common-
    wealth Secretariat, 1980.
Government of Rhodesia. *Report of the Constitutional Commission,
    1968.* Salisbury: Government Printer, April 1968.
——. *Proposals for a Settlement.* November 25, 1971. Salisbury:
    Government Printer, 1971.
Government of Rhodesia, Central Office of Statistics. *Rhodesia: In-
    come Tax Statistics: Analysis of Assessments and Loss. Statements
    issued during fiscal year 1968–69.* Salisbury: mimeo., October
    1969.
Joint Committee on Foreign Affairs and Defence. *Zimbabwe (May
    1980).* Canberra: Australian Government Printing Service,
    1980.
*Report of the Commission on Rhodesian Opinion under the Chairman-
    ship of the Right Honourable Lord Pearce.* Cmnd. 4964. London:
    HMSO, 1972.
Southern Rhodesia. *Report of the Franchise Commission.* Salisbury:
    Government Printer, 1957.
——. *Documents relating to the negotiations between the United
    Kingdom and Southern Rhodesian Governments, November
    1963–November 1965.* Presented to parliament, November
    1965. Cmnd. 2807. London: HMSO, 1965.

Published Materials

Achebe, Chinua. *There Was a Country: A Personal History of Biafra*. New York: Penguin, 2012.

Akyeampong, Emmanual K. "Race, Identity and Citizenship in Black Africa: The Case of the Lebanese in Ghana." *Africa* 76, no. 3 (2006): 297–322.

Alexander, Jocelyn. *The Unsettled Land: State-Making and the Politics of Land in Zimbabwe, 1893–2003*. Oxford: James Currey, 2006.

———, Joann McGregor, and Terence Ranger. *Violence and Memory: One Hundred Years in the 'Dark Forests' of Matabeleland*. Oxford: James Currey, 2000.

Allman, Jean Marie. *The Quills of the Porcupine: Asante Nationalism in Emergent Ghana*. Madison: University of Wisconsin Press, 1993.

Alport, Lord Cuthbert. *The Sudden Assignment: Central Africa 1961–63*. London: Hodder & Stoughton, 1965.

Anderson, Benedict. *Imagined Communities: Reflections on the Origins and Spread of Nationalism*. Rev. ed. London: Verso, 1991.

Anderson, Daphne. *The Toe-Rags: The Story of a Strange Up-Bringing in Southern Rhodesia*. London: Andre Deutsch, 1989.

Anderson, David. *Histories of the Hanged: The Dirty War in Kenya and the End of Empire*. New York: W. W. Norton, 2005.

———. " 'Yours in Struggle for Majimbo': Nationalism and the Party Politics of Decolonization in Kenya, 1955–64." *Journal of Contemporary History* 46, no. 3 (2005): 547–64.

Anderson, Jervis. *Bayard Rustin: Troubles I've Seen*. New York: Harper Collins, 1997.

Anderson, Warwick. *The Construction of Whiteness: Science, Health and Racial Destiny in Australia*. Melbourne: University of Melbourne Press, 2002.

Andreas, Peter. "Criminalizing Consequences of Sanctions: Embargo Busting and Its Legacy." *International Studies Quarterly* 49 (2005): 335–60.

Anghie, Anthony. *Imperialism, Sovereignty, and the Making of International Law*. Cambridge: Cambridge University Press, 2004.

Anglin, Douglas. "International Election Monitoring: the African Experience." *African Affairs* 97, no. 389 (1998): 471–95.

Anonymous. "Rhodesia: ANC and Others." *Africa Confidential* 13, no. 10 (May 19, 1972): 6–7.

———. "Rhodesia: Distant Prospects." *Africa Confidential* 13, no. 16 (August 11, 1972): 6–7.

———. "Zimbabwe Rhodesia: Conference Calculations," and "Zimbabwe: The Election Conundrum." *Africa Confidential* 20, no. 25 (December 12, 1979): 1–2.

Anthony, Douglas. " 'Resourceful and Progressive Blackmen': Modernity and Race in Biafra, 1967–68." *Journal of African History* 51, no. 1 (2010): 410–61.

Anti-Apartheid Movement. *Fireforce Exposed: The Rhodesian Security Forces and Their Role in Defending White Supremacy*. London: Anti-Apartheid Movement, 1979.

Armstrong, Peter. *Operation Zambezi: The Raid into Zambia*. Salisbury: Welston Press, 1979.

———. *Tobacco Spiced with Ginger: The Life of Ginger Freeman*. Harare: Welston Press, 1987.

Arnold, W. E. *The Goldbergs of Leigh Ranch*. Bulawayo: Books of Rhodesia, 1980.

Arsenault, Raymond. "White Chrome: Southern Congressmen and Rhodesia, 1962–71." *Issue: A Journal of Opinion* 3, no. 4 (1972): 46–57.

Atkins, Graham. *Once Upon a White Man: A Memoir of War and Peace in Africa*. Perth: n.p., 2008.

Auerbach, Sascha. "Negotiating Nationalism: Jewish Conscription and Russian Repatriation in London's East End, 1916–1918." *Journal of British Studies* 46, no. 3 (2007): 594–620.

Auret, Diana. *Reaching for Justice: The Catholic Commission for Justice and Peace*. Gweru: Mambo Press, 1992.

Bailey, Beth. *America's Army: Making an All-Volunteer Force*. Cambridge, MA: Harvard University Press, 2009.

Bailey, Martin. *Oilgate: The Sanctions Scandal*. London: Coronet Books, 1979.

Bailkin, Jordanna. *The Afterlife of Empire*. Berkeley: University of California Press, 2012.

Balibar, Etienne. "Propositions on Citizenship." *Ethics* 98 (1988): 723–30.

Barlow, James. *Goodbye, England*. London: Hamish Hamilton, 1969.

Bax, Tim. *Three Sips of Gin: Dominating the Battlespace with Rhodesia's Elite Selous Scouts*. Solihull: Helion, 2013.

Bennett, George, and Carl Rosberg. *The Kenyatta Election: Kenya 1960–1961*. Nairobi: Oxford University Press, 1961.

Berlyn, Phillipa. *The Quiet Man: A Biography of Ian Douglas Smith, I. D. Prime Minister of Rhodesia*. Salisbury: M. O. Collins, 1978.

Bernstein, Iver. *The New York City Draft Riots*. New York: Oxford University Press, 1990.

Bertrand, Romain, Jean-Louis Briquet, and Peter Pels, eds. *The Hidden History of the Secret Ballot*. Bloomington: Indiana University Press, 2006.

Bhebe, Ngwabi. *Simon Vengayi Muzenda and the Struggle for the Liberation of Zimbabwe*. Gweru: Mambo Press, 2004.

———, and T. Ranger, eds. *Soldiers in Zimbabwe's Liberation War*. Harare: University of Zimbabwe Press, 1995.

Binda, Alex. *Masodja: The History of the Rhodesian African Rifles and Its Forerunner the Rhodesia Native Regiment*. Johannesburg: 30 Degrees South, 2007.

———. *The Saints: The Rhodesian Light Infantry*. Johannesburg: 30 Degrees South, 2007.

Blake, Robert. *A History of Rhodesia*. London: Eyre Metheun, 1977.

Bond, Geoffrey. *The Incredibles: The Story of the 1st Battalion, the Rhodesian Light Infantry*. Salisbury: Sarum Imprint, 1977.

Bond, Patrick. *Uneven Zimbabwe: A Study of Finance, Development and Underdevelopment*. Trenton, NJ: Africa World Press, 1998.

————, and Msimba Manyanya. *Zimbabwe's Plunge: Exhausted Nationalism, Neoliberalism and the Search for Social Justice*. Pietermaritzburg: University of Natal Press, 2002.

Borstelmann, Thomas. *The Cold War and the Color Line*. Cambridge, MA: Harvard University Press, 2005.

Bowman, Larry W. "Organization, Power and Decision-Making with the Rhodesian Front." *Journal of Commonwealth Political Studies* 7 (1968): 145–65.

————. "Strains in the Rhodesian Front." *Africa Report* 13, no. 9 (1968): 16–22.

————. *Politics in Rhodesia: White Power in an African State*. Cambridge, MA: Harvard University Press, 1973.

Bozniak, Linda. *The Citizen and the Alien: Dilemmas of Contemporary Membership*. Princeton, NJ: Princeton University Press, 2012.

Bradbury, Mark. *Becoming Somaliland*. Oxford: James Currey, 2008.

Brennan, James R. *Taifa: Making Nation and Race in Urban Tanzania*. Athens: Ohio University Press, 2012.

Brent, Winston. *Rhodesian Air Force: The Sanctions Busters*. Nelspruit: Freeworld Publications, 2001.

Brinkley, Douglas. *Dean Acheson: The Cold War Years, 1953–71*. New Haven, CT: Yale University Press, 1992.

Brivati, Brian. *Lord Goodman*. London: Richard Cohen, 1999.

Brookfield, F. M. "The Courts, Kelsen, and the Rhodesian Revolution." *University of Toronto Law Journal* 19, no. 3 (1969): 326–52.

Brownell, Josiah. " 'A Sordid Tussle on the Strand': Rhodesia House during the UDI Rebellion (1965–80)." *Journal of Imperial and Commonwealth History* 38, no. 3 (2010): 471–99.

————. *The Collapse of Rhodesia: Population Demographics and the Politics of Race*. London: I. B. Taurus, 2011.

Brubaker, W. Rogers. "Citizenship Struggles in Successor States." *International Migration Review* 26, no. 2 (1992): 269–91.

————. "Migration, Membership, and the Modern Nation-State: Internal and External Dimensions of the Politics of Belonging." *Journal of Interdisciplinary History* 41, no. 1 (2010): 61–78.

Bullard, Audreen. "New York to Salisbury." Pages 101–11 in George M. Daniels, ed., *Drums of War: The Continuing Crisis in Rhodesia*. New York: The Third Press, 1974.

Burbank, Jane, and Frederick Cooper. *Empires in World History: Power and the Politics of Difference*. Princeton, NJ: Princeton University Press, 2010.

Burton, Lloyd. *The Yellow Mountain*. Salisbury: Regal Publishers, 1978.

Canfora, Luciano. *Democracy in Europe: A History of an Ideology*. Trans. Simon Jones. Oxford: Blackwell, 2006.

Carrington, Peter Lord. *Reflecting on Things Past*. New York: Harper & Row, 1988.

Caute, David. *Under the Skin: The Death of White Rhodesia*. London: Allen Lane, 1983.

Chan, Stephen. *The Commonwealth Observer Group in Zimbabwe.* Gweru: Mambo Press, 1985.

Chanock, Martin. *Unconsummated Union: Britain, Rhodesia, and South Africa 1900–45.* Manchester: Manchester University Press, 1977.

Charlton, Michael. *The Last Colony in Africa: Diplomacy and the Independence of Rhodesia.* Oxford: Basil Blackwell, 1990.

Chatterjee, Partha. *The Politics of the Governed: Reflections on Popular Politics in Most of the World.* New York: Columbia University Press, 2004.

Cheffers, John. *A Wilderness of Spite or Rhodesia Denied.* New York: Vantage Press, 1972.

Chennells, Anthony. "Rhodesian Discourse, Rhodesian Novels, and the Zimbabwe Liberation War." Pages 102–29 in N. Bhebe and T. Ranger, eds., *Society in Zimbabwe's Liberation War.* London: James Currey, 1995.

Cilliers, J. K. *Counter-Insurgency in Rhodesia.* London: Croom Helm, 1985.

Cliffe, Lionel, Joshua Mpofu, and Barry Munslow. "Nationalist Politics in Zimbabwe: The 1980 Election and Beyond?" *Review of African Political Economy* 18 (1980): 44–67.

Cocks, Chris. *Fireforce: One Man's War in the Rhodesian Light Infantry.* Weltevreden Park: Covos-Day, 1997 [1988].

———. *Survival Course.* Weltevreden Park: Covos-Day, 1999.

Coey, John Alan. *A Martyr Speaks: Journal of the Late John Alan Coey.* N.p., 1994 [1988].

Cohen, Andrew. "Lonrho and Oil Sanctions against Rhodesia in the 1960s." *Journal of Southern African Studies* 37, no. 4 (2011): 715–30.

Cohen, Barry. "The War in Rhodesia: A Dissenter's View." *African Affairs* 76, no. 305: 483–94.

Compagnon, Daniel. *A Predictable Tragedy: Robert Mugabe and the Collapse of Rhodesia.* Philadelphia: University of Pennsylvania Press, 2011.

Connelly, Mathew. "Taking Off the Cold War Lens: Visions of North-South Conflict during the Algerian War of Independence." *American Hist. Rev.* 105, no. 3 (2000): 739–69.

———. *A Diplomatic Revolution: Algeria's Fight for Independence and the Origins of the Post-Cold War World.* Oxford: Oxford University Press, 2002.

Conrad K. *In the Shadow of the Tokolosh.* Chelmsford: Silverling Inspired Publishing, 2010.

Cook, Adrian. *Armies of the Night: The New York City Draft Riots of 1863.* Lexington: University Press of Kentucky, 1974.

Cooper, Frederick. *On the African Waterfront: Urban Disorder and the Transformation of Work in Colonial Mombasa.* New Haven, CT: Yale University Press, 1987.

———. *Decolonization and African Society: The Labor Question in French and British Africa.* Cambridge: Cambridge University Press, 1996.

———. *Colonialism in Question: Theory, Knowledge, History.* Berkeley: University of California Press, 2005.

———. "Possibility and Constraint: African Independence in Historical Perspective." *Journal of African History* 40, no. 2 (2008): 167–97.

———. "Alternatives to Empire: France and Africa after World War II." Pages 94–123 in Howland and White, eds., *The State of Sovereignty*.

———. *Africa and the World: The McMillan-Stewart Lectures*. Cambridge, MA: Harvard University Press, 2014.

Cooper, Frederick and Ann Laura Stoler, eds. *Tensions of Empire: Colonial Cultures in a Bourgeois World*. Berkeley: University of California Press, 1997.

Cowen, Michael, and Liisa Laakso. "An Overview of Election Studies in Africa." *Journal of Modern African Studies* 35, no. 4 (1997): 717–44.

Craven, David. *Mapolisa: Some Reminiscences of a Rhodesian Policeman*. Weltevreden Park: Covos-Day, 1998.

Crawford, Neta C. "Trump Card or Theater? An Introduction to Two Sanctions Debates." Pages 2–24 in Crawford and Klotz, eds., *How Sanctions Work*.

———, and Audie Klotz, eds. *How Sanctions Work: Lessons from South Africa*. New York: St. Martin's Press, 1999.

Crook, Malcolm, and Tom Crook. "Reforming Voting Practices in a Global Age: The Making and Remaking of the Modern Secret Ballot in Britain, France and the United States, c. 1600–1950." *Past and Present* 212 (2011): 199–237.

Croukamp, Dennis. *Only My Friends Call Me "Crouks."* Cape Town: Pseudo Publishing, 2006.

Crowley, John. "The Uses and Abuses of the Secret Ballot in the American Age of Reform." Pages 43–68 in Bertrand et al., *The Hidden History of the Secret Ballot*.

Curtin, T. R. C. "Rhodesian Economic Development under Sanctions and the 'Long Haul.'" *African Affairs* 67, no. 267 (1968): 100–110.

Cutlack, Meredith. *Blood Running South*. London: Collins, 1972.

Darwin, John. *Britain and Decolonisation: The Retreat from Empire in the Post-War World*. New York: St. Martin's Press, 1988.

Davidow, Jeffrey. *A Peace in Southern Africa: The Lancaster House Conference on Rhodesia, 1979*. Boulder, CO: Westview Press, 1984.

Davis, John Gordon. *Hold My Hand I'm Dying*. London: Diamond Books, 1989 [1967].

Day, John. "Southern Rhodesian African Nationalists and the 1961 Constitution." *Journal of Modern African Studies* 7, no. 2 (1969): 221–47.

Delap, Mick. "The April 1979 Elections in Zimbabwe-Rhodesia." *African Affairs* 78, no. 313 (1979): 431–38.

DeRoche, Andrew. *Black, White and Chrome: The United States and Zimbabwe*. Trenton, NJ: Africa World Press, 2001.

Dibb, C. E. *Spotted Soldiers*. Salisbury: Leo Publications, 1978.

Doke, Graham. *First Born*. Cape Town: Book, 2000.

Douglas-Home, Sir Alec. *The Way the Wind Blows*. New York: Quadrangle, 1976.

Dudziak, Mary L. *Exporting American Dreams: Thurgood Marshall's African Journey.* Oxford: Oxford University Press, 2008.

———. *Cold War, Civil Rights: Race and the Image of American Democracy.* Princeton, NJ: Princeton University Press, 2011 [2000].

Dupont, Clifford. *The Reluctant President: The Memoirs of the Hon. Clifford Dupont.* Bulawayo: Books of Rhodesia, 1978.

Eekelaar, J. M. "Rhodesia: The Abdication of Constitutionalism." *Modern Law Review* 32, no. 1 (1969): 19–34.

Elkins, Caroline. *Imperial Reckoning: The Untold Story of Britain's Gulag in Kenya.* New York: Henry Holt, 2005.

———. "Race, Citizenship and Governance: Settler Tyranny and the End of Empire." Pages 203–22 in Elkins and Pedersen, eds., *Settler Colonialism in the Twentieth Century.*

———, and Susan Pedersen, eds. *Settler Colonialism in the Twentieth Century: Projects, Practices and Legacies.* New York: Routledge, 2005.

Evans, Peter, Dietrich Rusedchemeyer, and Theda Stocpole, eds. *Bringing the State Back In.* Cambridge: Cambridge University Press, 1985.

Fabry, Mikulas. *Recognizing States: International Society and the Recognition of New States since 1776.* Oxford: Oxford University Press, 2010.

Facchini, Manuele. "The 'Evil Genius' Sir Hugh Beadle and the Rhodesian Crisis, 1965–1972." *Journal of Southern African Studies* 33, no. 3 (2007): 673–89.

Flower, Ken. *Serving Secretly: Rhodesia's CIO Chief on Record.* Alberton: Galago, 1987.

Fothergill, Rowland. *Laboratory for Peace: The Story of Ken and Lillian Mew and Ranche House College.* Bulawayo: Louis Bolze Publishing, 1984.

Frantz, Charles, and Cyril A. Rogers. "Length of Residence and Race Attitudes in Southern Rhodesia." *Race* 3 (1962): 46.

French, Paul. *Shadows of a Forgotten Past: To the Edge with the Rhodesian SAS and Selous Scouts.* Solihull: Helion, 2012.

Fuller, Alexandra. *Don't Let's Go to the Dogs Tonight: An African Childhood.* New York: Random House, 2001.

Gagnin, Chip and Keith Brown, eds. *Post-Conflict Studies: An Interdisciplinary Approach.* New York: Routledge, 2014.

Galtung, John. "On the Effects of International Economic Sanctions: With Examples from the Case of Rhodesia." *World Politics* 19, no. 3 (1967): 378–416.

Gann, Lewis H. "From Ox Wagon to Armored Car in Rhodesia." *Military Review* 48, no. 4 (1968): 63–72.

———, and Peter Duignan. *White Settlers in Tropical Africa.* Baltimore: Penguin Books, 1962.

Geisler, Gisela. "Fair? What Has Fairness Got to Do with It? Vagaries of Election Observation and Democratic Standards." *Journal of Modern African Studies* 31, no. 4 (1993): 613–67.

Geschiere, Peter, and Stephen Jackson. "Autochthony and the Crisis of Citizenship: Democratization, Decentralization, and the Politics of Belonging." *African Studies Review* 49, no. 2 (2006): 1–7.

Geyer, Michael. "Insurrectionary Warfare: The German Debate about *Levée en Masse* in October 1918." *Journal of Modern History* 73, no. 3 (2001): 459–527.

Gibbs, Peter, and Hugh Phillips. *The History of the British South African Police, 1889–1980*. North Ringwood, Australia: Something of Value Press, 2000.

Gilmartin, David. "Towards a Global History of Voting: Sovereignty, the Diffusion of Ideas, and the Enchanted Individual." *Religions* 3 (2012): 407–23.

Glassman, Jonathon. "Sorting Out the Tribes: The Creation of Racial Identities in Colonial Zanzibar's Newspaper Wars." *Journal of African History* 41, no. 3 (2000): 395–428.

———. *War of Words, War of Stone: Racial Thought in Colonial Zanzibar*. Bloomington: Indiana University Press, 2011.

Gledhill, Richard. *One Commando*. Weltevreden Park: Covos-Day, 2001 [1997].

Godwin, Peter, and Ian Hancock. *"Rhodesians Never Die": The Impact of War and Political Change on White Rhodesia c. 1970–1980*. Harare: Baobab, 1995 [1993].

———. *Mukiwa. A White Boy in Africa*. London: Macmillan, 1996.

Goldin, Bennie. *The Judge, the Prince and the Usurper—from UDI to Zimbabwe*. New York: Vantage Press, 1990.

Good, Robert C. *U. D. I.: The International Politics of the Rhodesian Rebellion*. Princeton, NJ: Princeton University Press, 1973.

Goodwin-Gill, Guy S. *Free and Fair Elections: International Law and Practice*. Geneva: Inter-Parliamentary Union, 1994.

Gordon, David. "Owners of the Land and Lunda Lords: Colonial Chiefs in the Borderlands of Northern Rhodesia and the Belgian Congo." *International Journal of African Historical Studies* 34, no. 1 (2001): 315–38.

Gordon, Sarah Barringer. " 'The Liberty of Self-Degradation': Women, Suffrage, and Consent in Nineteenth- Century America." *Journal of American History* 83, no. 3 (1996): 815–47.

Gorman, Daniel. *Imperial Citizenship: Empire and the Question of Belonging*. Manchester: Manchester University Press, 2006.

Greenberg, Karl. *The Gokwe Kid: Dick of the Bushveld*. N.p.: Karl Greenberg, 2012.

Greenfield, J. M. *Testimony of a Rhodesian Federal*. Bulawayo: Books of Rhodesia, 1978.

Hancock, Ian. *White Liberals, Moderates and Radicals in Rhodesia, 1953–1980*. London: Croom Helm, 1984.

Handford, John. *Portrait of an Economy: Rhodesia under Sanctions*. Salisbury: Mercury Press, 1976.

Harper-Ronald, Jake, as told to Greg Budd. *Sunday, Bloody Sunday: A Soldier's War in Northern Ireland, Rhodesia, Mozambique, and Iraq*. Alberton: Galago, 2009.

Harris, P. B. "The Failure of a Constitution: The Whaley Report, Rhodesia, 1968." *International Affairs* 45, no. 2 (1969): 234–45.

Hartigan, John. "Establishing the Fact of Whiteness." *American Anthropologist* 99, no. 3 (1997): 495–505.

Hartmann, Michael. *Game for Vultures*. London: Pan Books, 1976 [1975].

Hartog, Hendrick. "The Constitution of Aspiration and 'The Rights That Belong to Us All.'" *Journal of American History* 74, no. 3 (1987): 1013–34.

Healy, Denis. *The Time of My Life*. New York: Norton, 1990 [1989].

Hecht, Gabrielle. *Being Nuclear: Africans in the Global Uranium Trade*. Cambridge, MA: MIT Press, 2012.

Hills, Denis. *Rebel People*. New York: Holmes & Meier, 1978.

———. *The Last Days of White Rhodesia*. London: Chatto & Windus, 1981.

Hintz, Stephen E. C. "The Political Transformation of Rhodesia, 1958–1965." *African Studies Review* 15, no. 2 (1971): 173–83.

Hirsch, Dr. I. M. *Focus on Southern Rhodesia: The Constitution and Independence*. Bulawayo: Stuart Manning, 1964.

Hitchens, Christopher. "Salisbury Diary." *New Statesman* 47, September 16, 1977, 365.

Hodder-Williams, Richard. "Rhodesia's Search for a Constitution. Or, Whatever Happened to Whaley?" *African Affairs* 69, no. 276 (1970): 217–35.

———. *White Farmers in Rhodesia: A History of Marandellas District*. London: Macmillan, 1983.

Hoffman, Bruce, Jennifer M. Tauw, and David Arnold. *Lessons for Counter-Insurgencies: Lessons from Rhodesia*. Santa Monica, CA: RAND, 1991.

Holderness, Hardwick. *Lost Chance: Southern Rhodesia 1945–58*. Harare: Zimbabwe Publishing House, 1985.

Holleman, J. F. *Chief, Council and Commissioner: Some Problems of Government in Rhodesia*. Assen: Royal VanGorcum, 1969.

Hopkins, A. G. "Rethinking Decolonization." *Past and Present* 200 (2008): 211–47.

Horne, Gerald. *From the Barrel of a Gun: The United States and the War against Zimbabwe, 1965–1980*. Chapel Hill: University of North Carolina Press, 2001.

Hotz, Paul. *Muzukuru: A Guerrilla's Story*. Johannesburg: Ravan, 1990.

Houser, George M. *No One Can Stop the Rain: Glimpses of Africa's Liberation Struggle*. New York: Pilgrim Press, 1989.

Howland, Douglas, and Luise White, eds. *The State of Sovereignty: Territories, Laws, Populations*. Bloomington: Indiana University Press, 2009.

Howman, H. R. G. *Provinicialisation in Rhodesia, 1968–1969: Rational and Irrational Elements*. Ed. G. C. Cashmore. Cambridge: African Studies Centre, 1985.

Hozic, Aida. "The Paradox of Sovereignty in the Balkins." Pages 243–60 in Howland and White, *The State of Sovereignty*.

———. "The Origins of Post-Conflict." Pages 19–38 in Chip Gagnin and Keith Brown, eds., *Post-Conflict Studies: An Interdisciplinary Approach*. New York; Routledge, 2014.

Hudson, Miles. *Triumph or Tragedy? Rhodesia to Zimbabwe*. London: Hamish Hamilton, 1981.

Hughes, David McDermott. *Whiteness in Zimbabwe: Race, Landscape, and the Problem of Belonging*. New York: Palgrave Macmillan, 2010.

Hughes, Richard. *Capricorn: David Stirling's Second Africa Campaign*. London: Radcliffe Press, 2003.

Hynes, Samuel. *The Soldiers' Tale: Bearing Witness to Modern War*. New York, Penguin, 1998.

Ignatiev, Noel. *How the Irish Became White*. New York: Routledge, 1996.

Igo, Sarah. *The Averaged American: Surveys, Citizens, and the Making of a Mass Public*. Cambridge, MA: Harvard University Press, 2007.

Iliffe, John. "Breaking the Chain at Its Weakest Link: TANU and the Colonial Office." Pages 168–97 in Maddox and Giblin, *In Search of a Nation*.

Jardim, Jorge. *Sanctions Double-Cross: Oil to Rhodesia*. Bulawayo: Books of Rhodesia, 1979.

Jones, J. D. F. *Storyteller: The Many Lives of Laurens van der Post*. London: John Murray, 2001.

Jones, Mervyn. *Rhodesia: The White Judge's Burden*. London: International Defence and Aid Fund, 1972.

Kann, Wendy. *Casting with a Fragile Thread: A Story of Sisters and Africa*. New York: Picador, 2006.

Kaplan, Marion. "Their Rhodesia." *Transition* 23 (1965): 32–34.

Keatley, Patrick. *The Politics of Partnership*. Baltimore: Penguin Books, 1963.

Keith, Jeanette. *Rich Man's War, Poor Man's Fight: Race, Class, and Power in the Rural South during the First World War*. Chapel Hill: University of North Carolina Press, 2004.

Kelly, John D., and Martha Kaplan. *Represented Communities: Fiji and World Decolonization*. Chicago: University of Chicago Press, 2001.

———. "Legal Fictions after Empire." Pages 169–95 in Howland and White, *The State of Sovereignty*.

Kentridge, Sir Sidney. "A Judge's Duty in a Revolution—the case of Madzimbamuto v. Lardner-Burke." *Commonwealth Judicial Journal* 15, no. 2 (2003): 32–42.

Keyssar, Alexander. *The Right to Vote: The Contested History of Democracy in the United States*. New York: Basic Books, 2000.

Kinzer, Bruce L. "The Un-Englishness of the Secret Ballot." *Albion: A Quarterly Journal Concerned with British Studies* 10, no. 3 (1978): 237–56.

Kirk, Tony. "Rhodesia's 'Pro-Settlement Groups' and the Anglo-Rhodesian Constitutional Dispute." *Issue: A Journal of Opinion* 3, no. 1 (1973): 2–5.

Kolchin, Peter. "Whiteness Studies: The New History of Race in America." *Journal of American History* 89, no. 1 (2002): 154–73.

Kriger, Norma. *Zimbabwe's Guerrilla War: Peasant Voices*. Cambridge: Cambridge University Press, 1992.

———. *Guerrilla Veterans in Post-war Zimbabwe: Symbolic and Violent Politics, 1980–1987*. Cambridge: Cambridge University Press, 2003.

———. "ZANU(PF) Strategies in General Elections, 1980–2000: Discourse and Coercion." *African Affairs* 104, no. 414 (2005): 1–34.

Lake, Anthony. *The 'Tar Baby' Option: American Policy toward Southern Rhodesia*. New York: Columbia University Press, 1976 [1973].

Lardner-Burke, Desmond. *Rhodesia: The Story of a Crisis*. London: Ouldborne Book Co., 1966.

Leaver, David. "Multiculturalism and Nationalisms: A Political Retrospective on 1950s Southern Rhodesia (Colonial Zimbabwe)." *Journal of Third World Studies* 23, no. 2 (2006): 167–88.

Lee, Christopher Joon-Hai. "The 'Native' Undefined: Colonial Categories, Anglo-American Status and the Politics of Kinship in British Central Africa, 1929–38." *Journal of African History* 46, no. 3 (2005): 455–78.

Lemon, Anthony. "Electoral Machinery and Voting Patterns in Rhodesia, 1962–1977." *African Affairs* 77, no. 309 (1978): 511–30.

Lemon, David. *Never Quite a Soldier: A Policeman's War 1971–1983*. Stroud: Albida, 2000.

Lessing, Doris. *Going Home*. New York: Harper Collins, 1996 [1957].

Lewis, Arthur R. *Too Bright the Vision? African Adventures of a Rhodesian Rebel*. London: Covenant, 1992.

Leys, Colin. *European Politics in Southern Rhodesia*. Oxford: Clarendon Press, 1960.

Lindberg, Staffan I. *Democracy and Elections in Africa*. Baltimore: Johns Hopkins University Press, 2006.

Linden, Ian. *Church and State in Rhodesia, 1959–1979*. Munich: Kaiser Verlag, 1979.

Lobban, Richard. "American Mercenaries in Rhodesia." *Journal of Southern African Affairs* 3 (1978): 219–25.

Lockwood, Edgar. "An Inside Look at the Sanctions Campaign." *Issue: A Journal of Opinion*. 4, no. 3 (1974): 73–75.

Lonsdale, John. "The State and Social Processes in Africa: An Historiographical Survey." *African Studies Review* 24, nos. 2/3 (1981): 139–225.

Losman, David L. *International Economic Sanctions: The Cases of Cuba, Israel, and Rhodesia*. Albuquerque: University of New Mexico Press, 1979.

Lowry, Donal. " 'White Woman's Country': Ethel Tawse Jollie and the Making of White Rhodesia." *Journal of Southern African Studies* 23, no. 2 (1997): 259–81.

———. "The Impact of Anti-communism on White Rhodesian Political Culture, c. 1920–1980." *Cold War History* 7, no. 2 (2007): 169–94.

MacBruce, James. *When the Going Was Rough: A Rhodesian Story*. Pretoria: Femina, 1983.

Mackay, Peter. *We Have Tomorrow: Stirrings in Africa 1959–1967*. Wilby: Michael Russell, 2008.

Mackenzie, W. J. M., and Kenneth Robinson, eds. *Five Elections in Africa*. Oxford: Clarendon Press, 1960.

Maddox, Gregory H., and James L. Giblin, eds., *In Search of a Nation: Histories of Authority and Dissonance in Tanzania*. Bloomington: Indiana University Press, 2009.

Mair, Lucy. *The Nyasaland Election of 1961*. London: Athlone Press, 1962.

Maisels, Isie. *A Life at Law: The Memoirs of I. A. Maisels, QC*. Johannesburg: Jonathan Ball, 1998.

Malkki, Liisa. "National Geographic: The Rootedness of People and Territorialization of National Identity among Scholars and Refugees." *Cultural Anthropology* 7, no. 1 (1992): 22–44.

Mamdani, Mahmood. *From Citizen to Refugee: Ugandan Asians Come to Britain.* London: Francis Pinter, 1973.

———. *Citizen and Subject: Contemporary Africa and the Legacy of Late Colonialism.* Princeton, NJ: Princeton University Press, 1996.

———. "Beyond Settler and Native as Political Identities: Overcoming the Political Legacy of Colonialism." *Comparative Studies in Society and History* 43, no. 4 (2001): 651–64.

Mandaza, Ibbo, ed. *Zimbabwe: The Political Economy of Transition, 1980–1986.* Dakar: Codesria Books, 1986.

Manela, Erez. *The Wilsonian Moment: Self-Determination and the International Origins of Anticolonial Nationalism.* Oxford: Oxford University Press, 2007.

Mann, Gregory. *Native Sons: West African Veterans and France in the Twentieth Century.* Durham, NC: Duke University Press, 2006.

Marshall, H. H. "The Legal Effects of U. D. I. (based on Madzimbamuto v. Lardner-Burke)." *International and Comparative Law Quarterly* 17, no. 1 (1988): 1022–34.

Martin, David, and Phyllis Johnson. *The Struggle for Zimbabwe.* London, Faber & Faber, 1981.

Mason, Philip. *Year of Decision: Rhodesia and Nyasaland in 1960.* London: Oxford University Press, 1960.

———. *A Thread of Silk.* London: Michael Russell, 1984.

Masunungure, E. V., ed. *Defying the Winds of Change: Zimbabwe's 2008 Elections.* Harare: Weaver Press, 2009.

Mazower, Mark. *No Enchanted Place: The End of Empire and the Ideological Origins of the United Nations.* Princeton, NJ: Princeton University Place, 2009.

McAleese, Peter. *No Mean Soldier: The Story of the Ultimate Professional Soldier in the SAS and Other Forces.* London: Cassell, 2000 [1993].

McGee, Gale W. "The US Congress and the Rhodesian Chrome Issue." *Issue: A Journal of Opinion* 2, no. 2 (1972): 1–7.

McIntyre, W. David. "The Strange Death of Dominion Status." *Journal of Imperial and Commonwealth History* 27, no. 2 (1999): 193–212.

McKeon, Nancy. "Rhodesia's Fighting Bishop." *Africa Report* 17, no. 3 (1972): 9.

McMahon, Robert J. *Dean Acheson and the Creation of an American World Order.* Washington, DC: Potomac, 2009.

McNeil, Daniel. " 'The rivers of Zimbabwe will run red with blood': Enoch Powell and the Post-Imperial Nostalgia of the Monday Club." *Journal of Southern African Studies* 37, no. 4 (2011): 731–45.

Meadows, Keith. *Sometimes When It Rains: White Africans in Black Africa.* Bulawayo: Thorntree Press, 1998.

Megahey, Alan. *Humphrey Gibbs: Beleaguered Governor: Southern Rhodesia, 1929–69.* London: Macmillan, 1998.

Mehta, Uday Singh. "Liberal Strategies of Exclusion." Pages 59–85 in Cooper and Stoler, eds., *Tensions of Empire*.

———. *Liberalism and Empire: A Study in Nineteenth Century British Liberal Thought*. Chicago: University of Chicago Press, 1999.

Meredith, Martin. *The Past Is Another Country: Rhodesia UDI to Zimbabwe*. London: Pan Books, 1980 [1979].

———. *Our Votes, Our Guns: Robert Mugabe and the Tragedy of Zimbabwe*. New York: Public Affairs, 2002.

Mhanda, Wilfred. *Dzino: Memoirs of a Freedom Fighter*. Harare: Weaver Press, 2011.

Miles, Robert. "Nationality, Citizenship, and Migration to Britain, 1945–1951." *Journal of Law and Society* 16, no. 4 (1989): 426–42.

Mill, John Stuart. *Considerations on Representative Government*. New York: Harper & Bros., 1862.

Millin, Sarah Gertrude, ed. *White Africans Are Also People*. Cape Town: Howard Timmons, 1967.

Minter, William, and Elizabeth Schmidt. "When Sanctions Worked: The Case of Rhodesia Reexamined." *African Affairs* 87, no. 347 (1988): 207–37.

Mitchell, Diana. "PARD on Me 'COSS I'm Non-Political." *Centre Point* 2, no. 5 (1972), 4.

Mittlebeeler, Emmet V. "The Settlement." *Africa Report* 17, no. 2 (1972): 11–13.

Mlambo, Alois. *White Immigration into Rhodesia: From Occupation to Federation*. Harare: University of Zimbabwe Press, 2002.

———. "Discordant Voices: The Organization of African Unity's Response to the Unilateral Declaration of Independence. 1965–75." *Afriche e Orineti* 2 (2011): 122–34.

Mlambo, Eshmael. *Rhodesia: The Struggle for a Birthright*. London: Hurst, 1972.

Moorcraft, Paul A. *A Short Thousand Years: The End of Rhodesia's Rebellion*. Salisbury: Galaxie, 1980.

———, and Peter McLaughlin. *Chimurenga! The War in Rhodesia 1965–1980*. Johannesburg: Sygma/Collins, 1982.

Moore, Donald S. *Suffering for Territory: Race, Place and Power in Zimbabwe*. Durham, NC: Duke University Press, 2005.

Moore, Robin. *Rhodesia*. New York: Condor, 1977.

———. *Major Mike*. New York: Ace, 1981 [1978].

———. *The White Tribe*. Publishers Encampment, WY: Affiliated Writers of America, 1991.

Morgan, Edmund S. *Inventing the People: The Rise of Popular Sovereignty in England and America*. New York: Norton, 1988.

Morris, Jan. *Destinations: Essays from Rolling Stone*. New York: Oxford University Press, 1982 [1980].

Moyn, Samuel. *The Last Utopia: Human Rights in History*. Cambridge, MA: Harvard University Press, 2010.

Mulford, David C. *The Northern Rhodesia General Election of 1962.* Nairobi: Oxford University Press, 1964.

Munro, William A. *The Moral Economy of the State: Conservation, Community Development, and State Making in Zimbabwe.* Athens: Ohio University Press, 1998.

Murphy, Philip. *Party Politics and Decolonization: The Conservative Party and British Colonial Policy in Tropical Africa.* Oxford: Clarendon Press, 1995.

——. " 'An intricate and distasteful subject': British Planning for the Use of Force against European Settlers in Central Africa, 1952–65." *English Hist. Review* 131, no. 492 (2006): 746–77.

Mutasa, Didymus. *Rhodesian Black Behind Bars.* London: Mowbrays, 1974.

Mutesa II, Kabaka of Buganda. *Desecration of My Kingdom.* London: Rex Collings, 1967.

Muzorewa, Bishop Abel. *Rise Up and Walk: An Autobiography.* Johannesburg: Jonathan Ball, 1978.

Nasson, Bill. "Why They Fought: Black Cape Colonists and Imperial Wars, 1899–1918." *Internatioanl Journal of African Historical Studies* 37, no. 1 (2004), 55–70.

Ndlovu-Gatsheni, Sabelo, and James Muzondidya, eds. *Redemptive or Grotesque Nationalism? Rethinking Contemporary Politics in Zimbabwe.* Bern: Peter Lang, 2011.

Nesbit, Francis Njubi. *Race for Sanctions: African Americans against Apartheid, 1946–94.* Bloomington: Indiana University Press, 2004.

Niesewand, Peter. "Settlement Brings about a Nationalist Rebirth." *Africa Report* 17, no. 2 (1972): 8–10.

——. *In Camera: Secret Justice in Rhodesia.* London: Weidenfeld & Nicholson, 1973.

Nkomo, Joshua. *My Life: The Story of Joshua Nkomo.* London: Methuen, 1984.

Nkrumah, Kwame. *Rhodesia File.* London: Panaf, n. d.

Nyagumbo, Maurice. *With the People: An Autobiography.* London: Allison & Busby, 1980.

Nyangoni, Christopher, and Gideon Nyandoro, eds. *Zimbabwe Independence Movements: Select Documents.* New York: Barnes & Noble Books, 1979.

Odhiambo, Atieno. "Woza Lugard? Rhetoric and Antiquarian Knowledge." *Canadian Journal of African Studies* 34, no. 2 (2000): 387–96.

O'Gorman, Frank. "The Secret Ballot in Nineteenth Century Britain." Pages 16–42 in Bertrand et al., *The Hidden History of the Secret Ballot.*

Ovendale, Ritchie. "Macmillan and the Wind of Change in Africa, 1957–1960." *The Historical Journal* 88, no. 2 (1995): 455–77.

Palley, Claire. *The Constitutional History of Southern Rhodesia, 1888–1965, with special reference to imperial control.* Oxford: Clarendon Press, 1966.

——. "The Judicial Process: U. D. I. and the Southern Rhodesian Judiciary." *Modern Law Review* 30, no. 3 (1967): 263–87.

———. "Rhodesia: The Time-Scale for Majority Rule." *Issue: A Journal of Opinion* 2, no. 2 (1972): 52–62.

Palloti, Arrigo. "Tanzania and the Decolonization of Rhodesia." *Afriche e Oriente* 2 (2011): 215–31.

Palmer, Robin. *Land and Racial Domination in Rhodesia.* London: Heinemann, 1977.

———. "Land Reform in Zimbabwe, 1980–1990." *African Affairs* 89, no. 355 (1990): 163–81.

Parker, Jim. *Assignment Selous Scouts: Inside Story of a Rhodesian Special Branch Officer.* Alberton: Galago, 2006.

Parker, John. *Little White Island.* London: Pitman Publishing, 1972.

Parpart, Jane. "Silenced Visions of Citizenship, Democracy and Nation: African MPs in Rhodesian Parliaments, 1963–1978." Pages 187–216 in Ndlovu-Gatsheni and Muzondidya, eds., *Redemptive or Grotesque Nationalism?*

Pels, Peter. "Imagining Elections: Modernity, Mediation and the Secret Ballot in Late Colonial Tanganyika." Pages 100–113 in Bertrand et al., *The Hidden History of the Secret Ballot.*

Petter-Bowyer, P. H. J. *Winds of Destruction.* Victoria, BC: Tafford, 2003.

Phimister, Ian. *An Economic and Social History of Zimbabwe, 1890–1948.* London: Longman, 1988.

———, and Charles van Onselen. *Studies in the History of African Mine Labour in Colonial Zimbabwe.* Salisbury: Mambo Press, 1978.

———. "Rethinking the Reserves: Southern Rhodesia's Land Husbandry Act Reviewed." *Journal of Southern African Studies* 19, no. 2 (1993): 225–39.

Phiri, Bizeck Jube. "The Capricorn African Society Revisited: The Impact of Liberalism on Zambia's Colonial History, 1949–1963." *International Journal of African Historical Studies* 24, no. 1 (1991): 65–83.

Pilossof, Rory. *The Unbearable Whiteness of Being: Farmers' Voices from Zimbabwe.* Harare: Weaver Press, 2012.

Pitman, Dick. *You Must Be New Around Here.* Bulawayo: Books of Rhodesia, 1979.

Pitts, Dennis. *Rogue Hercules.* New York: Atheneum, 1978.

Pollack, Oliver B. "Black Farmers and White Politics in Rhodesia." *African Affairs* 74, no. 296 (1975): 263–77.

Post, K. W. J. *The Nigerian Federal Election of 1959.* London: Oxford University Press, 1964.

Raftopoulos, Brian. "The Labour Movement in Zimbabwe, 1945–1965." Pages 55–90 in Raftopoulos and Phimister, eds., *Keep on Knocking.*

———. "Nationalism and Labour in Salisbury 1953–65." Pages 129–50 in Raftopoulos and Yoshikuni, eds., *Sites of Struggle.*

———, and Alois Mlambo. *Becoming Zimbabwe: A History from the Precolonial Period to 1980.* Harare: Weaver Press, 2009.

———, and Ian Phimister, eds. *Keep on Knocking: A History of the Labour Movement in Zimbabwe.* Harare: Weaver Press, 1997.

———, and Tsuneo Yoshikuni, eds. *Sites of Struggle: Essays in Zimbabwe's Urban History*. Harare: Weaver Press, 1999.

Ranger, Terence. *Voices from the Rocks: Nature, Culture and the History of the Matopos Hills of Zimbabwe*. Oxford: James Currey, 1999.

———. "Nationalist Historiography, Patriotic History and the History of the Nation: The Struggle over the Past in Zimbabwe." *Journal of Southern African Studies* 30, no. 2 (2005): 215–34.

———. *Bulawayo Burning: The Social History of a Southern African City, 1893–1960*. Harare: Weaver Press, 2010.

———. *Writing Revolt: An Engagement with African Nationalism 1957–67*. Harare: Weaver Press, 2013.

Rayner, William. *The Day of Chaminuka*. New York: Atheneum. 1977 [1976].

Reid-Daly, Ron, as told to Peter Stiff. *Selous Scouts: Top Secret War*. Alberton, South Africa: Galago, 1982.

———. *Pamwe Chete: The Legend of the Selous Scouts*. Weltevreden Park: Covos-Day, 1998.

Renwick, Robin. *Unconventional Diplomacy in Southern Africa*. New York: St. Martin's Press, 1997.

Reynolds, Andrew. "Reserved Seats in National Legislatures: A Research Note." *Legislative Studies Quarterly* 30, no. 2 (2005): 301–10.

Rhodesian Information Office. *Dean Acheson on the Rhodesian Question*. Washington, DC: Rhodesian Information Office, n. d.

Rich, Tony. "Legacies of the Past? The Results of the 1980 Election in Midlands Province, Zimbabwe." *Africa* 52, no. 3 (1982): 42–55.

Roberts, R. S. "The Armed Forces and Chimurenga: Ideology and History." *Heritage of Zimbabwe* 7 (1987): 31–47.

Roediger, David. *The Wages of Whiteness: The Making of the American Working Class*. London: Verso, 1990.

Rogers, Cyril A., and C. Frantz. *Racial Themes in Southern Rhodesia: The Attitudes and Behavior of the White Population*. New Haven, CT: Yale University Press, 1962.

Rowe, David M. *Manipulating the Market: Understanding Economic Sanctions, Institutional Change, and the Political Unity of White Rhodesia*. Ann Arbor: University of Michigan Press, 2001.

Rupert, Steven C. *A Most Promising Weed: A History of Tobacco Farming and Labor in Colonial Zimbabwe, 1890–1945*. Athens: Ohio University Press, 1998.

Rutherford, Blair. *Working on the Margins: Black Workers, White Farmers in Postcolonial Zimbabwe*. Harare: Weaver Press, 2001.

Sachikonye, Lloyd. *When a State Turns on Its Citizens: Instrumentalized Violence and Political Culture*. Harare: Weaver, 2011.

Salt, Beryl. *A Pride of Eagles: The Definitive History of the Rhodesian Air Force, 1920–1980*. Weltevreden Park: Covos-Day, 2001.

Scarnecchia, Timothy. *The Urban Roots of Democracy and Political Violence in Zimbabwe: Harare and Highfield, 1940–1964*. Rochester, NY: Rochester University Press, 2008.

Schmidt, Carl. *Political Theology: Four Chapters on the Concept of Sovereignty.* Trans. George Schwab. Chicago: University of Chicago Press, 1985.

Schmidt, Heike. *Colonialism and Violence in Zimbabwe: A History of Suffering.* Oxford: James Currey, 2012.

Scully, Pat. *Exit Rhodesia.* Ladysmith: Cotswold Press, 1984.

Seirils, J. K. "Undoing the United Front? Coloured Soldiers in Rhodesia, 1939–1980," *African Studies* 63, no. 1 (2004): 73–94.

Shamuyarira, Nathan. *Crisis in Rhodesia.* London: Andre Deutsch, 1965.

Shaw, Angus. *Kandaya: Another Time, Another Place.* Harare: Baobab Books, 1993.

———. *Mutoko Madness.* Harare: Boundary Books, 2013.

Shelley, Toby. *End Game in Western Sahara: What Future for Africa's Last Colony?* London: Zed Books, 2004.

Shepard, Todd. *The Invention of Decolonization: The Algerian War and the Remaking of France.* Ithaca, NY: Cornell University Press, 2006.

Shutt, Allison K. "Purchase Area Farmers and the Middle Class of Southern Rhodesia, c. 1931–1952." *International Journal of African Historical Studies* 30, no. 3 (1997): 555–81.

Shutz, Barry. "European Population Patterns, Cultural Persistence, and Political Change in Rhodesia." *Canadian Journal of African Studies* 7, no. 1 (1973): 3–26.

Sibanda, Eliakim M. *The Zimbabwe African People's Union.* Trenton, NJ: Red Sea Press, 2005.

Simpson, A. W. Brian. *Human Rights at the End of Empire: Britain and the Genesis of the European Convention.* Oxford: Oxford University Press, 2001.

Simpson, Gerry. *Great Powers and Outlaw States: Unequal Sovereigns in the International Legal Order.* Cambridge: Cambridge University Press, 2004.

Sinha, Mrinalini. *Specters of Mother India: The Global Restructuring of Empire.* Durham, NC: Duke University Press, 2006.

Sithole, Masipula. "The General Elections 1979–1980." Pages 75–97 in Mandaza, ed., *Zimbabwe: The Political Economy of Transition.*

Skeen, Brig. A. *Prelude to Independence: Skeen's 115 Days.* Cape Town: Boekhandel, 1966.

Skelton, Kenneth. *Bishop in Smith's Rhodesia: Notes from a Turbulent Octave.* Gweru: Mambo Press, 1983.

Slovo, Gillian. *Every Secret Thing: My Family, My Country.* London: Little, Brown, 1997.

Smith, Ian. *The Great Betrayal: The Memoirs of Ian Douglas Smith.* London: Blake, 1997. Reprinted as *Bitter Harvest: The Great Betrayal and Its Dreadful Aftermath.* London: John Blake, 2001.

Smith, Sylvia Bond. *Ginette.* Bulawayo: Black Eagle Press, 1980.

Stack, Harry B. *Sanctions: The Case of Rhodesia.* Syracuse, NY: Syracuse University Press, 1978.

Stapleton, Timothy. *African Police and Soldiers in Colonial Zimbabwe, 1913–1980.* Rochester, NY: University of Rochester Press, 2011.

Stedman, Stephen John. *Peacemaking in a Civil War: International Mediation in Zimbabwe, 1974–1980.* Boulder, CO: Lynne Reiner, 1988.

Stiff, Peter. *See You in November: Rhodesia's No-Holds-Barred Intelligence War.* Alberton, South Africa: Galago, 1985.

Stoler, Ann Laura. *Along the Archival Grain: Epistemic Anxieties and Colonial Common Sense.* Princeton, NJ: Princeton University Press, 2009.

Stulz, Newell M. "Multi-racial Voting and Nonracial Politics in Colonial East and Central Africa," *Phylon* 33, no.1 (1972): 67–78.

Stumbles, A. R. W. *Some Recollections of a Rhodesian Speaker.* Bulawayo: Books of Rhodesia, 1980.

Sutcliffe, Robert B. *Sanctions against Rhodesia: The Economic Background.* London: Africa Bureau, 1966.

Tagel, John. *Bolt from the Blue.* Cape Town: Howard Timmons, 1979.

Tamarkin, M. *The Making of Zimbabwe: Decolonization in Regional and International Politics.* London: Frank Cass, 1990.

Taylor, Stu. *Lost in Africa.* Johannesburg: 30 Degrees South, 2007.

Throup, David W. *The Social and Economic Origins of Mau Mau.* Oxford: James Currey, 1988.

Thrush, Alan. *Of Land and Spirits.* Guernsey: Transition Publishing, 1997.

Tilly, Charles. "War Making and State Making as Organized Crime." Pages 169–87 in Evans, Ruesdchemeyer, and Stocpole, eds., *Bringing the State Back In.*

Todd, Judith. *The Right to Say No.* London: Sidgewick & Johnson, 1972.

Tosh, John. "Colonial Chiefs in a Stateless Society: A Case Study from Northern Uganda." *Journal of African History* 14, no. 3 (1973): 473–90.

Tracey, C. G. *All for Nothing: My Life Remembered.* Harare: Weaver Press, 2009.

Tredgold, Sir Robert. *The Rhodesia That Was My Life.* London: George Allen & Unwin, 1968.

Trethowan, Anthony. *Delta Scout: Ground Coverage Operator.* Johannesburg: 30 Degree South, 2008.

Trillin, Calvin. "Letter from Salisbury." *The New Yorker* 42 (November 1966): 134–93.

Von Eschen, Penny M. *Race against Empire: Black Americans and Anticolonialism, 1937–1957.* Ithaca, NY: Cornell University Press, 1997.

Ward, Harvey. *Sanctions Buster.* Glasgow: William Maclellan Embryo, 1982.

Warren, Charlie. *Stick Leader RLI.* Durban: Just Done Productions, 2007.

Watson, Jack. *Conspire to Kill.* Salisbury: Penn Medos, 1976.

Watts, Carl Peter. "Killing Kith and Kin: The Viability of British Military Intervention in Rhodesia, 1964–5." *Twentieth-Century British History* 16, no. 4 (2005): 382–415.

———. *Rhodesia's Unilateral Declaration of Independence: An International History.* London: Macmillan, 2012.

Weiss, Ruth, with Jane Parpart. *Sir Garfield Todd and the Making of Zimbabwe.* London: British Academic Press, 1999.

Welensky, Sir Roy. "The United Nations and Colonialism in Africa." *Annals of the American Academy of Political and Social Science* 354 (1964): 145–52.

———. *Welensky's 4000 Days: The Life and Death of the Federation of Rhodesia and Nyasaland*. London: Collins, 1964.

Wells, Rob. *The Part-Time War*. Cambridge: Fern House, 2011.

Wessels, Hannes. *P. K. van der Byl: African Statesman*. Johannesburg: 30 Degrees South, 2010.

West, Michael. *The Rise of the African Middle Class in Colonial Zimbabwe*. Bloomington: Indiana University Press, 2002.

Westad, Odd Arne. *The Global Cold War: Third World Interventions and the Making of Our Times*. Cambridge: Cambridge University Press, 2005.

White, Luise. *The Comforts of Home: Prostitution in Colonial Nairobi*. Chicago: University of Chicago Press, 1990.

———. "Telling More: Secrets, Lies, and History." *History and Theory* 39 (2000): 11–22.

———. *The Assassination of Herbert Chitepo: Texts and Politics in Zimbabwe*. Bloomington: Indiana University Press, 2003.

———. " 'Whoever Saw a Country with Four Armies?' The Battle of Bulawayo Revisited." *Journal of Southern African Studies* 33, no. 3 (2007): 619–31.

———. " 'Heading for the Gun': Skills and Sophistication in an African Guerrilla War." *Comparative Studies in Society and History* 51, no. 2 (2009): 236–59.

Wigglesworth, Tom. *Perhaps Tomorrow*. Salisbury: Galaxie, 1980.

Wilkinson, Peter. *Msasa*. Workworth: C. E. Wilkinson, 1992.

Willis, Justin. " 'A Model of Its Kind': Representation and Performance in the Sudan Self-Government Election of 1953." *Journal of Imperial and Commonwealth History* 35, no. 3 (2007): 485–502.

———. " 'We Changed the Laws': Electoral Practice and Malpractice in Sudan since 1953." *African Affairs* 109, no. 435 (2010): 191–212.

Wood, J. R. T. *The War Diaries of Andre Dennison*. Gibraltar: Ashanti Publishing, 1989.

———. *So Far and No Further! Rhodesia's Bid for Independence during the Retreat from Empire 1959–65*. Victoria, BC: Tafford Publishing, 2005.

———. *A Matter of Weeks Rather than Months: The Impasse between Harold Wilson and Ian Smith, Sanctions, Aborted Settlements and War 1965–1969*. Victoria, BC: Tafford, 2008.

Wylie, Dan. *Dead Leaves: Two Years in the Rhodesian War*. Scottsville: University of Natal Press, 2000.

Yates, George T., III. "The Rhodesian Chrome Statute: The Congressional Response to United Nations Economic Sanctions against Southern Rhodesia." *Virginia Law Review* 58, no. 3 (1972): 511–51.

Young, Tom. "Elections and Electoral Politics in Africa." *Africa: Journal of the International African Institute* 63, no. 3 (1993): 299–312.

Zimudzi, Tapiwa B. "Spies and Informers on Campus: Vetting, Surveillance and Deportation of Expatriate University Lecturers in Colonial Zimbabwe, 1954–1963." *Journal of Southern African Studies* 33, no. 1 (2007): 193–208.

Unpublished Materials

Centre for Contemporary British History and the Cold War Studies Centre, London School of Economics. Rhodesia UDI, September 6, 2000.

————. Britain and Rhodesia: The Route to Settlement, July 5, 2005.

Comité Angola (Amsterdam), Anti-Apartheid Movement (London), Anti-Apartheid Movement (Dublin), et al. White Migration to Southern Africa. Mimeo., Centre Europe-Tiers Monde, Geneva, 1975.

Drinkwater, John Q. C. Report on the General Election held in April 1979 in Zimbabwe-Rhodesia, May 3, 1973.

Evans, Michael. The Role of Ideology in Rhodesian Front Rule, 1962–1980. Ph.D. dissertation, University of Western Australia, 1993.

Fraenkel, Jon. "'Equality of rights for every civilized man south of the Zambesi': The Origins of the Alternative Vote as a Tool for Ethnic Accommodation, Southern Rhodesia, 1958–65." Unpublished essay.

Freedom House. Report of the Freedom House Mission to Observe the Elections in Zimbabwe-Rhodesia, April 1979. Mimeo., Freedom House, New York, May 20, 1979.

Kandiah, Michael, and Sue Onslow, eds. Britain and Rhodesia: The Route to Settlement. London: Centre for Contemporary British Culture, 2008.

Moore, David B. The Contradictory Construction of Hegemony in Zimbabwe: Politics, Ideology, and Class Formation in a New African State. Ph.D. dissertation, York University, 1989.

Palley, Claire. The Rhodesian Election Campaign. On Whether Elections Were Fair and Free and Whether Principles Required for Rhodesian Independence Have Been Satisfied. Mimeo., Catholic Institute for Race Relations, London, April 1979.

————. Zimbabwe-Rhodesia: Should the Present Government Be Recognised? Minority Rights Group and the Catholic Institute for Race Relations, London, 1979.

Parliamentary Human Rights Group. Free and Fair? The 1979 Rhodesian Election. Mimeo., London, May 1979.

Viscount Boyd of Merton [Alan Lennox-Boys]. Report to the Prime Minister on the Election Held in Zimbabwe-Rhodesia in April 1979.

Index

Acheson, Dean, 130–31
African National Council. *See*
  ANC
Alport, Lord Cuthbert, 32, 93
American Committee on Africa,
  279n5, 293n63
ANC, 17, 87, 213, 214, 220, 222,
  223, 224, 225, 230
Anderson, Benedict, 142, 199
Anderson, Brig. John, 108, 111
Anglo-American proposals, 236–41,
  256. *See also* Graham, John;
  Low, Stephen
A roll, 52; in 1961 constitution,
  82–84, 94, 95, 102–4; and 1969
  constitution, 158, 160, 164–67
assembly points, 277, 279, 280–82,
  284, 284n31, 286, 290, 292

Banda, Hastings, 253
Baron, Leo Solomon, 30–31,
  119–23, 267, 271. See also
  *Madzimbamuto and Baron v.
  Lardner-Burke*
Bashford, Pat, 211, 224
Beadle, Sir Hugh, 114, 116, 120,
  122
Berlyn, Phillipa, 220, 224
Biafra, recognition of, 117
"blocking mechanism," 103, 237,
  250, 253, 264
Botha, P. W., 273–74
Botswana, 43n21; and Lancaster
  House, 268, 270; refugees in,
  234, 272, 294–95n69
Bottomley, Arthur, 102, 208

Boyd, Viscount (Alan Lennox-
  Boyd), 246, 247, 248
Boynton, Sir John, 287. *See also*
  Boynton commission; 1980
  election
Boynton commission, 287, 293,
  294, 295
Britain: and Anglo-American
  proposals, 236–41, 249, 250;
  and Anglo-Rhodesian proposals, 14–15, 207–13, 227; and
  Boynton commission, 287, 293,
  295; "Britain at its best," 3, 133;
  and Central African Federation,
  7–8, 10; and decolonization, 1,
  20–24, 25, 26, 37, 40, 81, 101–
  3, 107, 111–13; direct control of
  Rhodesia, 277, 304; emigration from, 4, 31, 194; and the
  five principles, 207–8; idea of
  Greater Britain, 27–28, 105–6;
  negotiations with Rhodesia, 75,
  84, 149–50, 155, 167, 175, 206,
  233; and Rhodesia, 11–12, 27,
  108–10, 117, 120, 126–28, 168,
  256; Rhodesian travel to, 116–
  18; and Southern Rhodesia,
  5–6, 45, 80–81, 97, 106; in UN,
  130–31, 133. *See also* Lancaster
  House conference; sanctions
British Electoral Commission. *See*
  Boynton commission
British South Africa Company
  (BSAC), 5
British South African Police. *See*
  BSAP

Commonwealth, 21; and Lancaster House, 256, 266, 276; UDI, 113–14, 118
Commonwealth Heads of Government Annual Meeting (CHOGAM), 251–54
Commonwealth Monitoring Force, 278, 280–81, 296
Commonwealth Observers Group. *See* COG
Commonwealth Relations Office (CRO), 8, 106
community development, 152, 161–62, 170, 171, 172
Congo, 11, 69
conscription: administration of, 185–86, 191–92; and admission to university, 187, 189, 191–92, 197; of Africans, 184, 202–4; and aliens, 182; and business owners, 191; and citizenship, 14, 178, 204; of Coloured youth, 184; deferments, 192–93; draft resisters, 185; and emigration, 181, 183, 193; exemptions, 191–93; increases in, 180–81; and international law, 180–81; of men, 38–50, 183; after 1970, 43; after 1980, 205; and patriotism, 187, 198–99, 203–4; success of, 184; and white families, 186–91, 200
Conservative Party, 14, 18; and Lancaster House, 256; and 1979 election, 249; Pearce Commission, 206–7, 208, 216, 226; and sanctions, 128–30
Conspire to Kill, 147n71
constitutions, 41, 60, 174; late colonial, 80–81, 239–40
Cooper, Frederick, 18, 19, 39, 47, 312
COSS, 215, 217, 225
Cummings, Sir Charles, 53, 76
currency, 14, 123–24, 146–48

Darwin, John, 20
Day of Chaminuka, The, 200
decolonization, 18–24; historiography of, 19–21; late, 2, 238
de facto government, 120–22. *See also* Rhodesia
deportations, 28, 41, 42–43; and citizenship, 64. *See also* prohibited immigrants
detention, and UDI, 106–8
Dissent. See Ranger, Terence
Dominion Party, 11, 53, 67, 69, 70, 73, 79, 91, 92, 96, 98, 100

Douglas-Home, Sir Alec, 209, 226, 230–31, 236
Duff, Sir Anthony, 302, 304, 305
Dunlop, Andrew, 134
Dupont, Clifford, 13n26, 13n28, 30, 106, 107

elections: democratic practices in, 24, 300–301; "fancy franchises," 20, 51, 86, 311; as foundational elections, 23, 287; in Kenya, 38, 242, 300; late colonial, 22–24, 37, 65, 66, 94, 237–38, 271, 294; multiracialism in, 20; in Nigeria, 23, 39; in Northern Rhodesia (Zambia), 23; in Nyasaland (Malawi), 23; in Sudan, 23–24, 301; in Tanganyika, 23, 24, 240, 260–61, 300; in Zanzibar, 242–43. *See also specific years*

Field, Winston, 98, 100, 107
"five principles." *See* Wilson, Harold
Flower, Ken, 108, 117, 133, 148, 302
Foreign and Commonwealth Office (FCO), 118, 249, 255, 256, 290, 306, 312
Foreign Office, 216, 227
Forum, the, 157, 168
Freedom House (New York), 246, 287
FRELIMO, 252, 257. *See also* Machel, Samora; Mozambique
frontline presidents, 268–69. *See also* Kaunda, Kenneth; Machel, Samora; Nyerere, Julius
frontline states, 107, 233–34, 249–50, 252, 254, 265, 272–73; and Commonwealth, 251–54. *See also* Botswana; Mozambique; Tanzania; Zambia

Gabon, 139–40
Game for Vultures, 200
Gaylard, J. F., 226–27, 231, 237–38, 251
Gayre, Robert, 153, 155, 171, 172
Geneva all-party conference (1976), 14, 234–36
Ghana, 48, 71, 79, 86; and Commonwealth, 113
Gibbs, Sir Humphrey, 107
Gilmour, Ian, 258, 261, 266, 267, 271, 273
Ginette, 146–47
Godwin, Peter, 187, 200
Goldin, Ian, 120

306; and Patriotic Front, 235; and Pearce Commission, 220, 222, 224, 225, 232
Zimbabwe: beginning of, 277; name of, 1–4, 239; as post-conflict society, 284–85
Zimbabwe African National Liberation Army. *See* ZANLA
Zimbabwe African National Union. *See* ZANU
Zimbabwe African People's Union. *See* ZAPU

Zimbabwe National Party, 86
Zimbabwe Peoples' Liberation Army. *See* ZIPRA
Zimbabwe-Rhodesia, 15, 248, 250; and Rhodesian army, 274
Zimbabwe United People's Organization (ZUPO), 239
ZIPRA, 16, 17, 79, 244, 254, 293; and assembly points, 280–82
Zog, king of Albania, 195
Zvobgo, Edison, 267